Early Anglo-Saxon cemeteries

MANCHESTER
1824

Manchester University Press

Social Archaeology and Material Worlds

Series editors
Chantal Conneller, Laura McAtackney and Joshua Pollard

Founding editors
Joshua Pollard and Duncan Sayer

Social Archaeology and Material Worlds aims to forefront dynamic and cutting-edge social approaches to archaeology. It brings together volumes about past people, social and material relations and landscape as explored through an archaeological lens. Topics covered may include memory, performance, identity, gender, life course, communities, materiality, landscape and archaeological politics and ethnography. The temporal scope runs from prehistory to the recent past, while the series' geographical scope is global. Books in this series bring innovative, interpretive approaches to important social questions within archaeology. Interdisciplinary methods which use up-to-date science, history or both, in combination with good theoretical insight, are encouraged. The series aims to publish research monographs and well-focused edited volumes that explore dynamic and complex questions, the why, how and who of archaeological research.

Previously published

Images in the making: Art, process, archaeology
Ing-Marie Back Danielsson and Andrew Meirion Jones (eds)

Neolithic cave burials: Agency, structure and environment
Rick Peterson

The Irish tower house: Society, economy and environment, c. 1300–1650
Victoria L. McAlister

*An archaeology of lunacy: Managing madness in early
nineteenth-century asylums*
Katherine Fennelly

Communities and knowledge production in archaeology
Julia Roberts, Kathleen Sheppard, Jonathan Trigg and Ulf Hansson (eds)

Forthcoming

Urban Zooarchaeology
James Morris

*An archaeology of innovation: Approaching social and technological
change in human society*
Catherine J. Frieman

Early Anglo-Saxon cemeteries

Kinship, community and identity

Duncan Sayer

Manchester University Press

Published by Manchester University Press
Altrincham Street, Manchester M1 7JA
www.manchesteruniversitypress.co.uk

British Library Cataloguing-in-Publication Data
A catalogue record for this book is available from the British Library

ISBN   978 1 5261 3556 8   hardback

First published 2020

Typeset by
Servis Filmsetting Ltd, Stockport, Cheshire

For my family; past, present and future

Contents

List of figures   viii
List of tables   xii
Preface   xiii
Note on terminology   xviii
Acknowledgements   xx

Prologue   1

1   Negotiating early Anglo-Saxon cemetery space   3

2   The syntax of cemetery space   37

3   Mortuary metre   87

4   The grammar of graves   143

5   Intonation on the individual   190

6   Early Anglo-Saxon community   239

Epilogue   273

Appendix: Dover Buckland chronology   276
References   286
Index   307

Figures

1.1 Grave 78 from Oakington (author photo) 5
1.2 The distribution of cemeteries mentioned in this book 8
1.3 Evison's 1987 interpretation of a horizontal chronology at Dover Buckland (from Evison 1987) 11
1.4 The complex chronology exhibited at Finglesham (after Sayer, 2009: Fig. 9.3) 13
1.5 Intercutting graves at Deal and Berinsfield 15
1.6 Orpington 16
1.7 Weapon burials at Orpington 19
1.8 The cemetery at Apple Down 23
1.9 An example of the objects within the different grave configurations at Apple Down 24
1.10 Trauma at Apple Down 26
2.1 Early Anglo-Saxon cemeteries at Orpington and Abingdon 41
2.2 Mucking II and Berinsfield 42
2.3 Wakerley and Norton 46
2.4 Orpington and Blacknall Field 48
2.5 Snells Corner, Sewerby and Holborough 49
2.6 Polhill and Deal in Kent have different internal organisations 51
2.7 Mucking II, a large and complex cemetery 53
2.8 West Heslerton 54
2.9 Buckland, a very complex mortuary landscape with multiple plots and different densities in the burial 56
2.10 Garton Slack II and Dunstable, two examples of row-grave cemeteries 58
2.11 Street House, a unique cemetery 59
2.12 Morning Thorpe, Lechlade and Bidford-on-Avon cemetery 61
2.13 Cemeteries at Berinsfield and Petersfinger 63
2.14 Great Chesterford 65
2.15 Spong Hill 69
2.16 Alwalton 71

2.17 Andover and Caistor-by-Norwich   72
2.18 Buckles and pins at Wakerley   76
2.19 Patterns in the distribution of objects at Deal   77
2.20 Apple Down, a compound cemetery that used a mixture of
      spatial tools   81
2.21 Wasperton, organised around a series of earlier ditches   82
2.22 Springfield Lyons, combined grave ritual, ancient features
      and spatial proximity   83
 3.1 Spong Hill, phase A cremations and phase A stamp groups,
      showing the southern concentration of cremation urns
      (image courtesy of the McDonald Institute)   104
 3.2 Spong Hill, phase B cremations and phase B stamp groups,
      showing the concentration of cremation urns around the
      whole area (image courtesy of the McDonald Institute)   105
 3.3 Spong Hill, phase C cremations and phase C stamp groups,
      showing the northern concentration of cremation urns and
      the tighter clustering in this phase (image courtesy of the
      McDonald Institute)   106
 3.4 Bossut-Gottechain, a Merovingian cemetery with three
      distinct phases   107
 3.5 Sewerby, the distribution of datable graves   110
 3.6 Sewerby, highlighting three phases of graves which focused
      around an earlier core in a concentric organisation   111
 3.7 Apple Down chronology   113
 3.8 Wakerley plot A   115
 3.9 Wakerley plot B   117
3.10 Wakerley plot C   119
3.11 Oakington: calibrated radiocarbon dates   120
3.12 Oakington Barrow burials   122
3.13 The 1951 and 1994 excavations at Dover Buckland with
      the location of burial plots labelled   124
3.14 Dover Buckland, plots A, B and L in the 1951 area   125
3.15 Dover Buckland, plots J and K in the 1994 area   126
3.16 Dover Buckland, plots E and F in the 1994 area   130
3.17 Dover Buckland, plots G, H and I in the 1994 area   133
3.18 Dover Buckland, plots C and D in the 1951 area   135
3.19 Dover Buckland, battleship chart to show the different
      chronological activity in the plots   141
 4.1 Wakerley, the spatial distribution of furnished graves in
      clusters at 5 m apart   150
 4.2 Core groups of furnished graves at Berinsfield   151
 4.3 West Heslerton   152
 4.4 Norton and Great Chesterford   154

 4.5 Holborough and Leighton Buzzard III   155
 4.6 Lechlade, Orpington and Oakington   157
 4.7 Wakerley   159
 4.8 Polhill   162
 4.9 Broadway Hill, Winterbourne Gunner and Lyminge II   165
4.10 Deal and West Heslerton (?)   166
4.11 Westgarth Gardens, Suffolk and Berinsfield   168
4.12 Apple Down and Westgarth Gardens   173
4.13 Oakington and Great Chesterford   175
4.14 St Peters and Broadstairs   178
4.15 Finglesham   180
4.16 Bradstow School and Ozengell   182
4.17 St Peters, Broadstairs and Finglesham   183
 5.1 Finglesham: the distribution of arthritis and weapons   195
 5.2 Finglesham dental pathology: caries and abscesses   196
 5.3 Finglesham dental pathology: enamel hypoplasia   198
 5.4 Berinsfield and generations   204
 5.5 Berinsfield: the distribution of arthritis and artefacts   205
 5.6 Deal: chronology and generations (after Sayer, 2010)   207
 5.7 Berinsfield: nitrogen isotopes δ15N box plots by burial
      area   211
 5.8 Berinsfield: carbon isotopes δ13C box plots by burial area 212
 5.9 Worthy Park: nitrogen isotopes δ15N box plots by burial
      area   213
5.10 Worthy Park: adult carbon isotopes δ13C box plots by
      burial area   214
5.11 Berinsfield: height data differences between weapon and
      non-weapon burials   217
5.12 Berinsfield: height data differences between weapon
      burials   218
5.13 Berinsfield: height data by gender   219
5.14 Berinsfield: height data with and without brooches   220
5.15 Berinsfield: height data with and without brooches by plot 221
5.16 Great Chesterford: female height   222
5.17 Great Chesterford: male height   222
5.18 Great Chesterford: weapon and non-weapon burials   223
5.19 Great Chesterford: brooch and non-brooch burials   224
5.20 Apple Down: men with weapons in configuration   225
5.21 Apple Down: height box plot by gender   226
5.22 Worthy Park cemetery plan, to illustrate the layout of the
      cemetery   227
5.23 Worthy Park: height and biological sex by area   227
5.24 Worthy Park: height data by orientation   228

5.25 Worthy Park: height and weapons by orientation in burial
     area   229
5.26 Lechlade: height by plot and gender   230
5.27 Lechlade: weapon burials in seventh-century burial areas   231
5.28 Lechlade: height and brooch burials   232
5.29 Lechlade: brooch burials in the seventh-century areas   233
6.1 Reconstruction based on archaeologists working
     at Oakington in 2014 (author photos and collage)   250
6.2 A busy excavation scene. This reconstruction, based on
     an open day at Oakington in 2012, includes site directors,
     excavation supervisors, excavators, members of the public
     and my father, with a spear (author photos and collage)   251
6.3 Different types of core graves within plots   253
6.4 Morning Thorpe, with kernel densities illustrated   257
6.5 Morning Thorpe: material culture   258
6.6 Morning Thorpe: distribution of pottery stamps where they
     were used for more than one pot (after Penn and Brugmann
     2007: 37, Fig. 4.7)   259
6.7 Morning Thorpe plot C. The light-grey circles illustrate the
     location of barrows based on presence of satellite graves
     that appear to circle around them   261
6.8 Lechlade split into two phases (grey are fifth- and sixth-
     century graves; black are the seventh-century graves)   263
6.9 Lechlade: fifth- and sixth-century graves (with kernel
     density set at 5 m to highlight the clustering of the graves)   264
6.10 Lechlade: seventh-century graves (with the kernel density
     set at 8 m)   266

Tables

1.1 Horizontal stratigraphy in Anglo-Saxon cemeteries   11

3.1 Datable graves from Dover Buckland's sixth- and seventh-century phases   93

3.2 Chronology of configuration A burials at Apple Down   114

4.1 Interpretations of social hierarchy based on the quality of gravegoods found in inhumation graves   147

4.2 The ratio of sex to gender and its statistical significance   169

4.3 Male-to-female contingency table: Great Chesterford   170

4.4 Male-to-female contingency table: Lechlade   171

4.5 Targets of grave robbers: barrows and graves with integral features   181

4.6 Targets of grave robbers: Bradstow School, Finglesham, Ozengell and St Peters   184

4.7 Targets of grave robbers: Finglesham and St Peters   184

4.8 Preference of grave robbers: flat graves and graves with integral features   185

4.9 Targets of grave robbers: barrows or flat graves   185

5.1 Skeletal trauma at Great Chesterford   201

5.2 Observations from cluster analysis for pooled sex comparisons from the combined cemetery and individual cemetery groups: Hatherdene, Oakington, Polhill and Eastry   235

Preface

Archaeology is frequently considered to be the study of artefacts, sites, graves or environments which result from the relationships that existed between people in the past. As a consequence, archaeology can be the study of people and their relationships with artefacts, with landscapes and, most importantly, with each other. Unfortunately, this last part, the interaction of people, is often overlooked because relationships are imprecise, difficult to define or have multiple qualities. Previously, for example, anthropologists have been critical of archaeological approaches to kinship, because they are often perceived as two-dimensional in nature, relying on rigid models derived from the metrics of artefact assemblages (Sayer, 2009: 147).

This book is informed equally by science and sociology; it is the result of over ten years of research and aims to revisit this vital subject from a holistic, multi-scaled perspective. My interest in early medieval cemeteries originated in 2002 when I read for a Master's degree titled *Death and Society*, based in the University of Reading's Sociology Department. Wishing to examine the topic further, I embarked on a PhD at Reading in 2003. The PhD was funded with a university studentship and was supervised by the shrewd and meticulous Dr Heinrich Härke. The degree was completed successfully in 2007 but I felt it was incomplete; there was a lot more to explore on the subject.

The nine sites I investigated in my PhD project provide a point of departure for this book, but my research has moved on profoundly since those postgraduate origins, and this comprehensive study has taken a further ten years to complete, with one hundred and eleven sites investigated in detail (see Figure 1.2). This more in-depth investigation has been as much a physical journey as an intellectual one. The project started in 2006 when I joined the teaching staff at the University of Bath to contribute to a new *Death and Society* Master's course. It was in this role as an adjunct teacher that I started to comprehend the value that social science subjects have for archaeology. In 2010 I moved to the

University of Central Lancashire and was able to explore statistics, geographical information systems and skeletal archaeology in more depth. The actual process of writing the book started in 2012 with a Livesey Fellowship. However, the project would not be thorough until, like the early Anglo-Saxons themselves, I had first-hand experience of early medieval mortuary space. This opportunity arose in 2010 when Richard Mortimer and I embarked on an ambitious five-year archaeological project at Oakington, Cambridgeshire. Funded by the University of Central Lancashire and the Institute of Field Archaeology we focused our attention on a large sixth-century cemetery. Through physical excavation the Oakington Project influenced my rationale, because climbing into a grave to locate, clean, record and lift artefacts or human remains is as close to the burial context as an archaeologist can be. The excavators, like the people who laid out the body, must climb into a grave, and in doing so they become entwined with the objects and the person, becoming part of their history. These events share another similarity because, where possible, the excavation of human remains, or the preparation of a corpse, is best done in collaboration with others.

Excavation is one method employed by a professional field science, but it is also a personal and sometimes an emotional experience. Many aspects of a funeral were intended to be emotive; for example, artefacts were selected deliberately for inclusion and so, once 'owned', they became invested with meaning and intertwined with emotion (Lupton, 1998: 143). When embedded with significance, material culture can take on a special character, becoming part of personhood (Gell, 1992). Consequently, we use our materiality to communicate things about ourselves and others, be it an outward identity or a group membership expressed from a cache of shared semiotic knowledge. Social relationships are themselves influenced by the space within which interaction takes place, and equally objects are entwined with social process, embedded within corporeal communication. Today, unfortunately, physical messages have often been undervalued in favour of the verbal or written form (see Moreland, 2001). Nevertheless, interpersonal communication is complex, where words originate from bodies and are enmeshed with materiality, place and the physical spaces of personhood, society and identity.

Our predecessors communicated in a variety of physical ways and, consequently, the archaeological record is as complex and diverse as was the human experience. This comparison has been made before. For example, Hope-Taylor sought to appreciate cemeteries as if they were a written account:

> The Anglo-Saxon cemetery in Britain has never been studied as a complete phenomenon, as the deeply revealing local entity it certainly is. It

ought by now to have been recognised as an unwritten form of historical document roughly equivalent (though at once broader in scope and less exact) to the parish register of later times, and investigated as such. (Hope-Taylor, 1977: 262)

This quote envisages cemeteries as a physical communication, like documents; they are capable of providing historical insights that parallel those of the parish register of the post-medieval period. The textual metaphor can also be seen in the work of some archaeologists, for example Arthur Saxe (1970: 7), who suggested that social personae operated within grammatical possibility; he argued that there were similar rules or universal ways in which society was organised. Ray Corbett (2009) and others have drawn on this approach to identify social 'norms' as the 'grammar and syntax of the dead'. Historian Guy Halsall considered that burial customs could be likened to grammar because, 'The norms act, in a way, as the grammar of display, necessary for any public symbolic act to be understood by its audience' (Halsall, 1995a: 44). Universal behaviours are not often visible in the archaeological evidence, and on closer inspection every burial was unique and each cemetery was different, in locally, regionally and chronologically significant ways. However, describing the combination of material culture and physical space as a form of communication remains a powerful metaphor.

Physical communication, like a book, needs a semantic structure, and each cemetery, and to a degree, each burial, relied on different shared semiotic knowledge as communities negotiated the cemetery space. In this book I extend the communication metaphor by investigating the 'Syntax of the cemetery' (Chapter 2) and considering each site as the multi-part composition of numerous agents. The 'Mortuary metre' (Chapter 3) refers to timing because those agents operated at different times with different influences, employing a complex localised grammar to create graves (Chapter 4) and express broader cultural elements like gender, age or social position. The decisions which assembled a funeral event were the results of the selective 'Intonation' (Chapter 5), stressing particular characteristics depending on situational circumstance, personal relationships and lifeways. These ideas intentionally use words which describe communication. For instance, in linguistics 'syntax' is the way in which elements come together, and poetic rhythm or time is called 'metre'. In writing, 'grammar' provides structure to allow comprehension, and for spoken delivery, 'intonation' is used to emphasise a particular point. Early Anglo-Saxon cemeteries provided a physical prop for poetry and a place for communities to tell stories about the dead, the living and their histories.

It was my ambition with this book to understand the early Anglo-Saxon cemetery as a complete phenomenon, one which existed at different scales, from the grave to the region and from a holistic multi-dimensional perspective. My approach is holistic because it combines the cemetery, grave, material culture, text and bodies as evidence, and it is multi-dimensional because it explores physical space, chronological difference and social time to arrive at social interpretation. By necessity each chapter builds on the last and contributes to an increasingly sophisticated examination of cemetery space.

Chapter 1, 'Negotiating early Anglo-Saxon cemetery space', provides an introduction to the subject by describing how archaeologists have approached early Anglo-Saxon cemeteries. It uses this historiography as a foundation upon which to describe several cemetery sites, starting with a double burial from Oakington and then focusing on the description of two complete cemeteries at Orpington, Kent and Apple Down, West Sussex. This chapter illustrates the problem with traditional monothematic approaches and describes how spatial layout, material culture and skeletal characteristics can be used together to explore the social arena. It also defines the philosophy which underpins the book. Based on interdisciplinary perspectives, Chapter 1 explores the causal agency embedded in relationships, material expressions of identity, transformative objects and aesthetic selection. Artefacts exist within the social world, and so the sociology of shoes and modern-day gravegoods are useful examples which are analogous to how more ancient objects interfaced with people. Society is pluralistic, but its physical remains are created from an amalgamation of factors, including the manifestation of identities and aesthetics derived from shared semiotic knowledge.

The 'Syntax of the cemetery' (Chapter 2), describes cemetery organisation thematically; it introduces the structural language of the cemetery and is the foundation of subsequent chapters. It starts by describing pre-existing topography and introduces the use of spatial statistics to identify distinct grave plots. The relative density of graves, rows of graves, the orientation of graves and the rituals used in the cemetery are alternative ways used to identify group affiliation(s). This chapter also investigates patterns in the material included within graves, and compares those patterns to the multiple methods used to organise funerary space. Chapter 3, 'Mortuary metre', considers the chronological construction of sites, investigating the development of cemeteries and the chronological transformation of funerary display. Building on the new chronologies proposed by John Hines and Alex Bayliss (2013), and Catherine Hills and Sam Lucy (2013) this chapter looks at seven sites: Spong Hill, Sewerby, Apple Down, Wakerley, Oakington, Deal and Orpington. It also presents an in-depth investigation of the chronology at Buckland, near Dover in Kent, because this site has been central to previous discussions of early Anglo-Saxon chronology. This chapter highlights discordant chronologies within sites, highlighting the use of different rituals by different identity groups within the same community.

Chapters 4 and 5 investigate graves and the people found in them. Chapter 4, 'The grammar of graves', explores *leitmotifs*, cultural themes in funerary display. These include social hierarchy, core burials, sex, gender and age. Plots or groups of graves were often arranged around significant burials. This focus may have been on the core groups of graves, which sometimes encircled specific individuals. Interestingly, graves with mounds on them were targeted by contemporary grave robbers, but some types of grave were deliberately avoided. Elaborate burials with exposed markers were a tool used by a community to distinguish key ancestors who formed powerful parts of the communal identity. Chapter 5, 'Intonation on the individual', builds on the previous three chapters to locate the lived experience. It uses skeletal archaeology to examine the distributions of skeletal trauma, diet and height. This focus on the body was developed in order to explore in more detail the differences in social attitudes expressed within the mortuary environment. Diet, and trauma, may provide insight into different lifeways, whereas height and teeth metrics may reveal a degree of relative biological connection across the cemeteries investigated.

Finally Chapter 6, 'Kinship and community', places the cemeteries back in their cultural context by discussing the legal and textual evidence. Whereas each preceding chapter built on the last to introduce new thematic elements, this chapter – like Chapter 1 – explores whole cemeteries as complete social phenomena. It establishes cemetery space as a unique and local creation. Each cemetery used different methods to differentiate between groups of graves and identify distinguished individuals from different generations. However, the creation of these burials was not solely to reconstruct the personhood of the deceased; it also recreated a community narrative with a 'scopic regime'. This localised way of seeing used gender and life course as well as situational, political and regional identities within a conglomerate, multi-layered mesh of characteristics. As a result, the dispositional difference between graves, between sites and across regions, can be used to discuss the nature of Anglo-Saxon society.

Note on terminology

During the writing of this book, an interesting question was raised for Anglo-Saxon scholars to consider: 'Is the term Anglo-Saxon racist?' This question was made international when the International Society of Anglo-Saxonists (ISAS) voted to change its name following accusations of racism, elitism, sexism and bigotry. *BBC History Magazine* (December 2019), *British Archaeology* 170 and several pieces in *The Times* covered this in the UK. In the United States in particular, the term Anglo-Saxon has been associated with white supremacists, who have been known to build identity around early medieval mythology and imagery, with a particular fascination for the Vikings as well as the Anglo-Saxons. I have witnessed this first-hand when rather unpleasantly I received death threats for writing popular articles about the biological diversity evident within early medieval peoples.

As archaeologists, our prehistoric colleagues might describe the study of the Anglo-Saxon period as 'culture-historical', because it appears to take its name from the name of a people. Importantly, however, the people themselves did not think of themselves as Anglo-Saxons, and the term describes a cultural and political situation. Nether Gildas, writing in the sixth century, nor Bede in the eighth century, used the term. In the ninth century, Alfred the Great described his unified realm as 'Anglo-Saxon' in opposition to the Dane Law, which was made up of people from Scandinavian countries, Ireland and Britain, as well as others from further afield. However, the Anglo-Saxon regions also consisted of a complex mix of people, and ancient DNA evidence points to that diversity. Importantly, the post-Roman people did not define themselves in biological terms; that is a more modern phenomenon and manifest from colonialism, apartheid and racial segregation. As Howard Williams pointed out in *British Archaeology* 170, 'abandoning the term Anglo-Saxon would not help us reach an audience beyond academia, and it would concede intellectual and historical territory to extremists and fringe narratives.'

This book does not use the term Anglo-Saxon to describe a race; it uses it to describe the cultural phenomenon of furnished burial that occurred in the fifth to eighth centuries AD across regions of England, a phenomenon related to a comparable Merovingian practice. Most importantly, this book is not about race; it is about cultural diversity, and this can be seen in the variations evident in localised expression of gender, status and identity in these burials.

Acknowledgements

This book is the result of over ten years' work and has involved the development of new methodological approaches, fieldwork and detailed scholarship. The first chapters were prepared during a Livesey Fellowship sabbatical grant, and I must acknowledge the support of the University of Central Lancashire (UCLan) in this for having confidence in my work. The editorial work was aided by funding from the School of Forensic and Applied Science at UCLan and was supported by Michael Mulqueen. Some of the case studies in this book were developed between 2004 and 2007 during my PhD, and I would like to thank Heinrich Härke for his tireless supervision during that period. Many thanks are also due to Tania Dickinson and Karen Høilund Neilson for advice. In particular, I would like to thank John Hines and Birte Brugmann for their advice and for access to prepublication copies of the four cemeteries volume (Penn and Brugmann 2007) and the early Anglo-Saxon chronologies volume (Hines and Bayliss 2013). In addition I would like to thank Josh Pollard for including this book in the Social Archaeology and Material Worlds series, and to Manchester University Press editors Alun Richards, Emma Brennan and Meredith Carroll for their hard work, editorial advice and support at various stages. I would like to acknowledge the valuable comments of two anonymous peer reviewers in shaping and improving this volume. I have been assisted by the comments of Helena Hamerow, Catherine Hills and Sarah Semple on various chapters, and must thank Sarah for her enthusiasm for this project; it helped me to see it to the end.

Richard Mortimer, Rob Wiseman and my sister-in-law Faye Sayer were all instrumental in the Oakington excavation, which took place between 2010 and 2014 and was fundamental to the evolution of ideas and directions in this volume. Furthermore, I am indebted to Michelle Wienhold for her contribution to the spatial statistics, James Morris for advice on geographic information systems (GIS) and statistics, Allison Stewart for her work on teeth, Erin Sebo for discussions about literature during our various collaborations, Patrick Randolph-Quinney for his advice on skeletal metrics and height, and Jenny Hockey for discussions about material culture, in particular the sociology of shoes. My thanks also to Susan Hirst for providing copies of the plans from Mucking to James Barrett, on behalf of the McDonald Institute, to Sam Lucy and Catherine Hills for permission to reproduce illustrations of Spong Hill, to Annia Cherryson for sharing a copy of her Master's thesis and to Indra Werthmann for illustrations and references relating to Frankish cemeteries.

Two people have seen this project evolve from beginning to end. Chris King was a partner during writing workshops which saw a number of chapters and illustrations completed, as well as in endless discussions about structure and style. Meredith Carroll has been the most supportive of all, having seen the process from the beginning, and I am truly sorry that she did not see the final phases of work. I must also thank Georgina Moore, Nick Baker and Natalie Hickie, who all tolerated, supported or encouraged my writing in various ways. My colleagues have been impeccable and must be recognised as a result because a project like this takes a considerable toll on a small team. In particular Vicki Cummings, James Morris, Seren Griffiths, Dave Robinson and Rick Peterson all made space and time to allow this work to happen. My PhD students must also be recognised for their tolerance in the final months; Justine Biddle and Allison Stewart in particular waited for me with patience as they journeyed through their own writing projects.

For a dyslexic author there is no doubt that some of the most important people in the process of preparing a monograph are the proofreaders and editors. As a consequence I would particularly like to thank Julia Roberts, who assisted me in the preparation of the chapters for the original book proposal, and Talya Bagwell who had the unenviable task of reading and assisting with the manuscript at various stages. Talya worked swiftly and professionally, and I am truly grateful to her for her efforts, without which this volume would not have been possible. Despite these many supporters, all of the errors in the archaeology, grammar or spelling within this volume remain my own.

Duncan Sayer

Prologue

This book takes a holistic approach to understanding cemetery development, and in its simplest reading it offers a new way to explore horizontal stratigraphy which depends on the local context and the layout of the cemetery. Mortuary archaeologists know that approaches to horizontal stratigraphy are problematic (Ucko, 1969; Parker Pearson, 1999). The same is true of using objects to describe gender, social hierarchy or social status, and yet these approaches reluctantly dominate the contemporary interpretive narrative (Gowland and Knüsel, 2006; Šmejda and Turek, 2004). Approaches to gender tend to be described in cultural terms defined by the difference between biological sex and the social construction gender; see, for example, Sofaer, 2006. Past approaches to gender can be embodied in cultural universality, but should not be seen as passive categories, for example 'housewife', 'warrior', 'slave' (Lucy, 1997: 164). Our own contemporary social context, however, does not support the use of these narratives because our experience of society is pluralistic and institutions like family or household influence the expectations and expressions of gender identity (Reay, 1998). Modern Australian, Welsh, Scottish, Irish, English or American societies all have subtly, and not so subtly, different approaches to the body, family, marriage, childbirth, social class, gender and age or education, based on wider cultural contexts like history, religion or law. Most importantly there is not in fact a single approach to these ideas in any of the places described. Indeed, your own attitude to family, for example, might depend on your past, your background and, importantly, the regional or class context of your upbringing. In this case then there are in fact multiple societal attitudes towards gender or the family, just as people's experience of family varies widely. This book uses a comprehensive exploration of the early Anglo-Saxon mortuary context to drill down into the local history and development of cemetery sites to explore the role of family and household and their impact on localised expressions of gender, life course and wealth.

This exploration is a case study in mortuary archaeology which proposes a way of looking at the visual aesthetics of mortuary space, to understand local *leitmotifs* as part of the expression of community history. Different agents working from different experiences within a unique and complex mortuary landscape created each funeral and, as a result, no two burials and no two cemeteries were the same. What this means is that any two persons' experiences were not the same. This book shows that each site contained a number of different attitudes towards the body, the display of gender, the use of the past or the use of objects in mortuary display. As a result, the attitudes of a funerary party, and the way they valued the location of a grave and its relationship to those graves around it might be a better indicator of social rank/identity than the number of objects within it. The past then is complex, dynamic and pluralistic, and this can be seen most obviously in the way that people negotiated the expression of mortuary identities within the public sphere. Many mortuary sites were intended to be visited: they were places to tell stories, places to build relationships and places to create or share identities (Price, 2010; Williams, 2002a). Uniquely, the approach outlined in this book places kinship, family and household in the foreground because it is these relational contexts that are at the heart of Anglo-Saxon society as seen in the poems and stories which reproduced it. The institutions of family determined and/or reproduced localised or personal attitudes towards gender, age, status and identity; and so an understanding of family and relational archaeology is essential: it is the keystone in the construction of a social approach that encapsulates the complexity of the lived past.

1

Negotiating early Anglo-Saxon cemetery space

Introduction

The dead aren't dead until the living have recorded their deaths in narratives. Death is a matter of archives. You are dead when stories are told about you, and when only stories are told about you (Lyotard and Benjamin, 1989: 126)

Today, ancient cemeteries are being rediscovered underneath rural landscapes, on the edges of ancient boundaries, or buried in the heart of villages and towns. But early medieval cemeteries were not forgotten places set aside for the dead, they were ancient repositories, archives where the dead and their stories were consigned to be recounted in the construction of community identities. The landscape acted as a meeting place for the living and their dead, making safe the bodies of relatives and associates, rooting community and memory into physical space. Cemeteries were not simply mortuary landscapes, they were pluralistic spaces used by the living who constructed them and who created experiences which situated cemeteries, performance and funerals within the spheres of personal and communal life.

Funerary narratives can be shared or internalised and may be supported with material culture: a spear placed in a grave or an heirloom brooch (Williams, 2007). Narratives can also take place at different scales using material and spatial foundations: burial under a mound, next to a partner, child, parent, grandparent or important person. As a result cemeteries are multi-generational histories, spatial representations of how a community described itself internally and to others. And, like other histories, dominant narratives were reinterpreted as each generation created its own discourses. Consequently, each cemetery is the unique and complex product of multiple agents working at different times. Each grave was the end result of a funeral designed by multiple architects working within specific chronological and personal circumstances and influenced by social agents which extended across peopled landscapes. At the graveside, funeral participants negotiated the details of a burial through participation. Part of this negotiation included decisions about the deceased's place within the contemporary community narrative – a choice was made to maintain or reject an existing epitome – and this negotiation affected the location of a grave, and the material culture included with a corpse. Consequently, the grave, the cemetery and the funeral were assembled within a familial circumstance which was part of a wider political situation; some individuals would have been buried locally, but others, influenced by regional agendas, may have been transported as corpses to another, specific site for burial (Sayer, 2014).

Material culture, burials, cemeteries and political landscapes were the product of social structures dependent on lifeways and objects, which are integral in expressing and transmitting human social relationships (Lupton, 1998: 143). In archaeology, as with many other social sciences, these structures can be understood to exist in the relationships between people. Archaeologically, we might consider the physical and the material remains of the past as an invention of interpersonal interaction. Thus we should consider that funerary decisions were the result of complex or incomplete social negotiations, with multiple layers and mutable agents presiding over different agendas and influence. Grave 78 from the early Anglo-Saxon cemetery at Oakington, Cambridgeshire, is a good example. This grave contained two individuals, an adult woman and a child (Figure 1.1), and the adult was placed prone with her legs crossed at the ankle as if tied, a position dissimilar to but reminiscent of the allegedly live burial from Sewerby, East Yorkshire (grave 41, Hirst, 1985). The prone body position seen in these two examples is a phenomenon seen in only 1 per cent of excavated early Anglo-Saxon graves and it seems to have re-emerged in the mid-sixth century AD (Stoodley, 1999: 55; Lucy, 2000a). This position has been described as a special burial rite and, as with the Sewerby example, archaeologists have associated prone burial with a violent death; or one in which the prone position made safe a dangerous corpse (Wilson, 1992; O'Brien, 1999; Reynolds, 2009: 75; Williams, 2007).

The interaction of the two individuals in grave 78 at Oakington is vital to its interpretation. The adult woman's right arm was located under her chest, her hand emerging at the shoulder and grasping a small, long brooch and glass beads. Her left arm was deliberately positioned under her abdomen so that her hand emerged on her right and rested on top of the child's upper left arm. The child had been placed lying on its right side, head facing or looking at the adult. Importantly the adult's wrist clasps were found on top of the child's arm; her arm had been positioned purposely to touch the child but this interaction

Figure 1.1 Grave 78 from Oakington. The double grave contained a woman and child. The woman was buried prone, holding a brooch and beads in her right hand. Her left hand rested on the child's arm.

was subsequently concealed with her sleeve. We can safely assume that the clasps were associated with the adult's wrist and not the child's dress because this dress item is commonly associated with adult females (over the age of about 20), and to a much lesser degree adolescents or older children, but never young children as in this case (Stoodley 1999: 231).

The grave soils in grave 78 contained no evidence of grave reopening, and the adult and child must have been buried at the same time.

The graveside experience was deliberately staged by the exhibition of a woman buried face down, and possibly bound to make her corpse safe. A second more subtle message was embedded within the funerary performance and would have been understood by just a few people, those who laid out the bodies and knew that the woman and child were intimately connected and buried together in the earth. The meanings entangled within this performance may have been deliberately ambiguous; her right hand clutched her beads, tightly protected by her shoulder, and away from an 'assailant' or observer. This is reminiscent of a live burial, but this intimacy is hard to reconcile with violence; it is a cherished position, subtle and too familiar. In this case, both arms were under the corpse and would have been hard to position without climbing into the grave, so the people who laid out her body would be close in with her, entangling their own bodies with the two corpses.

Funerals carried multiple messages; some were concealed, shared by just a few, and others were meant for many participants to witness. These messages were intended for a variety of people who shared different understandings, had different roles and different ways of participating in the funeral events. The example of Oakington's grave 78 is important because the physical concealment of a touch is not just a hidden gesture but could also be read as the manifestation of selective knowledge. Particular members of a funeral party might understand localised ways of preparing or dressing the dead (see Chapter 2); others may not have shared in that knowledge but participated in the event from a different perspective based on their relatedness to the funerary party, their role in the proceedings and previous experiences. Funerary negotiations can include scales of inclusion, scales of participation and practice. These conflicting perspectives are the essence of the constant renegotiation which ensues between generations of people who reinterpret their place within society as their life courses unfolded. So burial was a palimpsest, its purpose and meaning reinterpreted by individuals and generations, depending on community and personal circumstances. Because of these things each burial was the result of one set of decisions and depended on who was being interred and who was present at their funeral to make these decisions. Nevertheless, how a burial or cemetery was understood also depended on how previous inhumations were explained, who was relating that narrative, and the composition of their audience. These events entered social memory as an aural archive of stories replayed and reinterpreted at every retelling; recitations might also take place in between funerals, as part of routine life or at significant times and gatherings in the community calendar.

Importantly, the multi-scaled multi-dimensionality of the mortuary context means that archaeology can understand and interpret past behaviours. Past people created narratives and these stories were meant to be understood by dissimilar people with varying amounts of knowledge at different times. Past people cannot have imagined archaeological methods, and yet archaeologists are late audiences taking interpretive narratives from funeral spaces. These spaces are understandable because their multiple architects intended them to work as an *aide-mémoire* with which to negotiate community histories with shared semiotic understanding. This book describes a number of Anglo-Saxon cemeteries (Figure 1.2) and defines the archaeological evidence for the people found in those graves. It considers this evidence as being the result of a nexus of identities established by their relationship with others. It explores a variety of themes, including taphonomy, space, life course, gender, objects and osteology, within the context of cemetery organisation and regional circumstances. Early Anglo-Saxon cemeteries were the physical manifestation of community histories and early Anglo-Saxon societies; and they were textured, mutable, dynamic places within which personal, community and landscape identities were persistently negotiated, renegotiated and reinterpreted.

Approaching cemetery space

The earliest reports about Anglo-Saxon cemeteries were the results of eighteenth-century excavation. Attractive illustrations focused on gravegoods and occasionally reproduced images of the wealthiest graves (Williams, 2009). It was only in the 1930s that the less wealthy, but more typical, early Anglo-Saxon graves were also illustrated, albeit with a focus on the 'warrior burial' (Williams, 2009: 171–2). By the 1960s and 1970s, cemetery plans began to routinely appear in excavation reports. Sonia Chadwick Hawkes, as well as Calvin Wells and Charles Green, tried to connect this spatial information with deliberate behaviours and noted the presence of patterns in cemeteries. They investigated the location and orientation of graves and attempted to link these factors to the time of year that a burial was made (Chadwick Hawkes, 1977; Wells and Green, 1973). Called sunrise dating, this approach has been discredited because it tended to concentrate population mortality into the summer months, based on the angle of a grave and the position of the sun. Subsequent investigation of ethnographic evidence reveals that death in pre-industrial society was more likely in the winter because of the cold and the relative scarcity of food (Brown, 1983; Rahtz, 1978; Bullough, 1983; Boddington, 1990; Kendall, 1982).

Also in the 1970s, Lewis Binford observed that archaeological sites were the product of human agency and he hypothesised that they would contain spatial clustering, which could be investigated

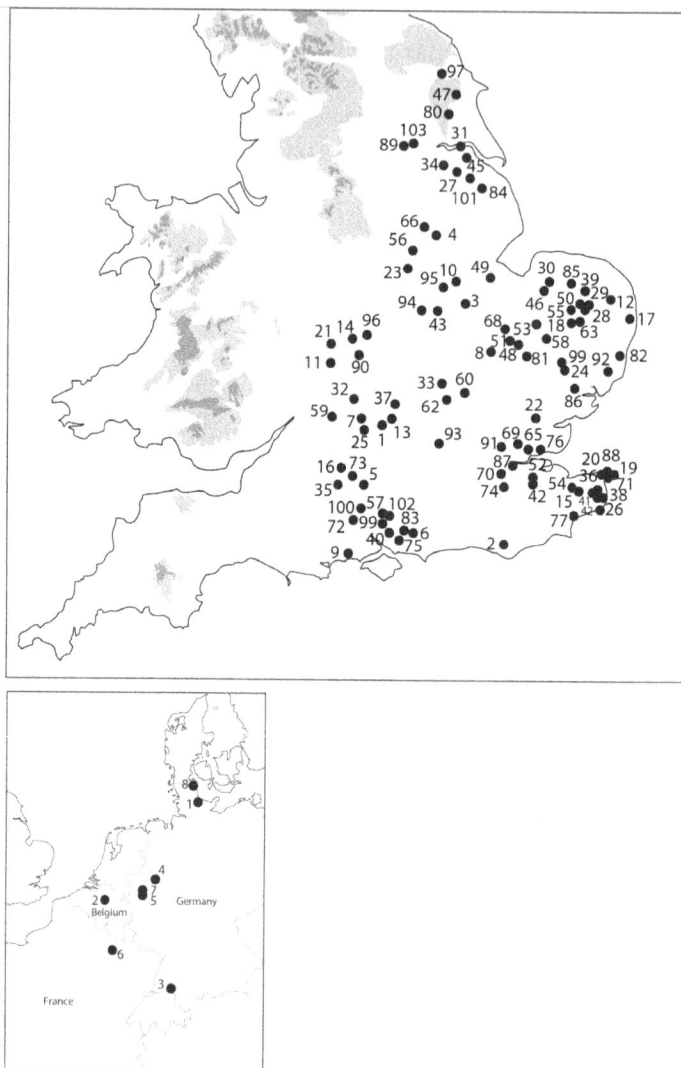

Figure 1.2 The distribution of cemeteries mentioned in this book:

1. Abingdon I, Upper Thames
2. Alfriston, Sussex
3. Alwalton, Cambridgeshire
4. Ancaster, Lincolnshire
5. Andover, Hampshire
6. Apple Down, West Sussex
7. Asthall, Oxfordshire
8. Barrington, Cambridgeshire
9. Bargates, Dorset
10. Baston, Lincolnshire

11. Beckford B, Worcestershire
12. Bergh Apton, Norfolk
13. Berinsfield, Oxfordshire
14. Bidford-on-Avon, Warwickshire
15. Bifrons, Kent
16. Blacknall Field, Wiltshire
17. Bloodmoor Hill, Suffolk
18. Brettenham, Norfolk
19. Bradstow School, Kent
20. Broadstairs I, Kent

21. Broadway Hill, Worcestershire
22. Broomfield, Essex
23. Broughton Lodge, Nottinghamshire
24. Boxford, Suffolk
25. Brighthampton, Oxfordshire
26. Buckland, Dover, Kent
27. Caenby, Lincolnshire
28. Caistor St Edmund, Norfolk
29. Caistor-by-Norwich, Norfolk
30. Castle Acre, Norfolk
31. Castledyke, North Lincolnshire
32. Chadlington, Oxfordshire
33. Chamberlains Barn II, Bedfordshire
34. Cleatham, Lincolnshire
35. Collingbourne Ducis, Wessex
36. Coombe, Kent
37. Cuddesdon, Oxfordshire
38. Deal, Kent
39. Drayton, Norfolk
40. Droxford, Hampshire
41. Eastry, Kent
42. Eccles, Kent
43. Empingham II, Rutland
44. Finglesham, Kent
45. Fonaby, Lincolnshire
46. Gallows Hill, Swaffham Prior, Cambridgeshire
47. Garton Slack II, East Yorkshire
48. Great Chesterford, Essex
49. Hall Hill, Lincolnshire
50. Harford Farm, Norfolk
51. Hatherdene, Cambridgeshire
52. Holborough, Kent
53. Holywell Row, Suffolk
54. Howletts, Kent
55. Illington, Norfolk
56. Kingston-on-Soar, Nottinghamshire
57. Kingsworthy, Hampshire
58. Lackford, Suffolk
59. Lechlade, Gloucestershire
60. Leighton Buzzard II and III, Bedfordshire
61. Lyminge, Kent
62. Marina Drive, Bedfordshire
63. Market Lavington, Wiltshire
64. Morning Thorpe, Norfolk
65. Mucking, Essex
66. Newark, Nottinghamshire
67. Norton, Cleveland (*was in* Co. Durham)
68. Oakington, Cambridgeshire

69. Orsett, Essex
70. Orpington, Kent
71. Ozengell, Kent
72. Petersfinger, Wiltshire
73. Pewsey, Wiltshire
74. Polhill, Kent
75. Ports Down I, Hampshire
76. Prittlewell, Essex
77. Saltwood, Kent
78. Sancton, East Yorkshire
79. Sarre, Kent
80. Sewerby, East Yorkshire
81. Shudy Camps, Cambridgeshire
82. Snape, Suffolk
83. Snell's Corner, Hampshire
84. South Elkington, Lincolnshire
85. Spong Hill, Norfolk
86. Springfield Lyons, Essex
87. Springhead, Northfleet, Kent
88. St Peters, Kent
89. Street House, Yorkshire
90. Stretton-on-Fosse, Warwickshire
91. Stifford Clays, Essex
92. Sutton Hoo, Suffolk
93. Taplow, Buckinghamshire
94. Thurmaston, Leicestershire
95. Wakerley, Northamptonshire
96. Wasperton, Warwickshire
97. West Heslerton, East Yorkshire
98. Westgarth Gardens, Suffolk
99. Winnall II, Hampshire
100. Winterbourne Gunner, Wiltshire
101. Wold Newton, Lincolnshire
102. Worthy Park, Kings Worthy, Hampshire
103. Tanner's Row, Pontefract, West Yorkshire

Continental Cemeteries

1. Bordesholm, Schleswig-Holstein, Germany
2. Bossut-Gottechain, Belgium
3. Bülach, Cologne, Germany
4. Dortmund-Wickede, Germany
5. Junkersdorf, Cologne, Germany
6. Lavoye, Le Haie des Vaches, Northern France
7. Müngersdorf, Cologne, Germany
8. Süderbrarup, Angeln, Schleswig-Holstein, Germany

by studying material remains (Binford, 1971). The simplicity of this notion was criticised by Ellen-Jane Pader who conducted a detailed investigation of two early Anglo-Saxon cemeteries, Holywell Row and Westgarth Gardens (both in Suffolk), and compared them to two sites that she studied in less detail, Bergh Apton, Norfolk, and Boxford, Suffolk (Pader, 1980; 1982). Using mathematical serration for grouping similarities in gravegood assemblages and body positions, Pader developed a multi-variate analysis, which considered differences in depositional practice between graves. Similarly, but without the statistics, Vera Evison (1987), produced a detailed spatial analysis of Dover Buckland. She identified spatial groups based on the physical clustering of graves, according to the location of adults of different genders. Both authors divided their respective cemeteries into small groups focused on a handful of furnished graves; however, their collective attention on the contents of each burial meant that their results tended to marginalise the physical clustering of the graves themselves. These two approaches also tended to ignore the chronological immediacy of burial, favouring instead the identification of small nuclear-family-like units.

The cemetery plans newly available to Hope-Taylor in the 1970s led him to observe that early Anglo-Saxon cemeteries had either a single focus or multiple foci around which the graves were clustered (Hope-Taylor, 1977: 262). After a prolonged study of 'inadequate records' he proposed that this monocentric or polycentric basis was chronological, with an earlier grave or monument defining a central point. Building on Brian Hope-Taylor's observations, and with access to more published and unpublished site plans, Heinrich Härke considered the foci of burial plots in conjunction with a generalised dating scheme based on male graves (Härke, 1992: 169–70). He compared the horizontal stratigraphy from twenty sites and concluded that there were four main types of cemetery (see Table 1.1): 1) horizontal, where a single direction of burial formed over time; 2) monocentric, where there was a single point from which burials radiated out over time in several directions; 3) polycentric, with the simultaneous development of several areas; 4) irregular, with no clear pattern.

These conceptualisations of cemetery space were a useful starting point and laid a foundation which has since been used to describe mortuary landscapes. Subsequent excavation reports have considered the horizontal development of cemeteries or the focus of burial. For example, Dover Buckland was considered to have a horizontal chronology from west [earlier] to east [later] (Evison, 1987: 136, 372–8, see Figure 1.3) whereas Blacknall Field, Wiltshire, has been interpreted as a polyfocal cemetery (Annable and Eagles, 2010: 103). Before the recent

Table 1.1 Horizontal stratigraphy in Anglo-Saxon cemeteries (adapted from Härke, 1992: 171, tab 26, and Härke, 1997: 138)

Horizontal stratigraphy	Cemetery	Region
horizontal	Finglesham	Kent
monocentral multi-directional	Petersfinger	Wessex
monocentral multi-directional	Collingbourne Ducis	Wessex
monocentral multi-directional	Berinsfield	Upper Thames
monocentral multi-directional	Bergh Apton	East Anglia
monocentral unclear development	Snell's Corner	Wessex
polycentric	Broadstairs I	Kent
polycentric	Polhill	Kent
polycentric	Mucking II	Essex
polycentric	Alfriston	Sussex
polycentric	Worthy Park	Wessex
polycentric	Andover	Wessex
polycentric	Pewsey	Wessex
polycentric	Stretton-on-Fosse	West Midlands
polycentric	Wakerley I	East Midlands
polycentric	Spong Hill (inhumations)	East Anglia
polycentric	Holywell Row	East Anglia
polycentric	Westgarth Gardens	East Anglia
polycentric	Sewerby	Northern England
irregular	Abingdon I	Upper Thames

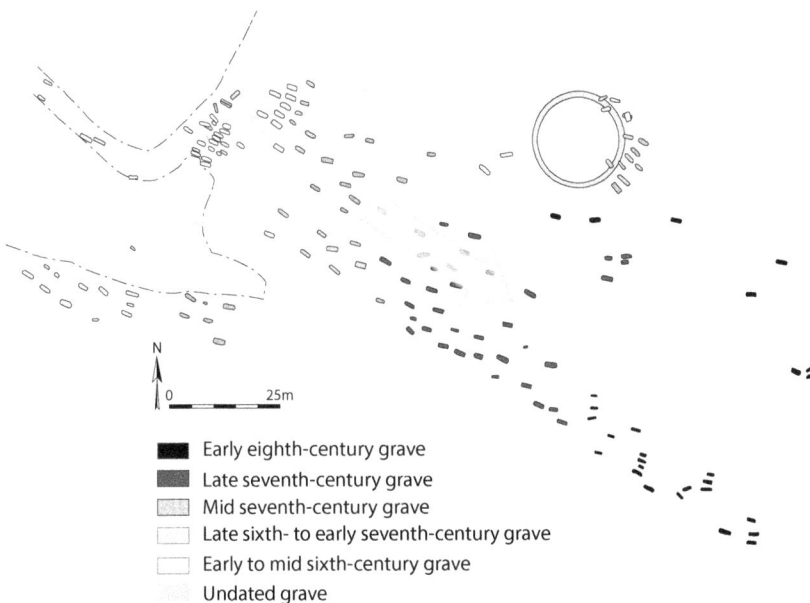

Figure 1.3 Evison's 1987 interpretation of a horizontal chronology at Dover Buckland, Kent. She considered the earliest graves to be in the north-west.

reassessment of its chronology, the large cremation cemetery found at Spong Hill, Norfolk, was considered to have radiated out from an earlier internal zone or zones (Hills, 1994: 42). Because it did not compare with other sites, Lechlade, Gloucestershire, was described as an irregular site with little evidence of clear spatial sequence (Boyle *et al.*, 2011: 129–45). As chapters 2 and 6 will show, Lechlade is complex and multi-phased but compares well with other sites. Spong Hill is very complex, with multi-phased activity, but each phase took a different pattern (Hills and Lucy, 2013: 213–32).

It is important to understand the chronology of a cemetery, but traditional methods expected adjacent graves to have comparable dates, an understanding that has been discredited (Ucko, 1969: 276–7). This approach is called 'horizontal stratigraphy' but, despite its name, it has very little to do with actual stratigraphy and is based on the assumption that cemeteries spread from an earlier point or points. In practice, most cemeteries are complex with multiple variables and many have no obvious single initial centre, so cannot be described as mono- or polycentral based on an exclusively chronological model. Burials were made by distinct groups of people at various times, and they chose to focus on different characteristics within the site. The studies by Härke and Hope-Taylor were based on the data available at the time of investigation, but they also tended to look for simple patterns to allow the comparison of cemeteries within and across regions. Finglesham, Kent, for example, exhibits a general trend for north-to-south drift over time and, based on male graves, Härke described it as horizontal (Härke, 1992: 171). However, when male and female graves are studied together, it becomes apparent that many later graves were placed on the northern part of the site and some early ones can be found in the southern part (Figure 1.4). Finglesham's seventh-century graves can be seen more frequently on the edges of the cemetery, suggesting a trend towards the placement of the dead at the edges of the site. But this is too simple. Finglesham actually exhibits multiple simultaneous chronological patterning with some burials placed at the edges of the cemetery and others focused around key burials positioned under mounds so that they become focal points (see chapters 2 and 3). Berinsfield, Oxfordshire, did not have a single earlier focus either, but exhibited multiple areas of continued emphasis throughout its sixth- and short-lived seventh-century use. Focal points rarely have one early date because they were visited and revisited during multiple generations and during different phases of activity as the architects of each grave chose to follow or reject the patterns established by their predecessors (Sayer, 2010).

In Härke's (1995) study of Berinsfield, based on the male gravegoods, he suggested that the cemetery developed horizontally in two cardinal

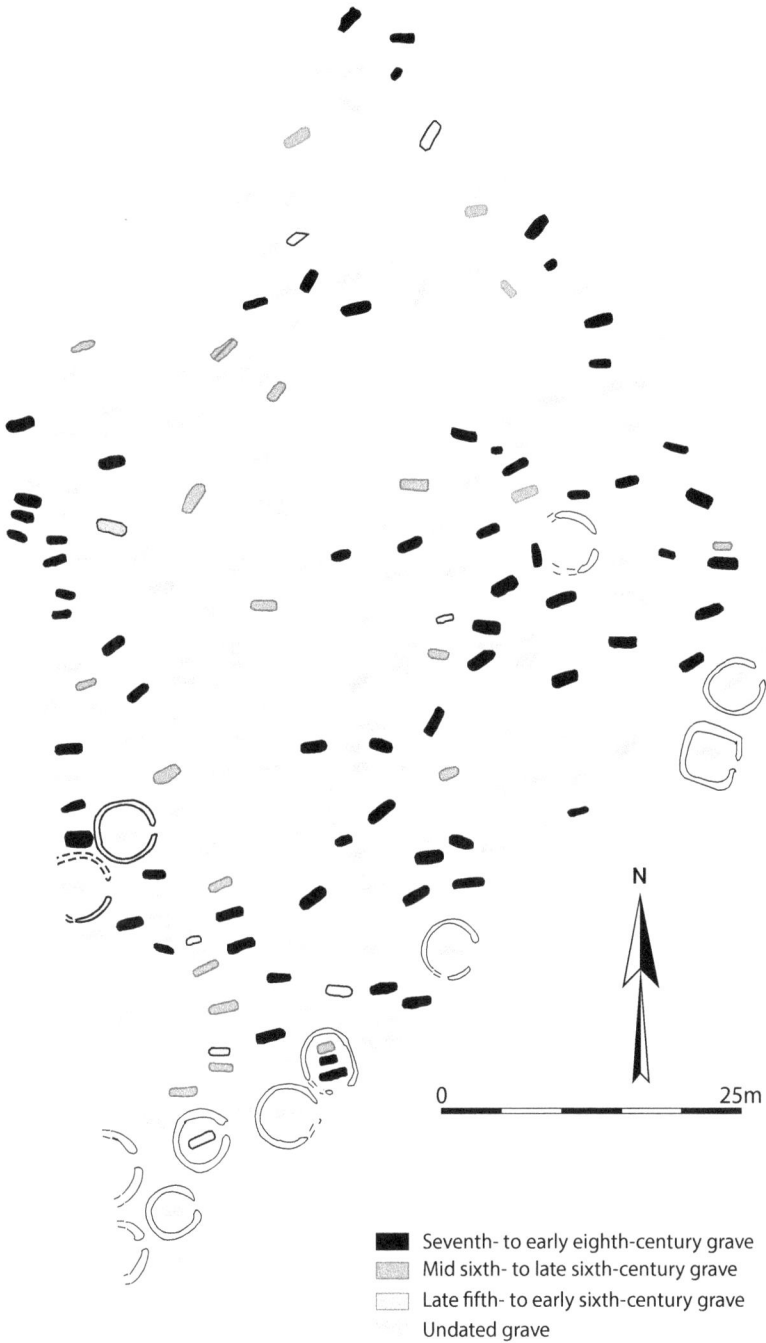

Figure 1.4 The complex chronology exhibited at Finglesham, Kent (after Sayer, 2009: Fig. 9.3).

directions: south to north and east to west. It has also been proposed that Deal, Kent, evidenced a horizontal stratigraphy which broadly operated from west to east (Sayer, 2007). However, at both Berinsfield and Deal several graves from different dates were placed adjacent to each other, and seventh-century graves deliberately cut early sixth-century inhumations (Figure 1.5). The development of these cemeteries must have been more complex than can be explained using chronology as the primary agent of examination, and other influences and changes in mortuary behaviour also motivated the cemetery's architectures.

Berinsfield was identified as a polyfocal cemetery because two or three groups of graves each contained a cluster of furnished inhumations, and other burials were placed around them. Berinsfield consisted of two contemporary collections of graves, and both contained a core group of inhumations. Around these cores the rest of the cemetery was arranged. However, not all groups of graves were contemporary. At Deal, for example, three groups of burials were separated around a single large Bronze-Age ring ditch, the remains of a round barrow. Two of these groups of graves, north and south of the ring ditch, were contemporary and were part of a first phase which was broadly early and middle sixth-century in date. The eastern group of graves, however, was part of a second phase that was broadly later sixth- and seventh-century in date.

Using horizontal stratigraphy also tends to equate chronology with spatial patterning; however, as already shown, these two factors independently influence the mortuary landscape. For example, Evison (1987: 165) considered that Orpington, in west Kent, was composed of a horizontal development east to west from a monocentred core. Orpington had one inhumation, grave 23, around which multiple male weapon graves were placed. The burials around grave 23 were all sixth-century, but they varied widely in date. The individuals from the latest graves found accompanied by weapons were very young or not yet born when grave 23 was constructed and when the first of the weapon graves was backfilled with earth (see Figure 1.6). This important inhumation became a focus for later burials, but the cemetery did not have an original contemporary core of graves; its centre was created through the repeated use of a particular place to inter children and men with weapons. At the same time, graves placed to the south and west of burial 23 created a multi-directional pattern. Orpington, then, is complex; simultaneously some inhumations were placed into a multi-phase core, whereas others were placed into more peripheral zones.

The spatial layout of early Anglo-Saxon cemeteries has been neglected in favour of death, objects and identities. Since the 1970s, studies which have investigated the organisation of the mortuary landscape have tended to combine interpretive discourse and spatial investigation, an

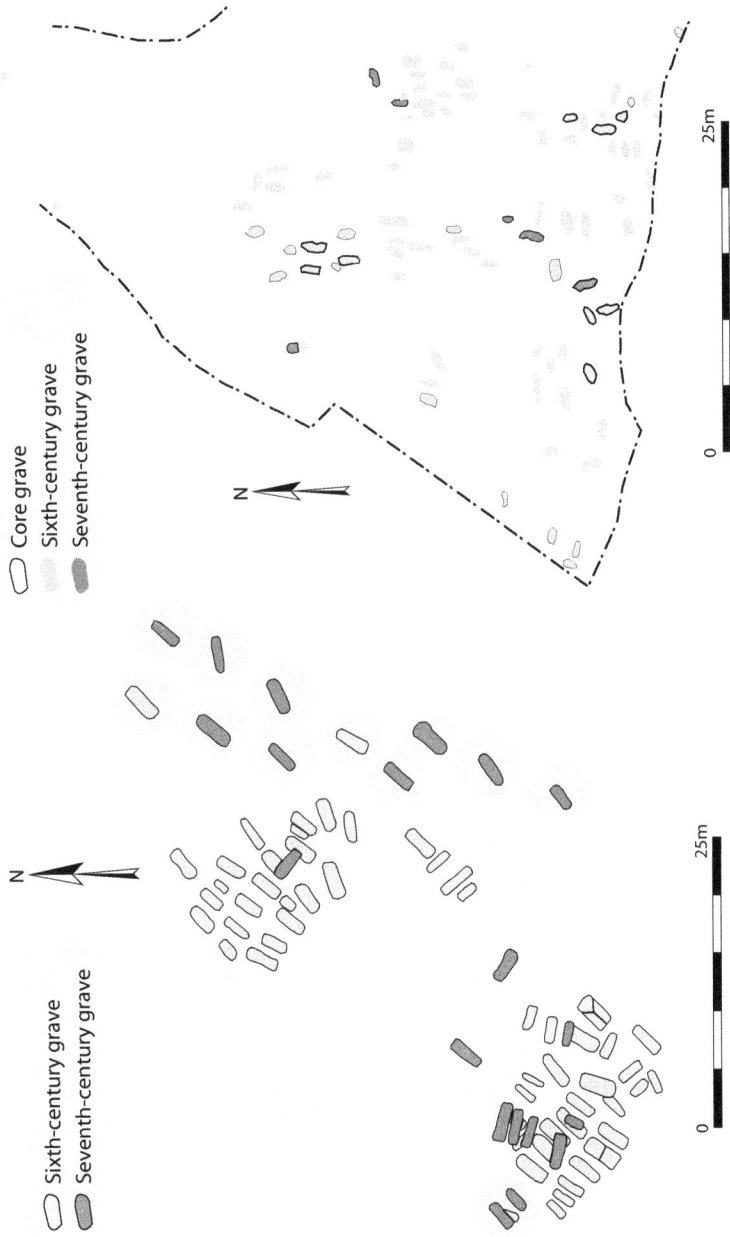

Figure 1.5 Intercutting graves at Deal, Kent (left) and Berinsfield, Oxfordshire (right). In both examples, later graves exhibited an intrusive quality, even cutting earlier inhumations.

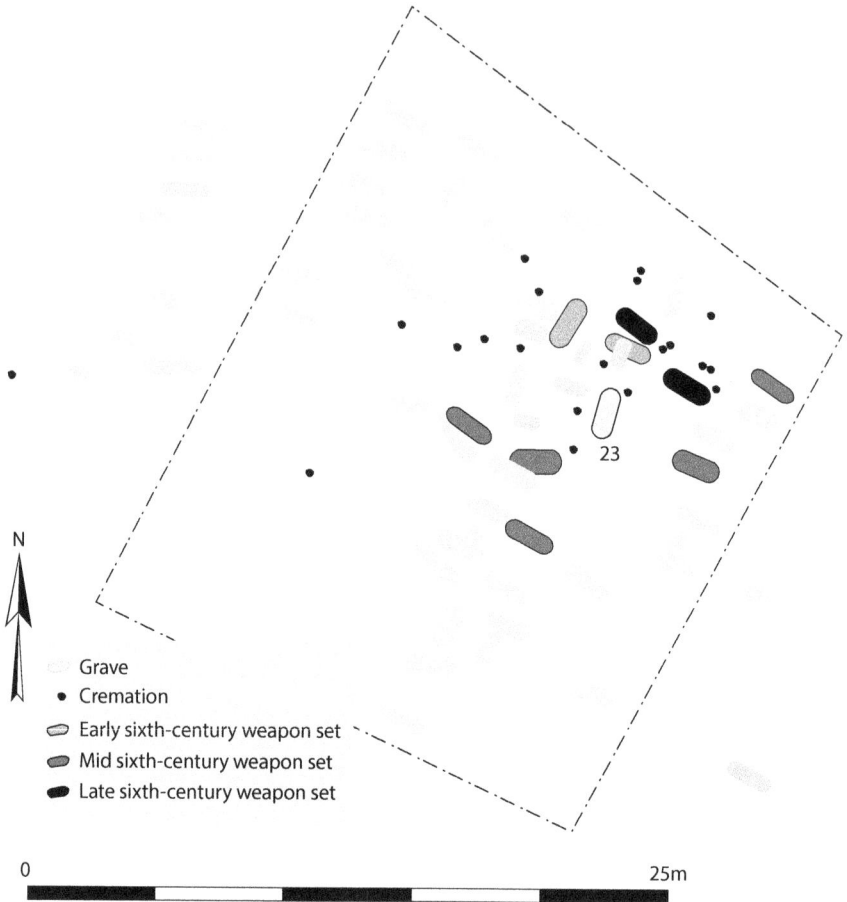

N

Grave
• Cremation
⬭ Early sixth-century weapon set
⬬ Mid sixth-century weapon set
⬮ Late sixth-century weapon set

0   25m

Figure 1.6 Orpington, Kent. Over the course of a hundred years or so, grave 23 was surrounded by multiple generations of weapon-set graves.

amalgamation of identity, chronology, space and belief which muddied these dimensions. As a result, few people have used space as the starting point for investigation. This book places the physical dimension of a cemetery at the centre of investigation, painting material and bodily data onto a canvas which allows for a study of mortuary behaviour and its motivations. However, space, materiality and bodies depend on time, both chronological and social. Where a grave was located, what was in it and who attended a funeral was dependent on the location of previous graves, the objects available and who was alive to contribute to the burial event (Sayer, 2010). Recent investigations into mortuary behaviour and the commemorative function of funerary semiotics have allowed archaeologists to move beyond an exploration of the individual dead into discussions of *thy death* (after Ariès, 1974: 55; 1981: 409). People make a funeral as a response to the death of another, but their behaviours and decisions encapsulate and reproduce mortuary culture and society in the moments adjoining burial and repurpose the ritualistic nature of burial to create new social identities (see Williams, 2006; Williams and Sayer, 2009; Fowler, 2010; Price, 2010). The living's response to bereavement embodies subjective decisions within the physical world because a funeral takes place at a specific time; the grave has a physical shape, and material things furnish it. But that grave does not exist in isolation: it is located in a space that includes other burials with their own histories. The very act of digging a grave enmeshes the newly dead within the narratives of a complex mortuary landscape, situating them within the materiality of the immediate past of living and changing community. The cemetery creates a tangible space which connects past generations with living populations and allows the living to construct themselves in relation to their dead.

Material and social perspectives

Entangled with ideas of horizontal stratigraphy and cemetery foci is the identification of 'founder's graves', an almost routine practice in the description of continental cemetery sites of late Iron Age or early medieval date (Härke, 2000a). A founder's grave is usually considered to be a single wealthy burial, or a pair of wealthy burials, identified as the earliest in the cemetery (Salin, 1952; James, 1979: 81–4). The identification of a founder's grave developed out of Germanic approaches to social structure based on literary sources, and is often linked to the horizontal development of a site where it is assumed that a cemetery expanded from those first burials (James, 1979; Härke, 1997). Lars Jørgensen (1987) considered this pattern to be the result of a social group, presumably a family, expressing its status with the burial of its principal parent, or parents, during the foundation of a cemetery. However, absolute dating is problematic, even with Merovingian numismatic dating, which underpins continental chronological schemes. The routine use of chronological groups with attributed artefact types means that it is impossible to definitively identify an earliest burial, and graves end up belonging to phases of costume or funerary practice (see Hines *et al.*, 1999). In early Anglo-Saxon cemeteries, fifth-century graves are often infrequent, poorly furnished and widely dispersed, which does not suit the character of a founder's grave (Dickinson, 2011: 230).

The concept of founder's graves has not been popular among Anglo-Saxon scholars, but has had its supporters. Sue Hirst (1985) preferred this interpretation to Hope-Taylor's foci, where Hope-Taylor suggested that groups of graves or plots were centred on early features, structures, or posts now absent (Hope-Taylor, 1977). Conversely, Hirst considered that Sewerby was the focus of an aristocratic family membership cult centred on a burial plot, or plots, within the cemetery. Like Hope-Taylor, Hirst complained that the absence of published sites and studies hindered the interpretation of Anglo-Saxon cemetery organisation (Hirst, 1985: 20; Hope-Taylor, 1977: 262). More recently Nick Stoodley (1999: 131–2) suggested that the burials at Andover, Hampshire, and Petersfinger, Wiltshire, were both organised around high-wealth individuals who seemed to be the central focus of burial plots; he argued that these graves were the cemeteries' founders. What is notable about this search for an originator's grave is that it often identifies the earliest wealthy burial, not the earliest burial, and as a result it might be seen as an overly romanticised approach which associates burial wealth, social status and horizontal stratigraphy.

The study of wealth and gravegoods prompted some critics to suggest that archaeologists investigate just a small number of wealthy burials in great detail, ignoring the majority of archaeological data. In the 1970s Hope-Taylor (1977: 262) lamented that many cemetery excavators were 'blinkered by their preoccupation with gravegoods'. He issued this challenge because early Anglo-Saxon archaeologists built regional typologies on objects and drew parallels between objects, not sites or people. Even studies of social stratification placed considerable emphasis on the quantity of objects found or their social value, based on modern perceptions of their meaning. For example, both J.B F. Shephard (1979), and C.B J. Arnold (1981) attributed specific importance to precious metals found within the grave. However, these approaches placed too much emphasis on archaeological data, including durable gravegoods; the amount of organic material originally included within the grave is rarely evident now, and sites like Snape, Suffolk, where some textile and other organic remains were preserved are rare (Filmer-Sankey and Pestell, 2001). In addition, archaeological categories are only of limited use for understanding early Anglo-Saxon actions; for instance, would the community who used the weapons recognise an archaeologist's definition of the weapon burial rite? The use and understanding of weapons in graves was multi-faceted and pluralistic (Sayer et al., 2019). Archaeological significance has been placed on the inclusion of a weapon or weapons in a burial, but the meanings and motivations of grave diggers might have varied between graves (Härke, 2014). For example, this variation might focus on ideas of the afterlife, personal need, personal or survivor authority, the authenticity of the weapon, the right to own or use it, warrior status, practical use, society's need for weapons or notions of masculinity, all of which would have intersected during graveside negotiations. These concepts and motivations have had uncertain boundaries overlapping and layering their use, and so emphasis on one or another might vary from grave to grave and from generation to generation.

The small cemetery at Orpington illustrates the problems associated with over-emphasising wealth. The cemetery, excavated in stages between 1965 and 1977, consisted of eighty-five burials, including both inhumations (sixty-five burials in sixty graves) and cremations (twenty), (Tester, 1968; 1969; 1977; Evison, 1987: 164). Orpington contained eleven adult male inhumation graves with weapons and five without (Figure 1.7). Two male burials, grave 26 and grave 23, were interred on a roughly N/S orientation (actually nearer NE/SW). Grave 26 was an early burial and included a spearhead, a knife and a shield boss, whereas burial 23 contained no gravegoods at all. However, the weapon burials found with a set of multiple weapons, for example a spear and shield, were all positioned 'enveloped' around grave 23, whereas those with

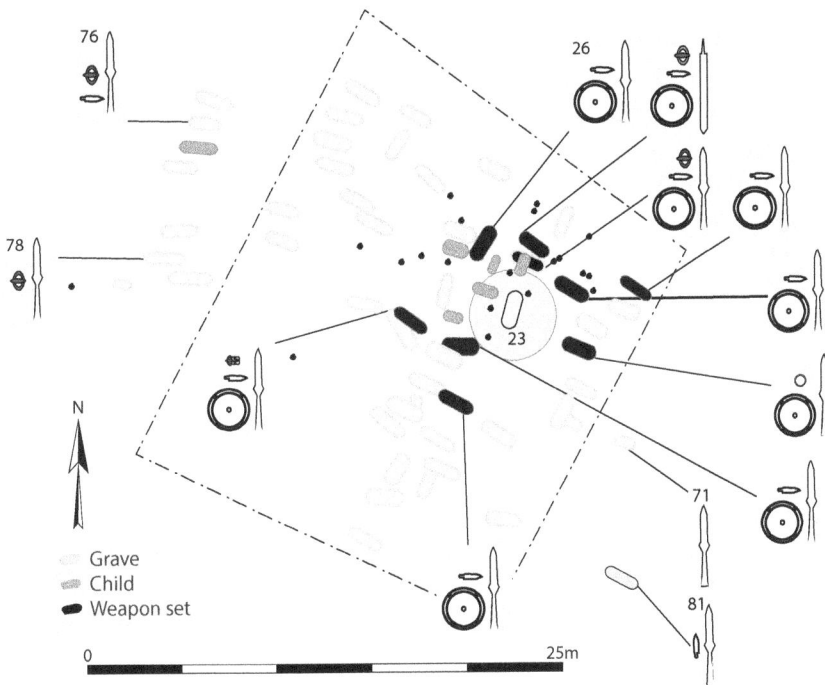

Figure 1.7 Weapon burials at Orpington, Kent. Note that grave 23 was not one of the eleven weapon burials from this site, but it was surrounded by weapon-set graves and those of children. Grave 23's continued use made it a focal point, a central place which probably had a small barrow erected over it to mark it out over generations.

a single spear were dispersed. The majority of children's graves were found adjacent to and immediately north of grave 23. Given that it was the focus of activity, grave 23 was probably marked with a small mound visible long after the soil had been backfilled and the grave closed.

Based on the uniformity of the Orpington weapon graves, Evison (1987: 164) proposed a militaristic interpretation, suggesting that minor differences were related to grades of rank, for example the presence or absence of a buckle. However, the spatial patterning of these inhumations placed grave 23 at the heart of activity for around a hundred years, and so this group could not have been a war band of contemporaries. Grave 23 was that of an older adult, over 45, whereas the weapon burials were younger men from later periods and many of them were probably not born when grave 23 was first dug. If this group of male burials was considered a *mannerbund* or male society in the sixth century, then it was a mythical association, part of a continuous but over-written narrative which was invented with the repeated placement of male weapon burials in this location. It is unlikely that this group was a contemporary uniformed military; instead the sixth-century community sought to construct a specifically masculine heritage with the appropriation of a significant ancestor. The community reinvented its mortuary tradition, introducing an inhumation grave which would become a focal point for later burials, and used it to germinate narratives about a multi-generational *comitatus*. The final abandonment of the cemetery may have been a deliberate rejection of this narrative, rather than motivated by religious observation.

Authors like Shephard (1979) and Arnold (1981) placed emphasis on objects and on precious metals, and yet at Orpington the three graves which contained gold or silver were all found on the periphery of the cemetery. Grave 23 had no objects and no precious metals. However, it would be unwise to assume that this absence of objects equated with inadequate access to wealth or power in life – one of the lessons from the astonishing finds of gold and art work from the Staffordshire hoard is that burial wealth may not have reflected the quality or quantity of wealth which was in circulation during the early and middle Anglo-Saxon period (Leahy and Bland, 2009). If there were larger quantities of good-quality material culture in circulation than we have predicted from burial data, then the things which are found in a grave are probably more about individuals than they are about conspicuous consumption. Of all the graves found at Orpington, grave 23 had the greatest influence on how the cemetery was to be shaped. Later narrators used mnemonic devices, like the central location or barrow, to describe the individual in grave 23 as a significant ancestor in ways that their contemporaries would have understood when retold.

Once a grave is closed, the memory of that grave is fragile; and with the retelling its afterimage need not resemble the events and objects which constructed the original funeral, especially generations on. In practice this means that a later sixth-century funerary party might have believed that grave 23 had been furnished like the burials they prepared themselves.

We must be wary of applying modern sentiment to the interpretation of a past people; a spear can be symbolic, but it was also a weapon, a practical artefact and a tool of aggression, defence or death. But objects like knives, spears and brooches can be inalienable from a person because bodies and material jointly created appearance and provided insights into personality; many objects are inseparable from the perception of a person (Fowler, 2004; Gell, 1998; also see Harper, 2012). These objects appeared in graves, according to age, gender or life course (Stoodley 1999; Härke 1989a), and had a role to play in the material aesthetic of society because people's multi-faceted identities were intertwined with material things, visual experiences, spaces and landscapes (Gosden, 2005). Moreover, objects are part of how people define themselves and each other, and are central to how people interact.

How a person looks will influence how someone responds to them within a specific cultural setting, because objects are situated intermediately in relationships and act as fulcrums for interpersonal interactions. The aesthetic of relationships reinforces perception – for example, some of the earliest law codes describe a penalty for inappropriate gift giving in Anglo-Saxon England, as in Ine's code 29:

> If anyone lends a sword to the servant of another man, and he makes off, he [the lender] shall pay him [the owner of the servant] a third [of his value]. If he provides [the servant] with a spear, [the lender] shall pay him half [of his value]. (Sexton, 2006: 67)

This seventh-century Law of Ine, King of Wessex, is important because it describes the penalty according to a weapon's blade length or its appearance; in particular, a sword brought a smaller fine than a spear but was a more potent symbol in early Anglo-Saxon allegory (Sexton, 2006: 67). This difference may have been because a sword required more training and skill to use than a spear, so a servant (or slave) would be less able to defend himself from capture. However, this may be an overly functionalist interpretation and the variations in individual circumstance which would be impossible to legislate for or enforce, since not all servants were born into servitude and many may have been taught how to use weapons by necessity or in a previous position (Pelteret, 1995). Significantly, however, this difference in the penalty might also have been because a servant was forbidden from using or carrying a sword and so a servant, or slave, looked incongruous with a sword but could be seen with a spear, if infrequently. A person chooses their appearance within the aesthetic of socially constructed norms, and this negotiation is subject to enduring scrutiny (Gell, 1998: 17).

Objects placed in graves are not simply gifts for the dead (King, 2004), and recent portable antiquities research suggests that, at least in Kent, objects commonly found outside the cemetery context were inconsistent with those from graves. This means that people dressed their dead especially for burial (McLean and Richardson, 2010), even if they did use older objects for burial. Dress objects found on the body were probably selected by a person or a group of people and had been chosen from a range of possibilities. They embodied aspects of how that person was perceived by those who survived them. These objects may have been inseparable from personal identity and they would have been chosen to create visual narratives because they were meaningful to the selectors (see Harper, 2012). The practicality of this is also important. An early medieval earthen grave was cut well below the ground surface; limbs, clothes and artefacts would have to be arranged and positioned or repositioned after the body was placed within it. To achieve this, an individual would have to climb into the grave in an intimate communion with the corpse, amalgamating clothing and bodies as part of an intimate, emotional and ultimately communal exhibition.

The early Anglo-Saxon cemetery at Apple Down, West Sussex, illustrates how material culture and skeletal characteristics can be combined with a cemetery plan and used to explore the social arena. The cemetery was discovered in 1981 and excavated between 1982 and 1987 by the Chichester Research Committee. It was a mixed-rite site containing inhumation and cremation burials dating from the fifth to the seventh century (Down and Welch, 1990). The decision to either cremate or bury the dead may have been the result of strategies intended to distinguish two or more separate social groups, a phenomenon seen in other contemporary cemeteries, for example Morning Thorpe, Spong Hill, Bergh Apton and Westgarth Gardens (Penn and Brugmann, 2007: 96–7). Alternatively, the choice may have been chronological, where cremation graves were mostly earlier than inhumations (see Chapter 2). Apple Down seems to be a mono-focal cemetery with central graves oriented E/W, surrounded by others oriented N/S (Figure 1.8; Sayer, 2010). Moreover, there were three distinct ways to prepare a grave at Apple Down: configuration A, inhumation graves oriented E/W and in an interior zone; configuration B, inhumation graves oriented N/S and in an exterior zone; and configuration C, cremation graves found with and without urns and in two zones across the site. Of the 121 inhumations, those which employed

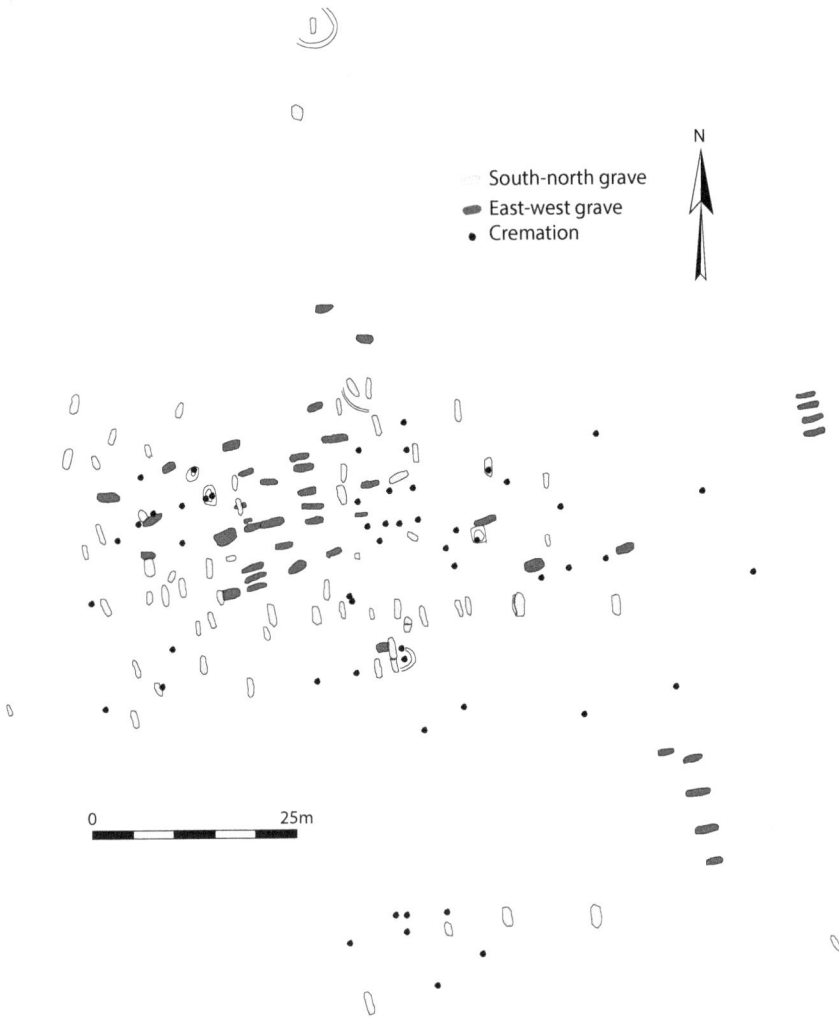

Figure 1.8 The cemetery at Apple Down, West Sussex. Grave orientation was used to define specific locations for inhumation graves at this site.

configuration A were located in the centre of the site and few of these had no gravegoods. The majority of furnished burials included a variety of artefacts, which included: swords, spears, shield bosses, seaxes, bow brooches, radiate-headed brooches, button brooches, bird brooches, saucer brooches, square-headed brooches, disc brooches, glass beakers and buckets. Configuration B, on the other hand, was more dispersed, the surviving artefacts were relatively infrequent or low in number and they included less remarkable or everyday objects like knives, beads, pins and buckles (see Figure 1.9).

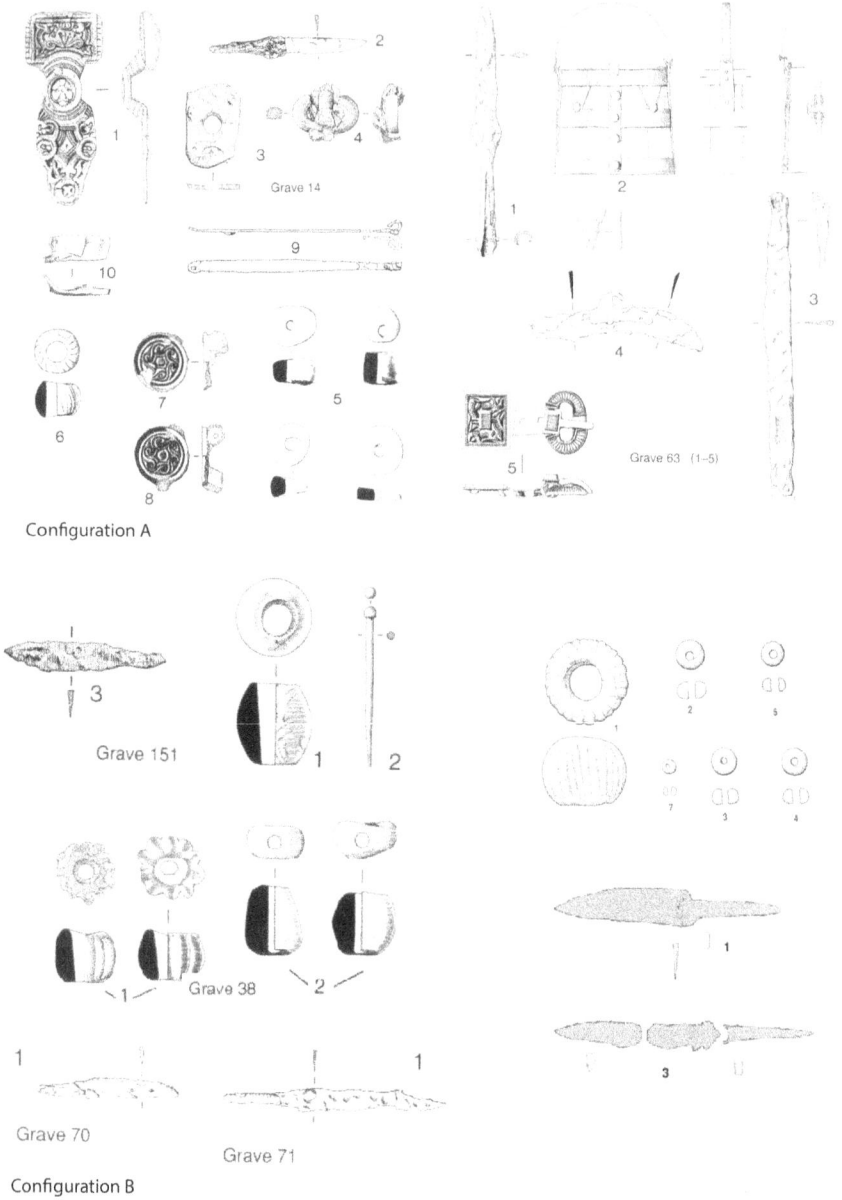

Figure 1.9 An example of the objects within the different grave configurations at Apple Down. These objects were contemporary with each other but suggest there were two distinct burial rites among the inhumation graves.

The inhumation burials at Apple Down were separated spatially in a visually powerful way defined by both their orientation, their location and the nature of the mortuary ritual. Each configuration was provided, broadly speaking, with its own physical space and so the mortuary architects of each configuration must have had a different agenda. They created disparate funeral rites which told dissimilar narratives and resulted in a different archaeological trace used to denote social difference, which is also observable in the skeletal evidence (see Chapter 4). Configuration A included the majority of older adults aged over 45 years and most of the children's graves. One of the most striking characteristics of the configuration B burials is the relative scarcity of children's graves. The early Anglo-Saxon burial rite treated children differently to adults in the type and quantities of gravegoods (Crawford, 1999; Sayer, 2014). It is important to note that at Apple Down the children's graves mainly cluster to the west of the centre, in the middle of the cemetery, adjacent to the oldest individuals.

Of the 121 inhumations at Apple Down, twenty showed evidence of skeletal trauma – fractures, periostitis (bone infection) or swollen limb-bone shafts, but only four of these (graves 14, 19, 28 and 67) belonged to configuration A. The individuals belonging to configuration B had been exposed to greater physical stress and had a higher risk of injury in life (Figure 1.10). Twenty-two of the twenty-five individuals (88 per cent) showed evidence of osteoarthritis and were found to have been interred without the types of artefacts predominantly found in configuration A graves. This pattern shows there were at least two different lifeways present within the sites; the configuration A burials included a higher proportion of adults aged over 45, whose longer life spans should have resulted in a higher, not lower, incidence of osteoarthritis and trauma. Furthermore, in a reassessment of the skeletal remains at Apple Down, Annia Cherryson calculated the mean muscle mass for the skeletons based on ligament attachment sites. She observed a difference between the muscle mass of the upper limbs in adult males aged 18 to 35, with and without weapons (Cherryson, 2000: 81–7; Robb, 1998). Cherryson noticed that those without weapons (loosely equating to configuration B burials) had a larger muscle mass across the whole sample. The males exposed to a higher risk of skeletal trauma had also done more physical work, enough to have increased the size of the muscle mass on their upper limbs in a different way to the males found in configuration A graves, those often found with full weapon kits.

Importantly, the graves around the edge of the cemetery were mostly configuration B, but exhibited important variations. Based on the artefacts found, two graves in this zone were configuration A inhumations, but had been deliberately located on the peripheries of the cemetery.

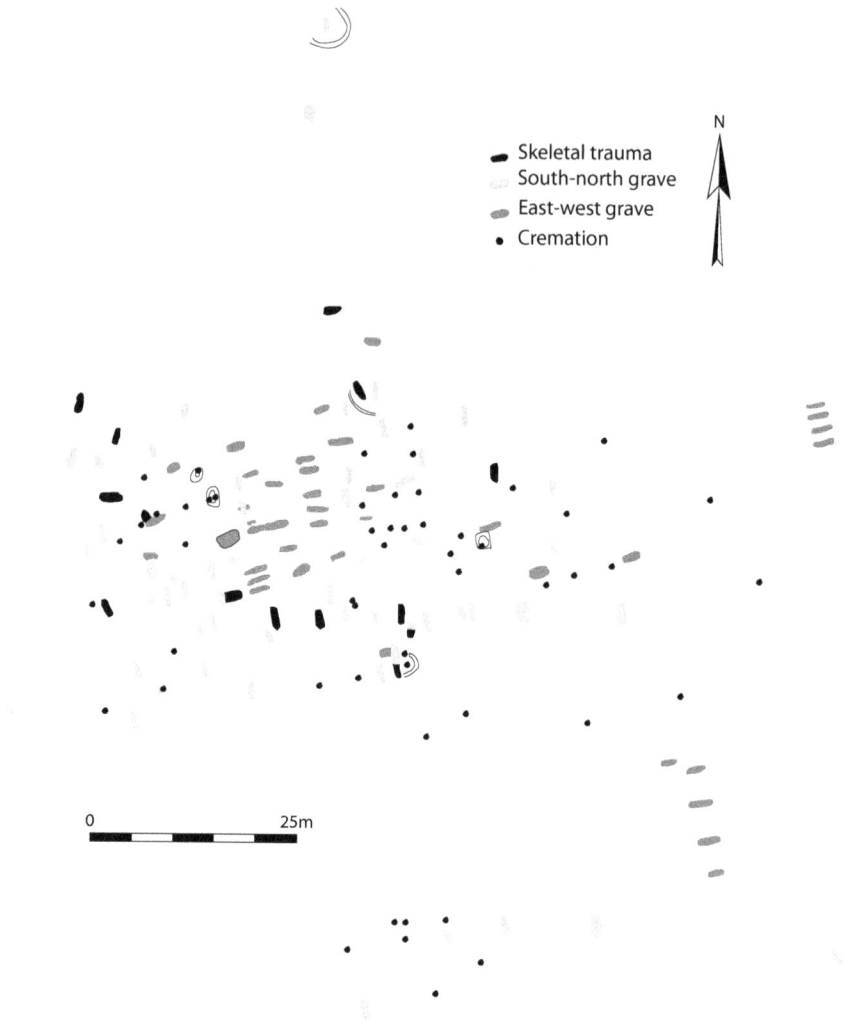

Figure 1.10 Trauma at Apple Down, West Sussex. The graves that contained evidence of skeletal trauma were found among the peripheral inhumations.

These graves (145 and 152) were both of males and both contained a full weapon kit with spear and shield. Both were positioned on an E/W orientation reminiscent of the configuration A graves in the centre. Perhaps these two individuals belonged to the social group or household, but not to the immediate kingroup, who buried their dead in the centre of the cemetery. Five individuals (113, 121, 122, 126 and 148) were buried with small spearheads but belong to configuration B. They did not contain full weapon kits, and burials 122 and 126 were both extreme outliers in Cherryson's study of muscle mass, having even larger muscle scores than the average for individuals in comparable non-weapon burials (Cherryson, 2000: 81–7). The man in burial 126 also showed signs of osteoarthritis and had a fractured vertebra. All five of these burials were found in the area of the cemetery dominated by configuration B burials, and their skeletal remains indicate a lifeway in common with those inhumations.

Apple Down was a cemetery with internal stratification according to burial ritual and location, and early Anglo-Saxon society was hier-archical, a detail that is evident in seventh-century legal codes such as Æthelberht's code:

[27]. If [a person] kills a freedman of the first rank, let him pay [with] 80 shillings.

[27.1] If he kills [one of] that second [rank], let him pay with 60 shillings.

[27.2] [For one of] that third [rank], let him pay with 40 shillings. (Oliver, 2002: 69)

These laws, and those of Hlothhere and Eadric, Wihtred or Ine preserve in a written, and therefore material form, a socially codified system of compensation outlining the value attached to a man's and a woman's life according to their status. However, that alone says very little about how this hierarchy influenced individual lives, if at all. At Apple Down, the two inhumation rituals appear to have deliberately distinguished between two groups buried together in the same cemetery and impor-tantly, they lived different lifeways, which can be seen in the skeletal remains. Perhaps they were two separate social units.

This Apple Down case study is similar to the one from Orpington because both require us to question the validity of blanket social cate-gories based on one strand of evidence. Although there can be no doubt that weapons were important symbols (Härke, 1989b; 1990), in both of these cases a multitude of factors influenced the final funerary assem-blage. At Orpington, the noteworthy, unfurnished grave 23 seems to have been placed under a small mound surrounded by weapon burials, indicating his continuing importance to narratives told by funerary parties. The Apple Down case puts us in a different predicament; sev-eral males (113, 121, 122, 126 and 148) were buried with a single spear and in the outer part of the cemetery. This zone and the greater degree of skeletal trauma within this group suggest that these people had been part of a separate and economically poorer lifeway. In the centre of the cemetery were found burials with the most wealth, also more children, but less evidence of skeletal trauma, and as a result we must consider that weapons were not themselves an indicator of rank. Rather, weapons encapsulated multiple ideas and singled out specific male identities (Gilchrist, 2009). Not all influential graves had spears, as Orpington burial 23 shows. He may have been buried before the full weapon kit became important to early Anglo-Saxon society, he may have been too old, his funerary party may not have been aware of this burial rite or he may not have been associated with the masculine virtues entangled with weapon burial. Equally, individuals from the poorer lifeways at Apple Down with small spears may have adopted weapon burial to enrich their own display, but this does not exclude association with a masculine identity that demanded a weapon burial. Equally, Apple Down inhumations 145 and 152 each contained two weapons, but they were outside the central burial area, and perhaps they reminded funeral participants about their separate place within living society.

Negotiating social interpretations

The previous two parts of this chapter have aimed to outline some problems with traditional monothematic archaeological interpretations and to present a holistic, multi-dimensional interpretation as an alternative. This approach was outlined in the Apple Down example, where a combination of gravegoods, mortuary space and skeletal elements provided an integrated case study. Both monothematic and multi-dimensional approaches are interpretative and seek to understand not just the creation of archaeological assemblages, but the social dynamic which made them. It is the social events within mortuary contexts, including the preparation of a body, digging a grave or contributing to a funeral, which created the archaeological record. Those events were attended by people whose decisions and actions organised and changed them. They were agents and, importantly, those agents operated within social structures that resulted in power, enslavement or reciprocal attitudes like gender differentiation, social status, kinship or belonging. In short the ability of people to influence the content of a grave, the structure of a cemetery or a social attitude is dependent on them being part of the relationships within society and social structures – for example, membership of the community or the kin group who prepared the corpse and laid it in the grave. However, individuals within these social structures are capable of conscious reflection and change; consequently it is a combination of agents and structure which affects social transformation and thereby materiality.

Inconsistent preservation and excavation methods mean that archaeology can be an imprecise science. This is true across a range of social sciences where the objects of study are inexact or have multiple qualities. As a result, social entities like power, gender, personhood or collective action require intellectualisation to be examined. The effect of these entities also requires conceptualisation, placing a considerable burden on abstraction in pursuit of understanding (Sayer, 1992). In archaeology this abstraction has created an apparent disharmony between agency, structuration, habitats or actor-network theories, which are measures of similar intellectual methodologies aimed at isolating internalised or externalised intentions and negotiations among past people (Robb, 2010). These social entities are embedded in the relationships between people and perhaps the ideas can be explored from this perspective. The dynamics between different generations, cultural contexts, genders and power relations enmesh individuals, places and material things with social structures and this can be used to explore the complex nature of a society. The philosopher Roy Bhaskar argued that:

> people, in their conscious activity, for the most part unconsciously reproduce (and occasionally transform) the structures governing their substantive activities of production. People do not marry to reproduce the nuclear family or work to reproduce the capitalist economy. Yet it is nevertheless the unintended consequence of … their activity. (Bhaskar, 1998: 38)

This causal agency is not embedded within social objects or individuals, but in social relations and the structures they form. For example, the powers of a university professor are not derived from their individual characteristics, but from their symbiotic relationship with students, colleagues, administrators, funding bodies and the employer or university (Sayer, 1992: 105). This will depend on a chronological context; for example, the early Anglo-Saxons did not have universities and so did not have professors. This equally applies to a multitude of other different types and shapes of institutions which structure society: land ownership, law, fostering, religion, nuclear families, prisons, servitude, class structures, gender attitude or kingship, which may exist in different forms or not at all, depending on the society in question. However, it is the associations between people which are crucial; the relation between master/mistress and servant, or king and subject, is internally necessary because each depends on the other to exist. There cannot be a monarch without subjects or a parent without children (real, deceased or metaphorical). This is not simply a social contrast or a tautology of personhood (Fowler, 2004, 2010). The servant does not give service because of social difference; it is the result of an involvement in a material social relationship. Neither master nor servant can exist without the other, but they can be separately identified by their contemporaries. As we discussed earlier, using Apple Down as an example, aspects of this recognition may manifest in material or physical difference between individuals.

The structuralism of the Binford or Durkheimian type was typified by the investigation of interchangeable macro phenomena, whereas the increasingly popular, but nonetheless reactionary, actor-network theory of Bruno Latour (2005) favours the micro – and proposed that *actants* (or agents) can be both human and non-human. This view is interesting, and increasingly built on by archaeologists either as actor-network theory (Robb, 2010) or as object-biography approaches because of the prevalence of objects within material evidence (Joy, 2009). However, Latour has been accused, like many 'recent French thinkers', of over dramatising his lines of thought, so those objects become living entities or nonperson characters in the social landscape (Alvesson and Sköldberg, 2010: 33). As archaeologists, we might consider relics to be an object where human and non-human *actants* have been combined. However, religious relics are saints reduced to component parts: skulls, fingernails, long bones or whole bodies. The objects are dry and anonymous, but in the context of the Catholic Church they can become the agents of pilgrimage and veneration. Without the Church these objects are human remains, but because of the symbiotic relationship between the objects, church administrators, the Catholic Church authorities and worshippers they become the subjects of veneration. It is the social structures in place within the Church, and between the Church and its worshippers, which are the agent and which provide authenticity, not the bones alone. In one of Latour's own examples (1996: 209–13), the computer processor and the red signal light which controls traffic are socially extended, forming an artefact which holds humans and non-humans together. When we stop at a red light, we are responding to the agency of a device which influences human designs (Alvesson and Sköldberg, 2010: 32). However, the red-light scenario is extremely problematic. Having acquired a driver's licence, the red light is a signal which a driver has pre-agreed means stop. He or she has entered into a social obligation to drive a vehicle within certain parameters – to obey traffic lights, speed limits and rules of conduct. The traffic light is not in fact a separate agent, but like the religious relic it is an object which embodies relationships – those between the driver and others, for example the authorities and any passengers.

As we saw with Oakington grave 78, Orpington and Apple Down gravegoods are intimate objects which were embedded with meanings and which were selected to commingle with buried bodies. Indeed, early Anglo-Saxon society placed emphasis on the aesthetic quality of material and dress. Sociologists have studied modern shoes in detail and as dress items they are varied and gender dependent, and they intermingle with bodies and identities in practical, semiotic and symbolic ways. As an analogy, shoes are symbiotic with the human body and have a role to play within relationships – sexy shoes, dress shoes, work shoes or sports shoes for example. Understanding this relationship between objects and people and the role of material culture in the interaction of people is important and so the sociology of shoes provides a more holistic way to understand early Anglo-Saxon dress than monothematic ranking systems based on quantity or material.

Shoes, like other apparel, are complex things consisting of multiple parts. At one level they are functional, keeping the foot warm and dry; however, shoes embody much more. They enclose and/or display parts of the body; they are status symbols; they are badges of class and group membership, which need to be learned to be used; and so they change us too (Dilley *et al.*, 2014; Kopytoff, 1986). Progression from girl to independent woman may be marked by the freedom to wear specific shoes, heels for example, and so the selection of a shoe varies by gender and stage in life course (Hockey *et al.*, 2014, Dilley *et al.*, 2014).

Shoes are transformative objects used to construct the individual (Hockey *et al.*, 2015). Likewise trainers are functional – for running, sport, informal socialising, dancing or dressing up. But they also identify a wearer's level of knowledge and engender a sense of exclusion, for example, the recognition of another skateboarder with tape or glue attached to their shoes in anticipation of damage caused by performing tricks (Steele, 1998). It can also be related to age – when the wearer lacks the semiotic knowledge shared by younger people. Equally, although trainers are used by men and women, this gender flexibility may be undermined as a woman gets older because the reproduction of asexual identities may not fit with clothing that she feels sexy or comfortable in (Hockey *et al.*, 2015; Hockey and James, 2003). Combinations of clothing may be unacceptable, such as white trainers and a suit on a man, or alternatively they may develop a degree of acceptance depending on context, for example a charismatic or eccentric academic may 'get away with' odd combinations, whereas a business leader could not (Hockey *et al.*, 2013). In the right combination, shoes and other clothes can produce an empowering aesthetic.

Men may wear highly polished shoes at key moments: weddings, funerals, job interviews, or simply with a dark suit in a professional role. Shoes can be status symbols which require a degree of knowledge or skill to use correctly, so shiny brown brogues require regular polishing, and Goodyear welted soles can be recognised and entirely replaced unlike glued soles. Like other material culture shoe construction may also merge with art and enchantment (Gell, 1992; 1998). For example, to quote the shoemaker Edward Green, 'We have half a dozen or so styles at Edward Green – most notably the Dover – which have the toe and apron carefully sewn by hand with a boar's bristle' (Green, 2017). The skill and time required to make these objects prices them as elite material culture but, like the skateboarder's shoes, only members of a specific community might have the semiotic knowledge needed to recognise particular expensive shoes.

Shoes and other apparel have multiple qualities and exist in the social world. Importantly, shoes 'need to be understood as [part of] an endlessly incomplete, embodied process' (Hockey et al., 2013: 5, 11). Objects like these are entangled with multiple forms of embodied identity; including life course, gender, sex and sexuality, materially grounded and socially differentiated, highlighting inequality which is manifested in gradations of knowledge or group membership. This fluidity of materiality mirrors Tim Ingold's (2010) concept of creative entanglement. However, contra Ingold, the material form is not itself an agent of this entanglement (Ingold, 2010: 12). Instead, embodiment is a creation of cohesive behaviours: individuals use this material culture in communication – signalling shared fraternity and reinforcing social structures. As described here, shoes are similar to all apparel, including weapons or jewellery, which are more than badges or props in social performances. They are also a metaphor for other aesthetic and physical qualities which enhance or define aspects of individual identity. These material manifestations require investment and in turn shape personae embodying inalienable identities influenced by social structures which impact on lifeways.

In modern cases there are examples of people preselecting burial costumes of their own, or choosing clothing for burial because of seasonal or specific contexts. In Sheila Harper's study of modern gravegoods one woman chose not to bury her husband in his shoes because 'shoes were for going to the doctor' (Harper, 2012: 48). Another group preferred to see a lady with her glasses on: 'She looks just like herself, doesn't she? I like her more with her glasses on' (Harper, 2012: 49). In both cases the presence or absence of objects reinforced the deceased's personhood in the eyes of the mourners. In these examples the use of an inalienable object within a grave required particular people to contribute, for example:

> 'We've put something in his top pocket, if that's alright.' I say: 'Whatever it is, is it to go with him?' He says: 'Yeah. It's just a cigarette, like. He liked a cigarette.' I say: 'That's not a problem.' The eldest brother says: 'No lighter, though. He'll have to get a light off someone else up there', and he gestures towards the sky as he says this. As they leave one of the

other brothers says to me: 'Thank you. He looks fantastic.' They walk out. When I go through and check the chapel, I see that, aside from a single cigarette, they have put a shot-sized bottle of Jack Daniels in Mr Atkinson's breast pocket as well. (Harper, 2012: 56)

One case study, often discussed by undertakers on the University of Bath's *Death and Society* Master's degree, was the inclusion of teddy bears and other objects in children's coffins, and the increasing need to have larger coffins for children to accommodate the extra material added for burial. By contrast, a crematorium might not allow a teddy bear to be cremated because burning artificial fibres is banned by many local authorities' environmental policy. The inclusion of a bear, shoes, glasses or cigarettes might depend on who dictates the funeral process. In the previous example, the wife may have disliked shoes because of her own values, or perhaps she associated her husband with a home environment; if they were an older couple, they may have left the house infrequently and only in a negative context, to see the doctor towards the end of his life. But the man's daughter might not have felt the same. As a result, we must see gravegoods as the end product of an ongoing social negotiation, not just between the funerary participants, but also other *actant* structures (like the crematorium or local government). But these processes are individual and specific and so may not always be obvious to archaeological enquiry.

Within the social world, objects and spaces may have multiple meanings where people have multiple disparate identities concurrently. Social archaeologists (like sociologists and anthropologists) are habitually challenged by situations in which multiple things happened simultaneously. It is therefore not possible to remove one factor, gender for example, from a mixture of other forces which include kinship, age, status or family and which might act on people's behaviour or perceptions. What is important is to recognise that the social world is not a fixed entity, but is in a state of constant unrest. This fluidity can be seen most obviously in archaeology, as opposed to sociology or social anthropology, because its subjects come from sites which span tens or hundreds of years and are not snapshots of social systems explored using focus groups, surveys or ethnographic observation. Archaeology is well placed to explore relations through societal change because society is not static, but consists of elastic identities expressed in a variety of ways which evolve and change over time, and it is this change that is identifiable.

Many of the underlying processes seen with shoes can also be considered for other objects which intersect with and enhance bodies: weapons, clothing or jewellery, for example. The spears from Apple Down and Orpington were not simply symbols added to a grave to signal rank or legal status. Like shoes, weapons were an extension of the person. A sword is worn perhaps regularly on a baldric or belt, so is visually associated with a person, and its shape may alter with wear, by a hand resting on it adding a patina and character (Sayer *et al.*, 2019; Brunning, 2019). When being worn, a sword may affect its wearer's stance, changing the body posture, and when it is left to one side a person may feel vulnerable, disempowered or naked. A spear regularly practised might leave calluses on its user's hands. Practice, as well as combat, is a physical activity with dangers that might leave recognisable scarring that could become part of a person's personality.

Both spears and swords need knowledge to use. Spears may have been hafted locally, with a handle cut from local wood, its head riveted or attached depending on local method or tradition. A whetstone is required to keep any blade sharp, and it might be wrapped, protected from the soil when it was placed into the grave; for example, grave 37 from Snape or the wrapped three-spear bundle also found at Snape in grave 47 (Filmer-Sankey and Pestell, 2001). Early Anglo-Saxon spear-heads are iron, so they had to be maintained, cleaned and looked after. A well-worn but well-maintained weapon conveys semiotic knowledge, whereas a broken haft, a haft of inappropriate size or a rusted or bent spearhead might engender exclusion or indicate a lost skill; for example grave 158 from West Heslerton, East Yorkshire, was accompanied by a spear with a deliberately bent blade. In the grave spears may be found alone, but swords are most often found in conjunction with other weapons. Out of the 534 weapon burials studied by Härke, 237 included just a spear whereas only nine examples included a solo sword, and there were sixty-two swords in total in this sample (Härke, 1989b: 56). Like shoes, swords might be visually empowering in weapon combinations, but jarring or disempowering when seen alone or with the wrong clothing and equipment.

Spears are transformative objects – a person holding a spear could be a guard, a fighter, a hunter – and the spear might be a threat, a danger or a reassuring presence. Previous studies show that weapons probably conveyed gender identities and were used in different ways over the life course (Stoodley, 2000; 2011; Härke, 1997). Early Anglo-Saxon swords were pattern welded; their fittings were often changed and some had great age before being buried. Epic poems describe swords as a 'hero's weapon' (Bone, 1989). Equally, however, some spears were pattern welded or carried embossed decoration or symbols, for example the ring-and-dot decorated spear from grave 51 at Great Chesterford, Essex (Evison, 1994: 150) – so while all swords probably carried cultural enchantment some spears were equally distinct, or made special with pattern welding or added decoration or symbols (Gell, 1992).

Leslie Alcock (1981), Rainer Christlein (1973) and J. F. Shephard (1979) directly associated weapons with rank. However, it is unlikely that specific subdivisions of rank were symbolised by weapon combinations, or by combinations with other material culture as with Evison's interpretation of Orpington (Evison, 1982: 165). Like dress shoes, the presence of a weapon in a grave probably embodied masculinity and formality. It conveyed authority and the knowledge to maintain and use it. That knowledge was gained from social associations, being taught, learning by copying and practice with comrades, and so a weapon conveys connection and association. The five small spears in graves 113, 121, 122, 126 and 148 from Apple Down may have been included because of their connection with social structures, masculinity and weapon use. Nonetheless they were outside the central areas of the cemetery, a phenomenon also seen at Orpington where graves 71, 76, 78 and 81 were neither spatially nor material similar to the other weapon burials (see Figure 1.7). All four of these graves were placed away from the centre of the burial ground. In both of these cemeteries the single spear entangled multiple qualities with overlapped messages. Importantly then, the spear did not convey the same associations for all people all of the time; instead it was a complex artefact with multiple layers of meaning which functioned differently within different social structures.

Anthropologists describe living society, and in a lived context weapons or clothing may help to construct the personhood of an individual. A person may choose to construct themselves using semiotic knowledge (Fowler, 2001: 160; 2004; 2010). In the mortuary context, however, it was social structures – shared cultural approaches to gender, age, common identity groups and local community – that dictated the nature of relationships and influenced how a person was treated, what they were buried with and who contributed to the material aesthetic of commemoration. The agents influencing burial existed (and exist) within the relationships between people and the relationships between objects and people.

Conclusion

Society has a pluralistic quality, which means we do not always know which combination of social factors is determining the archaeological record. However, social phenomena exist in history and geography, and meanings can be transient. Archaeologists see chronological phenomena muddied by preservation and recognition. We might understand how a particular quality changed in local, regional and national settings and how this quality was situated in relation to similar phenomena. What is harder to understand is what underlies a particular material pattern, but this does not suggest that social complexity, multiple determinations and ambiguity mean woolly interpretation. Socially situated phenomena like belief, personal motivation or affinity exist within material situations; they empowered *actants* with agency and created material expression, using the conceptual tools available, to create recognisable tropes or patterns in practice that others might also recognise in actual or conceptual terms. Together, objects and social relationships have causal powers which produce *leitmotifs*, shared themes, within and between sites and across different scales.

Each funeral event is different from the last; the dead are dissimilar people, and the social relationships and participants might be changed. But at each event there are similarities – participants have a relationship, and their social world is being reproduced by communication and interaction. Their individual attitudes towards status, gender, age and kinship have been shaped by interactions and relationships created or defined by social structures in the form of agreed canons. These principles are renegotiated as social situations are confirmed or challenged, creating new semiotic knowledge shared between participants. Objects are symbiotic to this situation because they are an aesthetic essential add-on to the layered and textured experience. In grave 78 at Oakington we saw a concealed touch, an act of body positioning which created knowledge and obscured it under a sleeve. The touch may have been a performance meant for just a few members of a subgroup of funerary participants, united with a shared memory and a shared connection to the deceased. Equally, the weapons located in the Apple Down and Orpington graves were part of an aesthetic combination appealing to the participants because they epitomised the qualities of a shared social class. Even at these two sites, spears had multiple meanings, appearing both in weapon combinations and singly within the graves of different people buried in separate areas of the cemeteries.

In doing social archaeology we are not comparing objective scientific phenomena, but events, outlooks and decisions with multiple qualities, so we must use qualitative and quantitative approaches simultaneously. For a cemetery this means a holistic approach because it explores artefacts and bodies together. A multi-dimensional perspective might employ spatial and temporal understandings, and a multiple-scale approach investigates single graves, cemetery patterns or regional distributions. With multiple methods applied to complementary evidence we can glimpse the shape of the social process which created observable phenomena. This chapter is an introduction to the philosophical perspective which underpins this book. Each community used its conceptual tools to create a unique site and they employed a language using grave orientation, chronology, grave plots and mounds to express that message.

2

The syntax of cemetery space

This chapter describes the physical organisation of early Anglo-Saxon cemetery space by detailing the repertoire of shared semiotics used to organise a cemetery, specifically: cemetery topography, clusters of graves or burial plots, grave density, grave orientation, burial rituals and material culture. It also considers cemeteries which combine multiple organisational strategies.

Introduction: structuring mortuary semiotics

Cemeteries are not simply places where people bury the dead; they are the product of social agents working within the confines of cultural practice and shared semiotic knowledge. Within cemetery space, people shared a conceptual understanding by participating in episodic narratives which were specific to that place and those people. Because of this, burial practice was not universal; it might be interpreted differently by local, regional and individual agents depending on their own circumstances and experiences. It is for these reasons that broad questions like ethnicity, religious practice or afterlife belief and cultural death ways have proved difficult to address (Lucy, 2000b). Sam Lucy (1998) touched on this issue when she considered the differences between cemeteries in East Yorkshire as the product of regional, rather than national, variations. This is a useful starting point: early Anglo-Saxon cemeteries do show regional variations, but they also show considerable localised variation where every site and every grave is different from others in a whole host of ways. Early Anglo-Saxon cemeteries were employed at a plurality of social scales simultaneously, from the individual to the local and regional, creating dissimilar sites which nonetheless shared broad conceptual ideas.

Early Anglo-Saxon burial grounds are recognisable because of the similarities to other sites – small barrows or mounds of earth cover some of the graves, and cemeteries are found in close proximity to a settlement and water (Arnold, 1997: 54–63). However, one cemetery is not all cemeteries, and the details will be unique to a particular community. For instance, only a few people in the Thames Valley, Kent or East Anglia would have been in a position to see another region's cemeteries, let alone participate in another group's funerals. Equally, a few people from one community might have travelled to another adjacent community to attend a single funeral event, but the primary influence on any specific site would have been from its contiguous populations. This means that cemeteries were not necessarily the product of societal-level decisions, but were organised locally using a repertoire of burial technologies which may, or may not, have shared similarities with any other site according to family, community and regional traditions operating within wider early medieval cultural boundaries.

The influences of individual agents operating locally would have had varying effects on cemetery aesthetic. Each burial and each cemetery had been 'designed' by different people, which would result in chronological and spatial variation. Each site and each grave would be different. From this perspective, it should not be a surprise to learn that all archaeologically excavated early Anglo-Saxon cemeteries look different, but the conceptual semiotics behind the organisation of many of these sites may have been very similar.

A useful perspective for considering mortuary rituals is to view funerals as staged events with active participants (Price, 2010). Each episode would have been different. Different people would have attended each funeral, depending on who was alive to be present at any one chronological point, and different people would have contributed to each funeral to degrees that were dictated by membership of a particular social group (Sayer, 2010). So, while we might see each cemetery as a single site and plausibly the product of a single community, it was also the result of various events at different times that included dissimilar participants who had their own unique experiences and perspectives. Each site had its own internal chronology and this dictated its shape and future development, as well as the nature of the burials. Therefore cemeteries were not just the focus of single-staged funeral events; they were an aesthetic, visually powerful tool that people used to recall the history of a community, their family and their genealogy. They were important for the development of individual and community memory (Williams, 2006; Devlin, 2007b). This was developed within the burial space where the living told stories about the dead and used the semiotic knowledge they shared literally to map the past onto a physical space. This story could change as further burials were added and as new generations reworked the contributions of their forerunners.

Early Anglo-Saxon cemeteries were frequently small and only a few contained more than a couple of hundred graves. Mucking in Essex, West Heslerton in East Yorkshire, Morning Thorpe and Spong Hill (both in Norfolk) were all particularly large sites, with either 200 to 400 inhumations or many thousands of cremations. However, most cemeteries contained around one hundred graves and were in use for 75 to 150 years; although Wasperton (in Warwickshire) and Spong Hill had their origins in the fourth century AD and so were used for considerably longer (Carver *et al.*, 2009; Hills and Lucy, 2013). Even at these large, long-lived sites burial did not take place every week, every month or even every year. Burials were infrequent but, because cemeteries are usually found adjacent to settlements, they would have hosted other gatherings too. In connecting the past and present, early Anglo-Saxon cemeteries became a narrative tool which contained semiotic messages in the form of mnemonic devices operating on an aesthetic level. This may have functioned at the scale of the grave where similarities in burial tradition and gravegoods are occasionally found in adjacent graves (Williams, 2006: 42). As we saw at Orpington (in Chapter 1), once a grave has been closed the memory of its contents is fragile and may be subject to change. Mnemonic devices would have been most effective at a cemetery scale visible for many years after the funeral. Some early Anglo-Saxon cemeteries were located next to ancient barrows, where old ditches were used to define one edge of the site and newly made small mounds were employed to highlight grave locations. Cemeteries also contained rows of graves, clusters of inhumations or (frequently) cremations and graves positioned on different orientations. These physical traits could be interpreted by members of the local community because they shared semiotic knowledge. Mortuary space was imbued with materially represented narratives, and while cemeteries may not have been mirrors of society they were constructed as representations of it, which went on to aid in the construction of contemporary community narratives (Williams and Sayer, 2009).

Cemetery topography

Early Anglo-Saxon cemeteries were often focused on earlier features such as monuments, buildings, ditches, roads and contemporary Anglo-Saxon barrows. Howard Williams (1997; 1998) investigated the reuse of prehistoric monuments as significant places for the location of burial grounds. He concluded that the use of visible ancient features enabled early Anglo-Saxon communities to ritually appropriate their environment, to propagate and generate myths about their origin and identity. The placement of seventh-century burials bordering the

Roman villa at Eccles in Kent (Williams 1997), or sixth-century burials alongside the Romano-British temple on Gallows Hill, Swaffham Prior in Cambridgeshire (Malim, 2006), and beside the Romano-British bath house at Orpington, Kent (Palmer, 1984), tell us a great deal about what was visible in the Early Middle Ages and the importance that these ancient structures may have had (Figure 2.1). Equally the fifth- and sixth-century cemetery at Abingdon, Oxfordshire, was adjacent to a Bronze Age ring ditch (Leeds and Harden, 1936), and the small seventh-century sites at Marina Drive (Dunstable, Bedfordshire), Ports Down I (Hampshire) and Bargates (Dorset) were all situated close to Bronze Age barrows (Matthews, 1962; Jarvis, 1983; Corney *et al.*, 1967). In fact, 61 per cent of those early Anglo-Saxon cemeteries that reused ancient features were located adjacent to round barrows (Williams, 1997: 17; 1998).

It is not enough simply to understand that the early Anglo-Saxons used ancient features to locate their cemeteries; it is also important to consider how they structured their sites around them. For example, Empingham II (Rutland), Morning Thorpe (Norfolk), Snape (Suffolk) and Shudy Camps (Cambridgeshire) all used earlier features to define one or more of their boundaries and shape at least one side of their site (Lucy, 2000b: 129–30; Devlin, 2007b: 57–8). Anglo-Saxon cemeteries did not just share adjacency with older monuments, they integrated them into their form and used them to provide structure. For example, an earlier ditch adjacent to the small seventh-century cemetery at Garton Slack II, East Yorkshire, influenced the location of burials, which were positioned on the same axis and in rows alongside it. The same is true for earlier cemeteries: Mucking II, Essex, was a large site consisting of more than 500 graves, the majority of which were situated between two parallel late Roman enclosure ditches (Hirst and Clark, 2009; Figure 2.2). In both of these examples the position of earlier, but still visible, topographic elements not only encouraged the placement of the cemetery, but also contributed to its shape and influenced how it developed. At Berinsfield, Oxfordshire, both the placement of burials and the orientation of the graves were determined by the location of a series of intersecting Roman ditches. The northernmost graves were positioned on a N/S axis along a Roman ditch oriented on the same axis; the southern graves were positioned parallel to an E/W aligned ditch, lost through later quarrying (Figure 2.2).

The graves on an E/W axis at Petersfinger, Wiltshire, appear to surround a now absent barrow and at Deal, Kent, the presence of a single large Bronze-Age ring ditch, presumably a round barrow, not only influenced the location of the site but was used to organise it. Two groups of sixth-century graves were positioned on opposite sides of the barrow, surrounding it and reinforcing the physical separation of these

Figure 2.1 Early Anglo-Saxon cemeteries at Orpington, Kent, and Abingdon, Oxfordshire. The Abingdon cemetery (top) was deliberately located next to a Bronze Age barrow and made use of the barrow ditch in its organisation. Orpington (bottom) was located to the west of a Roman building, presumably visible when the cemetery location was chosen.

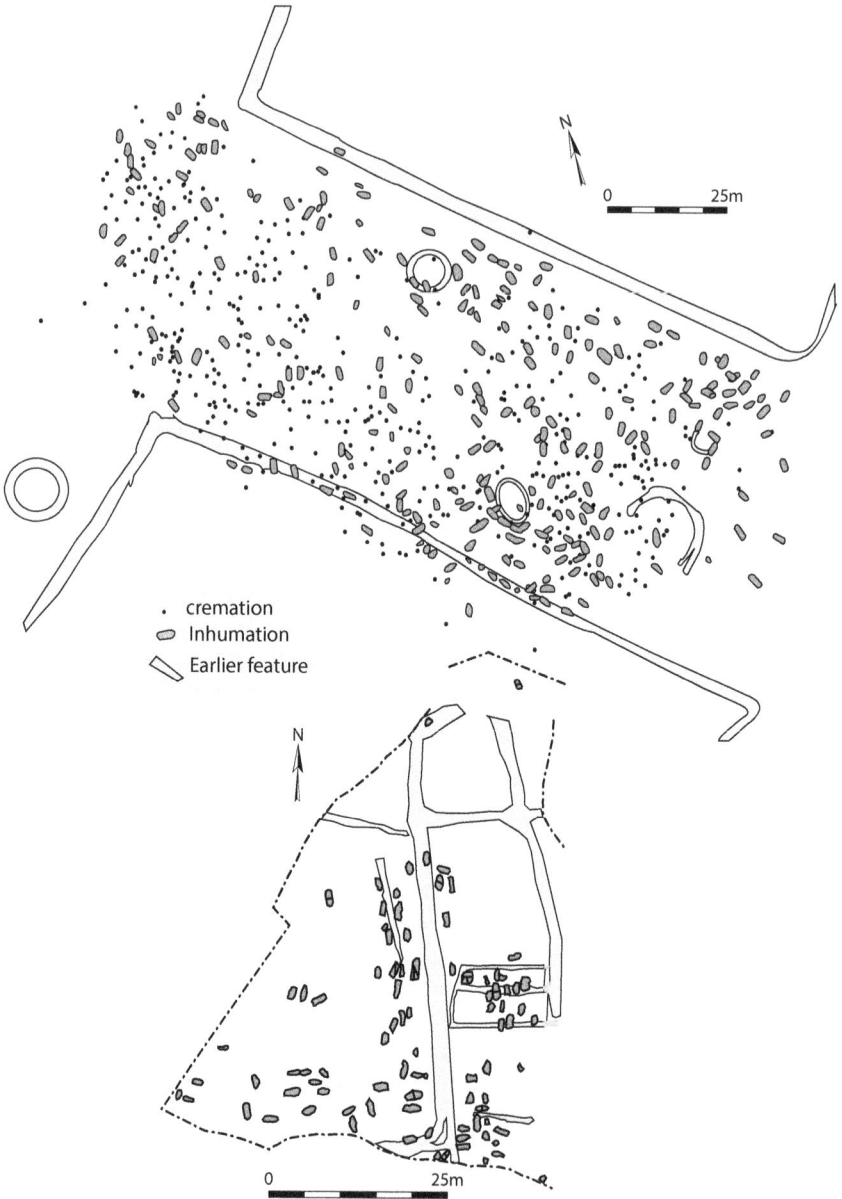

Figure 2.2 Mucking II, Essex (top), was a large and complex mixed-rite cemetery. The graves were positioned in between two late Roman ditches, which then shaped the cemetery. Berinsfield, Oxfordshire (bottom), also used a series of Roman ditches to provide structure; graves were adjacent to a N/S- or E/W-oriented ditch, and some were located within a small enclosed area.

two plots. The early Anglo-Saxon cemetery at Saltwood, Kent, was also divided between two Bronze-Age barrows, over 100 m apart, and the two groups of seventh-century burials at Caistor St Edmund, Norfolk, were separated by over 150 m and focused on two separate ring ditches (Penn, 2000). The ring ditches at the cemetery at Springfield Lyons, Essex, contained part of the site and housed a section of the cemetery whose ritual treatment was different to many of the inhumations found outside the ring ditches (see Chapter 4). Topography was an important part of the early Anglo-Saxon burial syntax. It influenced how people selected a location for their burial ground and continued to influence how that burial ground developed over time and how it was structured, defining similarities between individuals and differences between groups of graves. People created a site by selecting a location, but that location then influenced how they and later generations interacted with that space.

Grave plots

Of all of the ways to describe cemetery space, the most enduring are accounts of the clustering of graves into visually definable plots. For this study a plot is considered to be a group of graves with a clear demarcation separating it from other groups. Unfortunately, many earlier identifiers of plots have not always been clear about how they arrived at their boundaries. In an early and systematic investigation Ellen-Jane Pader (1982) used multivariate statistical methods to calculate differences between burials by identifying those which were most similar. Based primarily on artefacts and body positions, she was able to offer a detailed description of the organisation of four sites – Holywell Row and Westgarth Gardens, both in Suffolk, Bergh Apton, Norfolk, and Droxford, Hampshire. Mads Ravn (2003), attempted a similar study using serration-based statistics on the inhumation graves at Spong Hill, Norfolk. Unfortunately, he was unable to identify any groups in the inhumation graves, although the patterning he observed among cremation vessels showed far more spatial planning around age and gender than independent clusters of men, women and children (Ravn, 2003: 99–129).

These two different statistical methods were used by Pader and Ravn to investigate the content of graves and derive similarities, although Ravn implied that there was simply too much variation in the mortuary rite to identify meaningful similarities. Other scholars have shied away from computer methods and have relied on the visual appearance of a cemetery, with or without considering the content of individual graves, to conclude that cemeteries consisted of single or multiple-grave plots (see Chapter 1; Evison, 1987; Hirst, 1985; Stoodley, 1999; Härke, 1992). Alternative studies have used a combination of spatial layout and chronological information to understand or identify plots (Härke, 1995; Penn and Brugmann, 2007).

Just as there have been different methods employed to investigate the organisation of cemetery sites, there have also been two prevailing ways of describing the results. Pader (1982), Evison (1987) and Hirst (1985) preferred to see small clusters of burials as resembling small groups – mother, father and children, for example. Evison took this interpretation further and argued that the clusters of graves at Great Chesterford, Essex, were defined by large barrows overlying each of them (Evison, 1994: 46). In contrast, Heinrich Härke (1997), Nick Stoodley (1999) and Kenneth Penn and Birte Brugmann (2007), preferred to see larger, mixed burial plots that contained multiple adult inhumations. However, these two explanations are not always contradictory and Stoodley happily divided the Norton cemetery (Cleveland) into four small units based on the presence of gaps visible between groups of burials (Stoodley, 2011).

Recent developments in spatial analysis computer software – particularly spatially descriptive statistics and GIS (geographic information systems) – have made different types of statistical assessment possible. For example, Ripley's K-function analysis can be used to identify deviations from spatial homogeneity: the distance at which there is statistical significance in the proximity of groups of graves. This function can be used to investigate the mathematical evidence for clustering within a cemetery (Sayer and Wienhold, 2012).[1] Ripley's K-function provides statistical proof of clustering at multiple scales in graphical form, and provides a numerical distance between points at which clustering occurs. These distances can then be imaged as heat maps or kernel density plans which illustrate the density of burial by asking the computer to draw a heat map based on the value provided from the Ripley's K-function. Once established, this approach can be used to identify the size and extent of groups of graves within a cemetery, as the kernels plotted over a grave will overlap where there is statistically significant clustering. It is also useful to establish the presence of significant gaps around graves which may have hosted small barrows (see Chapter 4).

Burial plots can be identified in many different ways and scholars have focused variously on the presence of children's graves, the similarity of objects or the identification of groups of graves.[2] What the statistical assessment demonstrates is that there is, for numerous sites, significance in the grouping of some graves into clusters and that these were used in the arrangement of cemetery space. One of the key characteristics of the cemeteries described here is the variety of significant distances between burials. At Lechlade and Berinsfield, for example, the difference in the density of graves was itself a key difference between the sixth- and seventh-century burials (Sayer and Wienhold, 2012), and at other sites the density of each plot was a significant visual identifier used to differentiate between them. Grave plots were an important tool in organising early Anglo-Saxon cemeteries, but even these vary notice-ably, both between and within sites. Variable characteristics of plots include their density, date and shape.

One cemetery which is divided into three noticeably distinct plots is Wakerley, Northamptonshire; it consisted of eighty-five excavated skele-tons in seventy-two graves and it dates to the sixth century AD. When the cemetery was excavated in 1968 and 1969, the excavators visually iden-tified three major groups of burials: a western group, a central group and an eastern group (Adams and Jackson, 1988–9: 74–5). Re-analysis using the Ripley K-function showed statistically significant clustering among graves at approximately 3 m. When the density of graves was plotted at this distance, it showed three groups of burials: a large group to the east (C), a central cluster (B), and a less dense south-western cluster (A) (Figure 2.3). The gaps between plots can be identified because Ripley's L-function tells us how big they need to be to vary from homogeneity, in other words, the gap between the end of one cluster and the beginning of another. However, people at the time did not always make decisions which can be shown now in statistically meaningful ways and, as if to prove this, there is a small grave (grave 72) situated between the central (B) and western (A) plots at Wakerley. The grave sits on the midpoint between the two clusters and is more than 3 m from each. Grave 72 was intentionally located in this 'in-between area', positioned deliberately at odds with the cemetery's dominant arrangement.

The cemetery at Norton, in northern Cleveland, excavated between 1983 and 1985, is like Wakerley in that it was organised into deliber-ately separated groups of graves. However, these plots are much less dense and notably less distinct than those seen at Wakerley. The Norton site is a large Anglo-Saxon cemetery which consisted of three cremations and 117 inhumation graves, dating predominantly from the sixth cen-tury, but with a small number of graves from the early seventh century. The excavators suggested that it was laid out in rows rather than plots, and these were divided into two visible halves by a wide gap along the cemetery's central axis (Sherlock and Welch, 1992: 15). Nick Stoodley (2011: 654) preferred to interpret the whole site as consisting of four smaller plots, based on the appearance of groups of children's graves within these areas. The proximity of burials was statistically significant at 7 m, appreciably sparser than at Wakerley. The density of graves suggests the presence of two large burial plots separated by the central

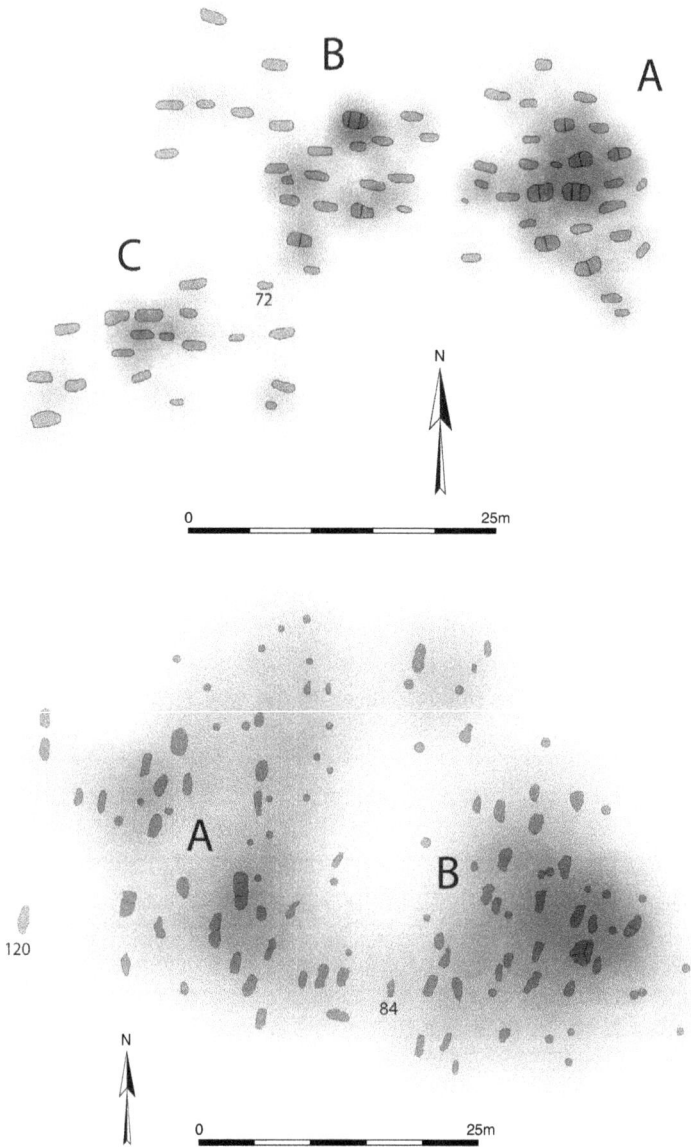

Figure 2.3 Wakerley, Northamptonshire (top) was divided into three groups of graves, A to the west, B in the middle and C to the east. Grave 72 was located in between plots B and C and over 3 m from burials in either plot. Norton, northern Cleveland (bottom), was divided into two groups, A to the west and B to the east. Grave 120 was on the western edge and grave 84 was placed in between the two plots.

gap, with each of these two plots denser in its interior than around its edges (Figure 2.3). Each of these two groups is roughly the same size and, by eye, there appears to be a separate group to the north of plot B, but these are within 7 m of the other inhumations in this area. There is just one outlying grave to the west of plot A (grave 120) but, as with Wakerley, the pattern has been challenged by just one grave (grave 84) placed deliberately part way between plots A and B.

The Wakerley and Norton cemeteries were divided into two or three groups of roughly equal proportions, but this is not always the case, as can be seen in the cemetery at Orpington which was described in Chapter 1. Orpington was a mixed-rite cemetery and consisted of eighty-five burials in eighty separate graves, excavated in stages between 1965 and 1977 (Tester, 1968; 1969; 1977; Evison, 1987: 164). The clustering of graves was statistically significant at 2.5 m (Figure 2.4). This cemetery seems to have been divided into two unequal but spatially distinct parts: a small group of nine graves on the west (B) and the remaining graves to the east (A), with a concentration of graves around the barrow burial, grave 23. Two inhumation graves and some cremations were placed well away from the plots in between them and not associated with either. Just like the graves at Norton and Wakerley, these burials were deliberately positioned in an indistinct location.

Similarly, the early Anglo-Saxon cemetery found at Blacknall Field, near Pewsey in Wiltshire, consisted of unequal groups of graves, with two large plots of similar size and two provably smaller but dissimilar ones in between. Blacknall Field dates to between the late fifth and mid-sixth centuries AD (Annable and Eagles, 2010). The site contained over 102 skeletons and four cremations from one hundred excavated graves. It was explored in stages between 1968 and 1976. The graves clustered with statistical significance at 3.5 m, with the two large plots in the north (A) and south (B) purposely separated by over 20 m (Figure 2.4). In between these were found two smaller and less dense groups of graves (C and D). Although parts of plot D remain unexcavated, its density suggests a smaller cluster of graves. Interestingly, the larger northern A and southern B plots had been constructed with similar densities and both clusters also included a number of solo satellite graves on their outer peripheries.

Despite these examples, not all early Anglo-Saxon cemeteries were deliberately separated into statistically significant groups of graves. The small site at Snell's Corner, Hampshire, contained thirty-two graves in one large group. Härke (1992: 171; 1997: 138) described Snell's Corner as monocentred and the Ripley K-test agreed, showing spatial homogeneity because deliberate gaps could not be found (Figure 2.5). Similarly, the forty-four graves at Winnall II, Hampshire, were not statistically

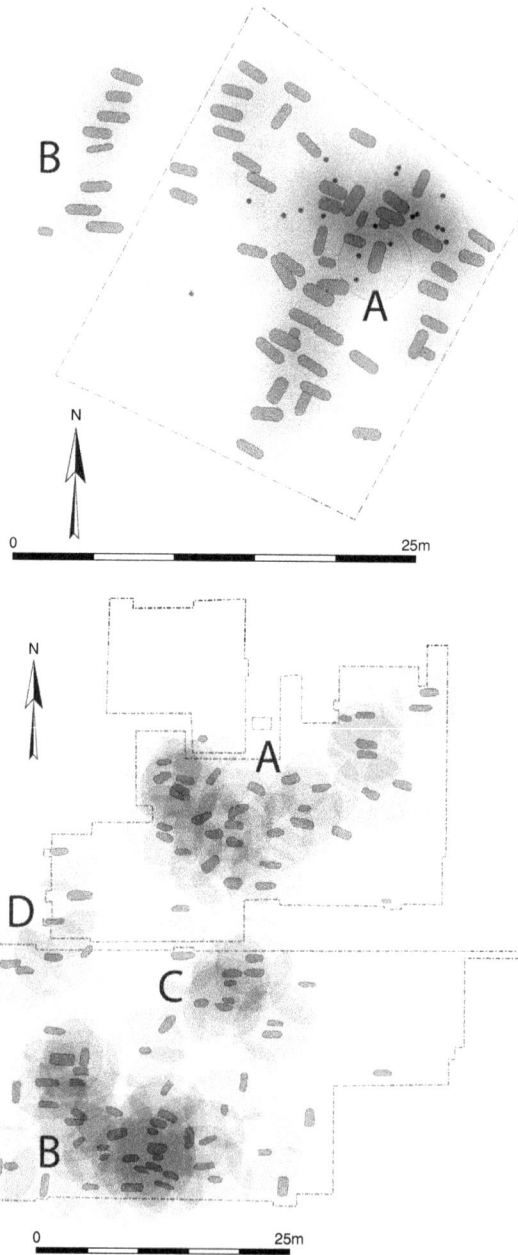

Figure 2.4 Orpington, Kent (top), consisted of two groups of graves, A to the east with the majority of burials, and nine others to the west in group B. Blacknall Field, Wiltshire (bottom), was divided into at least three plots, A to the north, B to the south and C, a small plot, in the middle. There was a further group of graves, D, to the west, which may have been a further plot, as yet unexcavated.

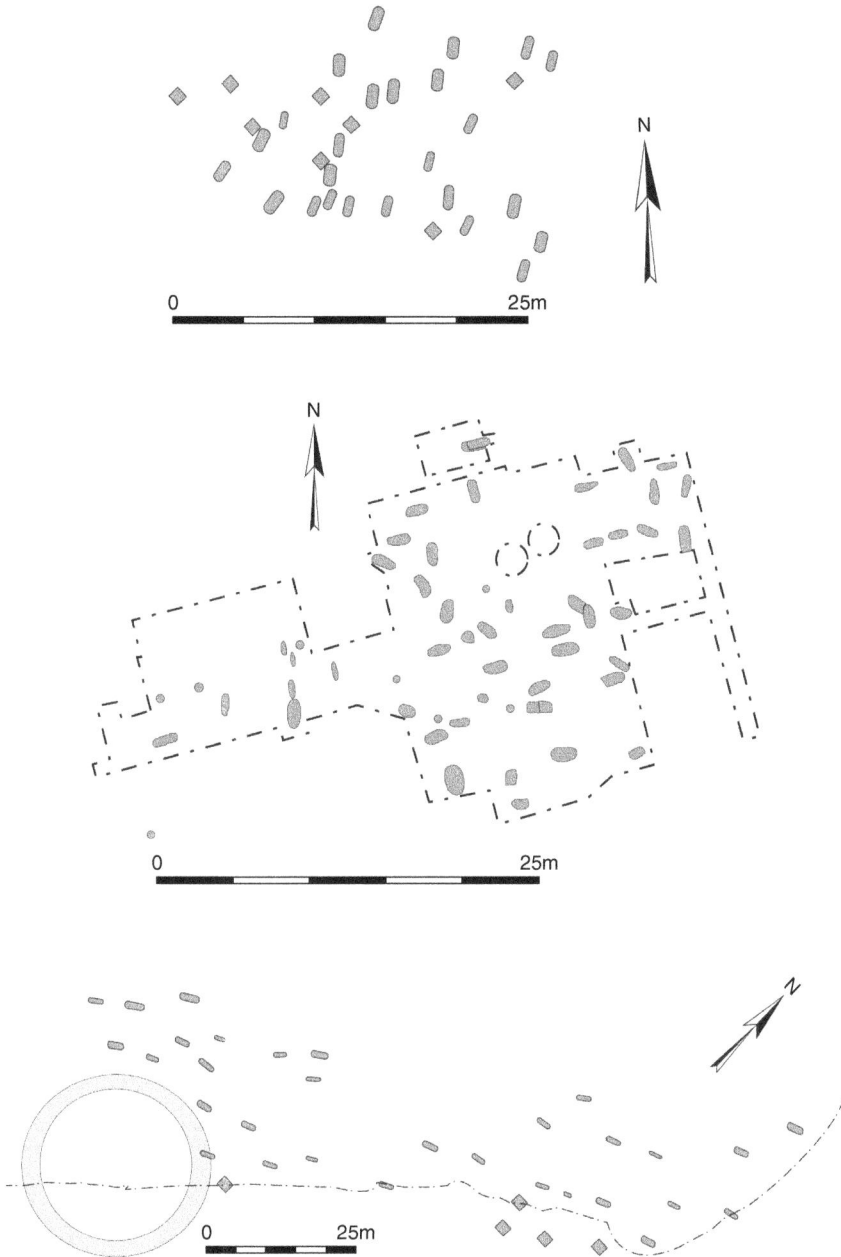

Figure 2.5 Snells Corner, Hampshire (top), consisted of one group of graves. Sewerby, East Yorkshire (middle), gave the impression of multiple plots but was homogeneous, although the excavated area may have been a small part of a larger cemetery. Holborough, Kent (bottom), looked like two groups of graves but in fact was entirely homogeneous.

clustered, and neither were the fifty-seven fifth- and sixth-century graves from Sewerby in the East Riding of Yorkshire (Hirst, 1985). The Sewerby cemetery highlights an important point here, because the graves were dispersed and could give the impression of multiple plots (see Stoodley, 1999: 131–4; Härke, 1992: 171; 1997: 138). Perhaps the site which is most surprising in its homogeneity, with no evident clustering, is the cemetery adjacent to an older ring ditch at Holborough, Kent. Although only partially excavated, these thirty-five graves were widely spaced and filled an area approximately 115 m long and 38 m wide. This is surprising because to the naked eye Holborough looks as if it had two clusters of graves, but in fact burials are spaced evenly throughout the burial area. The deliberateness of this spacing is particularly apparent when it is contrasted with the dense 374-grave cemetery at Morning Thorpe, which was found in a much smaller area than Holborough, just 75 m by 26 m (Green *et al.*, 1987).

Unfortunately, early Anglo-Saxon cemeteries cannot be described simply as either grouped into plots or dispersed. The cemeteries at Polhill and Deal, both in Kent, are particularly interesting because they combine two characteristics, where part of each cemetery was clustered unevenly and part was regularly dispersed. Polhill is a predominantly seventh- and eighth-century site, and importantly the main cemetery was subdivided into two groups of graves which were clustered at 5 m, (A) and (B), with a small satellite group to the south of the main cemetery (C) (Figure 2.6). The southern part of the main group (A) of graves was the larger of the two clusters and interestingly to the north of these was placed a deliberately homogeneous group of thirty-seven graves spread over an area of approximately 75 m by 70 m (D).

The dispersed graves at Polhill, Snell's Corner, Winnall II and Holborough are all seventh- or eighth-century cemeteries. It may be that all of these graves had small barrows erected over them, but this seems unlikely. Perhaps the later-sixth and seventh centuries saw a deliberate transformation in the burial rite, but also in the stimuli which structured that rite. For many communities, clustered graves were no longer an important part of the funerary message.

Grave density

Grave density is a characteristic of cemetery organisation tangled up with the construction of identifiable grave plots. Density is a powerful visual tool that may have been used to enhance physical proximity or difference. This is evident in two ways: firstly, different cemeteries display different densities of graves; and secondly, within some sites the density of graves varies between groups and may have been used

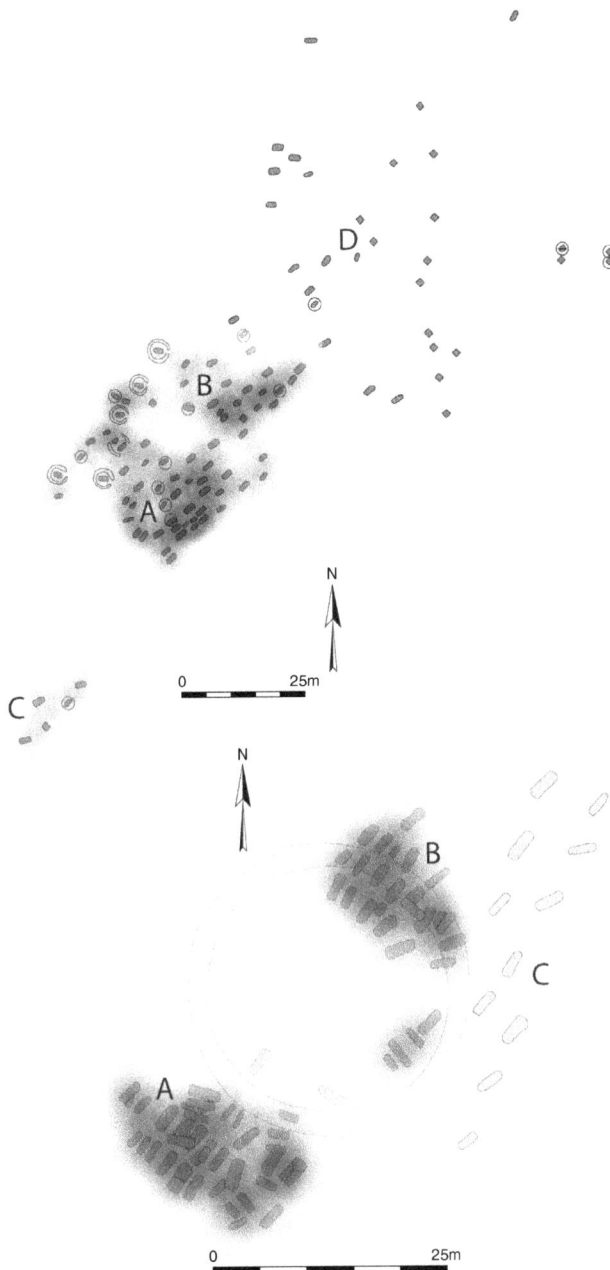

Figure 2.6 Polhill (top) and Deal (bottom) in Kent had different internal organisations. Polhill consisted of three groups of graves A, B and C. Two of these were in close proximity, A and B, and a number of inhumations were deliberately dispersed (D). Deal was similarly organised with two plots, A and B; the later graves were homogeneous (C).

to distinguish clustered grave plots and ungrouped graves. As we have seen above, the density of graves is closely related to the clustering of graves. For example, the Polhill cemetery was divided into two clustered groups of graves with a number of dispersed burials to the north and these graves were much less densely spaced than the clustered burials (see Figure 2.6). The site at Deal, by contrast, has a similar arrangement, but the groups are much more clearly defined and distinct (Figure 2.6). The cemetery was excavated between 1986 and 1989 and revealed seventy-six closely packed graves, divided into three plots. There were two tightly clustered groups of fifth- and sixth-century burials, one to the north and one to the south of a Bronze-Age ring ditch, (A) and (B) respectively, and these graves clustered at 5 m. To the east of these was a third, more homogeneous, group of less dense graves (C), placed more than 5 m apart. The difference was evidently deliberate and these graves were part of a second phase in the burial ritual: this new generation deliberately changed the burial ritual, rejecting the previous burial areas in favour of a new zone and a new organisation. Indeed, these newer graves of the later sixth century and the seventh century may have had small barrows constructed over them (Sayer, 2009). Nonetheless, these funeral organisers deliberately maintained the cemetery as a single burial site which highlighted the new burial form while maintaining their connection with the past through physical proximity.

In both the Deal and Polhill cemeteries, the density of the burials was related directly to the use or nature of grave plots: at Polhill the two plots contained the densest groups of graves and at Deal the density of burials was part of a chronologically specific burial practice. However, at sites with less well-defined plots of graves, the density of burial may have been the defining organisational principle. An example of this can be found with the large cemetery at Mucking, which showed significant clustering at 2 m, but with a few gaps between burial groups. However, the relative proximity of graves may have distinguished different groups of burials with dense areas in the south (A), west (C) and north (D), and less dense groups in the middle (B) and east (E) (Figure 2.7). Equally, there were no evident plots at Morning Thorpe, where the site was particularly densely packed, with significant clustering at 1.5 m. Notably, Morning Thorpe was organised into a series of groups of graves centred on two high-density areas in the centre of the site, areas A and B.

The use of contrasting burial density is particularly evident at West Heslerton, where grave proximity was employed differently between the burial plots (Figure 2.8). This large inhumation cemetery of 201 graves was discovered in 1977 and excavated between 1977 and 1987. West Heslerton was divided up into plots, two of which – to the south of the site (A and B) – clustered at around 2.5 m and were found within

Figure 2.7 Mucking II, Essex (top), was a large and complex cemetery. The graves seem to have been organised into a series of large groups: A, C and D were dense clusters, and B and E were less dense. Morning Thorpe, Norfolk (bottom), did not have identifiable plots with gaps, but there were two particularly dense areas of graves (labelled A and B).

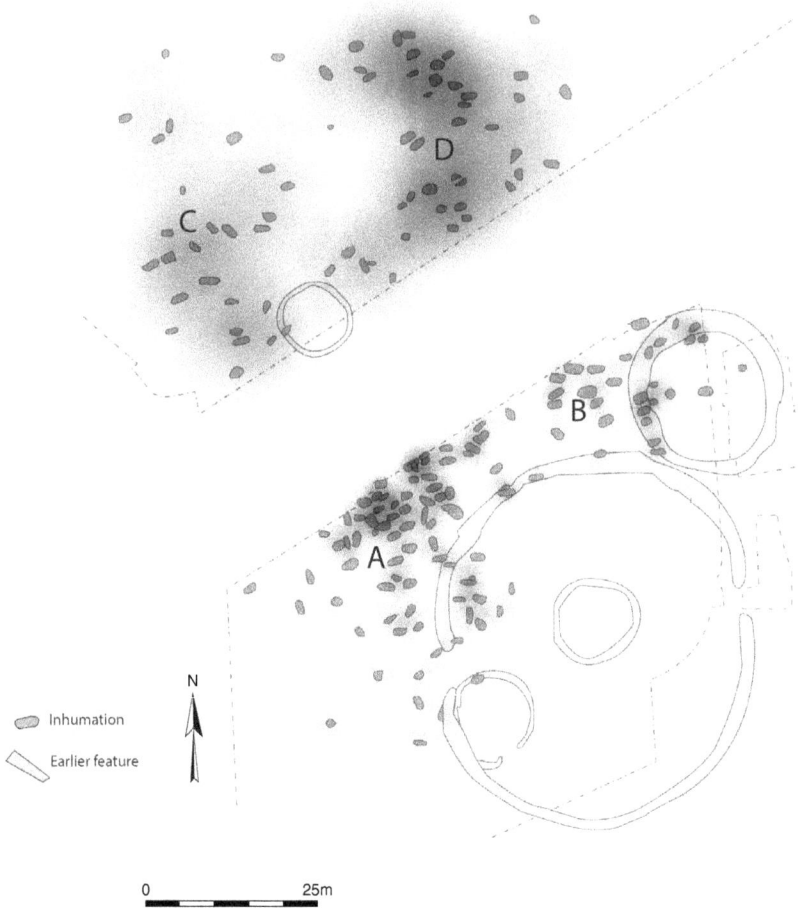

Figure 2.8 West Heslerton, East Yorkshire, had four plots A–D. The two southern ones (A and B) were densely packed at 2.5 m, the two northern plots (C and D) were less dense, with clustering at 10 m.

different areas of a complex of ring ditches; A being to the north-west of the large ring ditch, and B lying between the large ring ditch and a smaller one to the north-east. To the north of the modern road was found a much less dense group of burials with statistical clustering at 10 m. This group of burials seemed to be divided into two different groups, one on the east of a small ring ditch and one to the west. Both plots extended to the north, leaving a gap of between 11 m and 15 m in between. The spatial zoning of the four burial plots at West Heslerton differed, and funerary decisions may have focused on where and how to place the dead in a way that distinguished these different groups of individuals.

Similar difference can be seen at Dover Buckland, Kent; this large cemetery was subdivided into multiple plots or groups of graves and, like West Heslerton, these groups of graves had different densities in the north and south of the site. The Dover Buckland cemetery was first excavated in 1951 and again in 1994, and the sites of these excavations were separated by a railway, which had destroyed a limited number of graves (Parfitt and Anderson, 2012: 6). Together the two excavated elements included about 507 graves. Fascinatingly, these two elements (north and south) were organised in very different ways. The south-westernmost part of the cemetery, excavated in 1994, consisted of seven plots of graves all neatly separated and consistently clustered at 2 m (Figure 2.9). The 1951 graves in the north-east were clustered at different densities. Two groups of graves were most densely clustered at 3 m and one of these areas on the north of the site appears to have been divided into two plots, one larger one to the west (A) and one small one to the east (B). The other tightly spaced group, with a 3 m cluster, was found to the north-east of the 1951 excavation adjacent to an earlier ring ditch (C). However, the majority of graves were located between these two dense areas and have a less dense clustering at 9 m. These more dispersed graves seem to have been arranged into a series of smaller groups or plots. To the south-east of these areas the graves were placed homogeneously, but unfortunately this area was only partially excavated and so its extent and population is impossible to determine.

At Polhill, Deal, Mucking, West Heslerton and Dover Buckland, different funerary decisions were made which led to the varied organisation of these sites. This is compounded because there would have been dissimilar influences among funerary agents creating a contrasting use of space. Grouping graves together, or spreading them out, may have served as a way to create connections and mark difference within the mortuary environment. Grave density was used alongside other organisational characteristics like plots and created a rich and varied funerary aesthetic. Ultimately, this employment of space and differences in the origination of burial rituals led to the variations seen at these sites. At Deal, this was chronological: the last generations to use the site considered how that space had been used by its predecessors and opted for a different visual aesthetic. At West Heslerton and Mucking the variation existed between contrasting but contemporary groups. Perhaps burial practice differed because there were multiple strands to the burial tradition passed on between different community groups. Notably, at Polhill and Deal the least dense areas were not clustered at all, but there may have been very different reasons for this. At Deal, these later burials were among the wealthiest, whereas at Polhill few artefacts were associated with the more dispersed graves.

Figure 2.9 Buckland, at Dover in Kent, was a very complex mortuary landscape with multiple plots and different densities of burial. The part of the cemetery excavated in 1994 consisted of seven identifiable plots clustered at 2 m and with clear gaps between them. The north-eastern part, excavated in 1951, consisted of three plots (A, B and C) clustered at 3 m, and zone D, which consisted of at least seven groups of graves clustered at 9 m. Area L was homogeneous but only partly excavated.

Rows of graves

Many cemeteries either have rows or appear to be organised into rows or lines of graves. For clarity, rows are considered to be graves that are side-on to each other, whereas lines are lined up head to toe. Cemeteries organised in this way are seen more often in France and Germany, and date to the Iron Age and Early Middle Ages; they consisted of cemeteries with long rows of graves across them. The temptation is to assume that burials started at one end and were placed in chronological order until a particular row was finished and a new one started, a pattern reminiscent of some nineteenth-century practice (Sayer, 2011: 205).[3] However, this is not supported by the archaeological evidence, and adjacent burials can be chronologically separated by several decades or even hundreds of years (Hakenbeck, 2007a; 2011; Stapel, 2007). Rows of graves would not have been a series of neat lines when the cemetery was in use, even if they may seem that way to archaeologists looking at a cemetery plan. In many continental cemeteries, like Junkersdorf, Bülach, Müngersdorf (all near Cologne, Germany), or Lavoye or Le Haie des Vaches, in northern France, that appear to be organised in rows, there are clusters of wealthy graves in particular zones of the site and individual wealthy burials may have been located in clusters across several rows (Halsall, 1995b: 131; Christlein, 1973: 163–4).

A number of early Anglo-Saxon cemeteries contained rows – for example, Lechlade, St Peters (Kent), Orpington and Springhead (Northfleet, Kent). Few were true row-grave cemeteries, however, and these examples contained a single row (Lechlade) or a small group of rows (St Peters) in an otherwise non-linear cemetery pattern. Other sites like Norton, Cleveland (see below), did not contain any convincing rows, but instead displayed irregular lines of chronologically disparate burials which gave the impression of rows when looked at in their totality – a view that would not have been shared by the cemetery's users. One of the exceptions is Garton Slack II, East Yorkshire, which consisted of loosely defined lines organised into two clusters of twenty-nine and thirty-two burials, separated by a gap of 14 m (Figure 2.10; Mortimer, 1905: 247–57). Garton Slack II was a later cemetery and seems to have inherited its location and structure from its proximity to earlier ditches (Lucy, 2000a: 128). Another exception is the row-grave site at Marina Drive in Dunstable, Bedfordshire, which consisted of a cemetery organised into three rows. In two of the rows, the burials (nine and thirteen respectively) were N/S oriented, whereas the third group of burials, to the east, had ten burials aligned E/W (Matthews, 1962). The artefacts from Dunstable included a broad seax and a needle box, indicating that this site, like Garton Slack II and Springhead, dated to the seventh century and the end of the furnished burial rite, but the graves from Dunstable were probably later graves in a larger cemetery, not dissimilar to the two lines of graves from plot C, Deal.

In England, true row-grave cemeteries are often small and late in date, and individual burials within them cannot be dated easily because they contain few artefacts. They are part of a distinctive late sixth- to eighth-century phase of cemetery organisation. Garton Slack II and Springhead are similar to Street House, north-eastern Yorkshire, a

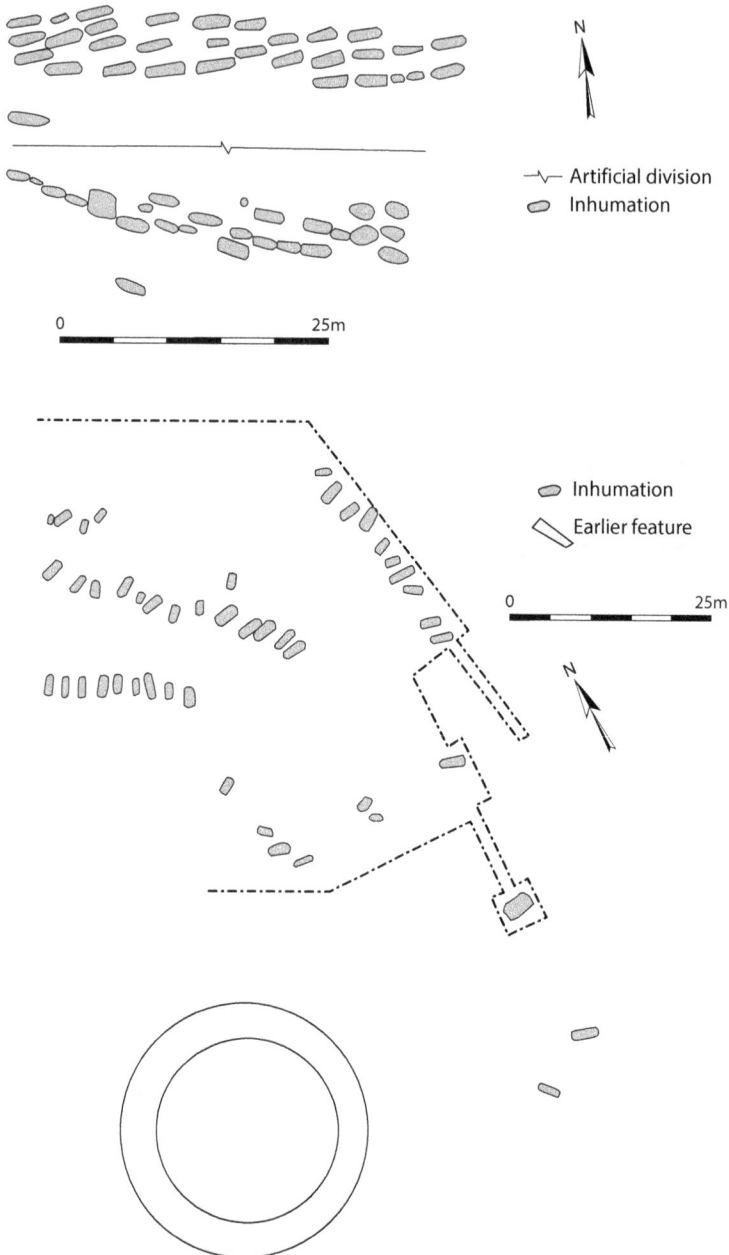

Figure 2.10 Garton Slack II, East Yorkshire (top), and Dunstable, Bedfordshire (bottom), are two examples of row-grave cemeteries. Garton Slack II consisted of two parts, separated by some distance, and Dunstable included three rows. The additional non-row graves at Dunstable, to the south, as well as the Bronze Age ring ditch, are evidence of an earlier and differently organised part of the cemetery.

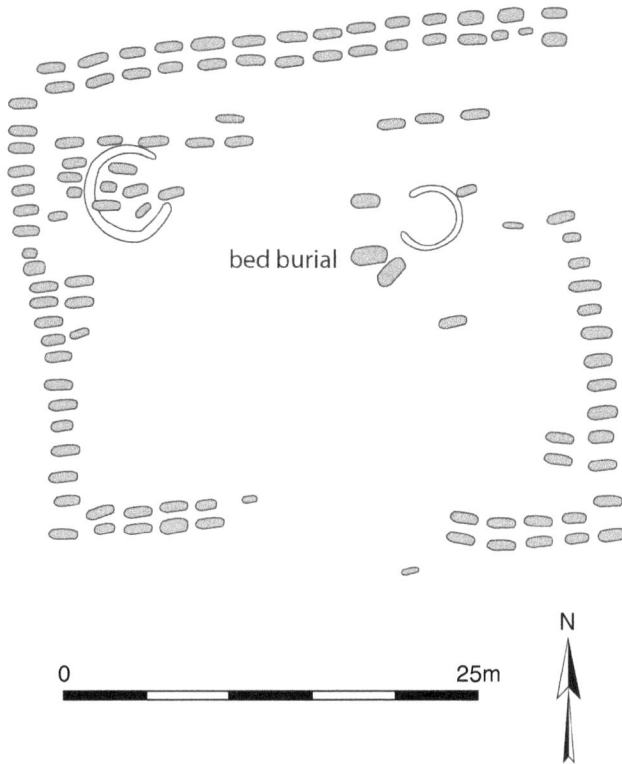

bed burial

0   25m

N

Figure 2.11 Street House, North Yorkshire, was a unique cemetery. A central bed burial, or small group of burials, was surrounded by a series of rows and lines of graves which formed a sub-rectangular shape.

site in which a series of graves was deliberately placed to construct a quadrilateral shape around a central mound and the bed burial (Figure 2.11; Sherlock, 2012). In many ways Street House is similar to many sixth-century cemeteries where graves are positioned in relation to a significant individual, but its deliberate and structured layout places it within a wider Merovingian tradition (for example Dortmund-Wickede, Germany; Stapel, 2007). In plain view, rows and lines of graves look very neat, and this organisation may have been utilised as part of a Merovingian tradition designed to create the impression of an ordered mortuary space, derived from an ordered hierarchical society. Even recognisable continental row-grave sites like Dortmund-Wickede would have looked that way only towards the end of their use (Stapel, 2007). Street House was deliberately conceived and constructed in a very short time and it was probably meant as a tribute for a royal dynasty (Sherlock, 2012).

Most grave cuts are roughly oblong in plan and so rows are a good and logical way to tightly cluster burials to the same orientation and prevent them from damaging older graves when dug. Rows are a useful strategy employed in the management of cemeteries over time and, at sites like Junkersdorf, they were used to create a particular aesthetic, as with the tightly packed, later burial grounds in England and on the Continent. However, individual rows may also have served a specific purpose. For example, along the eastern edge of the Bidford-on-Avon cemetery, Warwickshire (Figure 2.12), a densely packed row of graves (C) seems to have marked the limit of the cemetery, which was otherwise subdivided into two groups by density, plot A and group B, where A was clustered at 3 m and the northern graves (B) were deliberately spaced over 3 m apart. Similar rows of graves at Lechlade, Gloucestershire, and Morning Thorpe, Norfolk, seem to have defined the extent of an internal cemetery boundary (Figure 2.12). In the Morning Thorpe example, the line of graves divides a group of graves to the east of the site. At Lechlade, this row bounds a dispersed seventh-century group, dividing it from the main body of the cemetery.

The use of rows in cemeteries remains elusive, but was almost certainly part of a visual tradition. Many later sites, particularly in Kent and Yorkshire, may have used rows to create an aesthetic of order, influenced by Merovingian practice, which implies less flexibility in cemetery use. Such a tradition created an intent to the cemetery plan and this must have been influenced by a single agent – perhaps an influential individual or family. However, rows of graves were also used like a paling, a row of posts, creating a physical barrier which separated otherwise adjacent zones within a cemetery. This last practice is particularly evident in densely packed and complex cemeteries like Lechlade and Morning Thorpe; in these places, space was limited and the location of a grave was significant. The division of space was important in these sites and the row of graves would have taken many burials, and many years to construct. For example, the mortuary paling at Lechlade was not completed until the seventh century when it divided a group of largely unfurnished and dispersed graves from the cemetery proper.

Grave orientation

The orientation of graves has received considerable attention, especially where there are minor variations in the angles of those graves (Lucy, 2000b: 132). Discussion has focused on several factors, including the time of death – the solar arc model (see Chapter 1) – or as an important identifier in the performance of religion, where Christians were considered E/W oriented and pagans N/S (Rahtz, 1978). The orientation of

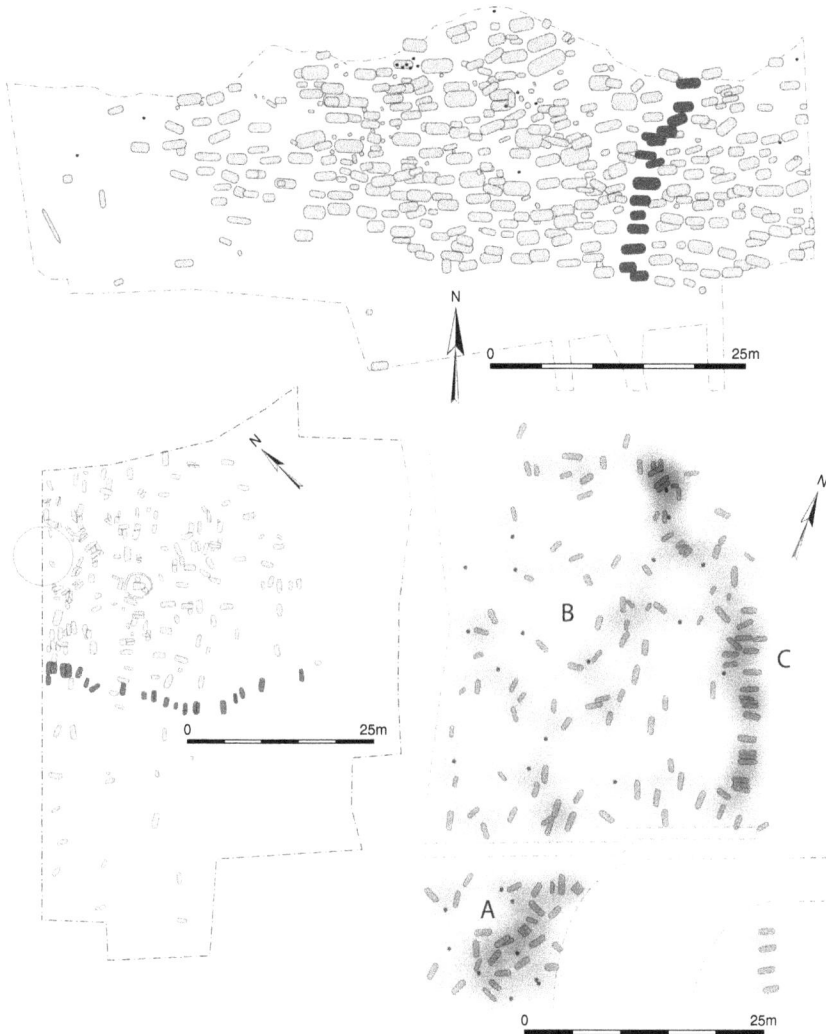

Figure 2.12 Morning Thorpe, Norfolk (top), Lechlade, Gloucestershire (bottom left), and Bidford-on-Avon, Warwickshire (bottom right). In each of these three cemeteries a row of graves may have marked an edge for the cemetery or may have defined a boundary between groups of graves.

a grave has been considered through analysis of the orientation of the body with the head at a particular end, whether the body is crouched or supine, and also more generally using the orientation of the grave. When discussing individual burials, the position of bodies and the orientation of heads may be important; however, in the wider context of cemetery organisation, it may not be particularly informative since the above ground circumstances may not distinguish body positions. Even though graves would have been marked in some way, only the archaeologist can see the position within a cemetery of each body, and each head, because when a site was in use the graves would have been closed. Individual body positions, on a 'reverse' orientation, prone or sitting, may have been a significant way for an individual to be treated at the funeral, but the orientation of a grave E/W, N/S or in between follows a pattern particular to each site. Many cemeteries contained a greater number of E/W oriented burials; for example, an E/W orientation was dominant at Westgarth Gardens, Bergh Apton and Morning Thorpe, whereas N/S was dominant at Beckford B, Worcestershire (Evison and Hill 1996), and Chamberlains Barn II, Bedfordshire (Hyslop, 1964), and both grave orientations were found in similar numbers at Great Chesterford, Apple Down and Berinsfield.

One of the most frequent interpretations made from grave orientation is that of religion, particularly Christian religion. It has often been assumed that Christian burials were interred E/W and without gravegoods. However, this is not the case; the orientation of graves and the presence or absence of crosses (for example cruciform brooches) or the absence of other objects has 'no particular Christian significance' (Hyslop, 1964: 72; also see Geake, 1992). Moreover, graves oriented on an E/W axis are the most commonly found burials in both pagan *and* Christian cemeteries (Meaney and Chadwick Hawkes, 1970: 53; Faull, 1977). Other arguments include ethnicity (Faull, 1977) or notions of a 'good or bad direction' (Devlin, 2007b: 51), or have focused on the presence of earlier features around which graves were oriented. Some of the burials at Deal had their head oriented towards the middle of the ring ditch, and a single burial at Dover Buckland also had its head oriented towards the centre of a barrow (Penn and Brugmann, 2007: 13; Evison, 1987: 152; Lucy, 2000b: 130). Stephen Sherlock and Martin Welch (1992: 17) argued that the rows in which burials had been arranged to the east of the Norton cemetery were deliberately oriented towards the grave within an ancient burial mound, but unfortunately this was only evidenced by a single piece of Bronze-Age pottery. Certainly, the location of cemeteries adjacent to earlier features, including barrows, is well known (Williams, 1998), but, even with radial arrangement like at Driffield, East Yorkshire, there is little evidence to suggest that graves were actively oriented towards a single point.

If the orientation of a grave was not influenced by date of death and does not signify religious affiliations or ethnicity, it could perhaps be considered a site-specific decision. Berinsfield is a good example of this since we have already established that there were at least two burial plots, in the north and the south of the cemetery. These groups were

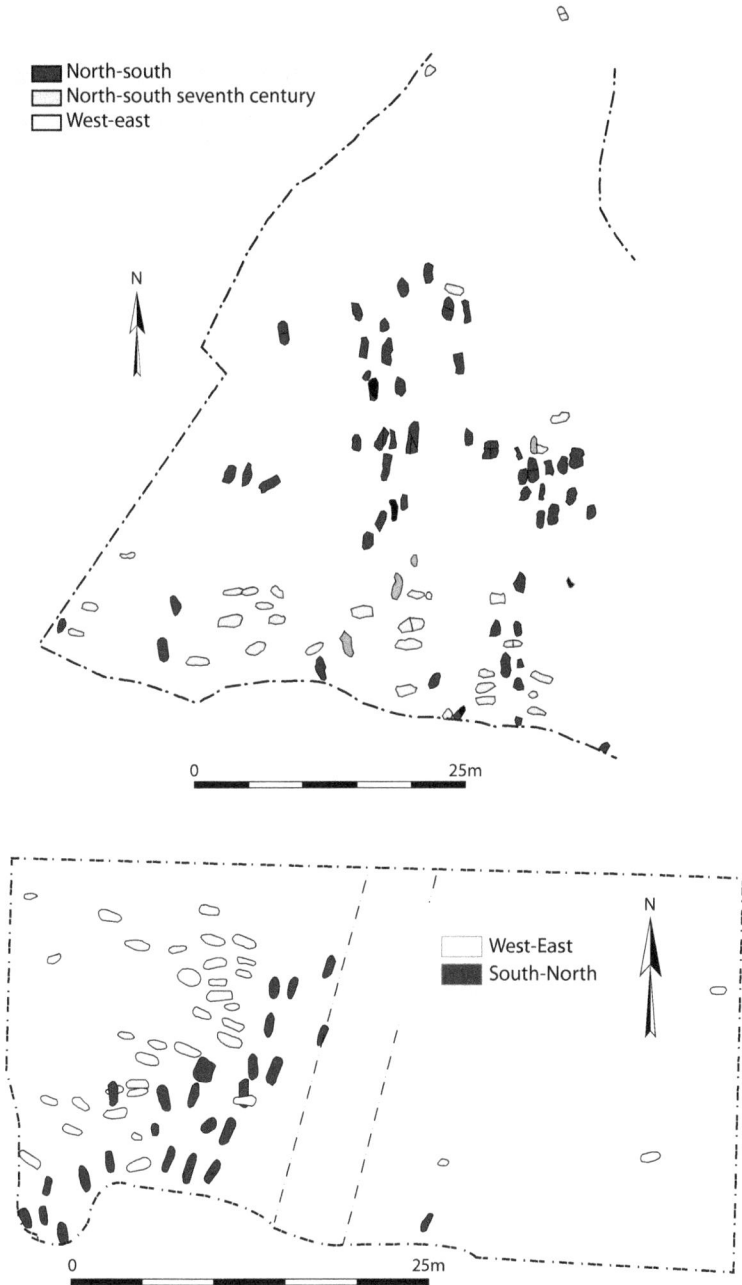

Figure 2.13 Cemeteries at Berinsfield, Oxfordshire (top), and Petersfinger, Wiltshire (bottom). Groups of graves here were spatially distinct and were also distinguished by their orientation. In both of these examples the difference in orientation is quite pronounced, with some graves broadly E/W and others N/S.

further defined by the orientation of graves within them, and strikingly the northern group with a N/S orientation juxtaposed the southern group with an E/W orientation (Figure 2.13). Another notable characteristic of Berinsfield is that the seventh-century graves were intrusive; they were placed in an existing part of the cemetery and were deliberately positioned on the opposite axis to the earlier graves. Three such seventh-century burials were found in the southern (E/W group). There was also one seventh-century burial in the northern group and, although this was N/S like most of the surrounding burials, it deliberately cut into one of the few E/W inhumations, creating a similarly deliberate juxtaposition.

The early Anglo-Saxon cemetery at Petersfinger, Wiltshire, showed a similar pattern. This site was partially excavated in 1948–51 and seventy-one inhumations were discovered (Leeds and Short, 1953). Unlike Berinsfield the graves were not organised into spatially defined plots, but seem to have been separated into two groups using their orientation to make this distinction. All of the N/S burials were located on the south and east of the site and most of the E/W burials were to the north and west of these. Interestingly, in the middle of the site there were two later graves that evidently cut earlier burials, and both of these graves were positioned on a different orientation to the ones they cut, intentionally contrasting with the earlier individual burial and the associated burial tradition.

One of the most complex uses of juxtaposed burials to define groups of graves and individual graves was seen at Great Chesterford, which was excavated in 1953–5 and revealed 161 inhumations and 33 cremations, though unfortunately only part of the cemetery had survived (Evison, 1994). Based on a small number of Roman cremations, Evison proposed that there had been a series of large Roman barrows on which the cemetery was focused. She went so far as to suggest that individual nuclear family units were placing their dead within particular Roman barrows. This is not a pattern that has been seen elsewhere; however, the orientation of each burial, as at our three previous cemeteries, did correspond to separate spatial clusters of graves oriented on the same axis and contrasting with the adjacent group (Figure 2.14). At the south of the site there was a group of predominantly N/S oriented burials, and to the north-west of those was a small group of E/W oriented burials, followed by a N/S oriented group with a large E/W oriented group in the middle of the site. Five N/S burials may have been deliberately placed within this cluster, and this central area seems to be the most densely clustered part of the site. To the north of this there were a series of N/S oriented burials. At the very northern tip of the excavated area another group of E/W burials was identified and, like the rest of these clusters, this group must extend into unexcavated areas. These groups of burials

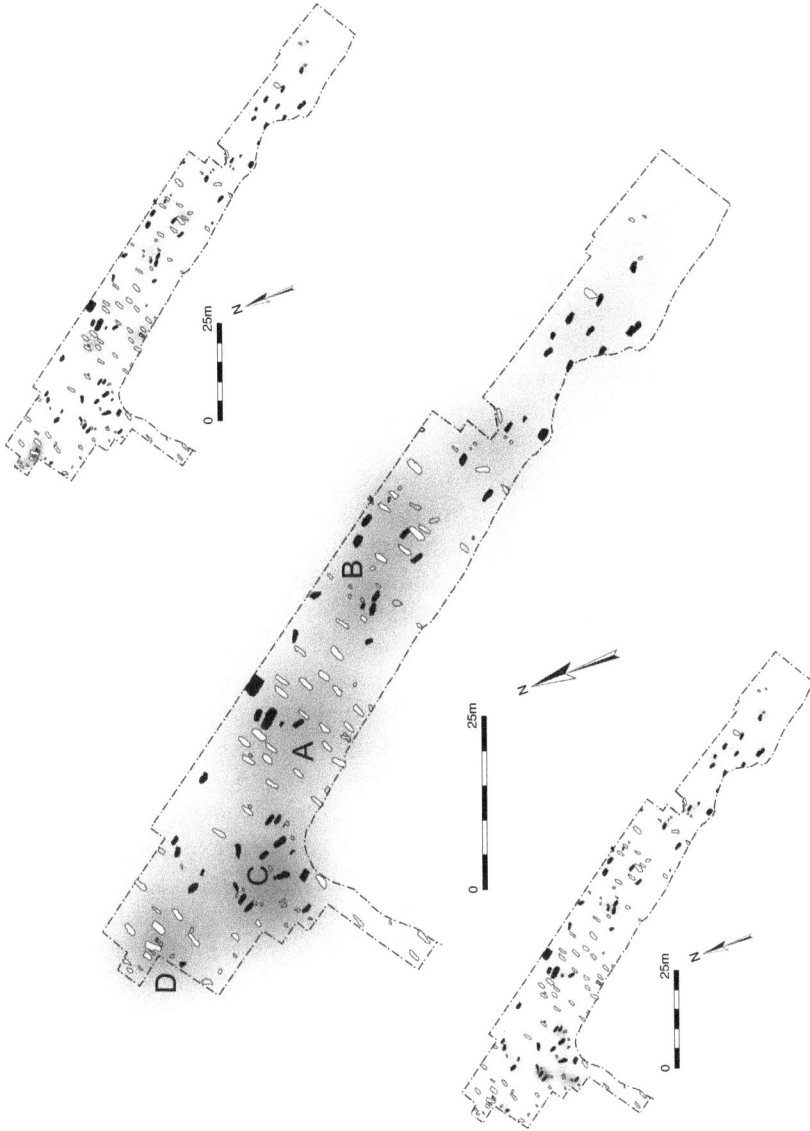

Figure 2.14 Great Chesterford, Essex, with the N/S-oriented graves shown in black. The middle illustration shows the cemetery with a heat map set at 10 m and illustrates the relative density of graves. The top illustration shows the E/W-oriented graves with the heat map set at 3 m. The bottom illustration shows the N/S graves with the heat map again set at 3 m. These plans show four deliberate clusters of graves (A–D), where D and C were defined by their orientation, A contained a core of N/S graves and B was a mixed-orientation plot. The southern part of the site contained dispersed graves.

may not have been individual clusters, as they were at Berinsfield and Petersfinger, but were subgroups of graves within more complex groups. The N/S burials were distributed in smaller groups which defined the extent of the densely packed E/W oriented graves. These were just like the E/W burials at Apple Down because they enclosed a more densely packed central area (see Chapter 4).

The orientation of graves at these four sites appears to have been used to subdivide each cemetery into different groups. These were used to define clusters separated by a gap, or as a method employed to define discrete plots of burials. At Berinsfield and Petersfinger, later burials were juxtaposed on different orientations to distinguish them from earlier burials where they were either placed within a pre-existing plot or else truncated an earlier inhumation. This use of orientation to define a new phase in burial practice is also seen at other sites, for example Deal (Sayer, 2009) or Lechlade (see Chapter 6). Orientation was, therefore, a tool which could be used at multiple scales within a repertoire of cemetery semiotics to distinguish different groups of burials within the same phase or to differentiate later inhumations.

Not all sites employed grave orientation to such an overtly organisational degree: Spong Hill, Morning Thorpe, West Heslerton, Deal and Sewerby had only a small number of burials on a different axis, but at these sites this contrast was a powerful visual tool utilised to distinguish individual inhumations. Like body position, grave orientation seems to have been used to distinguish a particular individual, or small groups of individuals. This was also the case at Oakington, Cambridgeshire, where a pregnant woman was found buried E/W in a cemetery of predominantly N/S graves (Sayer and Dickinson, 2013). Alternatively, when employed for a small number of burials, contrasting orientation could have been used to mark out special, prone or otherwise 'deviant' burials (Reynolds, 2009: 74). Given this variation, orientation was a cemetery-specific tool, and broader social concepts like religion, ethnicity or a 'good or bad' direction are too imprecise or grand to fit. Orientation was a multi-scale semiotic used within a community to separate individuals, for a variety of reasons, or groups of burials within a space; its effect was visually striking but it was not used consistently across all early Anglo-Saxon sites.

Burial rites

Two types of burial rite co-existed in the fifth and sixth centuries AD, inhumation and cremation. Previous scholars have suggested that cremation was the earlier of these two forms since it was the dominant burial rite on the Continent (Lucy, 2000b: 119–21). At Spong Hill, cremation started early in the fifth century (Hills and Lucy, 2013).

However, the dates for cremation and inhumation burials are generally contemporaneous. Cremation seems to go out of fashion by the end of the sixth century, but its use spans the fourth to seventh centuries with some notable late examples in barrows at Asthall, Oxfordshire and Sutton Hoo, Suffolk (Dickinson and Speake, 1992; Carver, 2005: 105). The cremation rite differs from the inhumation rite in a number of ways, including the technology that was used – cremation requires a funerary pyre and several more stages in the funerary process: the act of cremation, collecting the remains and burying them in an urn. However, there also seem to be variations in the materiality of the cremated corpse; for example, cremated males were interred with weapons less than 1 per cent of the time as opposed to 47 per cent of the time in inhumation graves. It would seem that the decisions which motivated the selection of cremation or inhumation may have been more complicated than simply selecting a type of funeral and a type of burial (Härke, 1990: 25; Härke, 1989: 49; Williams, 2005).

Cremation cemeteries

Archaeologists have often thought of cremation and inhumation rites as separate and as a result have investigated either inhumation burials or cremations and only occasionally both; this is particularly well illustrated by Howard Williams:

> Many communities in early Anglo-Saxon England had a choice between at least two contrasting mortuary technologies, cremation and inhumation ... It is also tempting to see the two rites as arbitrary distinctions: both rites were concerned with the visual display of the dead (in grave or pyre) and their subsequent interment albeit leaving very different archaeological traces. Alternatively, it is possible to regard the disposal methods in terms of binary opposites involving contrasting trajectories of the dead, perhaps linked to diametrically different 'meanings', attitudes towards social personal, and world views. (Williams, 2011: 241)

This wholly contrasting way of describing graves and particular burial rites has also been used to describe cemeteries. This convention probably stems from Audrey Meaney's *Gazetteer of Early Anglo-Saxon Burial Sites* which was used as source material for the Ordnance Survey's *Map of Britain in the Dark Ages* (Meaney, 1964: 15). Meaney assumed that the 'Angles cremated and Saxons and Jutes inhumed', and she divided these sites into cremation cemeteries, inhumation cemeteries or mixed-rite sites. However, at the time of the gazetteer's publication

Illington, Norfolk, was the only cremation site to have seen detailed archaeological investigation.

Unfortunately, at the time of writing, Illington has still been only partially excavated and its assemblage currently consists of 212 urns and three inhumations, implying that there may be more of both types of burial (Wells, 1960: 29; Meaney, 1964: 15; Davison et al., 1993). Illington is a mixed-rite cemetery and on closer examination so are numerous others from Meaney's gazetteer. For example Ancaster, Lincolnshire, was classed as a cremation cemetery, yet Meaney noted that skeletons had also been found (Meaney, 1964: 151). Subsequent excavations have revealed inhumation graves elsewhere, including at Spong Hill in Norfolk, Snape in Suffolk, and Cleatham in Lincolnshire where about 95 per cent of the site has now been excavated, revealing 1,014 cremation burials and sixty-two inhumations (Hills et al., 1984; Filmer-Sankey and Pestell, 2001; Leahy, 1998). Baston, also in Lincolnshire, has been only partially excavated, revealing sixty cremations to the south, but there have been enough good-quality early Anglo-Saxon metal artefacts identified by the Portable Antiquities Scheme to suggest the presence of inhumations (Mayes and Dean, 1976; Williams, 2002a: 352).

In total Meaney listed seventy-six cremation cemeteries; however, of these thirty-two consisted of just one cremation and eighteen consisted of fewer than ten. Of the larger sites, seventeen were partially excavated in the nineteenth century or before; Kingston-on-Soar in Nottinghamshire, for example, contained over 200 urns but only sixteen were rescued (Meaney, 1964: 200). Newark, Nottinghamshire, was first identified in the 1740s and was explored a number of times in the nineteenth century, yet few remains now survive (Meaney, 1964). South Elkington, Lincolnshire, consisted of 250 urns but has not been entirely excavated (Bennet, 2009). Other large sites like Wold Newton, Thurmaston or Hall Hill, in Leicestershire and Lincolnshire, have had only limited excavation (Williams, 2002a: 353). Older investigations at Brettenham, Castle Acre and Drayton, all in Norfolk, were not fully explored by their nineteenth-century finders because their intent was on discovering urns (Williams, 2002a). Even well-known sites like Lackford, Suffolk, or Sancton, Yorkshire, remain only partially excavated (Lethbridge, 1947; Myres and Southern, 1973). This incompleteness of excavation is problematic; at Spong Hill, for example, all the inhumations were concentrated in just one area with significant clustering at 1 m – a phenomenon which may have been repeated elsewhere (Figure 2.15).

There seems to be a consistent association between cremation and inhumation graves, and even sites which we routinely consider inhumation cemeteries, such as Norton, Great Chesterford, Sutton Hoo,

Figure 2.15 Spong Hill, Norfolk. The significant majority of inhumations were concentrated in the north of the site and the preponderance of cremations was found in the south, with some cremations and inhumations intermingled. This visually separated the two areas, since the south consisted of cremations and the north consisted of both cremations and inhumations, which were largely contemporary.

Blacknall Field or Berinsfield, often included a small number of cremations. Perhaps these different technologies were not considered to be wholly contrasting by their users. Rather, inhumation and cremation may have been at two ends of a range of a funerary syntax available for deployment at a cemetery or individual scale and to different degrees across Britain and between the fifth and seventh centuries AD. This view is shared by Penn and Brugmann, who looked in detail at four cemetery sites in East Anglia, where 'the differences between cremation and inhumation burial practice may not have been as fundamental as the archaeological evidence seem to suggest at first glance' (Penn and Brugmann, 2007: 96).

Mixed-rite cemeteries

Most, if not all, sites with cremations are mixed-rite cemeteries. They range from sites which contained large numbers of both ritual forms, such as Spong Hill, Caistor-by-Norwich, Andover or Apple Down, to sites which contained a small number of cremations, including Worthy Park, Hampshire, Norton and Berinsfield. This variation in the employment of cremation burial suggests that it was a multi-scale funerary technology used to distinguish either individuals within a predominantly inhumation site or specific groups of individuals within large mixed-rite cemeteries. Mads Ravn suggested that Spong Hill contained five or six burial plots consisting of cremations or inhumations (Ravn, 2003: 123). Visually, Spong Hill can be divided into two spatially distinct groups, the inhumations and cremations to the north and the majority of cremations to the south (Figure 2.15). Ravn also suggested that inhumation graves are evidence of an emerging elite group who used a separate burial form to distinguish themselves from the rest of society. This deliberate spatial and ritual differentiation is very similar from the burial plots visible at Wakerley and Berinsfield, or the different grave orientations seen at Apple Down and Petersfinger. The community using Spong Hill cemetery engaged separate spaces and juxtaposed different burial rites as a primary organising feature. This is an organisational characteristic which can also be seen at Alwalton, Cambridgeshire, where twenty-eight cremations were found in the western half of the excavated area and thirty-four inhumations in the eastern half (Figure 2.16; Gibson, 2007).

The division of mixed-rite sites into practice-related zones may have distinguished between two groups using the same site (Williams, 2002b), and patterns like this can be found at Andover (Cook and Dacre, 1985), where cremations were mostly located on the western side of the site with a small cluster of eight or nine inhumations in the middle of this area (Figure 2.17). These burials, both inhumation and cremation, were spatially distinct; by putting the different rituals in different physical spaces the funerary architects reinforced the semiotic division between two distinct groups within the community. Interestingly, Caistor-by-Norwich (Myres and Green, 1975) is similar to both Spong Hill and Andover, which seem to have been organised around a series of spatially distinct areas where the centrally located clusters have the highest concentration of cremations and also, notably, the largest number of inhumations.

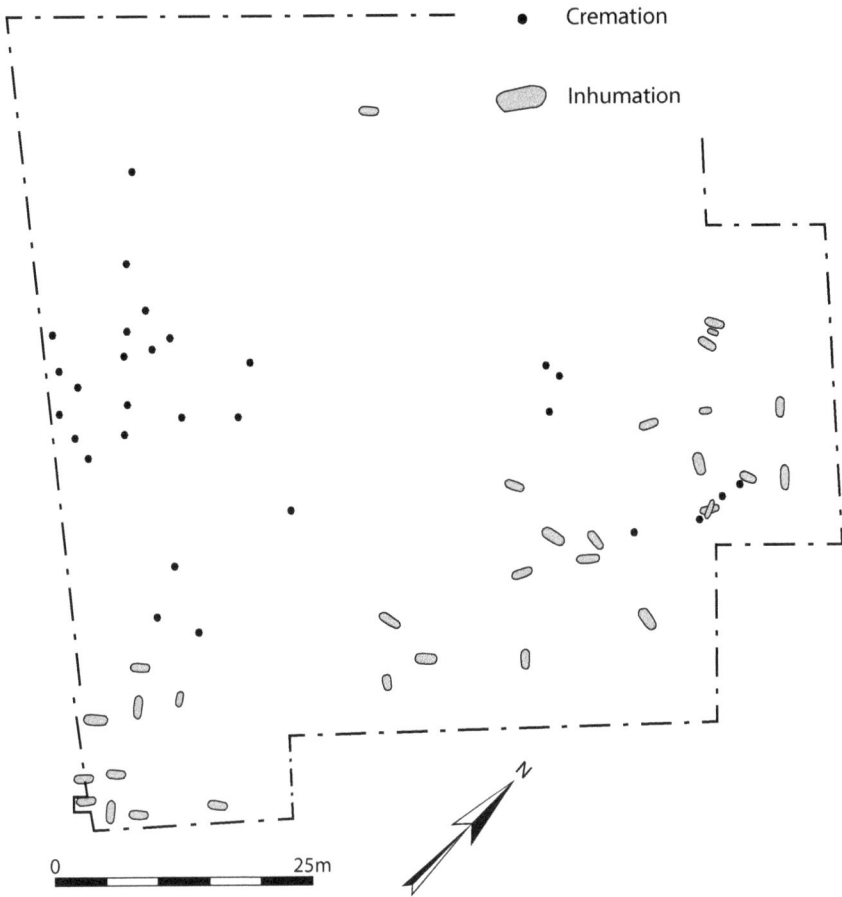

Figure 2.16 Alwalton, Cambridgeshire, was spatially separated into two groups: a cremation group and an inhumation group, which included just a few cremation graves.

Like Andover and Spong Hill, Caistor-by-Norwich seems to have been organised into distinct spatial areas. The clustering of graves was significant at 1 m separation, placing emphasis on high density of burial. Unlike Spong Hill, the plots at Andover and Caistor-by-Norwich combined inhumation and cremation burials, but (like Spong Hill) those at Caistor-by-Norwich were very dense, with many cremations clustering at 1 m and inhumations at 3 m. Cremation graves require less space than inhumation graves and so this high density suggests that Caistor-by-Norwich began as a closely packed cremation cemetery, like Spong Hill, and the inhumations were added later (see Chapter 3). The two groups who buried their dead in the middle of the cemetery used the

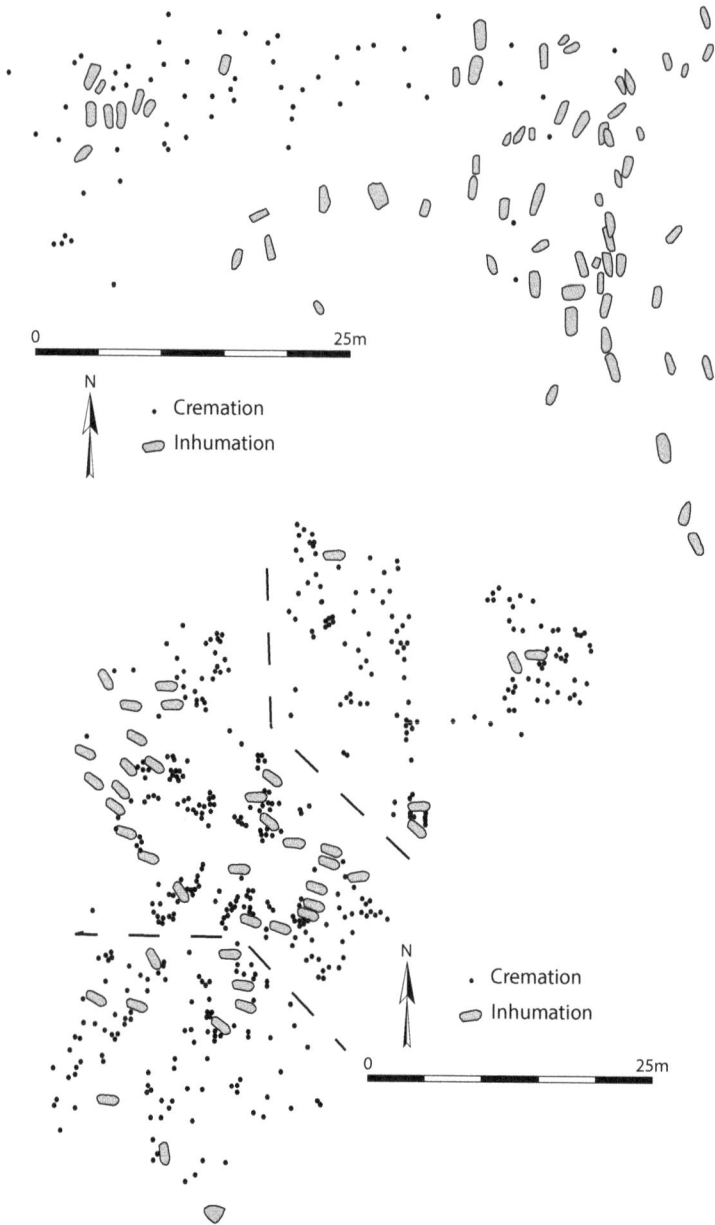

Figure 2.17 Andover, Hampshire (top), Caistor-by-Norwich, Norfolk (bottom). At Andover the majority of cremations were to the west of the site with a small cluster of nine inhumations in the middle. The east of the site included just a few cremations and the majority of graves were inhumations. The Caistor-by-Norwich graves clustered at 1 m, with evident groupings at 3 m; the central plots A, B, C and D were the densest groups of graves and contained the most inhumations.

most inhumations, and these may have been the longest-lived groups in the community. These spatial areas were large and the decision to cremate or inhume an individual may have taken place *within* particular social groups rather than *between* them, as at Spong Hill or Andover. Therefore, in these two examples cremation was a strategy employed to distinguish separate internal groups or identities within a particular extended social group.

As Howard Williams (2011) argued, cremation was a funerary technology that existed to contrast with inhumation but, just like grave orientation, burial plots and the density of graves, it was part of a semiotic toolkit used within the repertoire of cemetery-specific syntax. Cremation seems to have operated at different scales within different communities: at Spong Hill, cremation was used in combination with burial proximity to define the cemetery space; at Andover, cremation and clusters of inhumations were used in conjunction to mark out different groups; and, at both Andover and Caistor-by-Norwich, individual plots consisted of cremations and inhumations. By contrast, at Berinsfield and Worthy Park, cremation was used for only a few funerals, signalling their difference from the rest of the cemetery population.

Material culture

The types and distributions of material culture within Anglo-Saxon cemeteries have been discussed in several ways. The first of these is focused on the use of particular types of objects as identifiers of ethnicity, where certain brooch types appear to have been distributed across particular regions of the country (Leeds, 1913; 1936). Cruciform brooches are absent from many of the southern counties, where great square-headed brooches are more common. Girdle hangers, by contrast, seem to be more common in Kent and East Anglia, wrist clasps are found in Cambridgeshire and the Midlands, while cognate brooches are concentrated in Rutland and the Midlands. Applied brooches are found in the South-East of England, button brooches are concentrated in Kent and the Thames Valley and many disc brooch types are found in the Thames Valley region as well as the Midlands and East Anglia (Lucy, 2000b: 134–5). Distributions like these have led many authors to conclude that there were regional or group costumes (Hines, 1994: 52–3), which may have been used as indicators of the evolving expression of regional ethnicity – Saxons, Angles or Jutes for example (Böhme, 1974; Leeds, 1913; 1936; 1945; Chadwick Hawkes, 1969). This association of specific graves, and even objects, with regional variance resulted in them being assigned ethnicity (Lucy, 2000b: 169). However, Lucy (2000b: 174) also proposed an alternative: if these distributions did manifest

ethnicities, they were complex mixtures of political and ethnic affiliations. Susanne Hakenbeck, investigating Bavarian cemeteries that were
contemporary, identified the distribution of brooch types and weapon
burials within four sites as a plurality of expression. Objects, grave
locations and funerary rites were all locked up in a multi-layered set
of social circumstances that may have included ethnicity, kinship or
warrior status (Hakenbeck, 2007a; 2007b; 2011).

In the past, archaeologists have tried to use the distributions of
brooches to understand specific and individual ethnic affiliations within
cemetery sites (Koch, 1998; Hakenbeck, 2007b; 2011; Lucy, 2005).
One difficulty with this approach is its simplicity: male gravegoods
have been interpreted as indicators of status, and female gravegoods
as indicators of ethnicity (Härke, 1990; 2000; Stoodley, 1999; Lucy,
2000b). However, brooches, particularly elaborate brooches, like other
art forms are wrapped in multiple meanings associated with a plurality of underlying social factors like ethnicity, family identity, status
indicator and even personal choice.

Cemetery sites are not just places where people buried their dead;
they are also places where people remembered them. As a result, material culture may reflect a remembered continuity – a punctuated, ad
hoc similarity – where one grave is similar to, but not identical with, an
adjacent early burial because the funeral party remembered some of the
aspects of that earlier event but reinterpreted the rite, influenced by their
own relationships to the recently dead (Sayer, 2010). Williams (2006:
36–78) investigated combinations of material culture and gender/age
patterns in Berinsfield, Deal and Harford Farm, Norfolk, to approach
the question of cemetery structure, not from an organisational perspective, but from the question of burial ritual and memory. He used the
physical proximity and similarity of grave assemblages to discuss the
repetition of ritual and therefore the active memory of the participants
in the funerary rites. Equally, Zoe Devlin describes memory as an active,
not passive, process where the act recreates a past, and objects, rituals or
procedures can be forgotten and reinvented during that process (Devlin,
2007a; 2007b). Subsequently, objects were not simply transmitted and
interred, but were imbued with social and personal meanings which were
then considered, described and recreated in the placement of objects in
later graves.

Williams (2006: 36–78) focused on brooches and weapons to understand his cemetery sites; whereas previously Pader (1982) considered
that it was the less significant objects, such as tweezers and pins, which
might be indicators of divisions in cemeteries. This is an interesting idea
as ethnicity, family or social identity – expressed through the material
culture within relationships – can be reinterpreted or forgotten when

these identities are renegotiated by subsequent generations. What was a round disc brooch when put in a grave may have become subsequently a small square one when remembered through an oral tradition. The material associated with activities, for example the communal preparation of a corpse, may survive in a funeral rite as part of a localised but evolving ritual process.

As detailed above, Wakerley was divided into three contemporary groups of graves or plots; what is striking about this site is the distribution pattern of common dress objects, particularly buckles and pins (Figure 2.18). Two pins were found on the west side of the cemetery, only one pin on the east, yet in the middle there were five. However, even more notable is that six of the nine type-II buckles, those with a backplate, were concentrated in one of the three grave plots, the eastern group of burials (group C in Figure 2.3). This pattern is interesting when considered next to the distribution of brooches. Four of the six cruciform brooches were found in the eastern of the cemetery, whereas the less elaborate small-long brooches were found across the site. There were only two great square-headed brooches from this site, one on the east and one on the west, and there was just one imported small square-headed brooch from the west. This distribution of artefacts seems to confirm the spatial division of the cemetery into three plots with a western A, central B and eastern C group of burials. The distribution of objects suggests that the social groups who interred their dead in each of these areas treated their dead slightly differently: the eastern group in plot A dressed their dead in more elaborate costume, with more visually elaborate objects, illustrated by the presence of more ornamented brooches and more belt buckles with backplates; the central and western burial plots had a similar but less elaborate funerary costume.

This phenomenon is conceivably the result of several underlying social situations. The site seems to have contained evidence for a single style of female dress, which included annular brooches (not illustrated), small-long brooches and belt buckles. This tradition is common to the community at large, with a few burials in the eastern area showing a similar second tradition superimposed on this first one, and including cruciform and more elaborate brooches as well as more visually impressive buckles. Given that funerals are enacted by the living in the community, it is important to consider who was conducting and participating in these events. For the first, simpler, funeral tradition, the ritual is comparable across the site, so it was drawing on a collective communal memory, and it was this community who must have been the main audience for these funerals, as it was they who would have understood the symbols and associations made in each burial event. For the second, more selective, style the rite had been developed for a second group who

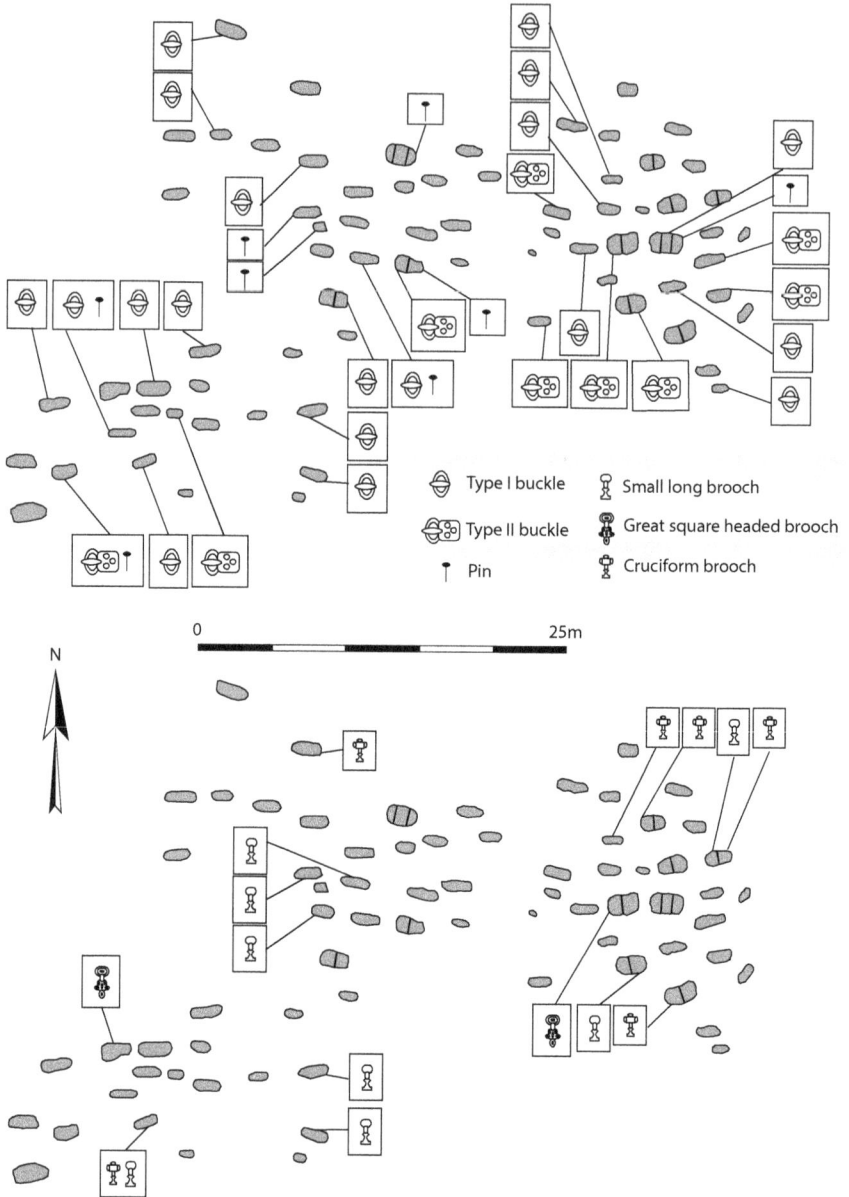

Figure 2.18 Buckles and pins at Wakerley, Northamptonshire (top). Notice that the type-II belt buckles were more common in the easternmost plot, and pins were commoner in the two western plots. Equally, the more elaborate brooches (bottom) were found to the east, with simple small-long brooches being most common in the two western plots.

may not have understood the particulars of the community tradition, but who would have understood the broader cultural references that were visually employed in this rite. This second dress style was more elaborate, suggesting these individuals were being identified as part of a wealthier group. As a result, we might conclude that the audience for the funeral probably included people from outside the immediate community who would have interpreted the social value of imported and decorative items within a wider societal context. Each individual or group participating in a particular funeral would have recognised certain elements of this rite at a personal, community and cultural level, both as an event and rooted within the plurality of meaning embedded within the objects and rites employed.

The Anglo-Saxon cemetery at Deal was largely sixth-century in date, but some of the graves dated to the early seventh century (Parfitt and Brugmann, 1997: 1–6). Like many Kentish cemeteries it was richly furnished, and most graves contained objects; however, as with Wakerley, there was a pattern to the distribution of some of these objects (Figure 2.19). For example, in the cluster of graves at the north

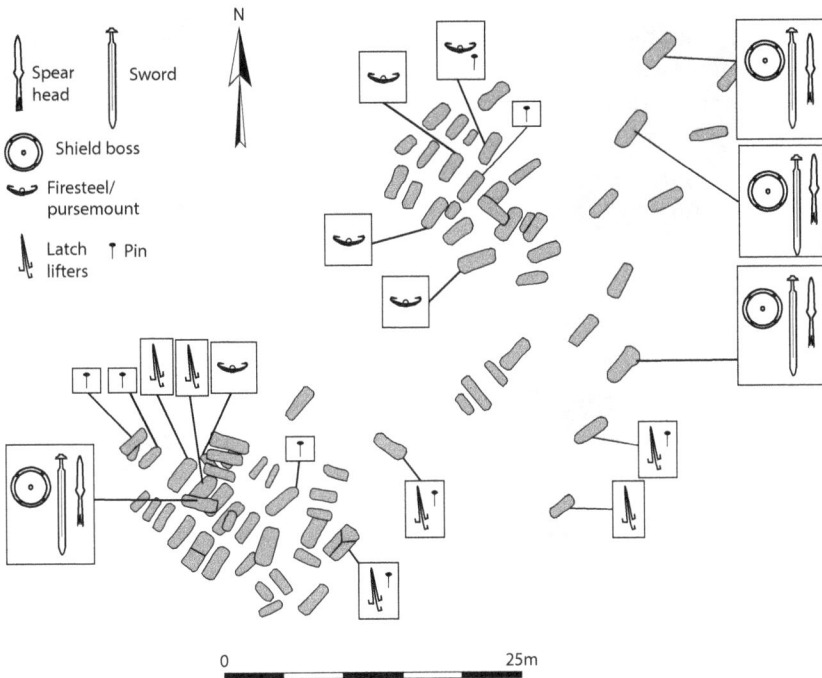

Figure 2.19 Patterns in the distribution of objects at Deal in Kent. Firesteels were more common north of the barrow, with pins and girdle-hangers to the south. Weapon burials with swords were more common in the line of graves to the east.

of the site there were four firesteels/pursemounts; whereas only a single one was found in the cluster in the south of the site. Similarly, six of the eight pins were found in graves in the southern part of the site, as were all six of the latch lifters. Many of the male graves at Deal contained weapons but, of those which included swords, three were in a group of burials in the eastern part, and only one was in the southern section.

The brooches found at Deal consisted of Kentish garnet discs, radial-headed, bird- and square-headed brooches. These objects were distributed around the site and their selection for burial probably depended on the individual choice of either the deceased or of the people who dressed their corpse. However, in the sixth-century burials it was the less conspicuous, functional objects which formed part of different localised funerary traditions. Presumably the use of these objects in graves was the result of two separate intra-community groups who passed on their own, independent traditions for dressing a corpse for burial. The male weapon burials were all late-sixth- or early seventh-century and were part of a second phase in the use of this site. However, the use of swords signalled a discontinuity from the older tradition and contributed to the creation of a new, localised male funerary rite, graves under mounds concentrated in a new, less dense and dispersed area of the cemetery (Sayer, 2010).

These examples demonstrate quite different distributions of material culture within each cemetery. In two cases, Wakerley and Deal, the distributions were evident in household objects, and in the selection of particular types of object. At Apple Down and Morning Thorpe (see Chapter 6), the difference manifested in the ritual, which dictated the type of burial assemblages to include within a grave, as much as in the material culture. 'Less significant' objects like pins, buckles and firesteels were part of these assemblages, but objects like brooches and weapons also displayed rather subtle patterns of deposit in early Anglo-Saxon cemeteries. Williams (2006: 52) investigated the early Anglo-Saxon cemetery at Berinsfield and suggested that great care had been taken in the selection and layout of gravegoods, particularly brooches. He discussed the attention to detail visible in graves 104 and 91, which were adjacent, oriented on the same axis, contained pots, small-long brooches and beads, and displayed similar body positions. However, there were also subtle differences between them: for instance, grave 104 did not have a copper-alloy pin, but did have twice the number of beads, and had charred logs along the graveside. This attention to detail is a universal part of the early Anglo-Saxon burial tradition, and it is interesting that the burials from Wakerley and Deal showed elements of continuity, indicating a desire to dress a corpse in similar ways among spatially similar burials. These details were learned, passed down and repeated for a number of burials within a particular social group. Identical adjacent graves are rare, so deliberate repetition was not the goal. However, elements of commonality ran through furnished burials in particular areas of each cemetery, suggesting uniformity of practice and detail with separate localised traditions that highlighted the individual.

How a corpse was dressed may have depended on the deceased, how old they were, and their gender (Stoodley, 2011), but it may also have depended on who was dressing that corpse and from whom they learned the techniques. Where bodies were laid out in graves fully dressed, surviving evidence such as brooches and pins can be used to reconstruct how women wore garments (Owen-Crocker, 1986; Rogers, 2007). Even burials found without dress items were probably clothed or wrapped. Burials may have been dressed in a specific way; evidence of veils, blankets, pillows or bags may have concealed or hidden objects, faces or other physical characteristics (Williams, 2006: 52). Knowing what was buried with an individual must have depended entirely on a person's level of participation in the funerary ritual. If a person cleaned, dressed or prepared a body and then laid it out in the grave, they would possess an intimate knowledge of the burial; whereas, if they only attended a funeral at the open graveside, they would have a more limited knowledge of the grave's secrets. Williams also suggested there were several phases to a funeral: preparing, laying out – in the ground or at a hall – and burial (Williams, 2006). The level of involvement a person or group had in a burial may have depended entirely on how they were connected to that person. Indeed, the distribution of objects at Wakerley, Deal, Morning Thorpe and Apple Down demonstrates that there were two or three different ways that bodies were prepared at each site.[4] These methods were transmitted among the people who used particular parts of the cemetery to locate their dead.

Compound cemeteries

Not all cemeteries used just one method to visually distinguish their dead. Large cemeteries like Lechlade, Spong Hill, Apple Down, Springfield Lyons and Wasperton used complex combinations of cremations, ancient features and clusters, plots and densities of burial to structure their graves and highlight difference. Each of these burial strategies was visually evidenced within the cemetery space and provided a set of structuring principles. These devices created divisions within the cemetery space and these were powerful ways to structure the experience, providing an aide-memoire for the narratives used in funeral display and local storytelling.

The early Anglo-Saxon cemetery at Apple Down, West Sussex, was discovered in 1981 and excavated between 1982 and 1987. The site contained 121 inhumation burials and sixty-four cremations and, although it was in use between the late-fifth and early seventh centuries, the majority of the burials dated to the sixth century. The excavators, Alec Down and Martin Welch (1990: 9), suggested that the cemetery was arranged around a core of early burials which dated to an initial phase in the late-fifth and early sixth centuries. However, this nucleus of inhumation was predominantly sixth-century in date, like the rest of the cemetery, so cannot have been an earlier arrangement.

As we saw in Chapter 1, Apple Down was striking in its organisation and consisted of one large central mixed-rite cluster with a series of satellite graves. As a whole, the graves clustered at around 2.5 m, but no patterning was evident when they were plotted as a kernel density map. This suggests a more subtle and internal organisation. This cemetery's major subdivision emphasised the differences between the E/W oriented inhumation graves, the N/S oriented inhumation graves and the cremations. Within the central area these burials were deliberately juxtaposed, by placement on different axes or using different rituals (Figure 2.20). Within the central mixed-rite group, cremations were clustered at 6 m and the E/W graves at 5 m, but the N/S graves were not deliberately clustered at all. This created a core of E/W oriented burials, two groups of cremations on both sides, and the N/S oriented group around the edges of the cemetery. Importantly, the N/S oriented graves did not cluster at all and so, although they were deliberately distinct from the N/S graves and the cremations, there was no attempt to structure their placement.

Apple Down is not the only cemetery which used multiple methods to divide its burial population. Wasperton, in Warwickshire, was excavated between 1980 and 1985, and 215 inhumation burials and twenty-six cremations were uncovered that used Roman, British and Anglo-Saxon burial rites (Carver et al., 2009). This early Anglo-Saxon cemetery was located mainly within a rectangular Romano-British field enclosure, which had been reused to create internal cemetery boundaries (Figure 2.21). The burials can be subdivided into two spatial groups separated by the surviving ditches, and the bulk of the cemetery was found within the larger quadrilateral enclosure, where graves concentrated with significant clustering at 3 m. This clustering divided these burials into four groups, the central one of which included twenty-two of the twenty-six cremations and the highest density of inhumation graves. Two similar clusters of inhumation graves were found to the south and east of the central group and a fourth more loosely clustered group of burials was found to the east, mostly within the second enclosure. If treated independently this fourth group was homogeneous and showed no internal clustering. Outside the field enclosure only inhumations were found; these graves were deliberately more spread out and formed

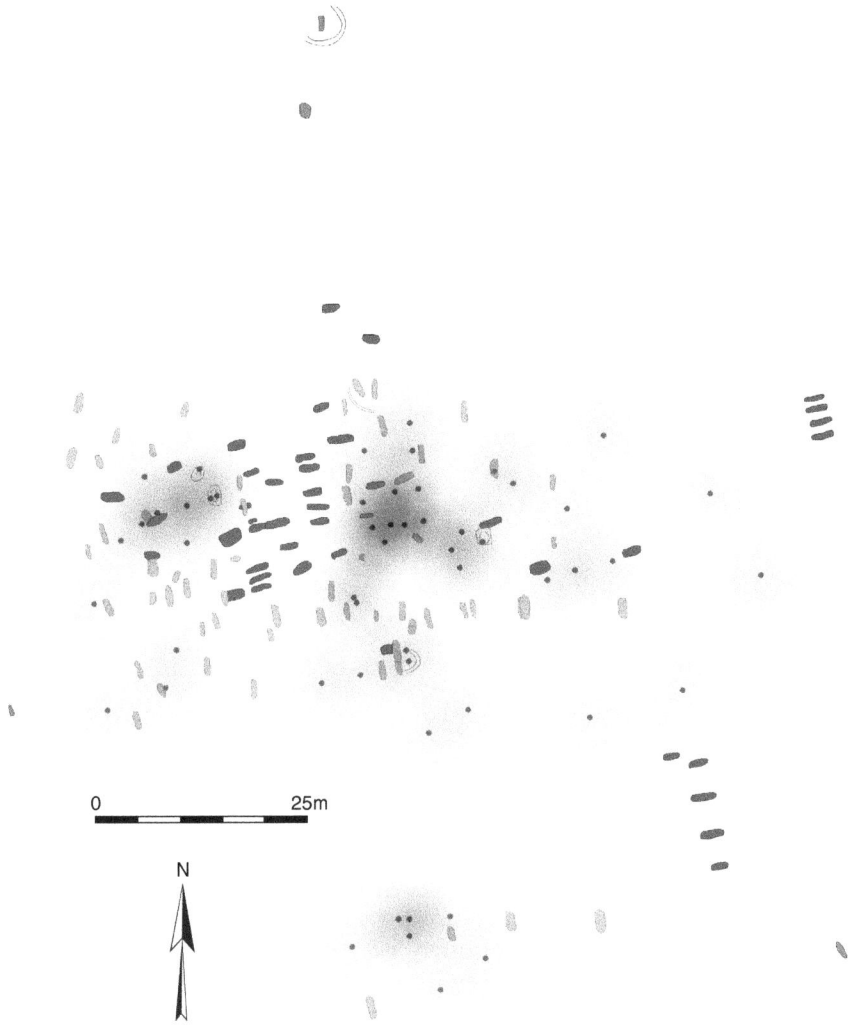

Figure 2.20 Apple Down, West Sussex, was a compound cemetery and used a mixture of spatial tools. The inhumations were distinguished by orientation with E/W and N/S graves; cremations were separated into two groups, clustering at 6 m on either side of the E/W inhumation graves.

three small groups of burials clustering at 5 m. The Wasperton cemetery employed a combination of plots, grave density and reused features to provide it with internal structure.

Springfield Lyons, Essex, used a different system and combined grave ritual, ancient features and spatial proximity. Like Apple Down and Wasperton, the cemetery was large, with over 250 individual burials

Figure 2.21 Wasperton, Wiltshire, was organised around a series of earlier ditches. Enclosed within the large sub-rectangular ditch were plots A, B and C, which were clustered at 3 m. Plot B had the greatest density and the most cremation graves, and Plot A exctended beyond the enclosure ditch. Within the ditch complex, but separated by a smaller ditch from plots A, B and C, was group D; these graves were almost all placed apart, in deliberate juxtaposition to the clustered plots. Outside the sub-rectangular enclosure, groups E, F and G included less densely spaced graves clustered at 4 m. There were a number of lone burials or small satellite groups around the edges of the cemetery.

(Tyler and Major, 2005). The graves statistically clustered at 2.5 m and, as at Apple Down and Andover, the cremations and inhumations were in different areas (Figure 2.22). In this case the clustered inhumations were to the south-west of a large Bronze-Age enclosure, with some burials placed within and on either side of the ditch. These were enveloped by the cremation burials on the south-eastern and south-western edges, and a small cluster of cremations were identified to the north-west of the enclosure. Unlike Caistor-by-Norwich and Spong Hill, the cremations

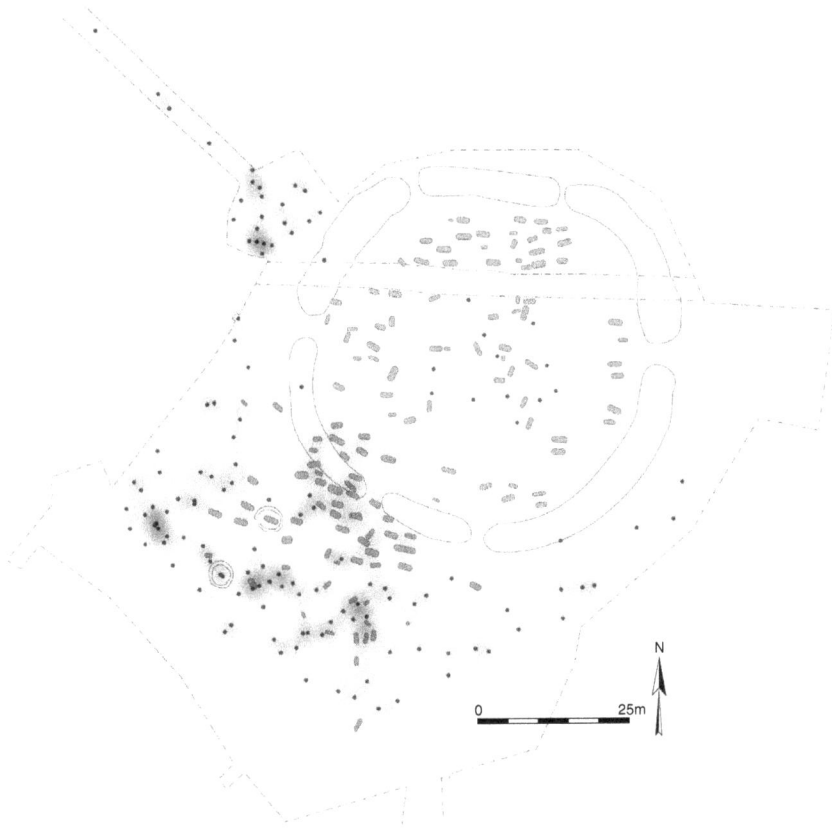

Figure 2.22 Springfield Lyons, Essex, combined grave ritual, ancient features and spatial proximity. The site was arranged around an earlier ring-ditch feature. Outside this, and overlapping the south-western portion of the ditch, was a tight group of graves that clustered at 2.5 m. Around this was a dispersed group of cremations, and within the ring ditch was a more dispersed group of inhumation burials.

were spaced out which may indicate that they were contemporary with the inhumations, the large graves establishing the relative density of burial. In this case, the spatial location and burial rite provided structure for the syntax of the cemetery space. Importantly, however, there was a second group of inhumations within the reused enclosure, and these were homogeneous and more spaced out than the cemetery's main cluster of inhumations. Springfield Lyons was not organised into obvious spatial plots, although other tools from the mortuary portfolio had been used to structure the site, combining different rituals, densities of burial and ancient monuments to create a narrative syntax which separated groups of graves.

Early Anglo-Saxon cemeteries were complex places without a single design. They were evolving mortuary landscapes created by a multitude of 'architects' for a variety of audiences. For archaeological investigation, understanding the space within the cemetery is as important as the contents of the graves. While simple sites might be divided into identifiable plots with groups of graves separated by a gap, almost sub-cemeteries within the larger site, the more complex sites were sub-divided on a basis of different knowledge or experience. The emphasis may have been on grave density, orientation or clustering around a significant ancestor, and so these cemeteries contained a range of different funerary rituals. Grave plots, grave orientation, density of burial or clustering groups of graves provided visual differentiation, changing the texture of burial areas within a site. Large cemeteries were more likely to be complex, with more variation in the interpretation of mortuary practice, and they combined many different ideas which contributed to the whole.

The structural syntax of early Anglo-Saxon cemeteries

At first glance each early Anglo-Saxon cemetery appears different. However, there were a number of underlying, but comparable, narratives that defined their organisation. The communities that interred their dead in these cemeteries drew from a repertoire of mortuary syntaxes and applied them at a cemetery scale to subdivide the site; in doing so they created divisions within the composition which structured shared semiotic knowledge. The application of these practices seems to have varied from cemetery to cemetery, depending on which other technologies had been adopted for previous graves and how they had already expressed existing aspects of group identity. In the sixth century, the utilisation of cemetery space resulted from an aggregate of multiple perspectives and so the syntax used to express meaning could change over time. But, inspired by Merovingian practice, the North-East of England and Kent in particular witnessed a new phase, a later sixth- and seventh-century arrangement, where rows of graves gave an impression of order – for example, the square-shaped layout of the Street House cemetery. In addition, both phases cemetery activity were influenced by existing topographic elements like barrows, or earlier ditches. The location of a cemetery may have been chosen because these mounds and ditches presented attractive ways to shape and order the mortuary space and subsequently influenced how the communities commemorated themselves. Nevertheless, pre-existing semiotics were no longer fit for purpose and did not adequately express the shape that society had taken. Similar methods were used to express a new narrative; the rows,

squares and dispersed cemeteries of the seventh century were akin to
Merovingian sites, and perhaps the members of an emerging familial
elite were using and adopting new styles of commemoration to fit their
purpose.

Brian Hope-Taylor (1977: 262) and Heinrich Härke (1992: 169)
described cemeteries as either monocentric or polycentric, based on
the clustering of graves. This is a useful starting position, but only the
smallest sites included just one method of organisation. Even the small
final-phase cemeteries like Dunstable, Garton Slack II, Bargates or
Caistor St Edmund consisted of several discrete groups of burials that
could be separated by up to 150 m. Moreover, visible burial semiotics
were employed by the cemetery architects to divide a site into different
groups, either by means of statistically observable grave clusters or
densities used to define specific groups of graves, as at Berinsfield,
Wakerley or Norton, or by creating a visible contrast by orienting
graves uniformly, as at Berinsfield, Petersfinger, Apple Down and Great
Chesterford. Nonetheless, orientation and grave plots were just two
methods and the very ritual itself – cremation or inhumation – was
also used to shape burial space at Springfield Lyons, Apple Down
and Andover. Most early Anglo-Saxon sites were either inhumation
cemeteries or mixed-rite cemeteries, and the latter used a combination
of cremation and orientation or grave plots to subdivide funeral space.
This practice can be seen at Spong Hill and Alwalton, where cremations
or inhumations were located in particular zones of the cemetery, or at
Caistor-by-Norwich, where cremation was employed to subdivide spatially distinct burial plots, probably by chronology. Cremation was used
at multiple scales, and the small number of urn burials at Berinsfield or
Worthy Park may have been used to distinguish individuals as opposed
to groups.

Early Anglo-Saxon cemeteries were both complex and culturally
specific, at both society-wide and local levels. They carried multiple
messages because they were constructed by many architects over
extended periods of time. They contained interpretations and reinter-
pretations, paradoxes and similarities, and they were designed as devices
to be understood by people situated within an early medieval attitude.
Individual sites contained continuities, and different funerary parties
shared semiotic knowledge of the cemeteries, but they interpreted them
according to their own rules using spatial patterning, grave orientation
or topography. For the most part cemeteries were neither homogeneous
nor random collections of unconnected burials (*contra* Barber, 2011: 6).
Early Anglo-Saxon cemeteries were the products of social agents operating at multiple scales and within an existing and predefined space.
Cemetery aesthetic was a mnemonic device used locally to communicate

at a cultural level; it provided the physical space to support narrative discourse and provides a unique resource for archaeological investigation. But these structures were not just used to divide up contemporary space; as we saw at Deal, cemeteries were a palimpsest of overwriting, where each generation reinterpreted the space for their own ends. Gravegoods, cemetery space and burial ritual were a physical manifestation, an overt expression, of the relationships which existed between people.

Notes

1 Sayer and Wienhold (2012) used ArcGIS 10 software to calculate Ripley's K-function, to establish the extent of deviation from spatial homogeneity at multiple scales. From this data they generated kernel density plots, which exploit the point of significant clustering. Unfortunately, ArcGIS 10 contains problems with edge correction. For this current study Ripley's K-function has been generated in R, a free statistic program, using the *maptools* and *spatstat* plugins. The graphs generated for this book are available on the ADS webite at https://archaeology dataservice.ac.uk/. The kernel density or heat maps have been generated with the QGIS *heatmap* plugin. The results of the two studies are comparable, but here the distances have been calculated using point data based on the centre of each grave to allow comparison between cremation and inhumation graves. Sayer and Wienhold (2012) took measurements from polyline shape files.

2 The assessment of grave homogeneity can be carried out using whole or partial cemeteries because the important value is the distance between graves, not the graves themselves. The statistic will account for any evident pattern even if further graves are found. When the kernel density map is plotted – using the Ripley K-value if no patterns are evident, or if there are patterns in only part of the cemetery – then the site can be broken down into subsections for independent investigation. This is discussed later in the chapter, for example, in the cremations and inhumations at Apple Down or the northern and southern graves at West Heslerton, which were buried using different densities and were part of a deliberate spatial patterning.

3 This system of rows developed to help manage mortuary space but, in fitting large numbers into an ordered and relatively small space, the orientation was not always E/W (Sayer, 2011: 205).

4 For patterns of material culture at Apple Down, see Chapter 1; and for similar patterns at Morning Thorpe, see Chapter 6.

3

Mortuary metre

Introduction: Horizontal stratigraphy in early Anglo-Saxon cemeteries

Metre is a measurement of cadence, of narrative time, and this chapter examines the chronological construction of cemetery space, employing the latest chronologies based on a detailed discussion of artefact typologies, as well as the new chronologies proposed by John Hines and Alex Bayliss (2013), and Catherine Hills and Sam Lucy (2013). A number of key early Anglo-Saxon cemeteries have been selected to illustrate different sequential characters in order to illustrate common patterns seen in the chronology of early Anglo-Saxon cemeteries, many of which are visible elsewhere in this book. Investigating the development of cemeteries and the transformation of funerary display over time, this chapter is by necessity both detailed and complex, exploring dating down to the burial plot, the individual grave and the artefact, so that we can understand the development of burial plots and sites as a whole. This detail reveals the complexities of horizontal stratigraphy, so we can begin to understand the generational cadence that underpins the changing attitudes towards artefacts, mortuary technologies and styles.

Beginning with Spong Hill, Norfolk, we investigate the use of new rituals as part of continually evolving social dynamics. Other sites include Bossut-Gottechain in Belgium, Sewerby, Apple Down, Wakerley, Oakington, Deal and Orpington, followed by a substantial reinvestigation of the chronology and horizontal stratigraphy at Dover Buckland. This draws on the previous case studies examined in this chapter to present a coherent dissection of the chronology of multiple-grave plots, each of which used different mortuary technologies to present similar and dissimilar characteristics as part of localised mortuary expressions. Each of these plots had different architects, and each grave was attended by a unique assembly of mourners. The mortuary metre highlights discordant identities, and sets the pace of chronological change.

As discussed in Chapter 1, traditional approaches to horizontal stratigraphy often expect adjacent graves to have comparable dates, and to have been positioned in sequential order. However, sometimes the fact that they were not adjacent in date is the important mortuary technology, in cases where mourners returned to particular spaces for generation after generation. In practice, most early Anglo-Saxon cemeteries were complex, with multiple changing variables, and many had no obvious initial single focus. As we have seen in Chapter 1, neither Finglesham, Kent nor Berinsfield, Oxfordshire, had a single early focus (Härke, 1992: 171). Both cemeteries actually exhibited multiple simultaneous chronological patterning. At Finglesham, some burials were placed at the edges of the cemetery, and others focused on key barrow burials so that these locations became chronologically specific focal points, a trend also seen at Dover Buckland and Oakington (see Chapter 2 and this chapter, below). Berinsfield did not have a single earlier focus either, but exhibited multiple areas of continued emphasis, where mourners returned to central areas throughout its sixth- and (short-lived) seventh-century use. Focal points rarely had one early date because they were visited and revisited, reinterpreted and represented throughout multiple generations and during different phases of activity. It is this reinterpretation that could refresh, or undermine, their importance for each subsequent generation.

Chapter 1 illustrated some chronological characteristics of Deal and Orpington that differed. Deal was organised around two plots which were returned to for generations, as well as a later group of graves. With these later graves the focus changed, and the earlier plots were altered and abandoned in favour of a new burial form. Grave location and individual groups of graves could have a chronological character, one plot following consecutively on from another. The burials at Deal consisted of two contemporary plots, or three groups of burials, which were separated around a single, large Bronze Age barrow. The two plots of graves were contemporaneous, part of a first phase broadly early and middle-sixth-century in date. Notably, however, some later-seventh-century graves truncated or partly obliterated earlier burials, and this seems to have been deliberate destruction, or the rewriting of the cemetery narrative by changing its aesthetic appearance and directing attention towards recently dead individuals rather than a long-deceased antecedent. It was part of a changing metre, with a new message, and the eastern group of graves was not a focused plot, but instead it was part of this second phase, dating broadly to the later sixth and seventh centuries. The character of these graves changed, placing new emphasis on groups of male-gendered weapon graves, a pattern also seen in a contemporaneous part of Dover Buckland.

Orpington had one inhumation, grave 23, around which multiple male weapon graves were placed. These graves dated throughout the whole of the sixth century, but many were not contemporaneous. At this sixth-century site, the emphasis was on a single biologically male antecedent, grave 23, and this may have engendered in subsequent generations a desire to highlight their martial identity, because it was weapon graves which seem to have dominated this mortuary space. As the chronology shows, the individuals within these weapon graves were very young or not yet born when grave 23 was constructed. They could not have been a contemporary group of warriors, unlike those at Deal or Dover Buckland (see below). Instead, they consisted of several generations of men who empathised with, or wanted to express, a similar identity. This centre was created through the repeated use of a particular place to inter children and also men with weapons. The placement of later graves around this centre shows how it was used and how these graves then shaped and contributed to the construction of community narratives. Perhaps Orpington was eventually abandoned as a burial site by a generation who did not feel connected to a previously highlighted ancestor, or this new generation may have wanted to focus the burial of their dead on a different part of their identity. This is the narrative that this chapter highlights, difference in the pace of change and difference in the cadence of cemetery space, particularly focusing on internal plot dynamics. This chronological character provides a key in our concluding discussions in Chapter 6, when we start to put all of these spatial, material and chronological cemetery technologies together to understand the cemetery space holistically.

Dating early Anglo-Saxon graves

Sam Lucy suggested that the development of artefact typologies, and the detailed chronologies which often accompany them, was a distraction from the important question of social relations (Lucy, 1997: 151). Similarly, Hope-Taylor (1977), indicated a frustration with his peers' obsession with artefacts over social and organisational aspects of Anglo-Saxon cemetery studies, criticisms that still could be levelled at some contemporary projects. Importantly, however, studies that ask social questions benefit from a good understanding of details. For example, the dating of artefacts is an important part of understanding how that object was used, circulated and deposited, and it affects the way it might be interpreted (see Sayer *et. al.*, 2019). We also need to understand who the living were, and how their experiences of cemetery space moulded their attitudes towards it. Who attended a funeral, and how did attitudes to the corpse, dress, material culture, gender and age change along with the context under investigation? The early Anglo-Saxons did not have one attitude, or a single approach, to community, death, burial or the corpse, but many, and these changed over time.

The early Anglo-Saxon period discussed in this book dates between the middle-fifth and the later-seventh or earliest-eighth centuries, a span of some 250 years. In the last 250 years Western societies have seen profound changes to gender and dress, and attitudes to the dead have undergone significant change as well, such as the secularisation of the deathbed and the funeral, and the adoption of cremation in the early twentieth century (Davies 2005; Walter 1994). Attitudes towards gender have changed substantially, so today women have the right to work, vote and own property, and are found in social spaces that would have been unlikely just one hundred years ago. Social attitudes to religion, and the use of religious spaces, have transformed profoundly, with the proliferation of nonconformity in the nineteenth century and the increasing secularisation of society in the twentieth (King and Sayer, 2011). How and where people live has changed, and sanitation rules and increasing home ownership have transformed the use of urban spaces completely. How, when and where we use formal attire has also changed generation by generation. Why, then, would we consider the early Anglo-Saxon period to be any less dynamic? We see profound changes within the period, for example, the decline in brooch and buckle wearing seen at the end of the sixth or beginning of the seventh century in female graves suggests changes to costume (Owen-Crocker, 1986; Walton Rogers, 2007). We also see the decline in cremation practice (Williams, 2002a), the adoption, or re-adoption, of Christianity and the rise of a new political elite in the form of local, then regional, kingdoms (Owen-Crocker, 1986; Arnold, 1997; Petts, 2011). As a result, it is very important to understand the context and fluctuation of change within mortuary landscapes. As this chapter aims to demonstrate, the pace of change was not always at the same speed from cemetery to cemetery, or even from grave plot to grave plot. To get at this pace, we must first understand how graves are dated, and explore the impact of new dating systems on cemetery chronologies.

Multiple objects, different dating systems

One of the challenges of producing cemetery chronologies in this period is a reliance on artefact typologies, and their associated chronologies, to date graves. Utilising artefacts as dating material is useful because similar artefacts are found in multiple graves in different combinations. As a result, objects can be compared to see a pattern, and this might be a group of artefacts which are repeatedly associated with each other and so must be contemporary. However, this is also challenging because of the different systems used by archaeologists to date objects. In addition, artefacts were portable and their use was open to individual or regional variations; for example, there are a number of heirloom objects which were old when buried. This complexity is compounded because there are several different systems for artefact dating in use among early medieval scholars. Early Anglo-Saxon artefact typologies often include a mixture of local comparison, comparison with continental equivalents where coin-dating evidence might be available, and/or art-historical methods which are used particularly for the presence of Salin style I animal art, or the emergence of Salin Style II, which occurred around AD 560–70 (Lucy, 2000b: 16–20; Evison, 1987). Some dating systems investigate single artefacts to understand their development and context, for example beads, buckles, shields or spears (Marzinzik, 2003; Brugmann, 2004; Dickinson and Härke, 1992; Swanton, 1973; 1974). Other dating systems investigate the range of objects found in a region, for example Tania Dickinson's (1976) study of the Thames Valley or Martin Welch's (1983) investigation of Sussex. Still others look at national assemblages to understand wider social phenomena, for example Stoodley's (1999) investigation of female graves, or Härke's (1992) investigation of weapon graves.

Alternatively, some studies set out to make national chronologies based on multiple selected artefacts, for example Hines and Bayliss' *Anglo-Saxon Graves and Grave Goods* (2013). By necessity, national systems use these regional- or artefact-specific studies to develop their methods, and these may differ. For example, Dickinson suggested that there were seven types of disc brooch, based on decorative elements, whereas Welch preferred to see four, based on the presence and/or absence of decoration, mainly stamps or ring-and-dot. Welch (1983: 57) preferred a predominantly fifth-century date with some examples of the brooch from the sixth century, whereas Dickinson (1976: 121) dated them between AD 450 and AD 550. Many typologies are based on the work of Nils Åberg (1926) and, like Barry Ager (1985); Richard Avent (1975); and Edwin Thurlow Leeds (1945), these tend to employ artistic styles to understand chronological change. As a result, these studies emphasise a changing character around the later-sixth century, whereas Kurt Böhner (1958), Elis Behmer (1939) and Wilfried Menghin (1974) analysed Merovingian material culture and based much of their dating on coins. This allowed Evison (1987) and others to build Anglo-Saxon chronologies, for example Evison's study of knives from Dover Buckland (1987: 113). Just like Dover Buckland's knives, some typologies were developed by cemetery excavators to make site-specific observations, and these could end up influencing national approaches, for example

Hirst (1985) on annular brooches from the cemetery at Sewerby. Some systems can prove to be complex or hard to work with outside the specific investigation. For example, Michael Swanton's spears can be difficult to delineate or separate into groups based on measurements (Dickinson, 1976: 291–2; Hines and Bayliss, 2013: 163). In this section I explore individual artefacts and their use in dating. In subsequent chapters I use these artefacts to describe a series of cemeteries highlighting different chronological characteristics.

Hines and Bayliss' chronological framework project (2013) aimed to make a chronological system for the later-sixth and seventh centuries based on Bayesian statistics and radiocarbon dating. This was an important piece of work, but, unfortunately, it had limitations for early Anglo-Saxon cemetery projects. Traditional artefact typologies start in the later-fifth century and often end in the early or mid-seventh century as artefacts were less frequently deposited in graves. The radiocarbon-dating project was able to explore seventh-century chronologies further, but its earliest dates are in the middle-sixth century, and so there is little crossover with earlier artefacts. In fact, one of the most notable differences is that traditional cemetery chronologies depend upon brooches, whereas the Hines and Bayliss chronological framework project dates around twenty brooches with wide definitions, as, for example, bow brooches or round brooches. In this dating system the early brooch types, disc brooches or cruciform brooches, tend to have distinct middle-sixth-century dates, but we know they have antecedents in the later-fifth and early sixth centuries. In fact, because of the absence of brooches in the Hines and Bayliss study, the chronology of female-gendered artefacts has changed little from artefact-typology systems. Notable exceptions include the identification of composite or garnet disc brooches in the middle-sixth century, an earlier development than was previously believed. Importantly, for female-gendered graves, beads (a common object) provide the most compatibility between an artefact-typology system and the radiocarbon-based dating systems, and the later bead combinations broadly correlate Hines and Bayliss' dates with Brugmann's phases. Nonetheless, there are considerable differences between Brugmann's (2004) national study and her regional study based on Dover Buckland (Brugmann, 2012). For example, grave 376 at Dover Buckland has beads of group B2 and so in the national framework dates to AD 580–650, but in the regional framework this grave is placed within phases 5–7 or AD 650–750 (Brugmann, 2004; Brugmann 2012: 324, 355; see Appendix 1 for a list of differently dated graves).

Another good point of crossover between the typology system and radiocarbon-dating system are buckles, which are found in male and female graves, with some gender differentiation according to type, in particular Sonja Marzinzik's (2003) typology. This is more complex than Hines and Bayliss' (2013) dating system for buckles, but these two approaches complement each other well. Weapons, notably shields and spears, however, provide something of a problem. Traditional spear and shield typologies consist of a combination of form and measurements, while the Hines and Bayliss chronological framework places greater emphasis on dimensions, and in particular the proportions of particular characteristics – height, length and breadth for example. This is similar to the existing object typologies, but different enough that compatibility has become an issue. This is a particular problem when looking at fifth- and sixth-century cemeteries because the earliest graves are identifiable using artefact types, and the middle-sixth-century and later graves have been dated using limited radiocarbon dating. As a result, the male and female chronologies behave differently. For example, based on an analysis of Dover Buckland (more below), there are thirty-six male-gendered graves which can be dated to within close-fitting margins, and similarly for fifty-five female-gendered graves (see Table 3.1). The male dating relies heavily on the Hines and Bayliss system and on buckles. Table 3.1 shows that this approach appears to bunch male-gendered graves to AD 530–60, over-emphasising the middle-sixth century.

Using Table 3.1 as a contingency table for a chi-square test, we can investigate this pattern statistically; chi-square is suitable for this 2 × 5 contingency table because there are two independent samples, and the expected values are greater than five. Nonetheless, the result is similar to that with Fisher's exact test. For this exercise the frequency of male-gendered versus female-gendered graves was attributed to four date bands between AD 450 and AD 650. The p-value for this chi-square test comes out at 0.009813, less than 0.05, meaning that the pattern we can see in this data is significant. Either there was an increased frequency of weapon burials around AD 530–60, or this method of dating the male-gendered graves bunches them in the middle-sixth century (see below). Notably, the weapon graves that were dated on the basis of buckles, using Brugmann's Kentish chronology (2012: 325–53), tend to be more evenly spread between dates. More weapon graves, eleven, are

Table 3.1 Datable graves from Dover Buckland's sixth- and seventh-century phases

	AD 450–530	AD 530–560	AD 560–600	AD 600–650	Totals
male	4	23	5	3	35
female	12	11	7	9	39

associated with the later-sixth-century or early seventh-century phases 3a, 3b or 3, than the middle-sixth-century phase 2 which has seven (see Appendix 1). Brugmann's correspondence analysis included the weapon graves. This incompatibility issue appears to be because different approaches use different assumptions, which are then used to date individual graves and their objects. For this national study of cemetery organisation, the male chronology used has relied heavily on Hines and Bayliss' approach, which has the advantage of the subdivision of the spearheads into finer date ranges, allowing for greater resolution than Swanton's typology (Swanton, 1973; 1974). However, at least for the earlier examples, we need to be cautious because there are only three radiocarbon dates associated with the earliest spears of types SP2-a2b2, SP2-b1a2 and SP2-b1a3 (Hines and Bayliss, 2013: 565–6). The Hines and Bayliss approach is just a beginning and a more detailed look at weapon chronologies would be welcomed to fine-tune the errors and explore the details more closely. Equally, associating more radiocarbon dates with earlier weapons and brooches, as well as exploring the regional distinctions, would be valuable, despite the radiocarbon curve plateau around the fifth and early sixth centuries.

By necessity, the dating system used in this book is a hybrid of artefact typologies and radiocarbon dating, for example Hines and Bayliss (2013). This system is described in detail in this chapter and uses 'gateway' artefacts, which can assist in the accurate dating of graves because they are associated with a specific date, or a range of dates. When these objects are identified in a grave, that grave should be associated with the same dates; the more artefacts there are in a grave, the more accurately it can be dated. These artefacts are outlined below. This section is necessarily detailed so that the errors and assumptions are visible, and so that the understanding of cemetery layouts can be adapted as the dating methods become increasingly sophisticated. In both the Hines and Bayliss' chronological framework (2013), and in the more traditional artefact-based dating systems, there are a few objects that prove most useful in exploring comparative dates.

The presence of a group 1 cruciform brooch, for example, would identify a grave as fifth century in date. A type I.12a–i buckle was in use for the whole of the early Anglo-Saxon period, but a type II.7 buckle, by contrast, is associated only with the second half of the sixth century, and it is unlikely to be found with a group 1 cruciform brooch – and, if it were, the brooch might be identified as an 'heirloom' object. It is also possible to separate graves into groups of a particular character, and this is done here where there are different areas of a cemetery that have distinct chronological characters. For this project, I am not approaching this with the formality of the *stufe* groups, like the phases or gravegood groups of Merovingian cemetery analysis (see, for example, Hines *et al.*, 1999). Rather, I intend to show the different characters of particular graves to highlight cemetery specific trends or chronological differences between individual graves, or spatially associated groups of graves, where these are possible.

It is vital that we understand the chronology of individual graves, and of parts of cemeteries, so we may understand the interactions and decisions that contributed to site construction. There is a certain generational cadence, or metre, that is specific to each individual cemetery (Sayer, 2010). Some sites saw the development of new areas triggered by generational change. In others we see the regular refocusing of graves around a particular barrow or key ancestor, and in yet other cemeteries we see the same areas of a site or plot returned to repeatedly, presumably to bury particular dead, even where a new burial will obliterate a previous one. In this way some communities reinforced antecedents within the cemetery space, and some rewrote the space constantly, turning the mortuary landscape into a palimpsest. What is fascinating is that the same system was not always consistently used across one site, and nor was a single system necessarily used at all times in the life of a particular cemetery. This explains the apparent complexity of larger or more long-lived sites, such as Dover Buckland or Lechlade, which are both explored in more detail here and in Chapter 6 in this volume.

Objects and their dates

In this section I present the dating system used here and discuss how the new radiocarbon project changes our perspectives. I start with female-gendered artefacts, and then focus on male artefacts and gender-neutral objects, because the radiocarbon dates have a different impact on these groups of objects.

Round brooches

Disc brooches are flat-cast copper-alloy brooches which may have simple stamped decoration in the form of lines, dots or perforated edges; it is likely that they date between the fifth and middle-sixth centuries (Welch, 1983: 57; Dickinson, 1976: 121). Applied brooches, by contrast, are composite objects, which have a flat copper-alloy plate with a decorated disc of thin metal fixed to the face of the brooch. They have been split into three types, dated from the fifth century to late-sixth century based on the presence of decorative elements and animal style I or II art, called Salin style I or II (Welch, 1983; Dickinson, 1976; 1979). Saucer brooches have been studied by Dickinson (1976; 1993) and are

primarily a sixth-century type, with eighteen different groups characterised by abstract designs. Abstract decoration is followed by animal
designs; larger, more elaborate types are dated to the late-sixth and early
seventh centuries. Hines and Bayliss (2013: 367, 221) dated six saucer
brooches and suggested that they have a chronologically distinct horizon
in the middle-sixth century.

Button brooches have a rounded human or stylised face, and are
around 19.8 mm in diameter. They were identified by Åberg (1926)
and Leeds (1945), who placed them in the later-sixth century as a
group; however, both Dickinson (1976) and Welch (1983) date them
earlier than that, with a later-fifth-century date. There are twelve basic
types, dating broadly within the fifth and sixth centuries. Avent (1975)
produced the only typology of composite or garnet disc brooches. He
divided them into four groups: keystone brooches (late-sixth to early
seventh century); plated brooches (early seventh century); composite
brooches (early to middle-seventh century); and a miscellaneous group.
However, the dating for these is problematic because it was based on
limited numbers of objects and on art-historical rather than contextual comparison. Hines and Bayliss' dating of these objects places the
BR2–1/b2 keystone brooches squarely in the mid-sixth century (Hines
and Bayliss, 2013: 367, 221).

Annular brooches are common, varied but usually plain, and
they defy conventional classification (Hines, 1984: 260–9; Penn and
Brugmann, 2007: 25). The only real attempt to classify these brooches
into chronological types was carried out by Sue Hirst (1985: 55–7),
in her report on Sewerby. She separated them into two types, earlier
flat-section or hammered, and later round- or D-section cast brooches,
and divided these into subcategories based on decoration. Hirst then
dated them around the early, middle or whole of the sixth century, with
one seventh-century-type in the case of type VII, which had a bird- or
animal-headed decoration. The radiocarbon-dated forms reported by
Hines and Bayliss are comparable with this model (Hines and Bayliss,
2013: 367). Cognate brooches were identified by Leeds (1945), with a
limited regional distribution, and date to the sixth century. Penannular
brooches are similar to annular brooches, but have terminals and are
also flat or D-section. These brooches have pre-Roman origins and
some of the types which Elizabeth Fowler identified as Roman are found
in Anglo-Saxon graves, used as bracelets (Fowler, 1960; 1963). Type
G brooch typologies were substantially revisited by Dickinson (1982),
who dated them broadly to the sixth and seventh centuries, and type
H ranges from the mid-fifth to the eighth century. The quoit-brooch
style is characterised by its zoomorphic and geomorphic elements and
is primarily mid- to late-fifth century (Ager, 1985); some heavily worn

examples come from early sixth-century contexts (Welch, 1983). Seiichi Suzuki carried out a more recent investigation of these objects but did not question the existing chronology (Suzuki, 2000).

Long/bow brooches

Cruciform brooches are derived from a Scandinavian brooch style. They were split into five types by Åberg (1926: 33–4) on the basis of stylistic elements, and this was further developed by Leeds (1945), Leeds and Pocock (1971), Mortimer (1990) and Martin (2015). They date from the early fifth century and continued with the later florid types to the mid-sixth century. Small-long brooches were first classified by Leeds (1945: 5), but have not seen any more comprehensive study. Midland (or mid-Anglian) examples may be sixth-century (Hirst, 1985), although Dickinson (1976: 174–82) regarded the Wessex examples as having a late-fifth-century origin. Welch (1983) dated the Sussex examples from the fifth to early sixth centuries. Great square-headed-brooches are elaborate gilt objects influenced by Scandinavian designs, and Leeds (1949) classified these by shape; however, Hines (1984; 1997) has reclassified them into three phases, dating the first two to the early sixth century and the last, and most common, type to the mid-sixth century. The great square-headed-brooches dated by Hines and Bayliss (2013: 367) were of the sixth century. There is no agreement about the date of small square-headed brooches which may fit best into the first three quarters of the sixth century (Leeds, 1949; Leigh, 1980; Welch, 1983; Dickinson, 1976; Brugmann, 1999: 35; Hines and Bayliss, 2013: 367). There are two types of equal-armed brooches: imported types from the fifth century, and early sixth-century copies, which are mainly found in East Anglia (Evison, 1977; Hines, 1984; Bruns, 2003). Likewise, supporting-arm brooches were imports from what is now northern Germany or Holland, and date to the later-fifth century (Evison, 1977). Bird and animal brooches are also rare and were imported from the Middle Rhine Valley or Frankish areas; the Mill Hill (Deal, Kent) examples are early sixth-century or more 'advanced' sixth-century (Parfitt and Brugmann, 1997: 44–5).

Other jewellery items

Beads are a common find in the burials of women and children, and are a critical component of the chronology of child and female graves (Hines and Bayliss, 2013: 203). There have been various attempts to date them, all of which recognise the importance of colour combinations (Chadwick Hawkes, 1973; Guido, 1999). Brugmann (2004) tightened up these categories and produced the most comprehensive study of glass beads. She dated combinations of beads according to three groups, A, B and C, which are in turn subdivided according to specific details: the presence of Roman types; biconical types; melon beads; polyhedral beads; or, in the later groups, the presence of white beads, dotted beads or annular twist beads. Brugmann's glass-bead chronologies are supported by Hines and Bayliss, with individual beads identified in the radiocarbon project fitting broadly with Brugmann's groups (Hines and Bayliss, 2013: 203–8). This correlation with the radiocarbon-dating project means they are one of the most reliable ways to date the graves of children and females. Beads provide a good crossover with the artefact-dating methods. In short, by relying on beads as a 'gateway' object the two systems become reasonably comparable.

Amethyst beads are found in relatively controlled contexts, and Helen Geake (1997) placed them at the end of the sixth century and into the third quarter of the seventh century, or Brugmann's group B. Cowrieshell beads fit into Brugmann's group C (Hines and Bayliss, 2013: 208). Rock-crystal beads have not been the subject of a detailed study, but Dickinson (1976: 206) suggested that they tend towards a sixth-century date. Pendants come in a variety of forms; bracteates, for example, have been studied because of their Scandinavian connection, and many English example are copper or silver, not gold. Mogens Mackeprang (1952) identified five classes and Marit Gaimster (1992) argued that they may have been in production for just two or three generations during the sixth century. Despite this, she proposed that the five groups fitted between the fifth and seventh centuries. Hines and Bayliss (2013: 365) indicated that PE2-a,d,e and PE2-b were sixth-century scutiform pendants, but they may also be earlier. The PE4 lunulate, PE5 cross pendant and PE11 suspended bead are seventh-century, but these dates are based on a small number of examples (Hines and Bayliss, 2013: 211–15, 364). These silver scutiform pendants, identifiable because of their central boss, were previously dated to the sixth century (Hirst, 1985: 70). Those with cross decorations may be of the late-sixth to seventh centuries (Hines and Bayliss, 2013: 365). Other pendants include gold disc pendants, bullae pendants, wire ring pendants, cabochon pendants and cloisonné-work pendants, and these mostly date to the seventh century (Dickinson, 1976: 200–1; Geake, 1997: 36–7).

Ornate pins and linked-pin sets tend to be dated to the seventh century, but unfortunately singular or plain pins remain largely undated despite the attempts of Welch and Dickinson (Owen-Crocker, 1986: 90–3; Welch, 1983; Dickinson, 1976: 193–7). Indeed, the only pin identified with a distinctive signature by Hines and Bayliss (2013: 370) was the P12-a linked pin, which confirmed a seventh-century date.

There is no agreement on the dating of bracelets because they vary so much between individual objects. They may have been most popular in the sixth century, with some decorated examples from the seventh (Dickinson, 1976: 200–1; Evison, 1987: 86; Hines, 1997: 268; Kennett, 1970: 27–8).

Personal equipment

Buckles are functional and decorative objects. Evison (1955), Chadwick Hawkes and Dunning (1961) and Geake (1994) all contributed to a patchy framework based on the presence of Salin type I and II animal art. However, the most comprehensive study is that of Marzinzik (2003), who started by dividing the buckles into groups with and without back plates. Subgroups were then based on the shape of elements which made up the buckle, and included the plate, tongue and decoration on the loop. As with beads, Marzinzik's buckle typology is based on continental chronologies, and Hines and Bayliss (2013: 332) agree that this relative sequence is plausible. They suggested that their first phase, BU2-d/BU2-h (AD 505–64), is followed by, second, BU3-a, BU3-g with BU3-c (AD 480–570), then third BU3-c, BU3-h, BU4-b and BU4-c (AD 570–650) followed by, fourth, BU3-d plus BU3-i (AD 610–80) and fifth and finally BU3-f (AD 635–710), presenting five abutting phases, a similar but simpler version of Marzinzik (2003). Buckles are less common in female graves of the seventh century (Owen-Crocker, 2004: 143; Walton Rogers, 2007: 187–9). Interestingly, one type, the BU8 (or Marzinzik type I.9–11), a simple oval-looped buckle dating AD 510–65, was probably placed in female graves a generation or so after it was placed in male graves (Hines and Bayliss, 2013: 245).

Hines (1993) made the most comprehensive study of both the chronology and typology of wrist clasps. Clasps have a chronological distribution between the fifth and seventh centuries, but are found most frequently and with the greatest diversity in the sixth century. Type B7, the most common form in England, was simply two plates, one with a hook and the other with a hole, which would have been sewn into the garment, and is a sixth-century type. Type B13a is similar, but each half of the clasp consisted of two elements, often a plate and bar, and is a late-fifth to early sixth-century form. David Brown (1977) published the only major corpus of firesteels, dividing them into three major groups based on decoration: bird-headed; horse-headed; and plain iron. Bird-headed examples, including the Portchester type, are probably fifth century, while horse-headed examples seem to be largely fifth- to late-sixth-century, and the plain iron ones are undated. Girdle hangers are bronze T-shaped or open-worked key-like objects, some with impressed

decorative elements on them; they date to the sixth century (Chadwick
Hawkes, 1973; Hines, 1997; Hines and Bayliss, 2013: 370). Chatelaines
are more elaborate girdle hangers, with a mixture of objects hanging
from a chain or loop, which date from the sixth and seventh centuries
(Chadwick Hawkes, 1973; Felder, 2015). Most cosmetic items are not
reliably dated, for example, tweezers (Dickinson, 1976: 220–4; Hines
and Bayliss, 2013: 370). However, combs of the fifth and sixth century are double-sided, whereas seventh-century combs are single-sided
(Dickinson, 1976: 216–19). Hincs and Bayliss (2013: 370) suggest that
combs do not appear in early Anglo-Saxon inhumation graves until
the later-sixth century. However, a recent dating project at Spong Hill,
Norfolk, showed that triangular-topped combs from cremations are
likely to appear in the fifth century (Hills and Lucy, 2013: 108).

Weapons

Swords are composite items and it is the pommel, scabbard, guard and
decorative elements which can inform us about type and date (Bone,
1989: 63; Cameron, 2000: 11–12). The blades themselves remain consistent, fitting into Behmer's (1939) Merovingian *schmal-blattig* or nar-
row-bladed type. Menghin's (1974) sword typology, based on pommels
and scabbard fittings, places English blades into three types, dating
to the fifth century, the early sixth century, and from the fifth to the
middle of the sixth century, respectively. Hines and Bayliss (2013: 332)
suggest two overlapping sequences broadly equivalent to Menghin's, but
unfortunately only the SW4, equivalent to Menghin's C, D and E, had
enough radiocarbon dates to be reliably dated. Swords probably came
into use as gravegoods between AD 420 and AD 560 and had gone out of
use by AD 650 (Brunning 2019). Hilt and guard types have been studied
by Behmer (1939) and Menghin (1974) for the fifth and sixth centuries,
whereas those of the eighth century and beyond have been looked at by
Dunning and Everson (1961), Evison (1967) and Wilson (1965). Evison
(1967: 67) looked at a number of sword rings and observed that the
mobile rings were earlier, while later ones had been fused to the hilt.
Other paraphernalia, such as pyramids and strap-holders, are of the
seventh century, and have been discussed in detail by Rupert Bruce-
Mitford (1978), and Hines and Bayliss (2013: 183–9). Despite dates for
some parts of swords, swords remain difficult to date, probably because
of their role as heirlooms, meaning that old swords can be found in later
graves (Dickinson, 1976; Härke, 2000b; Sayer *et al.*, 2019; Brunning,
2017; Brunning 2019).

   Spearheads have been studied in detail by Swanton (1973; 1974),
who grouped the typologies loosely on the profile, section, blade

length and socket length/blade ratios of individual blades. His types are simply: A–B, Germanic derivative forms (A being barbed and B including spikes and mid-ribbed examples); C, leaf-shaped blades with the socket shorter than the blade; D, leaf-shaped blades with the socket longer than the blade; E, angular straight-sided blades with the socket shorter than the blade; F, angular straight-sided blades with the socket longer than the blade; H, consisting of distinctively con-cave-bladed spearheads (including H2, the most common Anglo-Saxon spearhead); I and J types, which have corrugated blades; and K and L types, which have fullered blades. Several criticisms have been levelled at this typology; for example, minor uncertainties create considerable ambiguity (Dickinson, 1976: 291–2; Hines and Bayliss, 2013: 163). Hines and Bayliss' chronology (2013) is based on Karen Høilund Nielsen's typology, which uses ratios of blade length and width, a system which separates spears by profile (Hines and Bayliss, 2013: 168–80). Four types of spearhead – SP2-a2b; SP2-a2c; SPTip-212; SP2-a1a2; and SP2-b1a3 – fall at the start of the sequence, and probably date to the early and middle decades of the sixth century or earlier (Hines and Bayliss, 2013: 335). Types SP1-a3 and SP3-a fall into the second half of the sixth century, types SP1-a4 and SP4 have longer currency in the later-sixth and seventh centuries, and SP2-a2d and SP2-a1b1 appear to be restricted to the first half of the seventh century, but samples of these two types are limited (Hines and Bayliss, 2013: 336). In comparison with Swanton's, this system tends to put early spearheads into the mid-sixth century, but usefully it divides up the E-type with straight edges and H-type, broadly the SP2-bs with concave sides, into different dates based on the widest point on the blade.

Dickinson and Härke (1992) produced a typology for shield bosses and they identified: carinated, modified, derivative-type, 'transition', Merovingian, low-curved and sugar-loaf bosses. The first three are fifth- and early sixth-century types. Merovingian bosses and low-curved bosses are broadly sixth-century types, while sugar-loaf are later-sixth- and seventh-century. These forms are broadly based on the size and height of the boss, the width of the flange and the number of rivets on the flange. Hines and Bayliss' study identified five types of boss, SB1–5, where SB3 dates to the middle decades of the sixth century and SB4 is found in the decades around AD 600: AD 560–90 with probability of 68 per cent – AD 585–620, probability 68 per cent (Hines and Bayliss, 2013: 247–8, 334). Phyletic seriation produces a model that sees evolution from short to tall shield bosses. Shorter bosses (<130 mm) are earlier than taller bosses (>130 mm) and wider flanges (>17 mm) are earlier than smaller flanges (<17 mm), with the transition around AD 565–85 (Hines and Bayliss, 2013: 249–50).

The last weapon discussed here is the seax, which was a heavy, single-edged bladed weapon larger than most knives (Gale, 1989: 71). There were three main types of seax in early Anglo-Saxon England: the narrow seax, divided into triangular-bladed, small and large; the broad seax; and the long seax (Böhner, 1958: 135–45; Dickinson, 1976). Seaxes were a sixth-century innovation, first appearing around AD 525–60, but predominantly dated to the seventh century as swords declined in frequency. Phyletic seriation sees an evolution from smaller (<310 mm) to longer (>310 mm) seaxes around AD 600–35 – probability 68 per cent (Hines and Bayliss, 2013: 248–9). Their use as gravegoods ended around AD 670–705 and the radiocarbon dates are in broad agreement with continental parallels (Hines and Bayliss, 2013: 334).

Vessels

Donald Harden (1956; 1978) studied both Roman and Anglo-Saxon glass vessel types, including: stemmed beakers, claw beakers, cone beakers, horns, bell beakers, bag beakers, pouch bottles, squat jars, bottles, palm cups, bowls and buckets. Evison studied claw beakers and the Kempston-type cone beakers (Evison, 1972; 1982). As a result, glass vessels have been placed into three set date groups: fifth to early sixth century, sixth century or seventh century. Jean Cook (2004) produced a corpus of sixty-two copper-alloy-bound and twenty-four iron-bound buckets and fitted them into phases on the basis of an individual bucket's association with other gravegoods. Unfortunately there is no clear-cut typology. Nowell Myres' typology (1969; 1977) still stands as the only way to date Anglo-Saxon pottery, despite being very problematic and hard to repeat (Chadwick Hawkes, 1974; Morris, 1974). He split the corpus into several groups on the basis of quite generic shapes: biconical, globular, shouldered, necked, and bulbous or wide-mouthed. He dated other aspects as well, including handles, lugs, bosses and stamped decoration. The only significant addition is Evison's chronology (1979) of wheel-thrown pottery and continental wares.

Cemeteries' chronologies

The early Anglo-Saxon cemetery at Spong Hill, central Norfolk, was first excavated in 1968 and then systematically between 1972 and 1975 (Hills *et al.*, 1984: 32). It was a mixed-rite site with over 2500 cremations and fifty-seven inhumation graves. Antiquarian investigators may have removed many hundreds of cremations but, nonetheless, its large size means that much of the internal chronology can be understood (Hills and Lucy, 2013). The earliest cremation graves at Spong Hill, phase A, started around or just before the mid-fifth century, and the key artefacts used to date the site included antler combs and cruciform brooches. The latest phase, phase C, consisted of cremation and inhumation graves. This relative chronology led Catherine Hills to conclude that the majority of the cremation graves were deposited in the fifth century (Hills and Lucy, 2013; Hills, 2017: 248–50). Like other sites we have discussed, Spong Hill was neither a monocentric, nor a polycentric cemetery, but rather it had phases which changed between a single focus and multiple foci.

There were essentially two significant chronological changes. Phase A cremations and pottery stamps had a particular concentration on the south of the site (Figure 3.1) but were also found across the whole space. Phase A/B cremations were equally dispersed, but perhaps concentrated in the south of the cemetery, just to the east of the phase A burials. Significantly, in phase B, the southern part of the cemetery remained a focus for burial, but cremation urns became much denser across three areas more to the north of the site (Figure 3.2). Notably, in phase C, the cremations shifted their focus to the north-east of the site in between the contemporary inhumation graves (Figure 3.3). Unfortunately, large numbers of cremations, particularly from the middle spaces of Spong Hill cemetery, are not currently datable (Hills and Lucy, 2013).

Nonetheless, Spong Hill highlights the challenges presented by horizontal stratigraphy: instead of burial location changing from one place to another, it persisted in the southern part of the cemetery across phases A to C, although with significantly less emphasis in phase C. The southern area remained an important focus, returned to for over a hundred years or so. Several generations chose to bury their dead among the urns of their antecedents. The phase B cremations saw burial in existing areas continue, but significant new foci developed in the north. However, it was not until phase C that the focus and style of burial saw significant change. In phase C, burial persisted, but this phase saw the rejection of previous foci and the establishment of a new central location within which to bury cremations. At the same time, the introduction of inhumation burial was a break from the past, a recreation of burial practices according to a new narrative which took the previous mode and reinvented it. The physical proximity of the existing cemetery space remained important. Despite the change in style, a connection to the original cemetery seems to be part of why new graves were located within this space, and not within a new cemetery.

There are examples of sites which seem to maintain a single focus, even if they developed using different organisational methods. Bossut-Gottechain is a good example of a chronologically concentric site. Bossut-Gottechain is a Merovingian cemetery located in the province of

Phase A cremations

Phase A stamps

Figure 3.1 Spong Hill, Norfolk: phase A cremations and phase A stamp groups, showing the southern concentration of cremation urns.

Figure 3.2 Spong Hill, phase B cremations and phase B stamp groups, showing the concentration of cremation urns around the whole area.

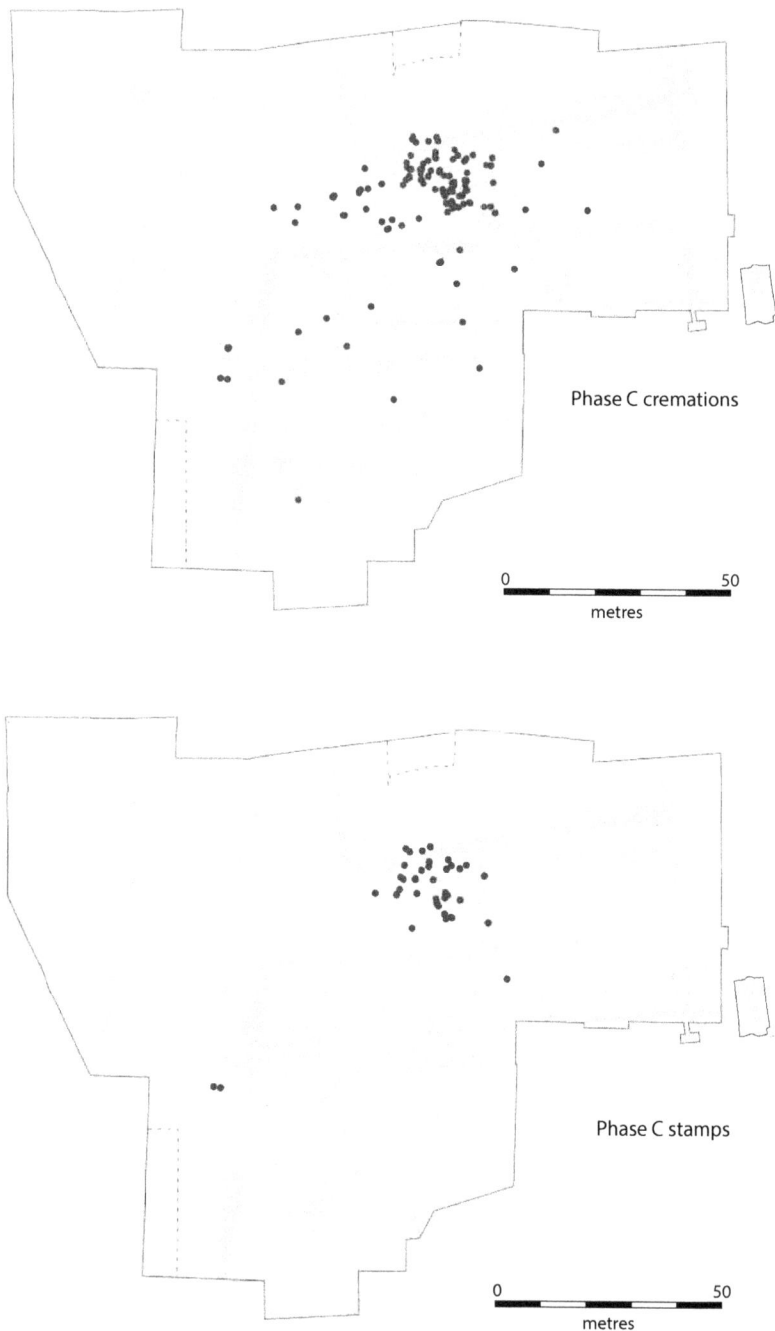

Figure 3.3 Spong Hill, phase C cremations and phase C stamp groups, showing the northern concentration of cremation urns, and the tighter clustering in this phase.

Brabant, 30 km south-east of Brussels, and was excavated between 2003 and 2006 in advance of road construction (Vrielynck, 2012). The excavated site consisted of 436 graves, but some were lost due to tree planting or surface erosion. It was in use for 180 years, from the last quarter of the fifth century to the middle of the seventh, making it contemporary with the early Anglo-Saxon cemeteries described elsewhere. The chronological assessment discussed here was developed based on some 8,300 beads from the site (Vrielynck, 2012). Notably, Bossut-Gottechain had a core of early burials (late-fifth century) on a roughly N/S orientation or a contrasting E/W orientation (Figure 3.4). On the edge of the earliest burial area had been placed a single horse grave. The early burials

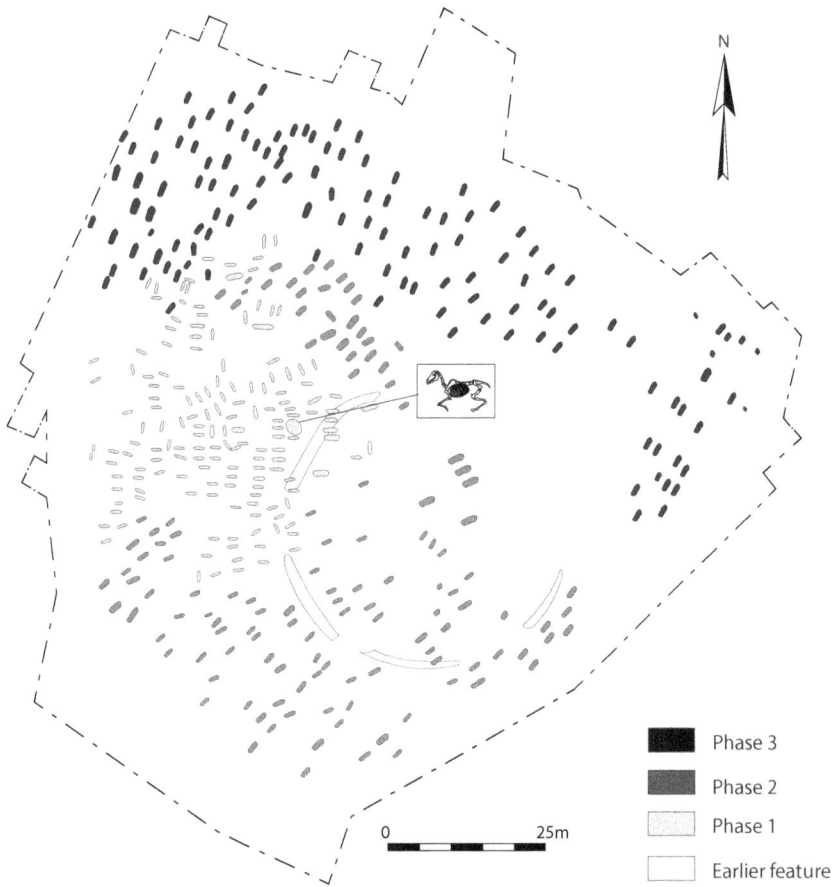

Figure 3.4 Bossut-Gottechain was a Merovingian cemetery with three distinct phases. A core of early inhumations was surrounded by increasingly ordered burials.

were described by the excavators as phase-one burials (Vanmechelen and Vrielynck, 2009) and showed a contrasting orientation, which distinguished burials within the fifth- and sixth-century area from the more regular later graves. Some twenty-one graves in the central part of the cemetery were on a N/S orientation, whereas the surrounding graves were E/W. This created an aesthetic contrast within the space, intercutting was limited and so presumably the graves were marked in some way and were visible. In the second and third phases orientation was used in a different way, and did not serve to highlight individual burials. The phase-two and three burials from the late-sixth and seventh centuries were interred on a NE/SW orientation, highlighting or creating a difference between them and the phase-one inhumations. This orientation created a deliberate contrast and was an important aspect of the aesthetics of the cemetery space. In this case, the orientation served two purposes. In the phase-one burials it distinguished particular inhumations. In the first few years, these newly NE/SW burials would have been noticeably at odds with the more numerous earlier inhumations. The phase-two graves were more widely spaced, regular and more ordered; indeed, from the cemetery plan they appear to be organised into rows. By the time of phase three, this ordered aesthetic had become the dominant visual form, with the smaller, more chaotic, phase-one area providing a contrasting visual experience. Nonetheless, phase-two and three burials wrapped around phase-one burials, 'foregrounding' them as the historic core of the site (Vanmechelen and Vrielynck, 2009). Despite the contrast the phase-one burials remained important to the successive community and contributed memories, mnemonic narratives and aesthetic qualities. This contrasting orientation at Bossut-Gottechain was deliberately cultivated and, like the spatial change in the later phases of Spong Hill, it must have helped contribute to the creation of an ancestral other, perhaps giving the impression that 'we are from them, but we are different to them'.

Interestingly, Sewerby, East Yorkshire, may also have had a chronological character to its organisation. The cemetery was first identified in 1958 during the building of a new farmhouse; following initial sampling work two preliminary excavations ensued in 1959 and 1974, but the site was not completely excavated. The excavated cemetery consisted of fifty-seven inhumations and was an exceptional find at the time (Hirst, 1985: xvii–17). As already discussed, Sewerby had no obvious differentiation by grave orientation, and statistical assessment showed spatial homogeneity, meaning there appears to have been no deliberate clustering (Chapter 2). Nonetheless, Sewerby had a structural component. This component was most evident in the earliest burials and, because of this, we must rely on artefact typologies, namely brooch, bead and buckle typologies, to help in our understanding of it. The artefact chronologies suggest three different groups, consisting of a core area with two later groups on either side of this.

The excavated area at Sewerby seems to have had a core of earlier burials; the datable graves that make this up consisted of inhumations 8, 12, 17, 28 and 45. Burial 8 was interred with beads of Brugmann's A1-type combination, and a cruciform brooch of the C2 type, and two undated annular brooches (Brugmann, 2004). Consequently, it is suggested that grave 8 had an early sixth-century date, although the cruciform brooch may suggest that burial came at the end of this range. Similarly, burial 12 included an A1 bead combination giving it an early date, with small-long and cruciform brooches of the Mortimer D2 and B2 variety, which suggest an early sixth-century date (Mortimer, 1990; Martin, 2015: 124). Burial 17 contained annular brooches and an A1 bead combination, also placing it in the early sixth century. Grave 28 had a cruciform brooch of the D2 type, and an A2 bead combination which overlapped somewhat with the A1 in the early sixth century, a date which fits the brooch.

To the north-east of these early graves was a series of later ones – 15, 19, 35, 38 and 50.1. These post-dated the core burials and had associated artefacts consistent with a broadly mid-sixth-century, or slightly later, date. These included grave 15 with annular IV and cruciform C2 brooches, wrist clasps of the B13a and B18 type, and a buckle of the common I.12a–i type. Notably, there was also a string of beads of the A2 combination. Grave 19 had annular IV brooches, a great square-headed brooch of type XXII, beads of the B1 combination, and buckles of the I.5a and II.17 type. Grave 35 had annular IV brooches, a cruciform brooch of the B3 type, common B7 wrist clasps, and a silver scutiform pendant, beads of the A2b combination, an I.12a–i buckle and a girdle-hanger. This area also included two burials, 38 and 50.1, unfortunately datable only broadly to the sixth century but which may be contemporary with each other: grave 38 had an annular IV brooch, B7 wrist clasps and a pendant. Grave 50.1 included an annular IV brooch and common B7 wrist clasps (Figure 3.5).

To the south of the early graves there was a series of much later ones, with a later-sixth-century, or potentially even early seventh-century, character. These included grave 16 with wrist clasps of type B18 and a type B bead combination, and grave 23 with annular IV brooches and buckles of types I.2 and II19a, as well as part of a small metal chain similar to one from grave 24. Grave 24 also contained a Salin animal style II silver penannular brooch with bird-head terminals. Hirst placed graves 23 and 24 in the seventh century (Hirst, 1985: 95), but animal art of style II can date to the later-sixth century, and the character and location of these graves is more congruent with a sixth-century date. Grave 49 also suggests a later-sixth-century date and contained over 200 beads,

Figure 3.5 Sewerby, the distribution of datable graves.

two small-long brooches, a cruciform brooch of type C3, wrist clasps of the B18 type, a bronze cauldron/vessel and a girdle-hanger. Overall, these later graves show a greater diversity in the range of associated objects identified than in the previous two phases.

These three phases of graves were about the same size, and were buried in different places in a concentric organisation (Figure 3.6). The early sixth-century core area consisted of eight or nine graves, adjacent to which was a mid-sixth-century area of similar size. The later-sixth- or early seventh-century area is to the south. Each of these three areas contained broadly the same number of graves, and so they may correspond with consecutive generations (see below). Each sequential generation may have been interred in its own space, adjacent to and slightly overlapping with, or enveloping, the earliest group of burials, which by the end of the sixth century had become a core area, central to this part of the cemetery. Unfortunately, Sewerby remains largely unexcavated and the identification of a small number of burials which do not fit this arrangement, to the east and west of those discussed, implies that this

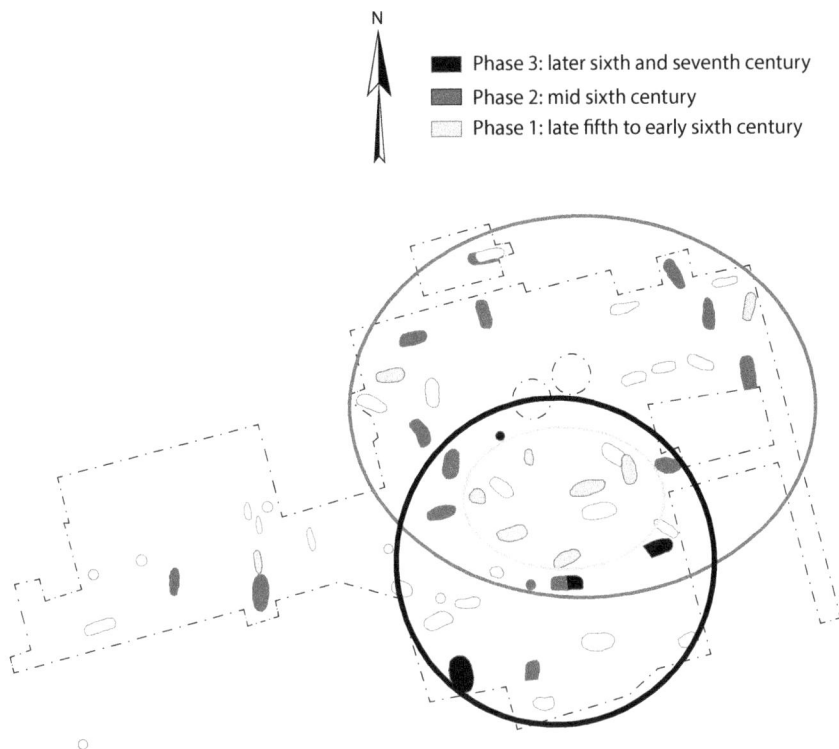

Figure 3.6 Sewerby, highlighting three phases of graves which focused around an earlier core in a concentric organisation.

concentric pattern does not describe the whole cemetery. Perhaps these concentric burials describe just a single plot within the larger cemetery. These occupants were organised by generation, but this pattern might be confined to this plot, becoming an internally distinguishing characteristic that was particular to a group of specific graves, and not a feature of the site as a whole. This organisational feature is something that is discussed in more detail in the description of Dover Buckland below.

As shown in Chapter 2, the early Anglo-Saxon cemetery at Apple Down had different configurations of burial, and these were based loosely on the type of mortuary ritual and the orientation of the grave. Configuration A consisted of inhumation graves oriented W/E and in an interior zone; configuration B included inhumation graves oriented S/N and found in an exterior zone; and configuration C were cremations found on either side of the central configuration A graves. From a chronological perspective, the cremations and exterior graves are hard to pinpoint because of the absence of diagnostic material culture;

configuration A burials, on the other hand, included a good number of datable graves and these came from a range of different overlapping dates from the later-fifth to the early seventh centuries (see Table 3.1). The configuration B burials are much harder to date because they contained fewer artefacts, and these artefacts are attributable to much broader dates. However, burials 54, 126, 128 and 145, in the north of the cemetery, had an early to mid-sixth century-character. They were buried with Swanton H2/3 spears or type SP2b1b and SP2a1b2 spears,[1] type 11.24b (–i) buckles, and a button brooch or shield from group 1.1 or SB2-a dated to AD 525–70 (Hines and Bayliss, 2013: 151, 458, 563). By contrast, burials 44, 46, 107, 113, 125, 130, 134, 138 and 151 had a later character and were found with type B2 and B2 b–c beads; knives of types C or D; a Swanton F1/SP1:b spear; pins; and buckles of a general Anglo-Saxon date of the 1.11a–i and 11.19a type (see Figure 1.9 and Figure 3.7). Overall, this pattern implies that the configuration B burials were treated differently. Instead of the vertical pattern presented in the centre of the cemetery among the configuration A burials, the configuration B inhumations had a more horizontal nature and were at least partially buried among groups of contemporaneous graves.

However, there were a couple of graves which complicate this. Grave 12 was of the A configuration, and was interesting because it consisted of two burials: 12A was a male burial with a scabbard mount of the SW6-e or Kempston-Mitcham type, placing it in the late-fifth or early sixth century; and then this grave was replaced/destroyed by 12B, another male buried with a spear, which unfortunately does not fit well into Karen Høilund Nielsen's typology (Hines and Bayliss, 2013) but must postdate 12A. Grave 99 was an exception as, although on a N/S orientation, it had a material assemblage more akin to configuration A. Notably, grave 99 had a spear of the SP3a type and a shield of SB4-b1 with a very small flange width, so probably from the last decades of the sixth century or the early seventh. Perhaps this later date suggests that the central burial system had begun to break down, and the occupants of grave 99 were not eligible for a full configuration A burial.

At Apple Down the different configurations of burials showed a different chronological treatment and importantly this different treatment is also seen among other groups of contemporary graves in early Anglo-Saxon cemeteries. For example, as already seen in Chapter 2, at Wakerley there were three separate plots of graves, and these included a mixture of furnished and unfurnished graves. In the eastern plot (C) there was a core of furnished burials which over successive, repeated burials created a central focus. The remaining two plots were more diffuse having no obvious core of furnished graves. Each of these three areas also contained very distinctive and dissimilar internal chronologies.

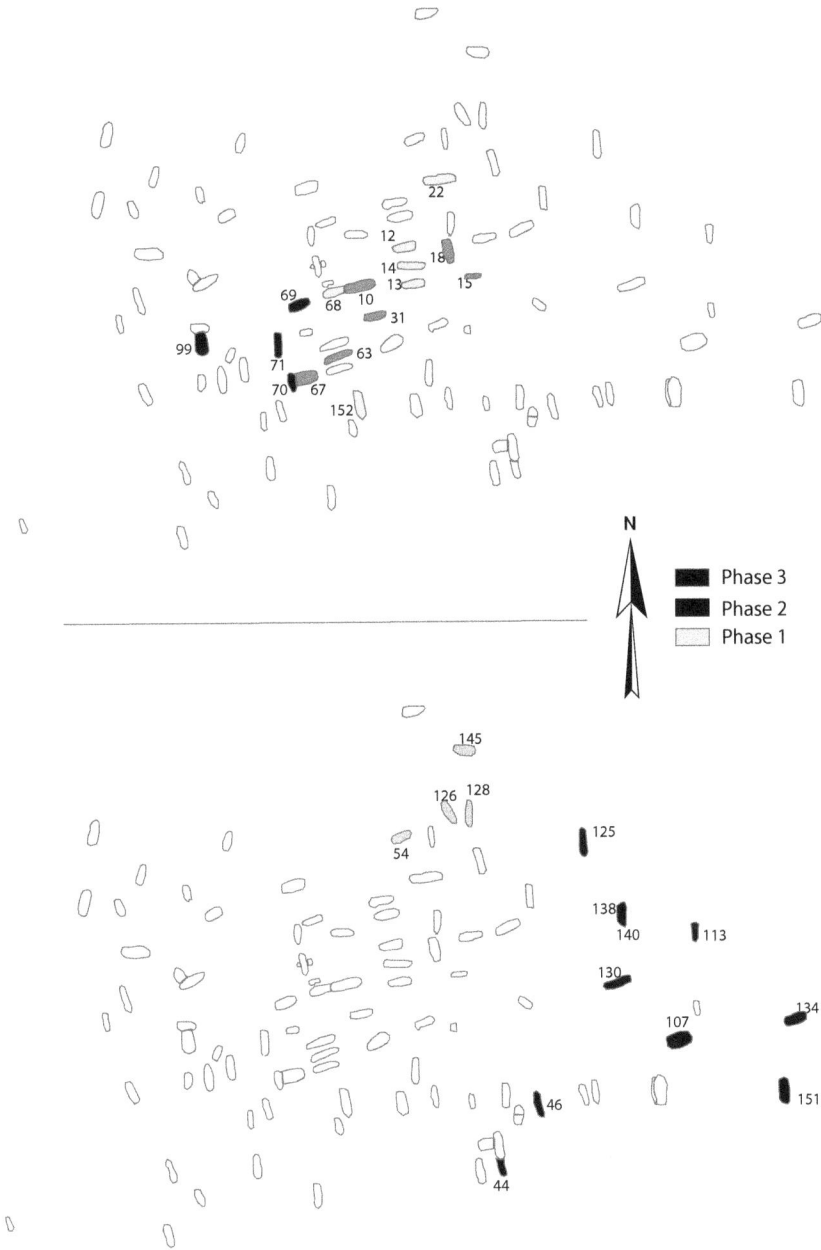

Figure 3.7 Apple Down: the chronology. Top, the core configuration A graves focused on one area that was returned to for generations. Bottom, the configuration B graves showed a more linear pattern with burial 'drifting' to the east of the cemetery.

Table 3.2 Chronology of configuration A burials at Apple Down

Period	Grave no.	Gravegoods
	12A	scabbard mount of the SW6-e or Kempston-Mitcham type
later-fifth to early sixth century	13	saucer brooch 2.1, snake-style ring, two spangles
	22	knife type B, buckle II.5
	68	knife type A, spear H3/SP2-bla4
	152	knife type A, spear of the H1/SP2:b1a2 type, shield from group 1.1/SB1-b, buckle I.11a-I
early sixth century	14	square-headed bow brooch, buckle I.5a, latch lifter
	18	bead group A2, two coins, a weaving comb, tube and purse bar
early to mid-sixth century	31	spear E1/SP2:b1b, I.10a buckle
	63	knife B, spear H2/SP2:b1b, small narrow seax/SX1:a, buckle II.14a, purse bar, tweezers, bucket male group A
	67	knife type A, spear H3/SP2:b1b, buckle I10a-I
mid-sixth century	10	saucer brooch 14.3, bead group A
	15	perforated annular brooch group G, bucket mounts
	69	strap end, buckle II.20
late-sixth to early seventh century	70	knife type C (cuts grave 67)
	71	knife type D
	99	spear SP3-a, shield SB4-1b (but E/W orientation)
unknown sixth century	76	knife B, buckle I.11a-I

In Wakerley plot A, burial 71 was probably the earliest, and was also the most easterly in this area. It contained small-long brooches, B12 wrist clasps and an I.12a–i buckle, giving it a date in the later-fifth century. Grave 70 included small-long brooches, wrist clasps of type B13a and a buckle of type I.7b, all of which associate it with a later-fifth- or early sixth-century date. Graves 73 and 74 both contained beads of group A2 and type B7 wrist clasps, and grave 74 also contained a cruciform brooch of the Z1 type, suggesting that both graves were from the early sixth century. Burial 78 contained a cognate brooch and burial 80 contained a number of objects, including a great square-headed brooch of type XV, which suggested a mid-sixth-century date as most suitable for these graves. Indeed, graves 82 and 84 both contained annular brooches of type IV and group A2 beads. Grave 82 also included a pin set and buckle of type II.19b that may suggest a sixth-century date, so perhaps the beads and artefact combination point to a mid-sixth century date. Similarly, male-grave 83 included a spear of Swanton's E2/SP2-bib variety and shield boss of type 3/SB3-b3, suggesting a mid-sixth-century date. Male-grave 85 contained spears of types H2/SP2-b1a1 and H3/SP2-b1a3 and a shield of type 1.1/SB1b, which are also objects dating to the mid-sixth century. Overall, these gravegoods suggest that plot A had a general east-to-west horizontal character, starting with easterly burials 70 and 71 in the later-fifth and early sixth centuries. The mid-sixth-century burials were all to the west, and the latest graves, including grave 79, were interred in the middle of the plot. Grave 79 seems almost to 'close' the burial space, and, interestingly, this individual was interred with an 'antique' spear, which must have been an heirloom artefact. Metaphorically at least, this spear connected this individual with the past, with the antecedent generations, and its inclusion in this grave may have been a useful way to separate the old and the new (Figure 3.8).

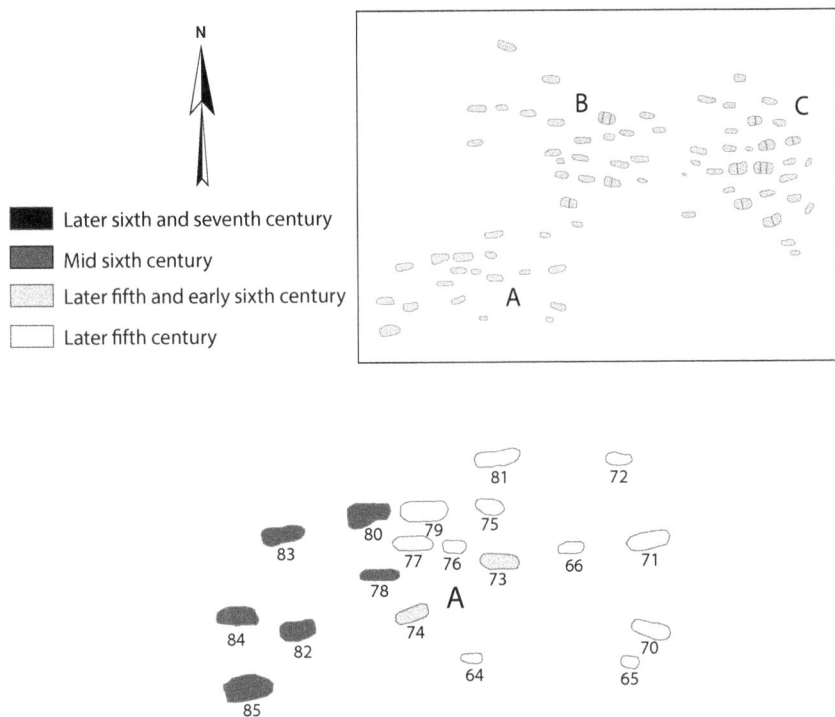

Figure 3.8 Wakerley: plot A had a linear chronological pattern, with burials placed to the west over time.

Plot B, by contrast, was a concentric plot with the earliest graves in the central area. Graves 4 and 58 appear to have been the earliest; both were found with small-long brooches of a trefoil type, which suggest a later-fifth- or early sixth-century date. To the north of this central area were a group of graves, 3, 8 and 57, most probably early sixth century in date. Grave 3 contained bronze mounts, an F1 spear/SP2-a1a1, a bucket of phase A and an I.12a–i buckle. Grave 8 had applied saucer brooches, and grave 57 included a pin and small-long brooches as well as type B7, B12 and B13c wrist clasps. These five graves, 3, 4, 8, 57 and 58 formed the core area, and on either side were a series of graves which had a different, and so probably later, character. These included graves 1, 61, 62 and 63 to the north-west of the centre. Also, to the east or south-east, were graves 5, 10, 14, and 69. Grave 1 had a cruciform brooch of type B/C and two of type SB2-s, as well as wrist clasps of type B7. Grave 61 finds comprised type B7 wrist clasps and a buckle of type I.10e. Grave 62 included wrist clasps of type B7 and grave 63 had annular brooches of type IV and a wide-mouthed pot (Myres, 1969: 168). Grave 5 finds were beads of type A2, type B13 wrist clasps, an I.11a–i buckle, a pin, a bronze vessel and a lugged pot. Grave 10 included two type IV annular brooches, a Roman coin and a pin. Grave 14 included a wide-mouthed pot which, although hard to date, Myres attributed by its appearance to the latter half of the sixth century. Grave 69 included B7 wrist clasps and a belt buckle of the I.11a–I type. Individually, these artefacts in grave 69 are datable broadly to the sixth century, but within this grave plot, and buried together, they are an assemblage which is of a very a different style to the previous burials, and probably dates to the middle- to later-sixth century. Inhumation 17 is the only one which was more obviously of the later-sixth century, it contained two type IV annular brooches, a penannular brooch, a silver bracteate, a scutiform pendant, type B7 wrist clasps, two II.21b buckles, as well as a girdle-hanger, a comb, keys and a pin (Figure 3.9). Overall, this area of the cemetery had a similar range of date to the plot A, with just a single, later grave marking its end.

The third area, plot C, contained seven of the ten double burials excavated, and this corresponded with a greater density in inhumations. None of these graves included evidence of reopening or of the second burial being added later, and so the two corpses were in all likelihood positioned in the grave at the same time. The earliest burial is probably grave(s) 31/32, where 31 had a small-long brooch, an A2b bead combination and a gilt/iron style I animal art mount. Grave 32 had an annular brooch fragment, a small-long brooch and a cruciform brooch of type D, a combination that implies an early sixth-century date. Double grave 42/43 was also early sixth century, where 42 had applied brooches, a

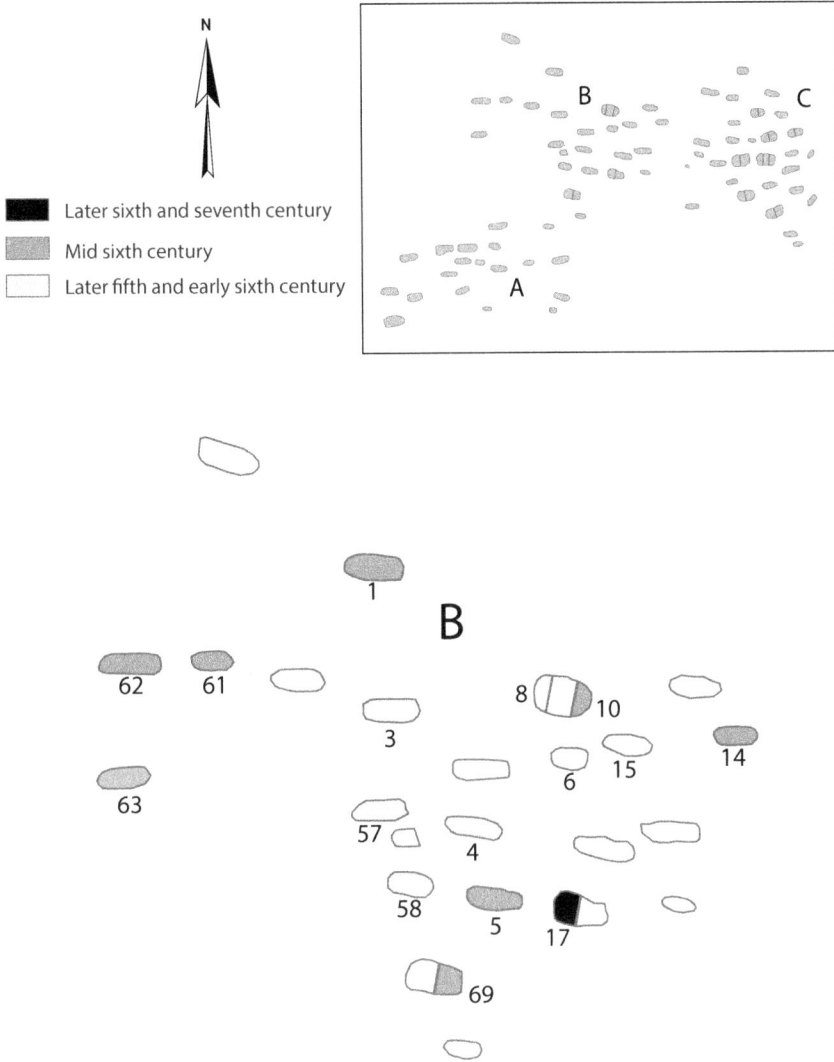

Figure 3.9 Wakerley: plot B had the early burials in a more concentric pattern, with earlier burials in the middle.

cruciform-type Z3 brooch, two silver ring pendants and a wire spiral wrist clasp of class A; however, no gravegoods were identified from grave 43. Graves 25/26 were found with cruciform brooches of type SB2 and B7 wrist clasps, suggesting a date in the first half of the sixth century. Chronologically, grave 22/23 straddled the early to mid-sixth century and contained an E3 spear/SP2-a, a type 3/SB1-b shield boss and a type1.1SB3-b2 shield boss, but most likely dated between AD 525 and 570. Given grave 23's later character, perhaps it fitted towards the end of this date range.

Similarly, grave(s) 50/51 also straddled the early to mid-sixth century. Grave 50 contained annular brooches, a great square-headed XV brooch, wrist clasps of B7 and B13c types, a string of A2 beads and a II.21a buckle, all of which place it in the middle decades of the sixth century. However, grave 51's L-type spear, and shield boss of type 1/SB1–b, might suggest an earlier date. The individual in grave 51 was an older man, and so perhaps the shield boss was old-fashioned when it was buried in or around the beginning of the middle-sixth century. Double grave 44/45 contained two women, and both sets of gravegoods tend towards the middle decades of the sixth century: grave 44 contained cognate brooches, an imported square-headed brooch, A2 beads, a Roman coin, a girdle-hanger and keys; grave 45 included small-long brooches, B13c wrist clasps, A2 beads and a type II.21b buckle. Finds from triple grave 52/53/54 also suggested a mid-sixth-century character. Grave 52 contained spears of H1, L and F1 forms (or types SP1-b, SP2-bib and SP5), grave 53 included an I.11b buckle, and grave 54 a pin and a ceramic vessel. The only later grave associated with plot C is burial 21, which had a type VII penannular brooch, B7 wrist clasps and a II.19b buckle. Other graves with a single individual within them dated to the early and mid-sixth centuries. Like the central burial area at Apple Down, this plot had a vertical chronological pattern, with successive burials placed adjacent to each other in a high-density area of the cemetery (Figure 3.10). Just as at Apple Down, these graves contained larger amounts of material culture relative to the rest of the cemetery. This depositional pattern took place across a series of generations, who each returned to the same central space within the cemetery to bury their dead.

Oakington, Cambridgeshire, had a rather different pattern. This early Anglo-Saxon cemetery was first identified in 1926 when three burials were found (Meaney, 1964). Subsequently, in 1994, a further twenty-six burials were excavated (Taylor et al., 1997) and in 2007 a further seventeen burials were excavated before construction of the parish recreational building (Mortimer et al., 2017). A further seventy-eight burials were excavated between 2010 and 2014 as part of a university research programme, taking the known cemetery total to 124 individuals. It is speculated that this is over 80 per cent of the total original extent of the site (Mortimer et al., 2017). Radiocarbon dates from Oakington help us to understand its chronological development. There are eight radiocarbon dates that point to a later fifth- and sixth-century range (see, for example, Schiffels et al., 2016; Mortimer et al., 2017). Based on material culture the site is understood as similar to Wakerley in that

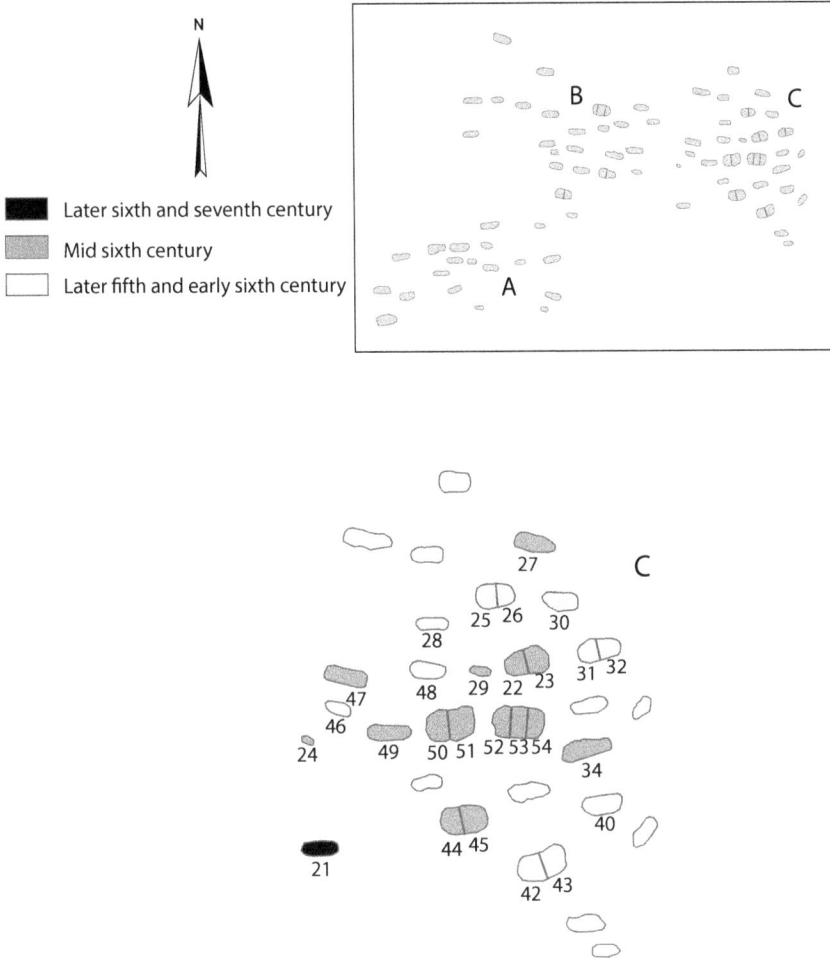

Figure 3.10 Wakerley: plot C consisted of densely packed multiple graves. Generation after generation returned to this area, which showed limited horizontal patterning as a result.

it was in use for about one hundred years between the later-fifth and later-sixth centuries (Figure 3.11).

Interestingly Oakington seems to have been organised around a series of key burials. For example, Burial 57, a pregnant woman, was interred in the later-fifth or early sixth century (also see Sayer and Dickinson, 2013). Her cruciform brooch was a typical example of type 3.3.1, belonging to cruciform brooch phase B and dating between c. AD 475 and c. AD 550, corroborated by radiocarbon dates. She was also found with two trefoil small-long brooches, a string of beads,

OxCal v4.2.2 Bronk Ramsey (2013); r:5 Atmospheric data from Reimer et al (2009);

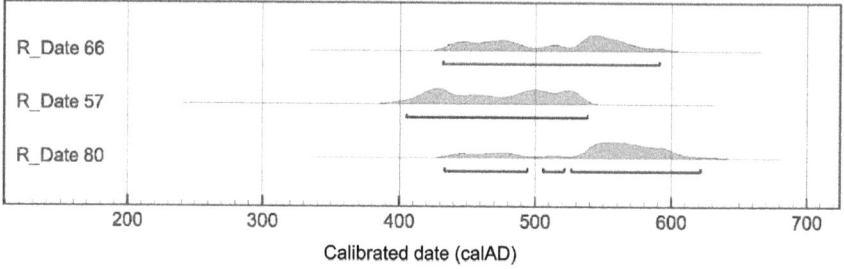

Calibrated date (calAD)

OxCal v4.2.2 Bronk Ramsey (2013); r:5 Atmospheric data from Reimer et al (2009);

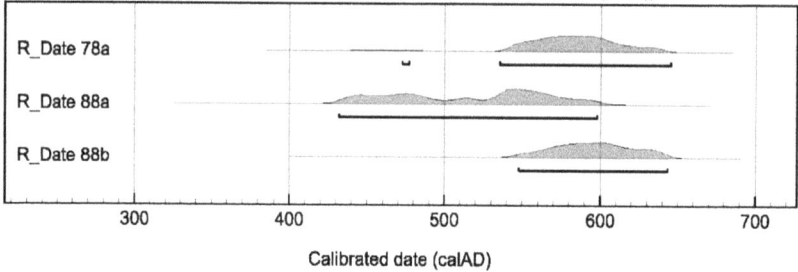

Calibrated date (calAD)

OxCal v4.2.2 Bronk Ramsey (2013); r:5 Atmospheric data from Reimer et al (2009);

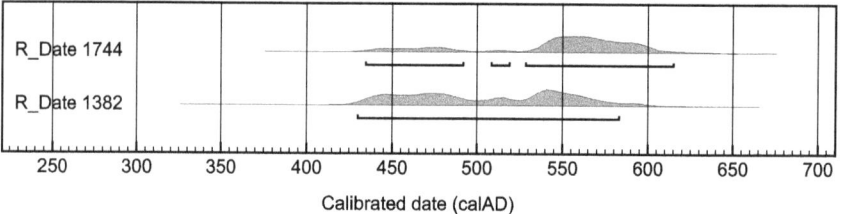

Calibrated date (calAD)

Figure 3.11 Oakington: calibrated radiocarbon dates for graves 66, 57, 80, 78a, 88a and 88b, as well as for horse burials 1744 and 1382.

two wrist clasps, an iron purse ring, copper-alloy belt fittings and an iron knife. Unfortunately, at the time of writing grave 109 does not have radiocarbon dates, but gravegoods including two applied saucer brooches imply a late-fifth- or early sixth-century date. In addition the grave included wrist clasps, a knife, a purse ring and a metal hinge, which may have been part of a box, and over forty amber beads. The child was found with a single copper-alloy ring resting on the chest area below the chin.

The female in grave 66 was found with a whole pot, keys, wrist clasps, a number of amber beads and two pierced copper-alloy pendants. She was also buried with two trefoil small-long brooches, found on her chest. She had wrist clasps of types B13b and B18c, a copper-alloy pin and an iron key or latch-lifter belt-hanging set, adjacent to which was hung a Roman spoon. In addition, her grave included a pottery fragment at her feet. The radiocarbon dates are less precise than for grave 57, but the burial was similar in character and so she was probably buried in the early/mid-sixth century. The occupant of grave 80 was buried with an almost complete cow. She also had forty-six amber beads and twenty-two glass beads. The beads were in at least two strings, one of which was draped over her arm and the other close to her body. She had two small, silvered disc brooches, two B7 wrist clasps and an iron girdle-hanger. Based on these objects and the radiocarbon dates, it is probable that this grave was created in the mid-sixth century. Curiously, four of the five prone burials excavated at Oakington were adjacent to this grave, and one of these was datable. Grave 78 was a double burial containing a prone adult female and a child, and it was dated to the mid-sixth century (see Chapter 1), a date supported by the radiocarbon results. She was found with seventeen beads, wrist clasps, a small-long brooch, an iron knife and a meat bone. Her burial was found in a satellite position around grave 80, indicating that burial 78 postdated it.

The dates for burials 88a and 88b overlapped and suggested they were part of the final phases of the site; perhaps they had been interred in the period AD 550–75, in the latter half of the mid-sixth century. The associated gravegoods included a shield boss (of the Dickinson and Härke group 1), a Marzinzik 11.19a buckle as well as a copper fitting from the shield, but unfortunately it is not possible to ascertain a further type at this stage.

All of these graves, with the exception of 78, are included here because they appear to have significant space and/or satellite burials around them. Indeed, 57, 80 and 88 were associated with a large mammal burial, either a horse or a cow. As with Lechlade, Finglesham and St Peters for example, these spaces were consistent with the location of small barrows, unfortunately no longer extant, which marked the burial. Graves 57, 66, 80 and 88 had satellite burials associated with them. Satellite graves are later graves which deliberately snaked around or were partially inserted into the barrow along one of its edges (Figure 3.12). These barrows created central places, and the subsequent burials show that they were returned to repeatedly after their creation. The discussion of artefacts and radiocarbon dates above suggests that these burials were deposited in sequence, probably starting with inhumation 57 in the late-fifth or early sixth century. This was followed by grave 66 in the early sixth century, then grave 80 in the middle-sixth century and grave 78 in the later-middle-sixth century. In short, these small-barrow burials were created roughly every generation. There was

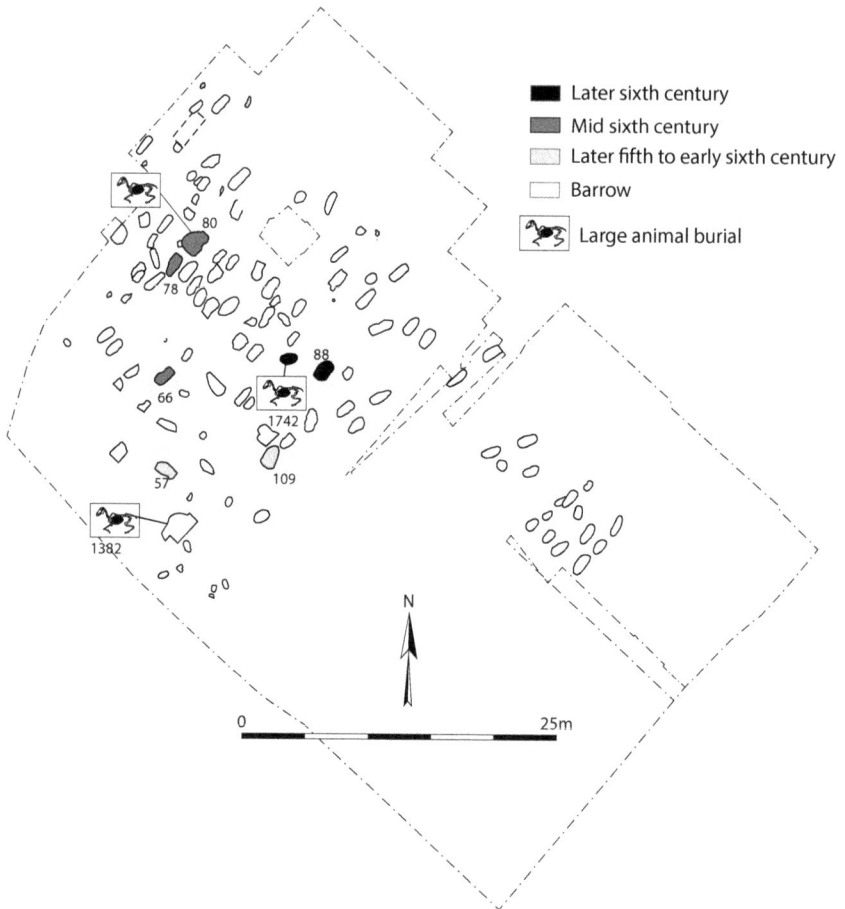

Figure 3.12 Oakington barrows: these burials were significant central points, but the focus seems to have shifted to a different barrow in each subsequent generation.

not a single central place where burials were returned to at Oakington, but instead the graves of individuals became short-lived central places that attracted later burials, often from the same generation. This is an ego-centred burial organisation because this scenario means that the community who used and returned to the cemetery space hung narratives upon, and told or retold stories about the individuals under these mounds, and they even placed the newly dead adjacent to particular mounds, highlighting a specific relationship. It looks as though each generation had a significant individual whose burial created a focal point for subsequent graves. Notably at this site these inhumations were mostly female graves, which may say quite a lot about the nature of this specific community (see chapters 4 and 5 for a further discussion of gender).

Dating Dover Buckland

We introduced the early Anglo-Saxon cemetery at Dover Buckland in chapters 1 and 2. The site was first excavated in 1951 and again in 1994. Together the two excavated elements included about 507 graves. Dover Buckland has been very influential in the development of Kentish, and indeed national, early Anglo-Saxon chronologies. As a result it makes sense to substantially revisit this site in this chapter. The 1951 project was the first long-lived Kentish cemetery excavation to be have been published since the nineteenth century, and so made an important contribution to chronology studies (Brugmann, 2012). In particular, the excavation developed its typology using absolute dates based on coins in graves and developed a chronological scheme of its own, one that influenced the dating of garnet brooches, shield bosses, swords and, in particular, knives (Evison, 1987: 21–121). This scheme received minor adjustments from Brugmann in her assessment of the later excavation because it showed a tendency to date graves too late, compared with earlier dates provided by subsequent radiocarbon dating. Nonetheless, the chronological phases established by Evison were left intact 'for ease of reference' or for comparison with the previously published volume, and further information could be used to subdivide date ranges providing better chronological resolution for some graves (Brugmann, 2012: 323). After these overlapping approaches were published, the Hines and Bayliss chronology project was completed. This project adds additional resolution, in particular for male-gendered graves, and this provides the starting point from which to revisit the dating of Dover Buckland and explore the organisation of the cemetery space. The dating scheme described in this chapter has been applied to Dover Buckland, and particular attention has been paid to the way Hines and Bayliss' chronology project impacts the male chronology. Appendix 1 lists each grave described here, and whether or not the dates in the two different schemes correspond.

Vera Evison used her chronological system to suggest that there was a single organising principle, an east-to-west burial direction (see Figure 1.3). To some degree this observation holds up with the new chronologies, but it does presuppose that there was a single architect, or narrative, which remained intact for the history of the site. Dover Buckland is a notably complex site and, like the other cemeteries discussed here, it had numerous architects with different and changing ideas about burial practice. This can be seen in the multiple chronological patterns which were in use at the same time. These individual parts are familiar because the same principles can be seen in the other cemeteries discussed in this chapter, and throughout this book.

The 1951 site is the northern part of the cemetery, and its earliest phase is to the west, described by Evison as plot A. However, area L also contained a single late-fifth/early sixth-century burial, grave D; otherwise it contained graves which dated between the later-fifth and mid-seventh centuries (Figure 3.13). Area L was dispersed and appears to have had no particular chronological character (Figure 3.14), and in this way it was similar to the westerly plot at Wakerley, Northamptonshire, if somewhat smaller. Graves 15 and 20 were the earliest datable graves. To the north of them, burial 87 was dated between the fifth and mid-sixth century, whereas graves 22, 48 and 92 contained mid-sixth-century objects (see

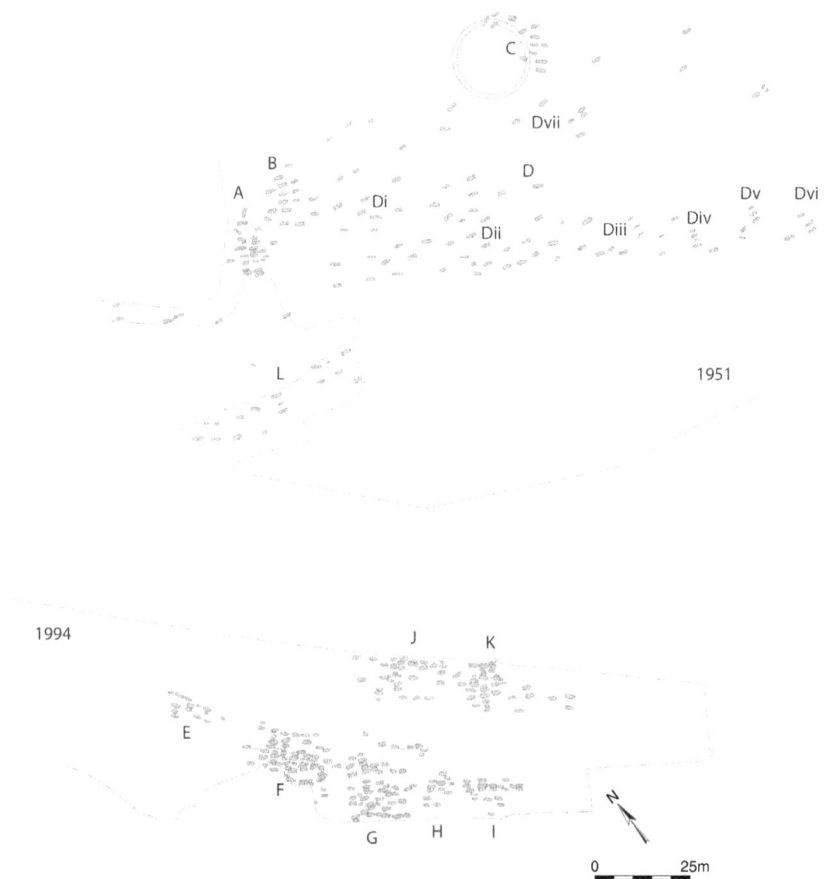

Figure 3.13 The 1951 and 1994 excavations at Dover Buckland, with the burial plots labelled.

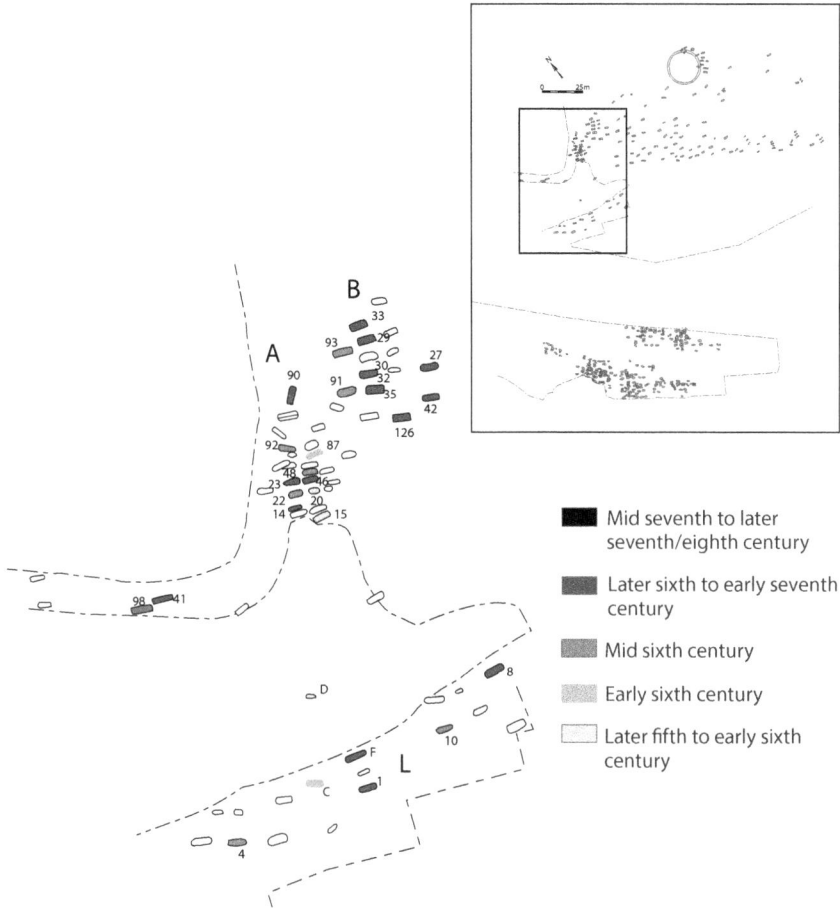

Figure 3.14 Dover Buckland: plots A, B and L in the 1951 excavation area. Plot A was an area of dense burial returned to repeatedly throughout the fifth and sixth centuries. Plot B, however, consisted primarily of a line of contemporary burials interred in the later-sixth century, as at Deal. Plot L contains some of the early burials and was among the first areas excavated, but large parts either remain unexcavated or have been lost.

Appendix 1). Most reminiscent of Wakerley, the later-sixth- and early seventh-century burials 14, 46, 23 and 90 were dispersed between, and placed around, these graves. At the same time, to the east, in an area described by Evison as plot B, burials 91 and 93 were placed in the middle-sixth century. In contrast the graves within plot A were densely packed, crowded into a particular space and were returned to for two or three generations. However, this burial style was short-lived, and to the east of burials 91 and 93 there was a row of broadly contemporary

■ Mid seventh to later seventh/eigth century
■ Later sixth to early seventh century
▨ Mid sixth century
▨ Early sixth century
▢ Later fifth to early sixth century

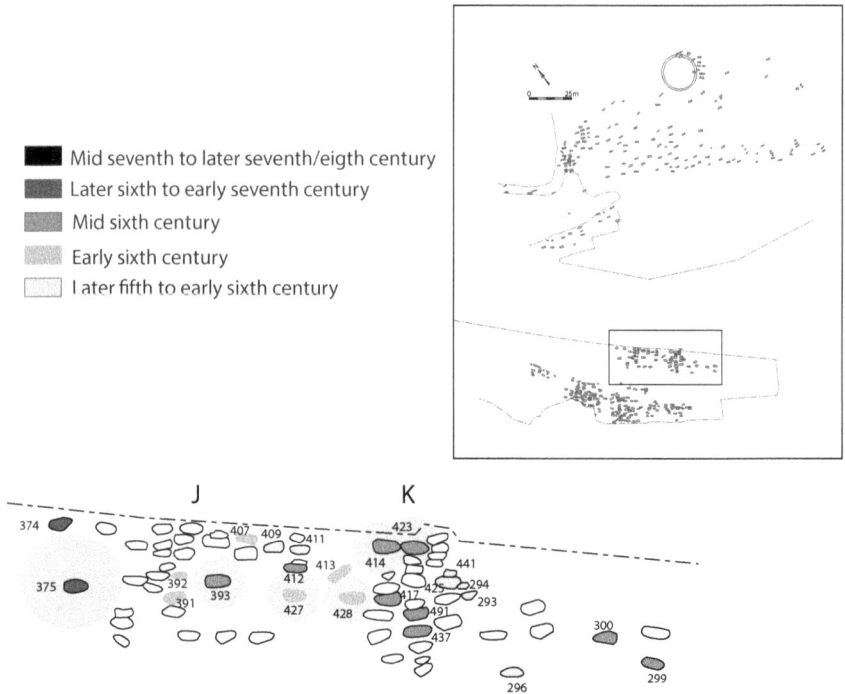

Figure 3.15 Dover Buckland: plots J and K in the 1994 excavation area. This was actually a single plot which had a pair of significant burials placed in each generation, then surrounded by satellite graves, as at Oakington.

graves, mostly dating to the later-sixth and early seventh centuries. This is strikingly similar to Mill Hill, Deal, where, as we have seen, a row of later-sixth and early seventh-century graves was placed next to the sixth-century plots (Figure 1.5). The mourners at Deal and in this part of Dover Buckland were changing the space and style of the burial, adapting the aesthetic of the mortuary landscape to suit a new idea, or a new way to identify their dead.

Interestingly, the 1994 excavated part of the cemetery had a similar origin. There were seven plots; E, F, G, H, I, J and K. The most striking of these was J–K, which was probably just one large plot (Figure 3.15). This is one plot because the 'gap' perceptible in plan was filled with several small barrows that joined it together, in a similar way to those we have also seen at Deal, Lechlade and Oakington (in this chapter; also see Chapter 4). Graves 393 and 427, in J–K, had ring gullies around them, providing direct evidence of these barrows. Grave 428 did not have a ring gully, but instead graves 413, 416, 417 and 429 enveloped it. Keith Parfitt and Ian Anderson (2012) proposed that burial 413 was originally beneath a barrow because it had a small amount of room around it. Notably this grave was on a different orientation to those adjacent to it, and graves 416, 417 and, in particular, 429 leave the shape of the barrow that they surrounded like a negative feature. Grave 428 was female-gendered, and contained two gilt saucer brooches, a buckle, beads and a perforated Roman *nummus*. Similarly, to the east of these graves was burial 423, a weapon burial. Enveloping this grave were burials 424, 442, 443 and 444, which seem to have been oriented to it, and, as we saw before, these graves 'dog-leg' around a circular or semi-circular space, where a barrow had been placed, and traced around its edges. Grave 422 marked the southern edge of this space. Grave 414, to the west of 423, was another weapon grave, with spear, shield and sword. These last objects were datable, and placed grave 414 in the mid-sixth century, a similar date to its pair, grave 423. The location of grave 414, the placement of grave 415 in a satellite position and the space around it suggested that both 414 and 423 had barrows over them. These two graves were dated at AD 525–95 for grave 414, and AD 525–50 for grave 423, which certainly allows them to be broadly contemporaneous.

To the south of these two barrows, inhumation 437 was another weapon burial. It contained a sword and, unusually, a hooked iron *atgeir*, a halberd-like weapon that the excavators described as a 'fauchard', which is a type of polearm weapon more common in the Middle Ages (Parfitt and Anderson, 2012: 450). This weapon is certainly extremely unusual if not unique within the mortuary record, and as a result it would have singled out its user and was probably associated with them in life (Sayer *et al.*, 2019). The space between this grave and graves 419, 434, 436 and 438 also implied that originally it was beneath a small barrow. The final barrow was associated with grave 375, which included a spear, sword and shield. This barrow was larger and later, and later graves 371, 374, 376, 385, 386 and 388 enveloped it, preserving the barrow's edges with their orientation. With these barrows located as described there would have been no significant gap between plots J and K, which should therefore be seen as a single large plot.

The chronology of plot J–K is notable and perhaps most resembles the description of Oakington, discussed above. Graves 293, 294, 425 and 441 were sparsely furnished female-gendered graves situated to the east, and were also among the earliest graves. Inhumation 294 contained group A beads (AD 450–80), burials 425 and 441 contained A2 beads (AD 450–530), and grave 239 contained A1 beads, dated AD 450–570. The different styles of these beads suggest that they were not contemporary, but these four burials seem to have been closely placed, so they were consecutive burials with stylistic similarities. They were probably interred in close succession in the later-fifth or early sixth centuries, and all were probably young adults or children, buried together by the adults that survived them, in a new cemetery space. In close association with these children's burials was inhumation 426, an adult female, aged 40–50, unfortunately not datable.

In the middle of plot J–K were two datable graves, 409 with A2 beads (AD 480–555), and 411 with a spear dated AD 450–525, dates which place these two graves among the earliest in the cemetery. The two barrow burials to the south, 427 and 428, were dated to the early part of the sixth century. Grave 427 was interred with A2 beads, like the other early female-gendered graves. Grave 428 was also interred with A2 beads and, as previously mentioned, two small gilt saucer brooches suggesting an early/mid-sixth-century date. As with the Orpington barrow burial (Chapter 1), these two examples were not richly furnished.

Clockwise from burials 427 and 428 were the double barrows 414 and 423, which have already been introduced as mid-sixth-century inhumations (see above). Grave 414 contained a type SP1-b spear and SB3-c shield boss with a combined date range of AD 525–95. Grave 423 continued a SP2-b1a3 spear dated AD 525–70. It therefore makes sense to suggest that grave 423 was the earlier of the two, especially given that the later satellite burials skirt around it, but have no direct relationship with 414. South of these two burials was grave 437, attributed by Brugmann to phase 2 and dating from AD 510/30–550/60 or the early/middle sixth century (Brugmann, 2012: 323). Its satellite burial 417 was probably interred later, and was a female-gendered grave with type-A beads, a great square-headed brooch, a radiate-headed brooch and a crystal ball, among other objects, which firmly dated it to the mid-sixth century, perhaps (as Brugmann suggests) the first part, placing both burials close to, but before, AD 550. Both graves were of adults, whereas the graves immediately to the north and all three southern burials contained adolescents.

Grave 393 had a similar date, and a spear of SP2-b1b suggests a date of AD 525–70. This male-gendered grave had a number of satellite burials, the two that were datable being burial 392, with a buckle (undatable) and A2 beads, and burial 391, which included A2 beads and a great square-headed brooch, placing it firmly in the middle of the sixth century. Also to the west of the plot was the latest barrow burial, grave 375, with spear of type SP3a and a shield of type SD4-b2 dated AD 525–645, for which Brugmann's phases within the 3b category suggest a date more like AD 580–645 (Brugmann, 2012: 323). Satellite burial 376 contained B2 beads, which dated it to AD 580–650, and twisted iron keys, which might imply that this burial was more sixth-century in date. The grave's location on the western edge of the plot, and its coherence with the location and material style of the other sixth-century graves, suggest that it had a later-sixth-century date. This burial and a few of its satellite graves marked the end of this sixth-century tradition in plot J–K.

Plot J–K is also very similar to Oakington in that it was organised around the burial of a number of significant individuals, highlighting an egocentric commemorative practice, with satellite burials placed around small pre-existing barrows. Plot J–K highlighted key members of the community, and it looks as if there were one or two of these individuals from each generation. These burials were returned to for a number of years; the positioning of subsequent satellite graves, and the digging and visiting of them would have allowed the community to remember not only the recent dead, but also the key ancestor buried beneath the associated adjacent small barrow.

Plot E was small and consisted of just fourteen graves (Figure 3.16). The datable ones included burials 204 and 207, which had the narrowest possible range. Grave 204 was dated probably AD 530–60, based on a garnet disc brooch and gold bracteate, while grave 207 dated to AD 450–580 based on associated bead finds. Overall, this area was characterised by a smaller number of finds. Burials 205 and 209 were placed into phases 2–3 (AD 530–80/600) and 1b–2 (c. AD 480–580/600), and together these four burials implied that this was a short-lived group that was in use for a generation or two.

Plot F was more substantial than plot E, and the associated artefacts suggested a wider range of dates that might imply that the artefacts were used between the later-fifth- and the early seventh centuries; however, this plot largely had a sixth-century character (Figure 3.16). The focus of the plot gradually shifted away from the earliest graves, which were later sidelined towards the edges of the plot. Graves 217 and 218 were the northernmost, and both were buried with A1 beads, although interestingly no other items of jewellery. Inhumation 398, to the east of them, had a broad chronological range, and was phased by Brugmann in 2b–3a (AD 530–80), which placed it in the middle-sixth century and therefore followed on from 217 and 218. Together, these three graves might imply that the group of graves to the north of plot F had a broadly linear chronological nature, starting in the east in the later-fifth century and ending in the middle-sixth century to the west. Unfortunately, graves 273 and 397 were not datable.

The southern part of plot F was interesting because it contained the most intercutting of any area within the Dover Buckland cemetery, and consequently it boasted the densest concentration of graves. This illustrates the degree of earlier burial, with a number of undated or unfurnished graves that had early dates because they were intersected by later graves. Inhumations 212, 229, 232, 235, 261, 263, 320, 347, 349,

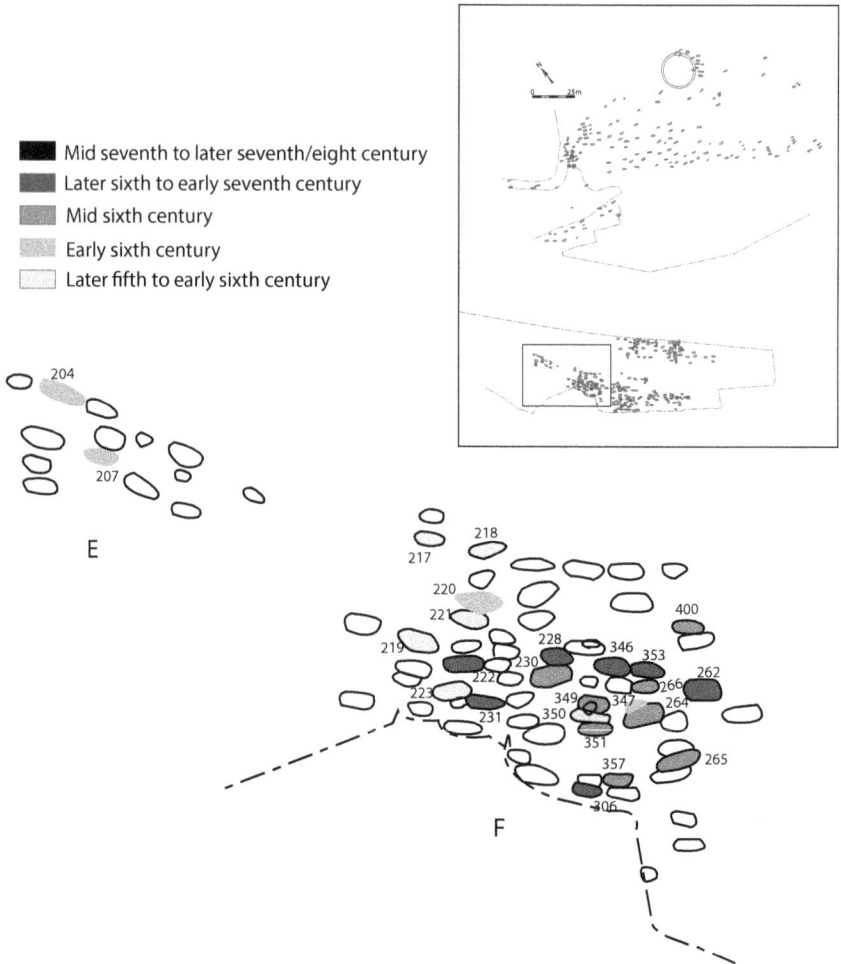

Figure 3.16 Dover Buckland: plots E and F in the 1994 excavation area. Plot F had a line of contemporary later graves which ran through the centre of the area. It may have had a loosely arranged linear organisation, with burials placed to the south-east.

351 and 352 were examples of graves cut by later ones. Burial 261 is of phase 1 because it was cut by grave 266, which was a grave dated to the first half of the sixth century, and female-gendered because it contained two silver radiate-headed brooches. Grave 347 was datable to the first half of the sixth century because it contained A2 beads, a glass cone beaker, a small square-headed brooch, a radiate brooch, and an open-work brooch, and was cut by burial 264, a mid-sixth-century grave.

The most obviously mid-sixth-century graves were placed across the centre of this densely populated area and included graves 230, 264 and

349. Grave 230 contained a SP2b1a3 spearhead and a SB1B shield boss, placing it between AD 525 and 570. Grave 264 had the same dates, and contained a SP1b spear and a SB3B3 shield boss. Grave 349 contained a SP2b1b spearhead, which Brugmann placed into phases 2–3, and probably dated AD 510–70. Notably, grave 265 to the south was also mid-sixth century (AD 525–70), with an SP2b1a2 spearhead and an SB3a shield. What is particularly interesting about these contemporararaneous graves is that they were all male-gendered weapon burials, placed to intercut with earlier graves in the centre of the plot, and so it was this mid-sixth-century phase that saw the density of burial in plot F becoming its defining feature. Notably, however, intercutting is not limited to male graves, since grave 354 was female-gendered and cut both 269 and 361, as did the later-sixth-century grave 360. Grave 354 contained A2b beads, and grave 360 had B2 beads of a different character, and so these individuals were probably from different generations.

There were a few later-sixth- and early seventh-century graves in plot F which appear to trace the middle of the plot. Grave 262, on the southern edge of the plot, was the earliest of these. It contained a SP1a1be spearhead giving it a depositional date range between the mid-sixth and early seventh centuries. This means that this grave could have belonged to either the group of mid-sixth-century intercutting graves, or to a similar group of later-sixth- or seventh-century graves. Its position on the edge of the plot, and in line with 346 and 353, tends to suggest the latter, placing it in the second half of the sixth century (see Figure 3.16). Grave 353 cut 352, partially obliterating it. Grave 346 was a weapon burial which contained a sword and a SP2-a2d spearhead, dating it AD 585–680. Grave 353's B2 beads dated it to AD 580–650, as did a garnet disc brooch with Salin Style II animal art. Grave 228 was further west than 353 and 352, and cut burial 231 which Brugmann placed in phase 3b, meaning that 228 must have dated to the later portion of the sixth or early seventh centuries. Graves 222 and 231 were to the western side of the plot. Grave 222 was dated with B2 beads between AD 580–650, and 231 contained an impressive decorated buckle and back plate; Brugmann placed it in phase 3b, dating it to the second half of the sixth century.

Plot F was defined by the density of its intercutting graves and by the degree of intercutting. Unlike plot J–K, many graves obliterated those of previous generations. Perhaps the ethos among this community focused on the immediate generation, and not on generations of particular antecedents. The density of burial created an aesthetic space and it highlighted the closeness of burial, perhaps a closeness of relationships within the community (Wiseman, 2015). It was an aesthetic that was particular to this plot and one that could be returned to, with the intention of telling stories, and retelling them in the funerals of others. This plot was a palimpsest and the rewriting, destruction and moulding of that space allowed the community to reinvent itself in its narrative creation. Just as with plots A and J–K, the space itself was important, and it was structured and shaped by each new generation for themselves, and their children, but this structuring of the internal plot space was not seen in all of the plots at Dover Buckland. Plots G, H and I were contemporary with A, F and J–K but contained fewer datable graves, and less internal organisation.

Plot G was the largest of these less-structured plots. Just six graves were tightly dated. Inhumations 306 and 308 were the earliest and both contained A1 beads, suggesting that they were interred around AD 450–530 (Figure 3.17). Birte Brugmann placed graves 281, 290, 334 and 335 into these earlier phases. Grave 290 contained a button brooch, and graves 334 and 335 contained buckles, whereas grave 281 contained a richer assemblage which included a small square-headed brooch and a great square-headed brooch, placing the four graves within phase 1 (AD 480–530). Graves 323 and 363 were dated to the mid-sixth century; grave 323 was a weapon burial with a SP2b spearhead and a SB2B3 shield boss, and dated to AD 525–70. Burial 363 was also a weapon burial, with an SP2-B1a3 spearhead; Brugmann dated it to her phase 3a, the latter half of the mid-sixth century (AD 550–80), because it cut grave 311. Burial 327 was dated to phase 2 on the basis of a buckle. On the southern edge of the plot, burials 333 and 335 were both dated by Brugmann to phases 1–2 on the basis of their buckles; they may date to AD 510–60.

On the opposite side of the plot, northern grave 302 contained a buckle and an arrowhead, whereas southern grave 336 contained a buckle and beads. Both were dated by Brugmann to the latter half of the sixth century. One grave, 303, dated to the later-sixth or seventh century on the basis of B2/C beads dating it to AD 580–720. Notably, these graves contained fewer goods than those in plot F, and they were also distributed evenly around the plot. A few graves intercut, but unlike plot F these were not concentrated in the central spaces of the plot.

Plots H and I were like J–K, in that these were probably one not two plots, so should be H–I (Figure 3.17). The latest two burials were 256 and 319, which dated to the later-sixth or seventh centuries. Therefore, for most of the sixth century these burials would not have been present, and throughout that time this area consisted of three small/medium-sized clusters of graves, rather than a coherent plot defined by the first burials, as we have seen elsewhere at Dover Buckland. The earliest graves, to the west, were 239, 245 and 247. Grave 239 had type A1 beads, a pair of early small-long brooches and a pin, graves 245 and 247 both had A2 beads and garnet jewellery, and so these were similar to, but stylistically different from, 239, where 239 was the earliest and probably

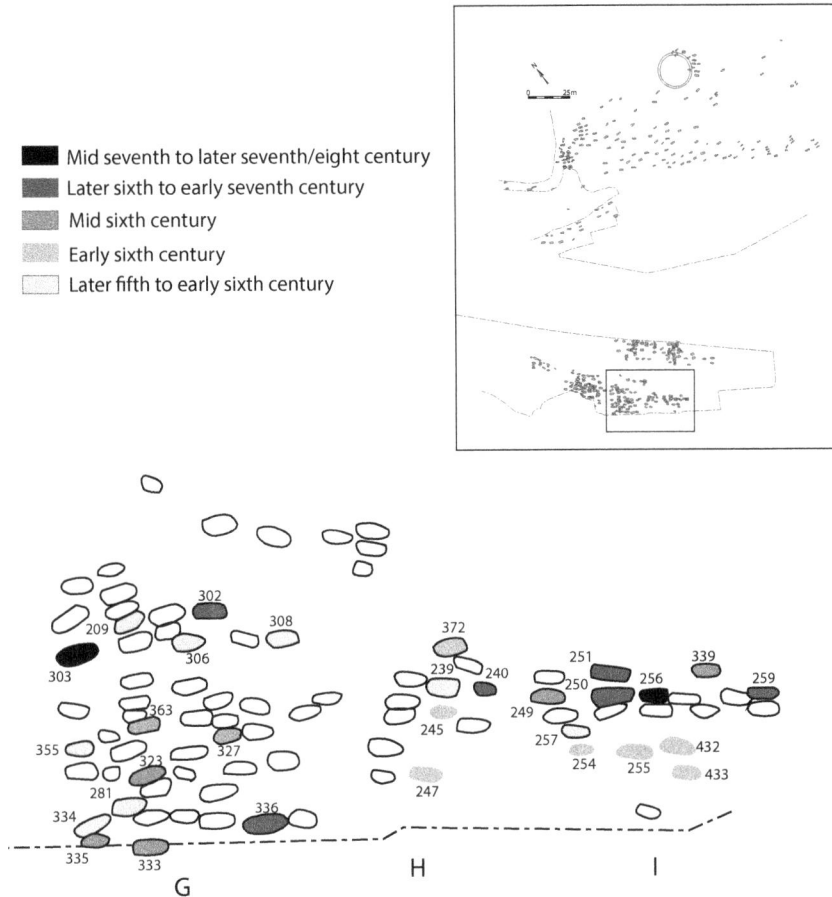

Figure 3.17 Dover Buckland: plots G, H and I in the 1994 excavation area. These three plots had less structure than the others.

fifth-century in date. Graves 254, 257 and 432 were also early, and grave 254 had A2 beads, a pin, a cone beaker, a button brooch and pair of small-long brooches. Grave 257 had A1 beads, a small-long brooch and a pin, putting it in the later-fifth or earliest-sixth century. Grave 432 had A2 beads, a cone beaker and a pin. Burials 255 and 433 were also earlier graves, and 255 contained a small square-headed brooch, a great square-headed brooch and a button brooch, which chronologically put it in into the first half of the sixth century. Grave 433 contained an openwork animal brooch of similar date. Even these earliest graves can be phased by artefact style.

The later graves were to the north-east, with mid-sixth-century burials 249, 339 and 372, where 249 was a weapon burial which contained an SP2-b1b spearhead (AD 510–70). Grave 339 was female-gendered with A2b beads dating to AD 530–80. Burial 372 was a wealthy female-gendered grave with a great square-headed brooch, an inlaid disc brooch and a claw beaker. Graves 250, 251 and 259 were of the later-sixth century. Grave 250 contained B1 beads, dating to AD 555–80, and 251 was male-gendered and contained an SP3-a spear, which probably dates the grave to AD 550–80. These two burials might well have felt like the middle of this group of graves when interred. Burial 259 by contrast was on the eastern edge and cut 260. It was a weapon burial with an SP2-a2a spearhead, dated to AD 550–615.

Grave 240 was later-sixth or seventh century in date, and was interred with a distinctive SP4 leaf-shaped spearhead with the socket longer than the blade. This grave might also have felt very central when interred. Grave 256 was another distinctive weapon burial found with a large SP1-a5 spear dating to the seventh century. It was truncated by 340, another male-gendered grave. Area H–I had some of the earliest graves in the cemetery, and some early wealthy female-gendered inhumations which outnumbered the later male-gendered weapon burials, but it remained largely dispersed until the very end of its use. There was no core, and there were no barrows. As we have seen, the earliest graves clustered in two groups and it seems that the later graves were buried around them with a loose chronological character that was not dissimilar to the plot organisation at Sewerby. However, in this group of graves at Dover Buckland the latest graves defined what was for them the middle, almost as if they were redefining the organisation with the location of latest graves. Certainly plot H–I was distinctive in that there was not the same importance placed on individuals, as seen in J–K, or on a central area, as seen in plot F. For the most part the graves in H–I were wealthier than those in plot G, but what is interesting is the changing nature of them, from wealthy female-gendered graves to a mixture of male and female and then male-gendered weapon graves. Perhaps this change was seen in the lived population who used this area. The inconstancy in the gender of the wealthy burials from generation to generation of the mortuary population might suggest a lack of stability in the lived population, and could help explain the absence of structure in the plot.

From the 1951 excavation, plot C was notable in a number of ways. The first was that it was positioned adjacent to and around a Bronze-Age round barrow and ring ditch (Figure 3.18). The graves respected the ditch and used it to structure their location. The second is that the burials here started at a later date than in the other plots we have discussed, and the plot was in use for a shorter period of time. Grave 65 was probably the earliest datable grave; it contained an SX-1c seax dated AD 525–70, and an SP2-b1a4 spearhead. Brugmann placed the burial in her phase 3

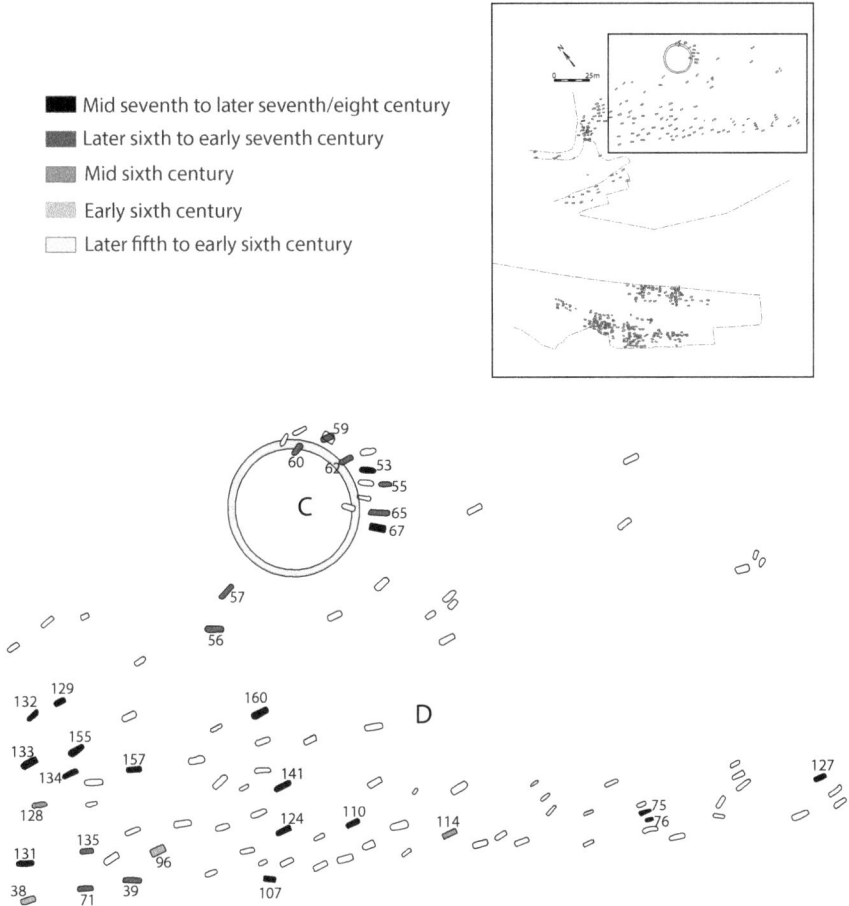

Mid seventh to later seventh/eight century
Later sixth to early seventh century
Mid sixth century
Early sixth century
Later fifth to early sixth century

Figure 3.18 Dover Buckland: plots C and D in the 1951 excavation area. Plot C largely consisted of contemporary graves situated around an earlier barrow. Plot D consisted of a dispersed group of graves dating to the last phases of activity. Its earliest burials were found to the north.

(AD 550–600 or later). This probably suggests that this grave dated to after AD 550, perhaps to the decades either side of AD 570, which means that the spearhead was probably an old or inherited object when it was deposited. Female-gendered grave 59 also dated to the second half of the sixth century, and with B1 beads and a BR2-b3 brooch had similar dates to grave 65. Interestingly, grave 59 cut grave 58, obliterating part of it; if 58 was contemporary with the foundation of the plot (i.e. grave 65) this might imply that grave 59 fell later in this range. Grave 62 contained B1 beads, giving it a date around AD 570 and making it contemporary with these examples. Later graves included 55 and 60, which were both of female-gendered individuals with B2 beads, dated to AD 580–650. Similarly, graves 53 and 67 both included B3 beads, dated to AD 650–720. A male-gendered weapon burial, grave 61, unfortunately was undated. There was little obvious structure to these graves, and more of them seem to have been female-gendered than male. Interestingly, graves 56 and 57 were opposite the graves attributed to plot C, across the other side of the barrow ditch. They were not physically associated with plot C, but they were chronologically contemporaneous. These burials were also male-gendered weapon burials, a category of grave that was otherwise distinctly absent from the datable burials in plot C.

Just to the south of plot C was a small cluster of graves referred to as 'Dvii' in Chapter 2, Figure 2.9, of this book, and as plots 'N' and 'L' by Evison (1994: 369). Unfortunately, these graves were not datable, but notably they did sit on a slightly different orientation to the others in the wider area D. As a result they seemed to have been oriented along or around the barrow ring ditch, a situation which aesthetically separated them from plot C.

Despite Evison's subdivision of these graves into different zones, area D seemed to consist of just two stylistically different groups of graves. Notably, the first of these groups consisted of the graves that Evison (1994: 369) attributed to a single plot, her plot F, with the addition of grave 128, which were chronologically and materially different from the rest of the burials in this area. Grave 38 was the only female-gendered grave, and with A2 beads and a garnet disc brooch of BR2b3 was mid-sixth century in date. All of the other datable graves were male-gendered, namely 39, 71, 96a, 96b, 128 and 135, and all contained spears of the SP2 varieties. Graves 39, 71 and 96a also contained shield bosses, while 96b contained a sword. Two graves, 128 and 131, and the double grave, 96, are most easily attributed to the mid-sixth century. The rest are more easily assigned a later-sixth-century date (Figure 3.18).

The rest of area D was a single area with 9 m clustering between graves (see Chapter 1); these inhumations had noticeably fewer artefacts, and those that were datable (graves 75, 76, 107, 124, 127, 129, 132, 133, 134, 141, 155 and 160) contained beads of group C, which date very broadly between AD 650 and 720. There was just one weapon burial, grave 114, and based on the proportions of its blade the spear interred within it was identifiable as a type SP2-a1a1 spear, dated AD 525–70. However, this weapon consisted of an odd little spike which fits the dimensions of this type, but is not otherwise consistent with weapons from this category. As a result, this spear must be considered of local manufacture and was probably contemporary with the seventh-century graves. Area D was the largest in the Dover Buckland cemetery, and it also had the latest graves with the least material culture. In this it resembles the last phases of Lechlade or Polhill. These area D graves contained the least material culture; this, with the wide gaps between graves, means they were probably of later-seventh-century date, making this plot unique, because most of the groups of graves and burial areas of Dover Buckland cemetery were pluralistic, containing generations of dead, whereas this one had a much 'flatter' chronology.

Dover Buckland: summary

The early Anglo-Saxon cemetery at Dover Buckland is very important for understanding the changes in behaviour found in mortuary landscapes. It was a very diverse cemetery, with ten or eleven burial areas which chronologically at least partially overlap. Plot A was small and dense, and was in use from the later-fifth/early sixth centuries through to the later-sixth or early seventh centuries. Area B may have been an extension of A, starting with a few graves in the middle-sixth century and it then included a row of five early seventh-century graves, just like Mill Hill, Deal. There were two changes to the tempo of burial, the first one around the middle/later-sixth century when the cemetery was discordant: some plots remained in use, while others were abandoned in favour of either a widely dispersed burial or a row-grave burial. The other change was in the seventh century when, for a single generation or so, a new burial form became popular: a small group was focused on a barrow, but others were buried dispersed and ordered, as if a single model was now informing decisions. That first change was complex because, at the same time as the row graves in area B were established, area D was developed too, and this consisted of a series of widely spaced weapon burials dating to the middle and later sixth century. In the last decades of the sixth century and the early seventh century, burial area C (located around a barrow) became important, and it is worth remembering at this point that the barrow had stood for some time without direct interaction from inhumations. Perhaps these new mourners were seeking to evoke a more ancient or mysterious ancestry. As the last two burials were dug in areas D and C, the larger, dispersed burial area D became the dominant burial area in the cemetery. Into the later seventh century, area D was the last place remaining in use. It was surrounded by earlier graves and is notable because of the 9 m gap between each grave. Unfortunately, as the furnished burial tradition ended there was a more limited use of gravegoods, and the relative absence of finely dated material culture means that it is impossible to see any internal structuring within area D.

The burials reported in the 1994 project (but actually excavated in the 1950s) also displayed a discordant tempo and areas E, F, G, H–I and J–K manifested different characters. Plot J–K was identifiable because of its size and because it consisted of a series of small barrows that defined and highlighted the graves of particular individuals. These would have dominated the mortuary aesthetic within this plot, and they would have been visible from each of the surrounding burial areas throughout the subsequent life of the Dover Buckland cemetery. It is probably significant that they remained unmolested (see Chapter 4), which may be evidence of how these monuments were valued by the wider community across generations. Around these barrows a number of satellite graves were placed. The plot furthest to the NW, plot E, was also notable because of its relatively short lifespan; it was in use between the fifth and later-sixth centuries, with just two datable graves and a small number of satellite graves dating to the later-sixth century. Area F was equally well structured, but instead of a focus on antecedents' graves, it had a single central space where funeral parties returned over and over again for generations, even partly obliterating older graves to place the newly dead. For them the focus does not seem to have been on longevity, but on the recently dead and the immediate family. Plot F was in use between the later-fifth and early sixth centuries and was still used regularly in the later-sixth century. In area G, graves were spaced out, had fewer intercutting graves and fewer datable artefacts, but this plot too was in use from the early sixth century until the early seventh. And in plot H–I, burials persisted from the fifth century well into the seventh century. Despite having little internal coherence, this plot contained some of the wealthiest graves in the cemetery.

It is possible to see that Dover Buckland had a broad east-to-west character, but this understates the organisational complexity. Instead, this detailed review has identified a series of distinct burial areas, with burial styles or tropes which were particular to them. Each area was chronologically unique, and some may have followed on directly from others as new emphases were found for commemoration (Sayer, 2009). It is evident there were phases in activity – the first phase focused on the grave plots, and in the second phase some of these plots persisted, while some were broken down towards the later-sixth century when a new commemorative style emerged. This new style focused on weapon burial or a row of graves, or the barrow, as at Deal. In the third phase the use of the previous two burial styles came to an end, beads were among the only significant gendered artefact, and burial style became homogenised into one that favoured a well-spaced, broadly E/W orientation. Previous mortuary technologies disappeared, and burial density, plots and gravegoods declined. In this seventh-century third phase, the underlying structure of the cemetery had broken down; burials were placed 9 m apart, were relatively poorly furnished and were not clustered at all. Being in the cemetery still mattered to some, and a few individuals were still interred in the old plots. For the most part, mortuary practice at Dover Buckland seems to have standardised in the middle- to later-seventh century after two phases of complex and colourful plurality. However, we should not get too distracted by notions of religious change; although important, these later-seventh-century graves were surrounded by the barrows and burials of their pagan ancestors in a location that would have been visually evident for hundreds of years.

Conclusion

Early Anglo-Saxon cemeteries were mutable, dynamic places and each burial saw participants negotiate around issues such as the location of a grave, how a corpse should be dressed and which objects went into, or were withheld from, the grave. The orientation of the grave – along a barrow, juxtaposed with core burials or conforming to those adjacent – was locally mediated and based on the expectations of mortuary partici-pants. The result was a continually negotiated expression, which changed generation by generation because the participants were different and because the *Zeitgeist* changed along with people's understanding of the space. New social perspectives and contexts mediated this change (Sayer, 2010). The nature of a negotiation might depend on who contributed, who was alive, who was present and what influences they had, or were given, by their peers. An exploration of cemetery chronology can show us when and how these negotiations differed by witnessing the changing of a cemetery pattern, or the rejection of one tradition in favour of another. This cadence might manifest in a generational focus for burial and, as a result, it might allow us to explore cemetery change as related to, but not dependent on, social change. Mortuary change was the result of a changed attitude towards the individual and deceased ancestor. Such an approach can be hugely informative and may allow us to begin writing life histories, or cemetery biographies, helping to identify specific groups or identities within them (Hines and Bayliss, 2013: 560). To understand the contrasting and changing attitudes towards cemetery space it is necessary, however, to understand the pace of this change, and the complexity of the mortuary landscapes.

Early Anglo-Saxon cemeteries have been described as monocentric or polycentric sites, which is helpful, but it assumes that there were a limited number of architects (see Chapter 1). Equally, the idea of a direction of burial also assumes there was a structure, or order, to the cemetery and that this was adhered to. These are useful starting positions, but, as we have seen, cemeteries were mutable landscapes with different dynamics across plots, by phase and within individual graves. In this chapter we have seen a number of different ways to organise cemetery space. At Orpington, a predominantly sixth-century site, a single grave provided a central point around which generations of subsequent weapon graves, children's graves and cremations were located. This principal antecedent provided a notable narrative point, and Orpington was probably abandoned by a generation that no longer felt a connection to this individual. Equally, early/mid-sixth-century plots at Oakington and plot J–K at Dover Buckland were organised around key individuals. Each subsequent generation interred key members of their community under small barrows that made them visible within the plot, but also created a striking aesthetic for the cemetery as a whole. This pattern of barrow use was also seen in several sites with substantial numbers of later-sixth- and seventh-century graves, for example St Peters, Lechlade and Finglesham. As we will see in chapters 5 and 6, later graves also had a flatter chronological nature, and this flatter nature is seen in plots B or D at Dover Buckland, which had a different character from the rest of the site. The excavated plot at Sewerby also contained a chronological character. These areas could be said to have a true horizontal stratigraphy because contemporary graves were positioned together and adjacent to their predecessors, a situation that was also seen among the configuration B burials at Apple Down and within plot H–I at Dover Buckland. Similarly, Bossut-Gottechain showed this character, but across multiple phases. Here the central burials were the earliest, and these were organised differently from the more regular later phases of burials. Importantly, at this site, the early cemetery remained relevant, becoming the historic core around which subsequent graves were placed.

Plot B at Wakerley showed a concentric pattern, one shared by the configuration A burials at Apple Down. At these sites, key individuals from successive generations were placed in a central location, a pattern also seen at Berinsfield (Sayer, 2010). The cores of plot F at Dover Buckland and plot C at Wakerley were comparatively densely packed. This pattern was also seen at Hatherdene cemetery, Cherry Hinton and Morning Thorpe, though not discussed in this chapter. In all of these cases, the high density of burial was paralleled with a greater degree of intercutting. In the case of the Wakerley plot C graves, this density was also highlighted by a greater degree of double burial (see Chapter 5). In many of the examples from Dover Buckland the later burials obliterated, or partly obliterated, previous graves. In these plots the prime narrative principle may not have been focused on key antecedents, as seen in plots J–K and at Oakington and Orpington, but on the generation being buried. It was their peers who organised the mortuary ritual, and it was probably how those people chose to express identity within the mortuary landscape that dictated the organisational character (see Chapter 6). Among these groups of people, emphasis was placed upon their immediate ancestor, who for these types of plot seemed to be more highly valued than those from their deeper past. Nonetheless, a core burial area remained and this helped to reinforce and legitimise these individuals' identities.

A number of smaller sixth-century burial plots at Dover Buckland, L, E or G for example, and the westernmost graves at Orpington, do not seem to have a chronological character. The groups of people using these burial areas do not seem to have placed the same aesthetic value onto the structuring of mortuary space. Perhaps they identified their connection to the past in different ways, in different places. Perhaps they did not share the same need or desire to express this part of their identity in community or public spaces.

Later-sixth- and seventh-century graves seem to have had more uniformity. At Dover Buckland, area D consisted of widely, but equally, spaced graves. A similar pattern is seen at Polhill and Lechlade, which are presented in Chapter 6. Indeed, as seen in Chapter 2, Street House, Garton Slack II and Dunstable were later-sixth- or seventh-century cemeteries which displayed regular, ordered or row-grave structures. However, this was not always the case, for Dover Buckland plots B, C and Di were later, or transitional, phases between the early/mid-sixth and seventh centuries. All of these had a much flatter chronological organisation, and this structure highlighted a number of comparable graves from the same generation, a pattern also seen at Lechlade and Finglesham.

These three transitional plots at Dover Buckland all highlight an important aspect of the site. Not all of the plots, or groups of graves, shared the same pace of change. Figure 3.19 presents a battleship-style

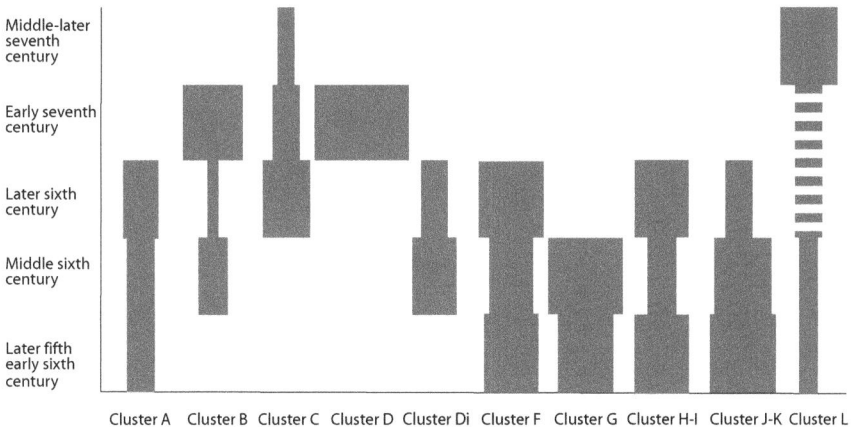

Figure 3.19 Dover Buckland: 'battleship' histogram. This shows the different chronological activity in the various plots (clusters), illustrating that these areas were not all contemporary and, importantly, that not all of the plots shared the same pace of change, some being long-lived, others short-lived.

histogram that illustrates the changes in frequency of datable graves for each of the ten plots at Dover Buckland. Chronologically, plot G mostly received early/middle-sixth-century inhumations while four plots (A, F, H–I, J–K) were used predominantly between the early and later-sixth century. Plot D was in use between the middle- and later-sixth centuries. Plot B was used between the middle-sixth and early seventh centuries and plot C was in use between the later-sixth century and the end of the seventh century. Burials in plot D were isolated to the early seventh century, whereas the infrequent burials in area L were placed there for the whole period that the cemetery was in use. This pattern is notable in highlighting an important watershed between the later-sixth and seventh centuries, but it also identifies a number of other important chronological transitions around the middle-sixth and early seventh centuries. Each of these burial plots had a different style – some were densely packed, some marked by barrows, others used external features or rows of graves as part of their structure – but they also each had their own different metre or cadence. Plots G and J–K were used intensely and early, and then declined quickly, whereas A and L took just a few burials over a hundred or more years. This cadence was also seen at Spong Hill, where burial areas waxed and waned in importance across the life of the site, until the final phase where focus shifted to the north, and the inhumation burials.

As we have discussed here, this chronological metre may have resulted from the way that users of a particular burial space saw their past, how they interacted with their dead and how they valued, or not, the graves of their antecedents. Understanding the chronology of burial is not just a way to date graves, but to understand the context of burial. There were a number of ways to organise mortuary space, and these were the result of negotiations around differences in attitude toward the dead. Differences in these attitudes probably reflect how communities used mortuary spaces as ways to express, maintain and reproduce communal identities. These ideas are discussed further in chapters 5 and 6.

Note

1 The spears from graves 54 and 126 are of type SP2b1b and are attributed to an early phase which ended around AD 570–650. Grave 145 included a type SP2a1b2 spear and has a middle- to late-sixth-/early seventh-century range of AD 525–615 (Hines and Bayliss, 2013: 163, 485, 565–6). Grave 145 also included a shield of type SB2 – with a date between AD 525 and 570, providing a tighter date for this burial (Hines and Bayliss, 2013: 151, 458, 563).

4

The grammar of graves

Introduction:
mortuary grammar and community identity

Cemeteries were spaces in which to dispose of the dead, to remove social and physical pollution by partitioning the dangerous decomposing body away from living space; and so prevent exposure to noxious odours. But disposal alone is too simplistic and perfunctory to explain the role of a burial ground because cemetery spaces hosted funerals, which were temporal events that recreated social bonds, allowing them to be forged anew following loss (Metcalf and Huntington, 1991). As a consequence, cemeteries were places for living people and communities, and it was these communities who adopted the material, visual and linguistic means to describe their deceased and in doing so they described themselves as well (Williams and Sayer, 2009). Cemeteries were social apparatus, resources which could be employed in the construction and maintenance of living and evolving identities. Part of this expression described the dead's relationships to the living funeral goers using shared processes: memory, performance, language and physical knowledge, such as material culture, aesthetic and space. The dead were placed in a grave using a communication that described their relationship to others among the funeral party, within the cemetery and among the wider world. The dead did not lie down to die in the grave, but their affiliations were captured in a mortuary culture that resulted from multiple agents engaged in internalised and articulated negotiations which included emotional, familial, community, political and economic changes.

Social identity is not a simple phenomenon, but the result of a nexus of nested and competing concerns. Which aspects of identity are externally expressed and to whom they are expressed all depend on an individual's circumstances, both immediate and personal (Sayer, 2010). The way an individual behaves will be different in the presence of a war band, a family or a religious community, and is dependent on that person's political affiliation and belief system, as well as age and gender among other things. But identity is as much a set of different cultural constructions as it is an ongoing, evolving process changing over a life's course, as circumstance and relationships themselves change. This *persona* depends on participants who make sense of the world around them though a matrix of semiotics expressed as conceptual, material and physical cultures consumed within social life and through communication. The result is a way of perceiving difference and creating similarities that identify, define or create networks between people and communities, but also utilises material things, visual processes and language in the expression of those relationships. In short, people use a combination of mythology, material culture and speech to construct coherent individual and group identities that provide a way to understand and structure their association with others.

The negotiations embedded in early Anglo-Saxon mortuary behaviour employed a mixture of semiotics expressed through a combination of spoken and visual knowledge. Some of these visual tools survive in the archaeological record and are described in Chapter 2, and they included grave clusters, grave orientation, grave density and choice of burial rite, where relational situations were articulated though the juxtaposition of similarity and difference. Other expressive technologies were part of individual funerary display and these included grave location, gravegoods, body positions or proximity to barrows, or other features that were embedded in cemetery architecture. In combination, these things provided ways for funeral celebrants to express and recognise their association with the deceased and other participants, and it is because this message was meant to be understood, even physical and verbally articulated, that we can discover it.

Mortuary variation is not a mirror of living society (Williams and Sayer, 2009; Chapman *et al.*, 1981; Parker Pearson, 1999: 73). Gravegoods were deliberately used to dress a corpse or placed into a grave, and so they may convey specific and meaningful messages to different groups of people. The nature of the message is entangled within their relationships; however, some of these messages can be explored. Furnished graves often included sets of objects: a furnished male burial is one with a weapon set, a shield and spear; a woman's burial is furnished with a pair of brooches (Härke, 1994; Stoodley, 1999). These material characteristics carried important visual messages at specific times: for example, a combination of high-resolution radiocarbon dates and Bayesian statistics reveals that furnished burials of these types were most popular in the mid-sixth century (Hines and Bayliss, 2013). As a result, gravegoods and gravegood combinations are important ways to study a site, but they may be misleading if relied upon to the exclusion of other evidence. The implication of Hines and Bayliss' discovery is that a person of high social rank may be buried with limited or no gravegoods in the early and the late-sixth century. Nonetheless, the cemetery space was a tool to structure narrative portrayals of the past, and so this chapter explores the methods that were employed to organise grave plots, to create central places or to mark out people and relationships. This chapter looks at the internal organisation of early Anglo-Saxon cemeteries by exploring how burial wealth, gender, sex and age were expressed at the point of burial. It will also examine the afterlife of a grave, looking at subsequent burial locations and grave robbing, because all of these *leitmotifs* are an expression of personality and intercommunity relationships.

Social status, wealth and core burials

Social status is, quite rightly, a problematic term and a contentious issue, but the presence of social rank in past societies, and particularly the Early Middle Ages, is not an issue of dispute; it is how archaeologists investigate it that is problematic. Previous scholars have relied on the presence or absence of gravegoods to investigate the social elite (Parker Pearson, 1999: 78). Among Anglo-Saxon archaeologists, these investigations have often focused on the quantity or quality of material in the graves, or relied on a knowledge of the character of specific objects to make conjectures (Arnold, 1981). The principle behind these investigations was the assumption that in a stratified society the elite displayed their status in the grave. This is viewed as a form of competitive consumption used to signal their identity or rank in a way that allowed the surviving family, or remaining elite, to legitimate their own position within the community (Parker Pearson, 1982; 1984; Morris, 1991).

Burial display is not simply focused on wealth, and Arthur Saxe (1970) suggested that the number and range of gravegoods may relate to the role of the deceased in society, and how many people attended a funeral. For example, a single adult male may have had nothing, or simply a knife, but a married adult male was also a husband and so his wife may have placed additional objects in the grave. The greater an individual's investment in society, Saxe speculated, the more people had a connection with them and so many more people would have contributed to the funeral or placed objects in the grave. In Saxe's model a father or mother, a general, king or religious leader would have people from each social role attending and contributing to their funeral. Thus the more of these categories they belonged to, the more people from each group attended – for example, children, subjects, soldiers or congregations. As a result the funeral event signalled their importance and allowed a broader range of people to renew their social bonds in that person's absence. Consequently, wealth positioned in the grave may have been placed there directly, or indirectly, by funeral participants, or because the surviving funeral organisers created an opportunity to show off their own importance and wealth at a local, regional or national scale. This is an important concept because it connects the objects found in a grave with the community who placed them there. However, this concept also highlights one of the key problems: members of the funeral party selected how the dead were dressed, with what they were accompanied, who attended a funeral and how the commemoration was structured. This means that an individual was prepared, presented, buried and commemorated in a way meaningful to the funerary party and relevant at a specific point in time and for a particular generation or group of people.

The presence of gravegoods in early medieval cemeteries has a long tradition of being associated with rank; for example, Heiko Steuer (1968) analysed Frankish and Alemannic cemeteries and connected wealthy individuals with an elite defined in the Merovingian legal codes. This system influenced C. J. Arnold (1981), who similarly identified ranks defined in the Anglo-Saxon legal codes within Bernicia's cemeteries (although no codes survive from this kingdom). Christlein (1973) and Shephard (1979) both proposed comparable systems of qualitative investigation, suggesting three or five social ranks identifiable from the gravegoods (see Table 4.1). These systems are based around a tripartite ranking scheme – with the absence of gravegoods, or the presence of just basic equipment such as a knife, bead or single buckle, being at the lowest rank, an average set of equipment in the middle rank or ranks, and exceptional equipment including gold, silver or equine equipment at the top. Shephard subdivided the bottom rank into two, those with and without gravegoods. However, the fact that organic material such as soft furnishings, clothing, filleted meat and wooden objects would not survive for the archaeologist means that these categories are largely artificial. Shephard also subdivided the middle rank into two, separating men with a single weapon and women with a single brooch from those with a full, if not spectacular, set of equipment, usually defined as a two-weapon combination, or a pair of brooches and a set of beads (see Chapter 1).

These studies are problematic, firstly because they do not address regional or chronological variants. For example, graves in Kent are significantly wealthier on average than the graves found in West Sussex or the Thames Valley. At Deal, Kent, for example, the majority of burials, some 53 per cent (of seventy-six inhumations) would fit into Shephard's A, B or C categories, with ten individuals at the very top of the social spectrum. By contrast, at Apple Down, West Sussex, 69 per cent (of 121

Table 4.1 Interpretations of social hierarchy based on the quality of gravegoods found in inhumation graves (based on Arnold 1981, Christlein 1973 and Shephard 1979)

Social rank (Arnold)	Quality group (Christlein)	Social hierarchy (Shephard)	Male grave goods	Female grave goods	General significance
unfree	A	E	No gravegoods	No gravegoods	Poor graves
		D	Knife buckle (bow, axe)	Glass beads, knife, buckle	
ceorls	B	C	Single weapon	Single brooch, short chain of beads	Average wealth
		B	Weapon set	Full female dress set	Wealthy
thegn	C	A	Exceptional full weapon set, decorated buckles, horse equipment	Full female dress set with silver or gilt objects	Exceptional/ above average wealth

inhumations) would have been in Shephard's D and E categories, where only seven individuals could have been placed in ranks A or B. While it is possible that Deal was the burial ground for an exclusive sixth- or seventh-century elite, this is unlikely because it is at least materially comparable to many sites in East Kent: Lyminge, Bifrons, Sarre, Bucklands or Finglesham for example (Parfitt and Brugmann, 1997: 96). Apple Down is comparable to other sites in West Sussex, so this difference is more likely to be the result of regional access to wealth and objects, or regional attitudes to the deposition of that wealth which defined what went into or stayed out of the grave. This is not just a geographic phenomenon and is also seen chronologically. It was not until the seventh century that truly outstanding wealth was to be found in 'princely' graves like those from Asthall, Oxfordshire, Broomfield, Essex, Caenby, Lincolnshire, Coombe, Kent, Cuddesdon, Oxfordshire, Prittlewell, Essex, Sutton Hoo, Suffolk, or Taplow, Buckinghamshire. There was also more regional variation in brooch types in the sixth century – a phenomenon connected to the emergence of the 'Heptarchy', the seven Anglo-Saxon kingdoms of the *Historia Anglorum* (Northumbria, Mercia, East Anglia, Essex, Kent, Sussex, and Wessex), though the political reality was more complex than that, with many micro-kingdoms, fluctuating authority and instability – and the appearance of distinctive regional costumes, triggered by the evolution of regional identities that emerged alongside these kingdoms (Hines, 1994). The same is true for weapons: fewer weapons are found from graves created in times of greater conflict, such as the early sixth or early seventh centuries. As a result, Härke argued, weapons may have been easily dispensed with in quiet times and more common in graves when they were less critical to the living community (Härke, 1994).

Objects were not just tied to social rank and had a complex role to play within society because they were bound up with images, memories and associations, and suggested different things to different people (Joy, 2009; Gosden and Marshall, 1999). Many objects were symbolic, like swords or weapon sets, which may not have been associated with actual warriors, but with ideas about gender roles, identity or appearance (Härke, 1994). As a result the displays of social status cannot have been as rigid and fixed as Shephard, Arnold or Christlein imagined, varying not just because of social rank, but also due to time of death and who buried the dead. Equally, a gilt brooch was not just a badge of wealth for an adult woman; it was also used in the creation and/or display of regional and personal identities (see, for example, Hakenbeck, 2009). Some individuals have been discovered buried with heirloom objects, many with considerable wear or damage from heavy or long-term use (Eckardt and Williams, 2003; White, 1988; White 1990). These may have been seen as amulets or of personal significance and so became inalienable from the dead person's identity in the eyes of the funeral party. Perhaps they were significant for a particular group of people at a particular time: Grandmother's brooch inherited and buried with a young woman or child, for example. All of these concepts were inter-connected and the decisions that led to the creation of a grave assem-blage would have been an amalgamation of ideas, concepts, images and negotiations shared by multiple people; buried objects became 'enchanted' and enmeshed with perceived *personae* (Gell, 1992). The choice of whether to dress a corpse, and what to dress it in or what to furnish the grave with, were as personal and specific to individuals as they were particular to kin groups, communities, regions or cultures. For this reason the wealth within a grave has to be understood within its community context. The location of a grave and its relationship to other graves provides evidence about how a community saw and used a grave after earth had filled it.

While social status is a difficult phrase (having often been used to describe rank), grave wealth is too crude a concept to properly describe the act of dressing a corpse, cutting a grave and celebrating a funeral. Wealth is only part of why objects were selected for display, whereas societal situations and relationships define the significance of an individual to others, and so display must be intended for an audience specific to a location and period. This social status is a mutable concept and a good way to think about part of a grave and cemetery's messages, but it must be considered alongside other factors like gender, age and location within the broader cemetery organisation. Such ephemeral concepts cannot be derived from burial wealth alone. Moreover, while it is possible to criticise the segregation of cemeteries into ranks based on the numbers of objects, it is not possible to study cemeteries without conceding that wealthy burials were significant. Many marked out specific people and events, reconstructing personhood *post mortem* and marking out a particular episode as important (Theuws, 2013). The inclusion of rich, elaborate or just specific, artefact assemblages was used to create a *persona* for the deceased, but in the creation of a significant, shared ancestor the entire burial community made a statement about their own communal identity.

In Chapter 2, the seventy-two-grave cemetery at Wakerley, Northamptonshire, was discussed in detail. The site was subdivided into three separate burial plots each demarcated by gaps larger than 3 m. For this site it was also possible to plot the distribution of wealthy graves, defined for the statistical investigation as furnished graves containing men with two or more weapons and women with two or more brooches (after Stoodley, 1999; Härke, 1994; see Chapter 1). Interestingly, this more detailed investigation showed clustering at 3 m for the cemetery and 5 m for furnished burials, suggesting some further internal organisation where the eastern plot had a group of multiple furnished graves positioned deliberately close together, but the western and central plots did not; in each case just two wealthy graves were in close proximity (Figure 4.1). This positioning constituted an internal cluster, or core, to that eastern plot and shows differential organisation between zones of the cemetery.

Nick Stoodley (1999: 131–2) observed that the cemeteries at Andover and Petersfinger were both organised around the high-wealth individuals who were the central focus of burial plots. However, the three plots at Wakerley present us with two different types of internal organisation. All three plots contained a mixture of furnished and unfurnished graves. In the eastern plot, a core of the furnished burials created a central focus, but the remaining two plots were more diffuse, having no obvious core. These two types of burial plot can be seen across the corpus of early Anglo-Saxon cemeteries. For example, the hundred graves at Berinsfield were organised between two or more burial plots, with the northern plot separated spatially and with N/S oriented graves. This northern group contained a core of three clustered furnished burials (Figure 4.2). Berinsfield's plot B contained four furnished burials positioned together at its core, with three more buried on the eastern edge suggesting the

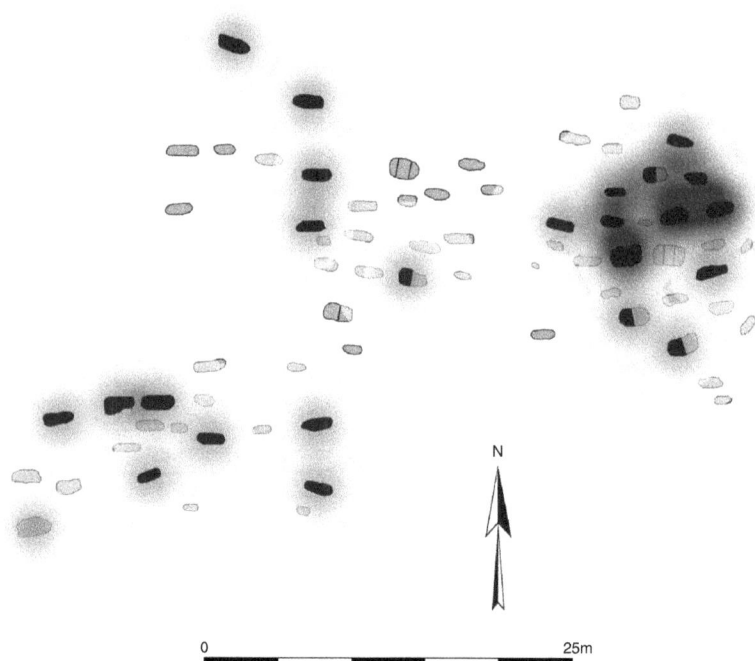

Figure 4.1 Wakerley, Northamptonshire: the spatial distribution of furnished graves clustered at 5 m. This clustering was evident in the eastern graves, which can be seen here deliberately grouped together as a core group within this plot.

focus of a third group, plot C, but many of these graves have been lost during quarrying to the south of the site.

Apple Down is another cemetery in which mortuary practice centred on a core of furnished or wealthy burials (Figure 4.2). Three of the wealthiest graves from the site were located at the heart of the cemetery and surrounded by less wealthy, but mostly furnished, inhumations clustered at 5 m (see Chapter 1). Three further furnished burials were distributed around the site, seemingly at random. However, the richest burials were placed at the centre of the group of E/W oriented graves and so they were at the core of the sixth-century cemetery. These graves were not just furnished, but similar and comparatively wealthy: graves 10, 13 and 14 contained gilded saucer brooches, sets of beads, and knives, while grave 14 also included a gilt great square-headed brooch. A similarly wealthy male burial nearby, grave 63, contained a spear, bucket, seax, firesteel, buckle, knife and set of tweezers.

The excavation at West Heslerton, East Yorkshire, identified 201 individual graves. To the south the cemetery was divided into two plots,

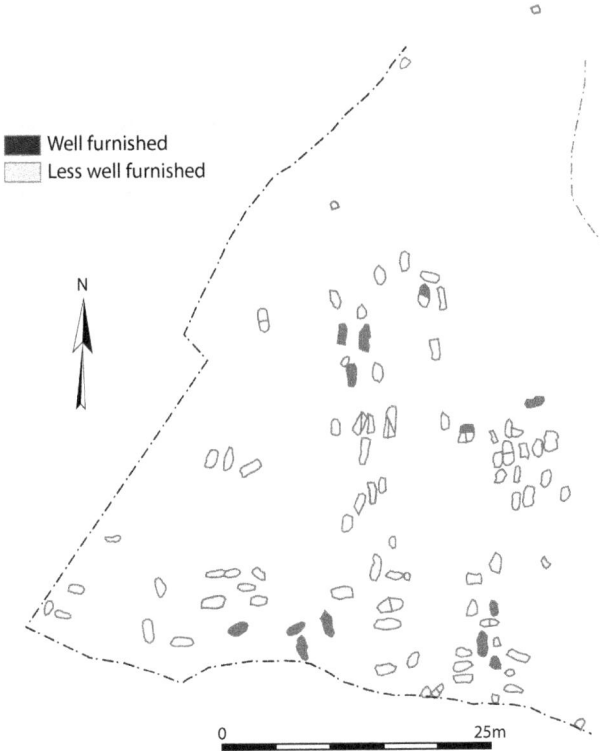

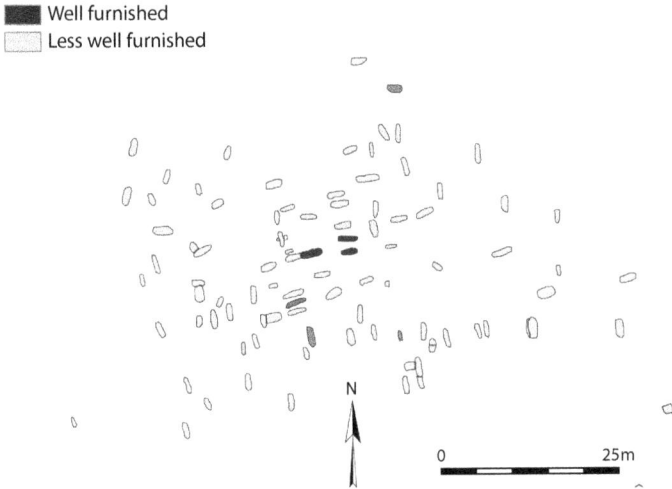

Figure 4.2 Core groups of furnished graves were also seen at Berinsfield, Oxfordshire (top), where groups of three or four graves made up clusters within the different plots. At Apple Down, West Sussex (bottom), the three wealthiest graves were found together in the centre of the E/W oriented burials.

each on either side of a Bronze Age ring ditch. In the north of the cemetery was found a less dense group of graves also divided into two widely spaced groups. The largest plot, A, had a core of wealthy burials consisting of five double or triple weapon graves (Figure 4.3), and these included one central burial with a sword, shield and two spears, as well as a number of female graves with great square-headed and cruciform brooches. These brooches are significant because the common dress items in the cemetery consisted of annular or penannular brooches and beads,

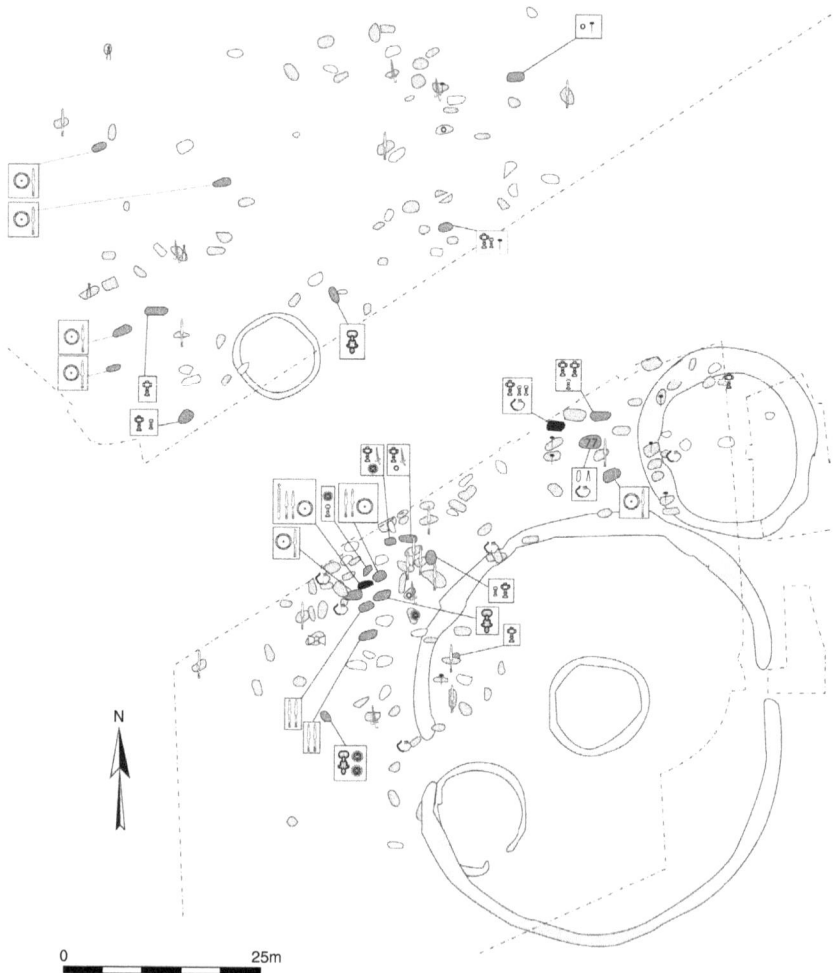

Figure 4.3 At West Heslerton, East Yorkshire, the cemetery was divided into four plots. To the south were found clustered plots of graves; and the largest group, A, contained a core of furnished burials in the centre.

or a buckle and knife. This core was surrounded by more graves that had common brooch types, or single weapons, and these burials contained knives, buckles, beads or brooches. The smaller plot to the east also had a core of burials just outside the western edge of a Bronze-Age ring ditch. This group consisted of two female burials, with cruciform and small-long brooches, and two weapon burials, with another grave, 77, in the middle. Grave 77 was not a weapon grave, but was notable for its unusual assemblage that included two knives, one 79 mm and one 151 mm in length. The burial also included a buckle, awl, tweezers, blue-green glass cullet from a cone beaker, the remains of three pottery vessels and a whetstone. This range of goods was unique within the cemetery and is certainly unusual, suggesting an artisan but one buried in a central and significant location. The northern groups of graves had no obvious centres, although two weapon burials and two cruciform brooch burials were placed in close proximity on the south-western edge.

At Great Chesterford, Essex, there were also a number of differ-ent plots of burials, signalled by the density and orientation of graves, and the wealthy N/S-oriented graves seemed to constitute core burials in plot A. In the middle of the cemetery there were two particularly wealthy graves, grave 122, which contained a globular pot, Roman coin, glass claw beaker, spearhead, sword and shield boss, and grave 142, which held a spearhead, pottery vessel, shield boss and horse (Figure 4.4, bottom). Six other furnished inhumations were found in close proximity. This cluster constituted a core of wealthy burials at the heart of a spatial group of inhumations (plot A). Similarly, to the south of this burial plot was found a second, smaller plot with six furnished burials creating a core (plot B). The N/S graves at Great Chesterford clustered at 3 m, and were organised around two large multi-directional plots in the middle of the cemetery. Plot A's core graves were N/S oriented and formed a centre; plot B's core graves were not all oriented the same way, but nonetheless a core of wealthy inhumations was located in the middle of this group of burials (Figure 4.4). To the south of plot B a less dense cluster of burials contained furnished graves but no obvious core. Similarly, to the north of plot A there were a number of less dense burials with furnished graves throughout and no obvious cores or pattern to the orientation of graves.

The contrast between plots A and B at Great Chesterford shows that not all plots had similar cores of graves, and these central areas may have been identified in any number of ways. Ripley K analysis of the 117 graves at Norton showed statistical significance at 7 m, and conse-quently the Norton cemetery was organised into two plots, an eastern and a western plot, divided by a single 5 m gap (Chapter 2). The eastern plot, B, contained fifty-eight inhumations and the furnished graves were found in two groups. Three of these graves were to the west on the edge

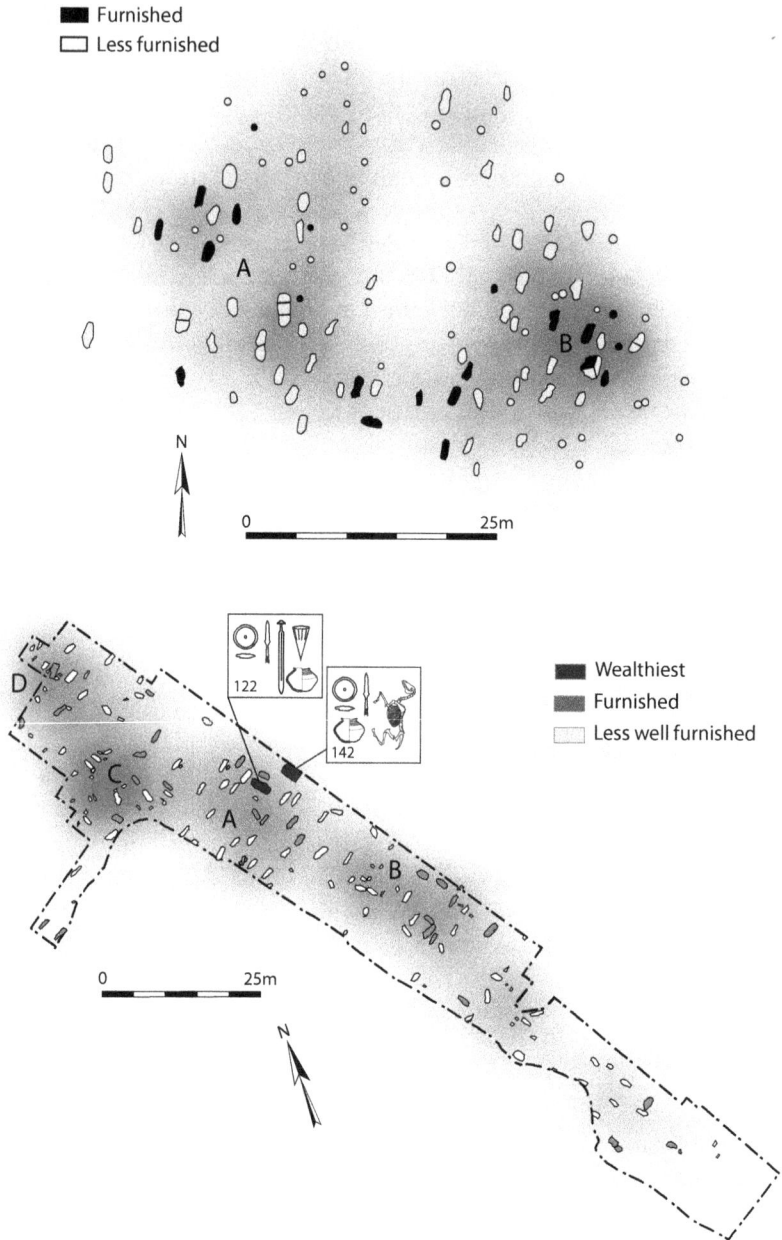

Figure 4.4 Norton, northern Cleveland (top), and Great Chesterford, Essex (bottom). These two cemeteries contained different core groups of burials. At Norton, the furnished graves in plot B were split between two groups, one in the highest-density areas and one to the western edge of the group. At Great Chesterford, both plots A and B had a core of furnished burials, but plot A centred around two particularly wealthy burials, 122 and 142.

of the plot and a further six, or seven, in the central area within 7 m of each other. This area was the densest in the cemetery and so was a core for this cemetery, with multiple burials placed deliberately in the space (Figure 4.4). The western plot contained fifty-nine inhumations with ten furnished graves dispersed around the plot, and the four westernmost inhumations formed a higher-density group, but there was no obvious centre to this plot. Only in one plot at Norton did the furnished burials form a core, but the graves were much more dispersed than at West Heslerton or Great Chesterford, which fits the general character of this cemetery with more widely separated graves.

Similarly, at Holborough, west Kent, thirty-nine graves were excavated as part of rescue excavations in the 1950s, by which time many more to the south had been lost. These graves appear to have been loosely clustered into two plots of burials, but in fact this was not statistically significant (Figure 4.5); the thirty-nine graves covered the same

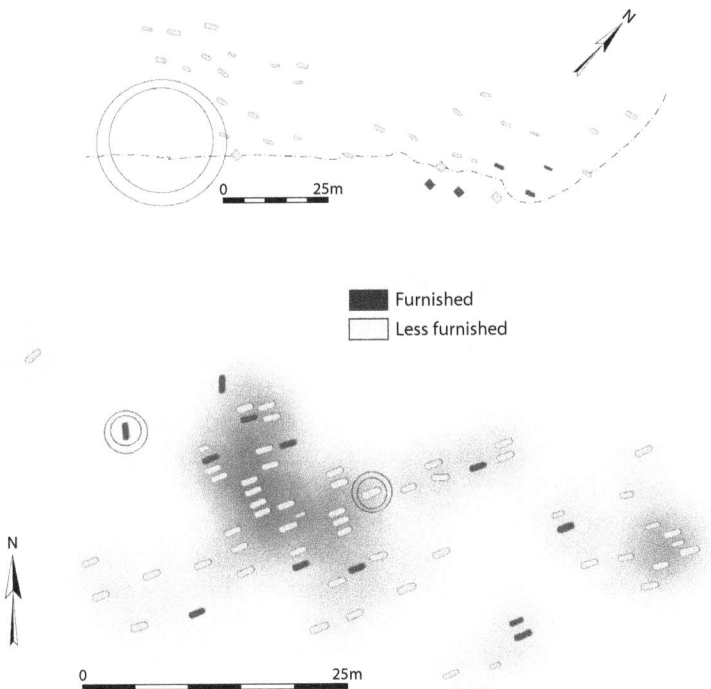

Figure 4.5 Holborough, western Kent (top), had just five furnished burials, all found towards the eastern end of the site. Leighton Buzzard III, Bedfordshire (bottom), had one large group of graves or plots with several smaller groups of graves to the east. The furnished graves were dispersed around the site with no obvious clustering. Both Holborough and Leighton Buzzard were seventh-century sites.

area as the whole of the diffuse Norton cemetery with its 117 graves (Evison, 1956). Only the eastern part of Holborough contained any furnished burials, with just five graves in close proximity to the south-east. Equally, Leighton Buzzard III, Bedfordshire, consisted of sixty-eight graves (Figure 4.5; Hyslop, 1964). It was more ordered than Norton, but was more dispersed, with two plots clustering at 5 m. Plot A was a large group of burials to the west, and plot B was a much smaller plot to the east. The furnished graves from this site were dispersed around the cemetery and showed no internal clustering whatsoever. Leighton Buzzard III was a seventh-century cemetery and, like Holborough, it had a much more dispersed internal organisation. Seventh-century cemeteries, like Holborough, Leighton Buzzard II or III and Bargates, and second-phase zones in earlier cemeteries, like those at Lechlade or Polhill (see below), seem less likely to be focused on a core of higher-status graves, with the exception of the royal graves at Street House (Sherlock, 2012). By way of contrast, many fifth- and sixth-century cemeteries (for example, West Heslerton, Great Chesterford, Deal or Bergh Apton) had a cluster of graves which formed a central focus for the cemetery. Other fifth- and sixth-century sites, like Apple Down, Wakerley and Great Chesterford, had been organised around multiple plots with different structures within each plot. In either case one plot, or one core of one plot, consisted of notably wealthy individuals.

Not all cemeteries had a core of wealthy graves, but many did contain notable burials. Four obvious examples are Lechlade, Orpington, Oakington and Finglesham (Chapter 6). These four sites had a dispersed set of high-status graves, a combination that we also saw in the plots at Great Chesterford, Apple Down or Berinsfield. These furnished graves were still the focus of specific commemorative activity. For example, Orpington in west Kent, a sixth-century site with sixty-four excavated graves (Palmer, 1984), is significant because the furnished burials were located around the core, rather than within the heart of the cemetery, and they seemed to snake around a small barrow burial which made a central focus for the cemetery (Figure 4.6, right; see also Chapter 1; Stoodley, 1999: 128). Intriguingly, this barrow burial was not furnished at all, but seems to have been the focus of the furnished burials and the whole cemetery, cremations included, providing a central point around which the site continued to develop. This can be seen because the densest area of burial on the site encircled grave 23. Equally, grave 80 at Oakington was the focus of a tight cluster of inhumations which enclosed it (Figure 4.6, bottom). This group of graves was a central focus of the northern grave plot around the middle-sixth century. However, burial 80 was not a founder's grave because it truncated an earlier burial, grave 92. The early medieval excavators of grave 80 came across

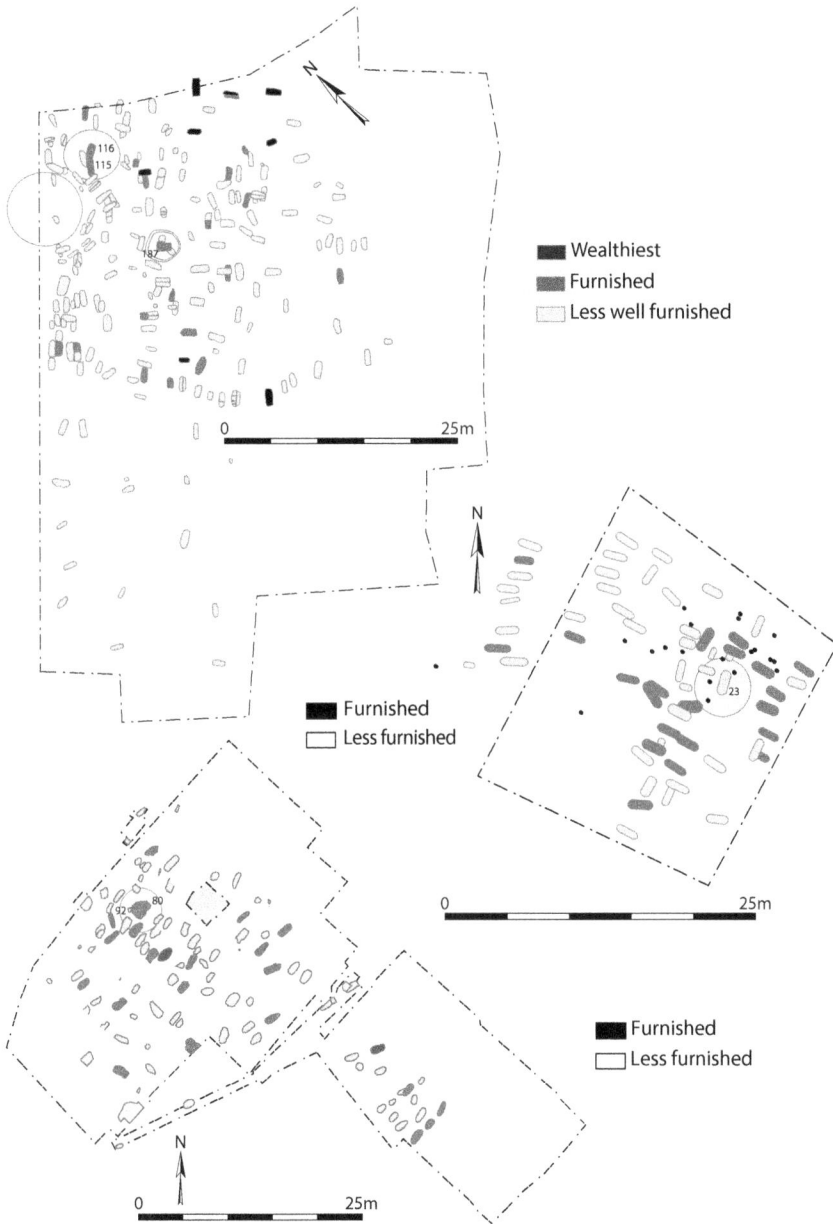

Figure 4.6 Lechlade, Gloucestershire (top), Orpington, eastern Kent (right), and Oakington, Cambridgeshire (bottom). At Lechlade the adjacent burials 116 and 115, and nearby 187, were central places around which other graves were placed in satellite positions. This phenomenon is also evident at Orpington, around grave 23, and Oakington, with grave 80. All of these graves probably had small barrows erected over them, marking their location.

foot bones from the child in grave 92 and deliberately placed them back on top of the child's exposed leg bones.

A similar pattern is observed at Lechlade where furnished burials 116 and 115 were adjacent and formed a two-grave core within the northern burial plot (Figure 4.6, top; see also Chapter 6). Interestingly, the other burials in that area left a gap around the two graves, presumably because there had been a barrow over the top of them. These satellite graves enclosed the two central barrow burials, augmenting this focus of activity at the heart of the burial plot. A third inhumation, to the west of this pair of seventh-century graves, was inserted deliberately and dug directly into the overburden of the barrow. Burial 187 was also seventh-century and seems to have truncated the two earlier burials. This group has a ring ditch around it and a series of burials to the north and west actively enclosed them, highlighting this place for continued focus and consecutive inhumation. Other seventh-century burials at Lechlade may also have had small barrows on top of them, and so this pattern of activity was repeated for particular individuals throughout the site. The result was an ego-focused commemorative space which highlighted particular individuals instead of groups of important graves.

In all three examples, Orpington, Oakington and Lechlade, the sixth-century burials which focused later activity were probably mounded, and in each example later graves or cremations had been inserted directly into these features. At Orpington, these interleaved burials were of children and cremations (Stoodley, 1999: 128). At Oakington, they were children and prone burials; four prone burials were placed south of grave 80 in the area directly around, the barrow (Figure 4.6, bottom). At Lechlade, the interleaved burial was a third male inhumation dug into the barrow in the seventh century, and many of the graves immediately around this centre contained children. This small Anglo-Saxon barrow may have been purposely placed adjacent to a pre-existing Bronze-Age monument, around which other graves had been placed in satellite positions. In all three examples we speculate about the presence of barrows, and certainly the evidence presented by the satellite graves supports this hypothesis. None of these examples were discovered with a surviving barrow, but they were a central focus highlighted in a significant way. And so we venture that small mounds of earth marked each grave (Devlin, 2007b: 56) and these small barrows, witnessed by early antiquaries, do seem a logical way to have marked central focal points and significant graves (see below).

In these examples furnished, wealthy or mounded graves created central places which contributed to the subsequent structure of the cemetery. These graves could be gathered into a collective core group located within a space, or they might have formed individual places around which groups of burials were located. The two strategies for burial may say quite a lot about the community's decisions and it is of note that some communities placed emphasis on collective, multi-generational groups, whereas others seem to have structured burial places around particular egos.

The location of furnished graves was an important part of cemetery organisation, although this may have manifested in a number of different ways. In all of these cases, the furnished graves made places for mnemonic and commemorative activities and provided a structure, or grammar, for the site. But not all grave plots had these features, and in many cemeteries the second or third burial plots did not have a central focus, instead having a number of dispersed and furnished inhumations. Interestingly, the plots which contained a core, or central focus, were often richer than those with a dispersed core. This is seen at Wakerley, where the easternmost plot included a core of inhumations, and this was also where the majority of type II belt buckles and cruciform brooches were found (Figure 4.7). This grave plot, with the

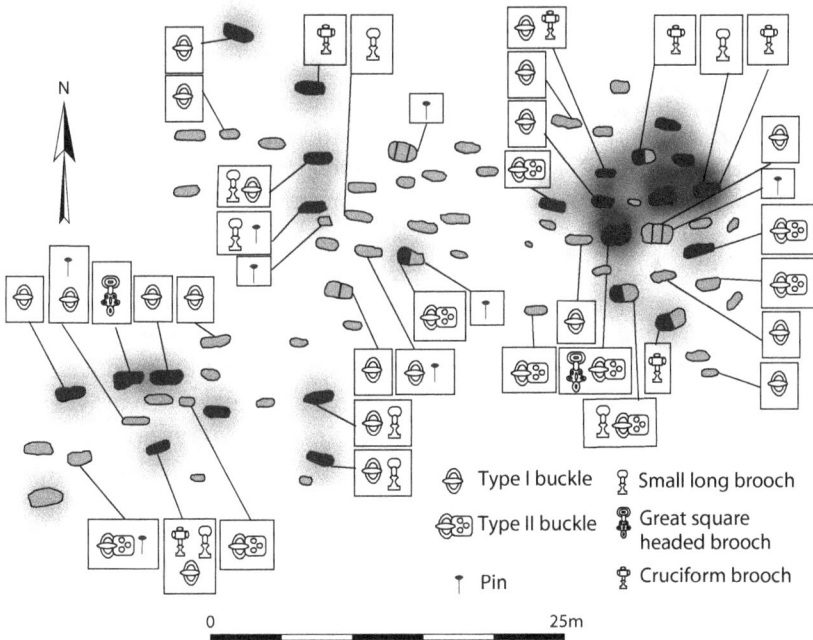

Figure 4.7 At Wakerley, Northamptonshire, the core inhumations were found in the eastern plot, corresponding with the more display-oriented objects; in this case the type-II belt buckles and the cruciform brooches were more common in the eastern burials.

core, contained objects that placed more emphasis on display compared with the other contemporary burial plots. The same is true at Lechlade and Oakington, where the richer graves were found in the plots that contained central barrow burials. The physical situation of a grave was key to understanding individual graves and cemeteries, but it is also important to consider other *leitmotifs* like age and gender, which are central to social perceptions.

Sex and gender

Among the most influential contributions of theoretical archaeology has been the development of sophisticated ways to think about gender differences (Gilchrist, 1991; Barrett, 1988; Sørensen, 1992) – not just as the biological sexes, but as identities and physical bodies, both of which need to be negotiated and managed during the progress of a life course (Gilchrist, 2012). In British archaeology, gender developed as an important topic for research in the 1990s after a series of influential investigations (for example: Gilchrist, 1991; Gero and Conkey, 1991; Moore and Scott, 1997). Early Anglo-Saxon female objects, brooches for example, had been a central component of research, but the focus of that research was firmly set on regional object types, style and chronology (Brush 1988; Dickinson, 1976; Welch, 1983). There was no investigation of the woman within the costume or the man behind the shield boss. However, in the 1990s, there were two scholars who stood out as leaders in this field, Sam Lucy (1997) and Nick Stoodley (1999; 2000). Stoodley conducted a large, quantitative study based on the investigation of forty-six cemeteries; he indicated that women's burials were not any richer than men's but that the rituals associated with women placed more emphasis on the body and on life course and that femininity transcended social status – unlike masculinity, which was tied to social rank. Lucy's investigation was more qualitative and she identified five genders: male with gravegoods, male with female gravegoods, female with gravegoods, female with male gravegoods and burial with no gravegoods.

Both Härke (1997) and Stoodley (1999) considered early Anglo-Saxon gender identities to be without rigidity. They regarded them as fluid negotiations taking place within a 'frontier-like' society where lifetime roles and daily routines had to be completed regardless of social distinctions. Such a situation required a degree of transaction between sexes and it is this flexibility, they argued, that gave rise to definite gender identities expressed during the construction of funerals. In this context display was used as a reaffirmation of social differences largely absent in life (Härke, 1997; Stoodley, 1999). Härke questioned the identification of manifold gender identities and, returning to the data, he suggested that the individuals assigned third and fourth gender distinctions could be explained as part of the error margins for skeletal sexing. This he estimated to be between 5 and 10 per cent, with only 1.16 per cent of males found with dress items and 0.24 per cent of females with weapons (based on a database of forty-five cemeteries, Härke, 2011). This problem is particularly significant at some cemeteries, like Empingham II, which contained a number of third and fourth gender burials. Unfortunately, Empingham II was plagued with post-excavation problems, such as missing objects and doubtful associations between some objects and graves (Timby, 1996: 6).

The sex–gender phenomenon is also seen in well-excavated sites, such as grave 104 at Berinsfield. Skeletally an adult male, the occupant was found with two small-long brooches and amber beads, more often associated with a female gender (Boyle *et al.*, 1995: 52). Another example, grave 144 from West Heslerton, included a female skeleton with a spear (Haughton and Powlesland, 1999b: 249). These individuals were not otherwise treated differently, or located in 'deviant' burial locations on the edge of cemeteries or plots (Reynolds, 2009), as we might expect if they occupied unusual social categories – this is well attested in the anthropological literature, where third and fourth genders are accepted but separated by social norms (Metcalf and Huntington, 1991). Perhaps defining third genders in early Anglo-Saxon archaeology is a circular argument – the assumption is that weapons were associated with the male sex and therefore were masculine artefacts, but when a weapon is identified with a member of the female sex she has taken on a different gender. If we reduce this to basic principles then this circumstance proves only that weapons were not exclusively associated with men, and so perhaps the mesh of concepts bound up with a spear included masculinity but also other important elements which became especially important when buried with a woman. An unusual object, in this case a spear, may have promoted a number of different overlapping elements, for example, asexual or sexualised female identities, and so interpreting this subtlety in terms of gender divisions is at best simplistic. In two cases at West Heslerton, graves 144 and 164, women were buried with a spear, but the absence of brooches neither confirms nor refutes that they were also dressed in male clothes; many females were buried without surviving artefacts and presumably organic fasteners held their costume in place.

The concepts enmeshed with gender identities are complex and multi-faceted, linked with age (Stoodley, 2000) and the expression of identity (Lucy, 1997). Gender is an important part of social life and as a result scholars have tried to find patterns within the archaeological record by looking at changes in costume or burial practice. Ellen-Jane Pader took a multi-variant approach connecting age, body positions and artefact assemblages, but obvious patterns are not common (Pader, 1982). One of the most obvious is in the layout of a cemetery, and for some sites limited patterning is evident.

The location of male and female graves has been identified as significant to the organisation of some cemeteries, for example Howletts in Kent, Lechlade and Polhill (Lucy, 2000: 132) or Broadstairs and Worthy Park (Stoodley, 1999: 135). All of these sites organised different genders into different areas, but many of these sites were complex or

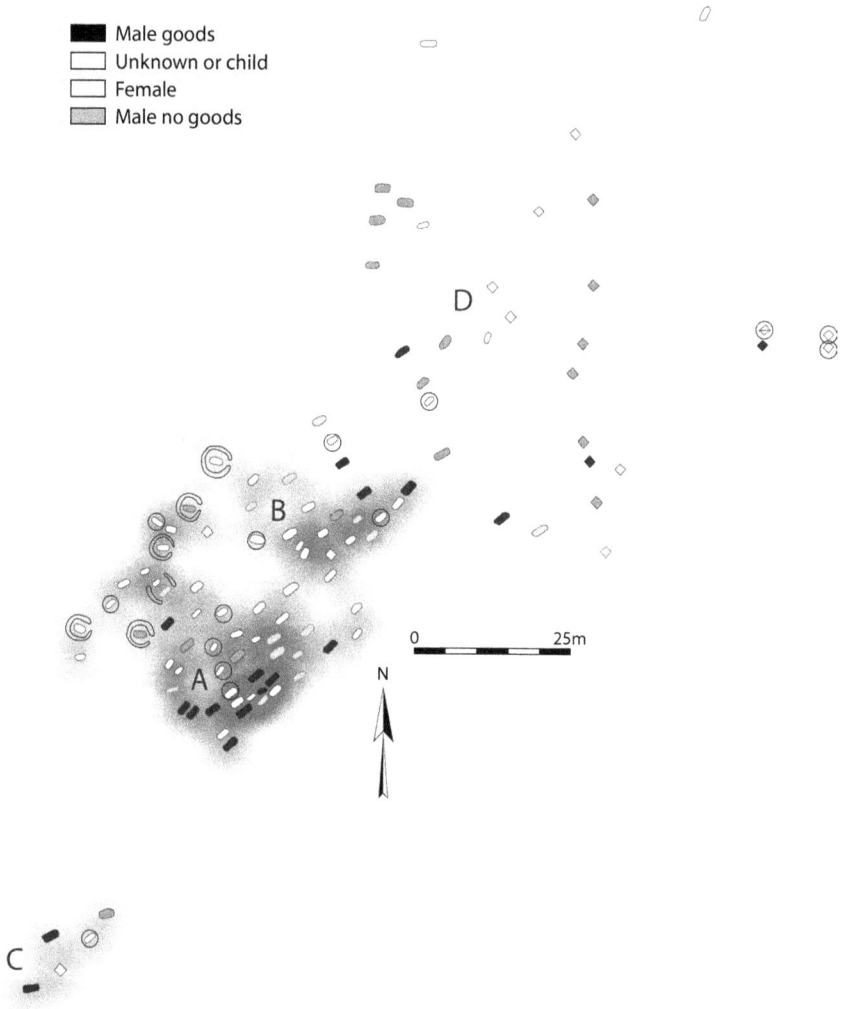

Figure 4.8 Polhill, Kent, was divided into three plots of graves, A, B and C, with one group of homogeneous graves, D, to the north. Plot A contained a specific concentration of male-weapon burials to the south.

have been only partly excavated. Regardless, a considerable endeavour has been made to identify gender patterning in early Anglo-Saxon cemeteries – in cemetery organisation at Polhill and Westgarth Gardens, or in small numbers of comparable graves at sites like Empingham II or Lechlade, for example. However, few sites actually contained patterns. Cemeteries like Pewsey, Bergh Apton and Finglesham show no obvious difference and are by far the norm. Indeed, Lechlade cemetery also shows little evidence of gender differentiation at a site scale. These types of investigation serve to demonstrate the considerable variation within the archaeological record (Huggett, 1996; McHugh, 1999). Gender has rarely been considered as a structuring principle within groups of graves or plots, and so it is the social unit that arranged the plots which may be of some consequence in gender distinction. With gender display, social differences might be apparent because of localised decisions, such as who prepared a body or selected a location for the grave, and so specific practices might only have been common among specific sub-social groups. Patterns within some cemeteries are perhaps more interesting than patterns across all cemeteries because local patterns tell us about local decision-making, power relationships, behaviours and local histories. Localised patterning emphasises the power of the individual and community as the agent(s) of early medieval cemetery architecture.

The separation of small numbers of gender-specific graves is seen elsewhere, for example with the graves of a specific gender, or biological sex, in the seventh- and eighth-century cemetery at Polhill, Kent. Polhill is a large site with 130 burials in 111 graves (Philp, 1973; 1979; 2002). The gender division was evident in its internal organisation: some graves were clustered at 5 m, making up two plots, a large plot to the south-west (A) and a smaller one to the north-east (B), and there was a group of statistically dispersed graves north-east of plot B. The excavators identified a series of six ring ditches to the north-west of the site and these, as with contemporary Kentish cemeteries like Deal, Finglesham or Dover Buckland, are probably seventh-century. A group of eight male-gendered weapon graves were found to the south of plot A, and to the north-east of these were found five furnished female graves, deliberately positioned and creating a gender-divided core of furnished burials (Figure 4.8). This group of graves was accompanied by four burials with small barrows over the top (Philp, 1973; 1979; 2002). Interestingly, this core of significant inhumations was divided loosely into two halves structured by gender. Plot B had no core, and there was no evidence of gender separation. However, the dispersed graves to the east had two groups of male graves; to the north was a group of males without weapons, and to the east a row of seven male graves, of which only one included a weapon. In this dispersed zone the unfurnished male graves were on the peripheries of the site, separated from the two plots (A and B) and also from the deliberate gender segregation seen among the wealthy graves at the heart of plot A.

The pattern seen in plot A at Polhill is seen elsewhere in early Anglo-Saxon cemeteries, for example, the two small sites at Broadway Hill, Hereford and Worcester, and Winterbourne Gunner, Salisbury and South Wiltshire (Figure 4.9). Broadway Hill is a late-fifth- and sixth-century cemetery consisting of eight graves and was identified during quarrying (Cook, 1958). This site had a strong gender-oriented organisation, with male graves in the west and females in the east. Similarly, Winterbourne Gunner, consisting of ten graves, was also a late-fifth- and sixth-century cemetery with males to the west and women to the east (Musty and Stratton, 1964). Other sites, like Lyminge II in Kent, also showed strong gender patterning within specific parts of the site. However, all of these sites were fragmentary, and excavation comprised fewer than 50 per cent of the graves originally present; so these patterns may be found only in localised areas of the cemetery (Hurd, 1913; Hurd and Smith, 1910; Warhurst, 1955).

The deliberate grouping of male burials was also seen in the late-sixth- and seventh-century furnished graves. At Deal, seven of the east-ernmost burials formed a line of male graves, and all dated to this latest phase (Figure 4.10). It has been proposed that this was an expression of divisions within rank (Stoodley, 1999: 128), but it may also have been the result of a subdivision of the male household. At West Heslerton, 201 graves were excavated and subdivided into statistically significant plots (see Chapter 2). Plot A was the wealthiest and contained a cluster of sixth-century weapon burials. Williams (2007: 116) suggested that the objects placed within these graves were a response to the memory of previous graves and included a range of material selected to identify similarity and masculine status. Their organisation is reminiscent of Orpington (see Chapter 2), the weapon graves were placed in a T shape and each was given a slightly different range of equipment – including multiple spears, shields and a sword – showing their martial equality but marking each one as different. Interestingly, just a few metres to the east of these a group of four single-weapon spear burials were positioned in a cluster. There were no comparable groupings for the women's graves, which were positioned around these two groups. None of the other plots in this cemetery contained such a marked gender division, and plot A at West Heslerton was the wealthiest and largest plot in the cemetery.

Strong gender patterning was also present within Westgarth Gardens, Suffolk (West, 1988; Penn and Brugmann, 2007). Stoodley suggested that gender played a major role in the organisation of this

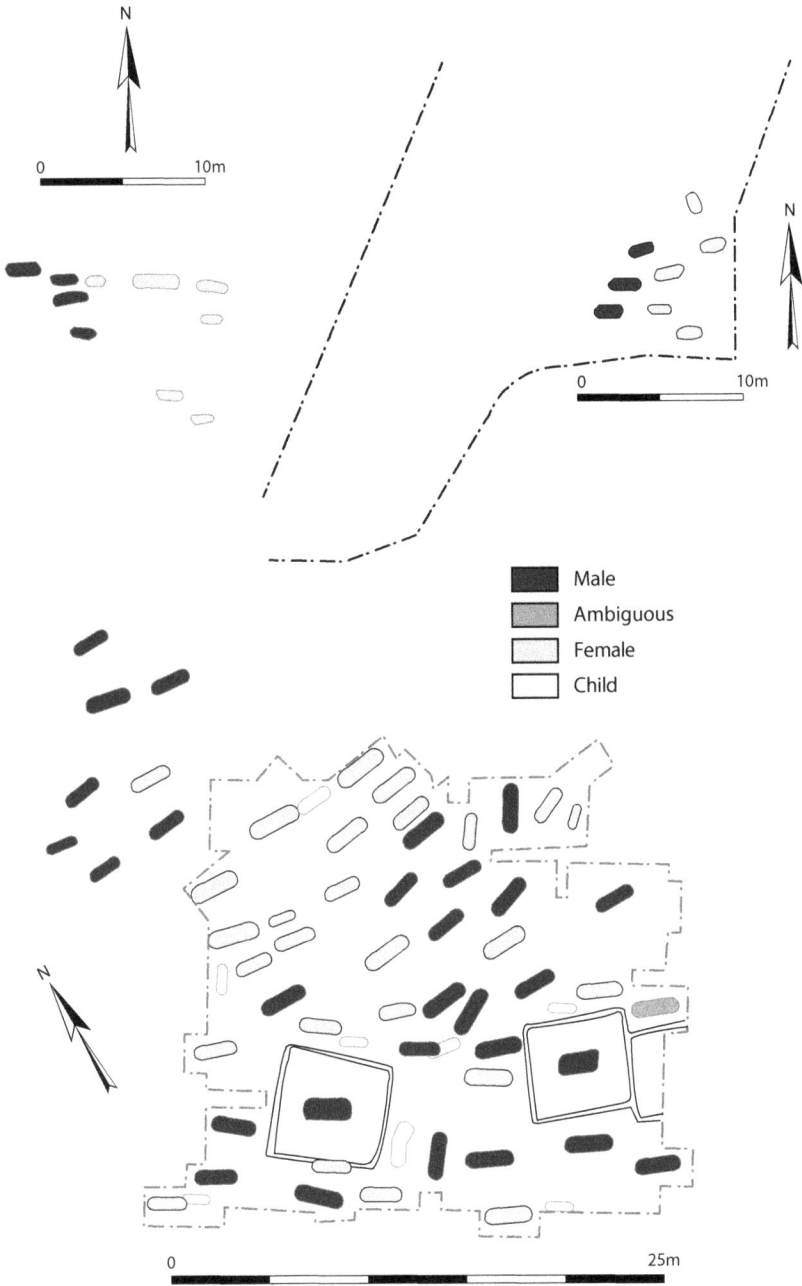

Figure 4.9 Broadway Hill, Worcestershire (top left), Winterbourne Gunner, near Salisbury, Wiltshire (top right), and Lyminge II, Kent (bottom). In each of these cemeteries male and female graves were located in different parts of the site, creating a gender zoning within the known burials.

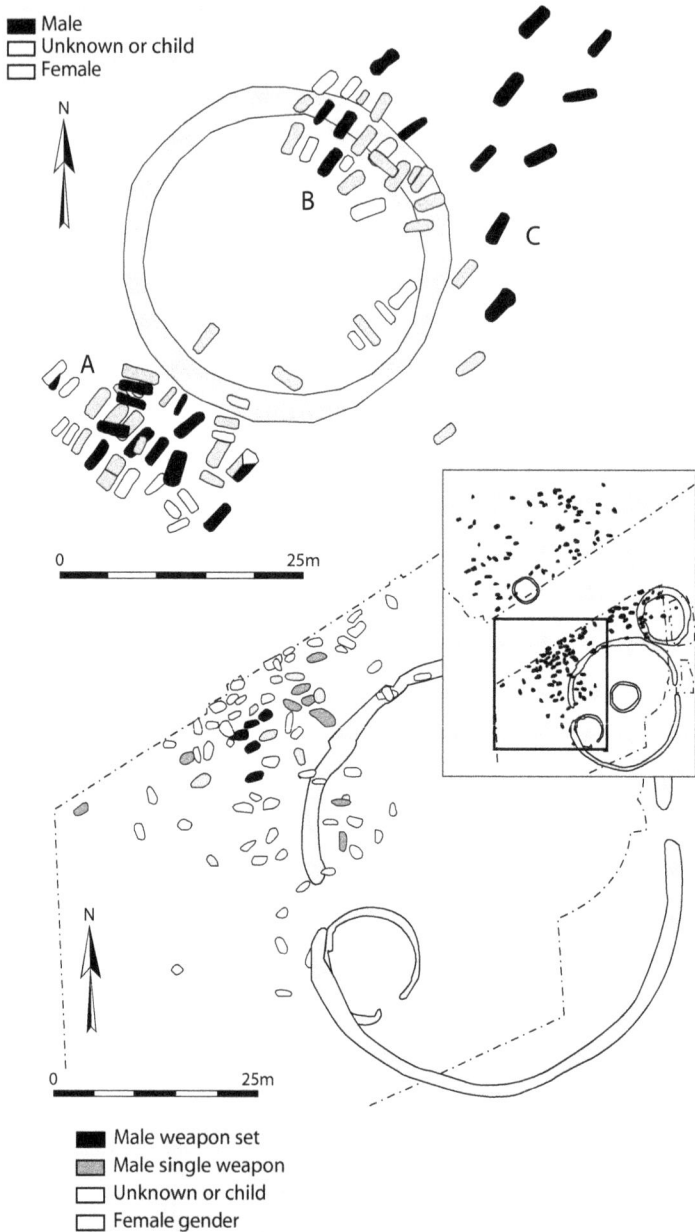

Figure 4.10 Deal, eastern Kent (top), and West Heslerton, East Yorkshire (bottom). At Deal, the two sixth-century plots, A and B, showed some internal clustering of gendered graves, with groups of males and females. This pattern was most evident in the later eastern group C, where all of the male graves were found in the northern area of the plot. At West Heslerton, the males with weapon sets were found in a group in the centre of the largest and wealthiest cluster of graves.

cemetery (Stoodley, 1999: 131). Penn and Brugmann agreed but argued that Westgarth Gardens cannot be organised into different plots for men, women and children (Penn and Brugmann, 2007: 86). However, the sixty-six burials, in sixty-one graves, do show strong gender segregation, with women buried to the north and men to the south. Interestingly, children's graves were placed between these two areas (Figure 4.11). This site does not appear to have been organised into different plots, but this was also not a complete cemetery, being one part of a larger site. This excavated area probably included just the core of the cemetery, identified because the metalwork was discovered with a metal detector, and subsequently seven male burials have been found to the north. A further burial was found 50 m to the east of the excavated cemetery, but the intervening area was not excavated (West, 1988: 2).

The Westgarth Gardens pattern is also seen elsewhere. Berinsfield is a good example of segregated zoning among elite inhumations: the core graves in plot A all had female artefacts, the core in plot B consisted of three male burials and just a single female grave (Figure 4.11) and the core in plot C consisted of two females and one male. This arrangement focused on gender affinity, and was the deliberate result of decisions and negotiations made by the people who attended each funeral and who contributed to the cemetery architecture. Not all cemeteries had cores divided by gender – Norton and Wakerley, for example, showed no internal subdivision – and so the decision to segregate focal space by gender must have been the result of community-specific decisions affecting only individuals from affluent – and/or dominant – families.

There were probably identity motivations to divide cores (or plots) along gender lines, and small-scale gendered distributions were also evident in seventh-century cemeteries such as Bargates (male), Fonaby, Lincolnshire (female) and Snell's Corner (male) (Stoodley, 1999: 135). This bias or clustering in favour of one gender may have been the consequence of prejudice embedded in the expression of belonging to a particular local group who preferred to express male or female characteristics in funeral narrative. Specific costume was favoured for display in a mortuary drama whose most numerous participants would have been the immediate community and regional elite. This emphasis was intended to highlight the progress of a specific lineage though one gender line, defining a principal family as either matriarchal or patriarchal. In this scenario, members of the community who 'married in', or otherwise came from outside, would not have been placed in a central position. The differentiation shown was aimed at the regional audiences to whom the accentuation of gender-determined lineages would have been significant.

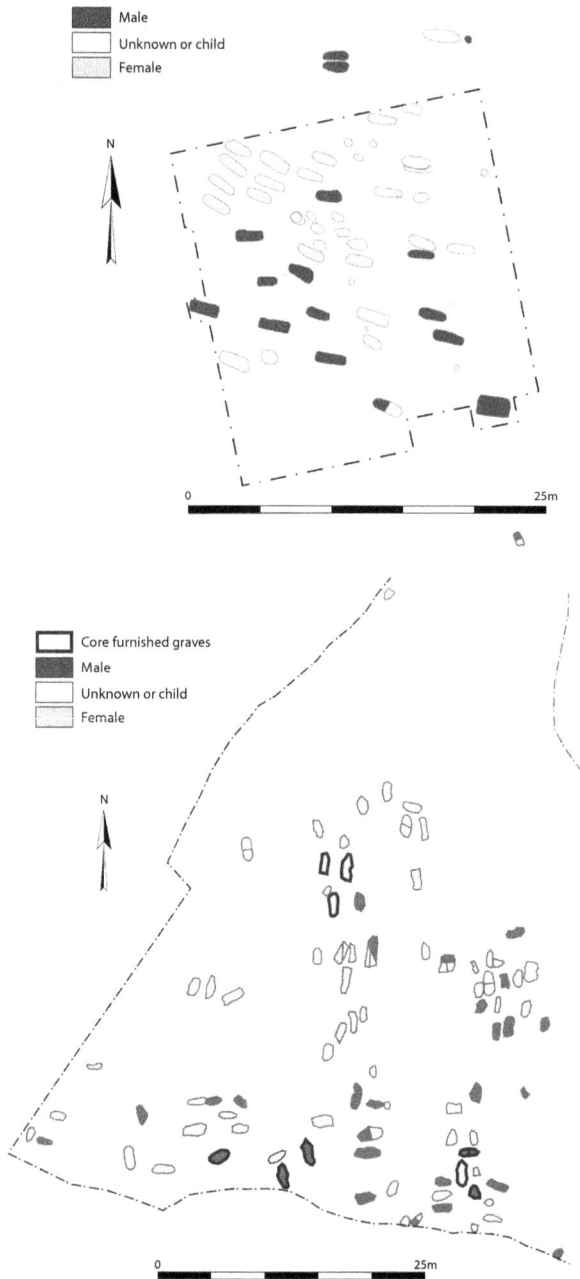

Figure 4.11 Westgarth Gardens, Suffolk (top), and Berinsfield, Oxfordshire (bottom). The burials at Westgarth Gardens seem to have been divided into male and female spaces. This excavated area was probably a core area within a large plot and a larger cemetery. The segregation of elite burials is seen at Berinsfield too.

Another way that gender was emphasised can also be seen by comparing cemeteries. This can be seen clearly in a sample of twenty cemeteries with good skeletal and artefact data (Table 4.2). In these cemeteries, five show significant proportions of gendered artefacts to biological sexes, and a further site shows borderline significance. For example, from the identifiable adult skeletons at Apple Down, forty-three were male and forty-four were female. This was not an unusual ratio; however, sixteen male skeletons were buried with weapons and only six female skeletons with female-gendered gravegoods. This is statistically significant and shows a deliberate localised bias against interring females with gendered objects.

Apple Down is the only cemetery from this sample with a bias against the female gender; the other four or five sites show the reverse bias, with a greater proportion of female to male skeletons found with female-gendered artefacts. These sites include Broughton Lodge (Nottinghamshire), Castledyke South (North Lincolnshire), Norton and Sewerby. West Heslerton is a borderline case and, with a ratio of sixty-nine females to twenty-four males, nearly three times the number of gendered-female burials to male burials, it may be that this is a

Table 4.2 The ratio of sex to gender and its statistical significance

Cemetery	Sex (skeleton)		Gender (goods)		Fisher's Test p value	Significant
	M	F	M	F		
Apple Down	43	44	16	06	0.041	Yes
Barrington	58	40	22	21	0.241	No
Beckford B	34	55	26	31	0.236	No
Berinsfield	30	32	19	11	0.130	No
Blacknall Field	29	32	18	26	0.318	No
Broughton Lodge	6	12	37	25	0.044	Yes
Castledyke South	51	69	13	35	0.045	Yes
Deal	17	16	18	16	0.550	No
Dover	129	117	58	54	0.500	No
Empingham II	43	38	44	52	0.209	No
Finglesham	76	75	27	27	0.546	No
Great Chesterford	22	43	18	37	0.530	No
Kingsworthy	32	39	19	12	0.098	No
Lechlade	52	89	29	57	0.369	No
Market Lavington	10	09	09	07	0.550	No
Norton	32	27	10	41	0.0002	Yes
Sewerby	11	12	04	17	0.044	Yes
Wakerley	18	31	18	33	0.523	No
West Heslerton	15	20	24	69	0.0509	Borderline
Westgarth Gardens	24	22	21	12	0.217	No

definite bias in favour of the female gender. In the above discussion, gendered artefacts are taken to include male graves with a weapon, such as a sword, shield or spear, and female graves with a single brooch or pair of brooches. To avoid the chronological drop-off in brooch burials at the end of the sixth century, seventh-century graves with pairs of dress pins and significant pendants (for example, see Finglesham) have been included as gendered graves.

Note that Table 4.2 uses Fisher's exact test, which is more accurate than chi-square, both because it is an exact test, not an estimate, and because it is also accurate with small numbers. The equation for Fisher's exact test is $(p = (a+b)!(c+d)!(a+c)!(b+d)!/n!a!b!c!d1)$ (Fisher, 1922). For this test, significance is taken to be a p value of 0.05.

Alongside the localised bias in favour of a specific gender expression, seen above, there is also evidence for differences in the treatment of one biological sex over another, and two sites from this sample of twenty are numerical outliers for biological sex ratios. Both Great Chesterford and Lechlade contain nearly twice as many women to men, although the proportions of gendered graves remain within expected norms. If we consider these two sites to be abnormal, then the ratio of male-to-female sexed skeletons from the remaining eighteen sites is 658:690 (48.8 per cent men, 51.2 per cent women). Interestingly, in the 2011 census the British population was 63.182 million, 31.029 million men (49.1 per cent) and 32.153 million women (50.9 per cent) (Office of National Statistics, 2012: tab 1). The Great Chesterford and Lechlade variation is statistically significant, and so these populations were not the result of a random variation but of deliberate behaviour. The female corpse was more likely to be interred in these sites and, given that whole areas of early Anglo-Saxon cemeteries are not defined by sex or gender differences, as discussed above, this is unlikely to be the result of under-excavation.

Contingency tables 4.3 and 4.4 outline the data for Great Chesterford and Lechlade respectively. The predicted value was calculated using the proportion of male-to-female graves from eighteen cemeteries and calculating the expected proportion based on the size of each site. The null hypothesis for these tests asked if the proportion of men to women was an expectable average or 'normal' value based on the sample. To check the results given by Fisher's exact test, Pearson's chi-square

Table 4.3 Male-to-female contingency table: Great Chesterford

	Males	Females	Totals
actual numbers	43	22	65
predicted numbers	32	33	65
total	75	55	

Table 4.4 Male-to-female contingency table: Lechlade

	Males	Females	Totals
actual numbers	52	89	141
predicted numbers	69	72	141
total	121	161	

was also used to test this hypothesis at $P = < .05$. It was rejected at Great Chesterford with a P value of $p = .05$ [$X^2(1, n = 65) = 3.8$], and also at Lechlade, where the P value was $p = .04$ [$X^2(1, n = 141) = 4.18$], so the larger populations of women at these sites were significant and were probably the result of deliberate cultural behaviours.

Anglo-Saxon burial customs allowed patterns in the placement of gendered graves, but these are not as pronounced as the patterns displayed in the large cremation cemeteries on the Continent. Süderbrarup in Angeln Schleswig-Holstein, Germany, contained 1,234 second- to sixth-century graves with predominantly male gravegoods and a biological population which included 51 per cent male graves *versus* ten per cent female graves; the rest remained unsexed or were juvenile (Bantelmann, 1988; Wahl, 1988). By contrast, Bordesholm, near Kiel in Schleswig-Holstein, contained over 5,000 cremations with predominantly female gravegoods, including a range of brooch types. It was in use from the Roman Iron Age to the fifth and sixth centuries but, with just one martial object, a single scabbard chape, this was a predominantly female-gendered cemetery (Saggau, 1981; Saggau, 1986; Wahl, 1988). This comparison highlights an important difference: early Anglo-Saxon cemeteries expressed limited organisation by gender and, unlike these large continental cemeteries, they did not serve whole regions. Anglo-Saxon differentiation was specific to a particular localised elite, who interred their dead as core burials at the centre of grave plots. Internal patterns were evident at Broadstairs I, Lyminge II, Winterbourne Gunner, Bargates, Fonaby, Snell's Corner, Lyminge, Deal, Orpington, Berinsfield, West Heslerton, Westgarth Gardens and Polhill – with a specific bias towards female-gendered burials at Broughton Lodge, Castledyke South, Norton and Sewerby, and possibly at West Heslerton too. In these sites the placement of furnished burials sent a message to a regional audience, just as it did in continental migration-period cemeteries; but, rather than highlighting the joint inheritance of a community, these funerals focused on a specific lineage, the local elite family, and conveyed the value that the family placed on gender in this locality, so that gender expression is contingent on social group and location. Indeed, at Apple Down it was the male lineage which dominated the cemetery. At Great Chesterford and at Lechlade, however, there were significantly more women in proportion to men than would be expected from a single community. Presumably, women's bodies were specifically transported to these sites for burial, a phenomenon which is also seen in age differentiation.

Age

Developments in gender archaeology have led to an increased focus on life course and, in particular, infancy (see Sayer, 2014; Crawford, 1999, 2000, 2011). There are differences in the distribution of infant graves in later Anglo-Saxon sites. Minsters and the later-emerging parish church-yards were more likely to attract infant burials than contemporary field cemeteries, and many infant burials were found around the church or under the eaves, for example, at Raunds, Northamptonshire, Cherry Hinton, Cambridgeshire, and Tanner's Row, West Yorkshire (Sayer, 2012; Hadley, 2011). When looking at earlier sites, a number of authors have suggested that the style of a child's burial and their body position often mimic those of adults in close proximity, either just the women or both men and women (Pader, 1982). However, there remains a problem. Few studies have looked at the distribution of ages in cemeteries with the intention of deriving patterns. Many reports simply state that children are under-represented in early Anglo-Saxon cemeteries (Buckberry, 2000; Lucy, 1994). Penn and Brugmann even warned against such investigations based on the distribution of graves at the partly excavated Norton cemetery (Penn and Brugmann, 2007: 88). Stoodley has investigated the ages of furnished graves at Deal, Pewsey and Norton. He observed just one pattern at Norton and noticed that 'in each of the main plots the burials of children, but also youths, are on the outer edges, with the adult burials making up the core' (Stoodley, 2011: 654).

In many cemetery sites children, particularly infants, are absent or in fewer numbers than expected. For example, the cemetery at Alwalton, Cambridgeshire, was a small cemetery of around thirty-six graves with just two children, both found disarticulated in hollows and pits having been disturbed (Gibson, 2007). But under-representation is only part of the situation, and there were significant differences between cemeteries in how infants' and children's graves had been managed (Sayer, 2014). In the majority of cases, Norton included, there was no obvious pattern-ing to the distribution of specific age groups, even children, who were consistently distributed throughout early medieval cemeteries. However, perhaps for underlying social reasons, several cemeteries stand out.

As we saw in Chapter 1, at Apple Down the burials of infants and children seem to have been spread around the cemetery, but there was a specific concentration of burials in the middle of the site, clustered along-side a similar concentration of adults over the age of 45 (Figure 4.12).

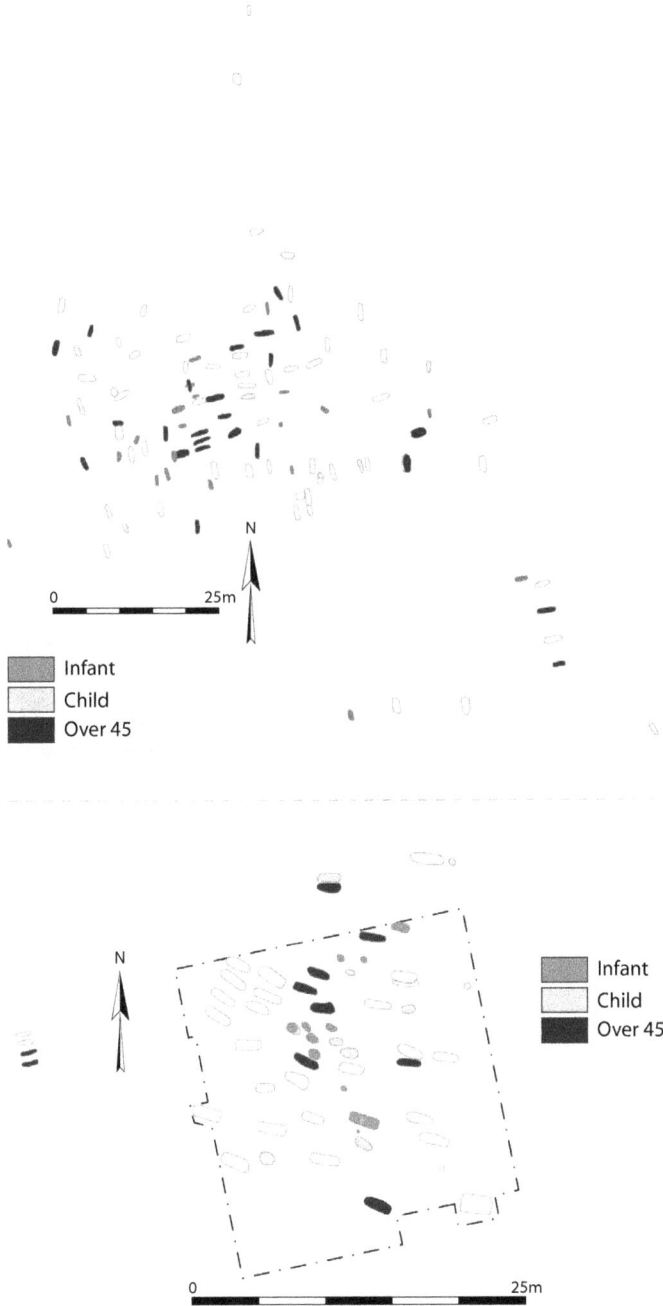

Figure 4.12 Apple Down, West Sussex (top), and Westgarth Gardens, Suffolk (bottom). These two cemeteries had a concentration of infants, or infants and children, associated with graves of older adult.

Many of these adults were also part of the furnished core at the centre of the cemetery and most of them were on the same orientation, a strategy that defined the central area of the site. Westgarth Gardens contained a similar pattern, with a core of furnished burials divided into a male (south) and female (north) zone. This core seems to have included a cluster of older adults, and in its centre was placed a group of infants and children. Similarly, the Oakington cemetery, in Cambridgeshire, had a particular distribution of infants and children in the south of the site (Figure 4.13). In these three cases the sites included infants and children distributed throughout, but with a particular concentration in one area, sometimes associated with older adults. This pattern was also seen at Morning Thorpe where plot B, the western of two wealthy plots, had a figurative barrier of furnished graves defining its extent and inside the boundary established by these graves were the smallest graves, suggesting that many infants and children could be found within the middle of this plot. Unfortunately, however, bone preservation was very poor (see Chapter 6).

At these three sites children were placed within central, or off-centre, zones within the cemetery. At Great Chesterford, Essex, a different pattern was evident. Great Chesterford was excavated between 1953 and 1955 and revealed 161 inhumations and thirty-three cremations (Evison, 1994). As outlined in Chapter 2, the site was organised with a recurring pattern based on the orientation of graves with tight clusters, and interestingly infant and child graves were found in particular zones (Figure 4.13). To the north a cluster of thirty-five children occupied a wide area of approximately 35 sq.m interspersed with adults, but with two specific concentrations of infants in two zones: one consisted of seven infants, the other of eight. A second cluster of twenty infants and children was placed in the south of the cemetery, although this was interspersed with adults. There were also specific clusters of infant graves. The largest, to the north of this cluster, contained seven graves. Importantly, what defined these two zones of infant burial was the comparative absence of infants and children in the cemetery's central area. This centre consisted of the furnished adult graves on an E/W orientation and the two most richly furnished graves.

Children and infants are often under-represented in cemeteries (Crawford, 1991; Buckberry, 2000), and so it is interesting that there were particular concentrations of them at Great Chesterford, Morning Thorpe, Westgarth Gardens and Oakington. In these sites there was a demographic over-representation of infants, where 11 per cent mortality was expected (Crawford, 1993; 2000; Sayer, 2014), and so they appear to have been central places to inter infants, and adults may have carried the children for some distance to be interred in a specific place. It is

Figure 4.13 Oakington, Cambridgeshire (lower left), and Great Chesterford, Essex (right). These two cemeteries had a distribution of infants and children throughout the cemetery and in particular zones. There were very few infants in the central areas at Great Chesterford, but there were clusters of them in the surrounding plots and zones. Equally, there was a particular grouping of infants' graves in the southern part of the Oakington cemetery.

interesting to see a similar pattern among women and infants, and in some places this *post mortem* mobility must have drawn women or infants from outside the immediate community, transported specifically for burial. Perhaps these social categories had more geographic mobility, moving between communities for marriage, or were associated with particular localised identity units.

Grave structures, identity and grave robbing

In East Kent there was a group of cemeteries, including Finglesham near Dover, Ozengell at Ramsgate, and St Peters and Bradstow School, both in Broadstairs, all of which had extra features used to distinguish particular burials (Hogarth, 1974). These features included two or more sockets cut out of the side of the graves, and ledges or sideboards cut into any or multiple-grave walls. A. C. Hogarth classified these structural features as integral to a grave and also identified external features such as postholes, ring ditches, curb slots or square ditches which are seen more widely across England. He considered that integral features should be regarded as later-seventh-century, although many examples, like grave 108 from Finglesham found with a ledge, are best dated to the first half of the seventh century, in the case of 108 because it contained a Marzinzik II.19b buckle (Marzinzik, 2003). The recent revised chronology of the mid-sixth and seventh-century graves simplified Marzinzik's typology and places many objects previously believed to be later into an earlier date range (Hines and Bayliss, 2013). This means that all of the graves with integral features can be dated to the whole seventh century and not just its twilight.

External features like ring ditches were certainly more common in these cemeteries, but they were also used in the sixth century (Shephard, 1979). The early antiquarian investigators William Stukeley, Bryan Faussett and James Douglas noted the presence of small mounds in many of their cemetery sites (Lucy, 1999: 101). Ring ditches were found in sites like Spong Hill (Hills *et al.*, 1984), or associated with cremations at Apple Down, Orsett (Essex), Springfield Lyons or Stifford Clays (Essex) (Down and Welch, 1990; Tyler, 1996: 108–13). The fifth- and sixth-century burials at Lechlade, Orpington and Oakington had small above-ground barrows which created a central place that focused attention. Without ring ditches these small mounds were not as obvious during excavation but their positioning over a grave meant that a space was left where other burials were not positioned because of the earth which surrounded them. These mounds were central places important to the cemetery narrative and so they also attracted satellite graves placed intentionally around them. The deliberate arrangement of space made barrows a focal point and a highly visual marker, used to convey messages about the deceased interred beneath them.

The sites from east Kent are particularly thought-provoking because these features were the foundation for structures, posts, canopies, planks or other visually identifiable features used alongside the preparation of a corpse and the furnishing of a grave in conveying the mortuary narrative. Sideboards, ledges and posthole features were deployed in these cemeteries, and probably others in Thanet and east Kent because each funeral influenced its participants. Within a regional setting, people from across these communities attended each other's funerals and witnessed the use of structures in funerary display; they also deployed them to enrich their own practice. Grave features are not well understood because many of the sites are only partially, or poorly, published (but see Avent, 1975: 4, 32; Evison, 1979: 69–83; Geake, 1997: 161–2; Hogarth, 1974; Klevnäs, 2013).

St Peters in Broadstairs was excavated between 1969 and 1971, in advance of an extension to the local authority refuse tip. Some 388 graves were identified and dated between the mid-sixth and mid-eighth centuries, with most dating to the seventh and eighth, although some of the cemetery remains unexcavated to the north-west of the site (Richardson, 2005: 15). The excavated graves from St Peters clustered with statistical significance at 4 m, but at that distance only one separate group of graves is visible to the north. However, just like Apple Down, Berinsfield, Petersfinger and Great Chesterford, this large cemetery was organised by grave orientation. At St Peters this is subtle, but nonetheless deliberate, with grave orientation varying slightly between E/W and NW/SE (Figure 4.14). This variation in axis divided the cemetery into three groups, B to the west with a NW/SE axis, A to the south with an E/W axis and C to the north-east divided from the rest of the cemetery by a significant gap and consisting of a series of rows with graves on an E/W axis. Notably, graves located on the edges of each of these plots were likely to be oriented differently, or in an indeterminate way. This was also evident in between the western and southern plots of graves, a particularly high-density area. In the middle of plots A and B several graves were located with significant (4 m or more) gaps, and many of these had satellite graves enveloping them, evidence that there were once barrows raised there. Interestingly, the graves with integral features were located in the highest-density areas of the site, particularly in between plots A and B, with only one associated with a grave that may have had a barrow (the only published, but much reproduced, plan is Hogarth, 1974). These integral-feature graves were positioned between barrows, between plots and not associated with the most prominent graves.

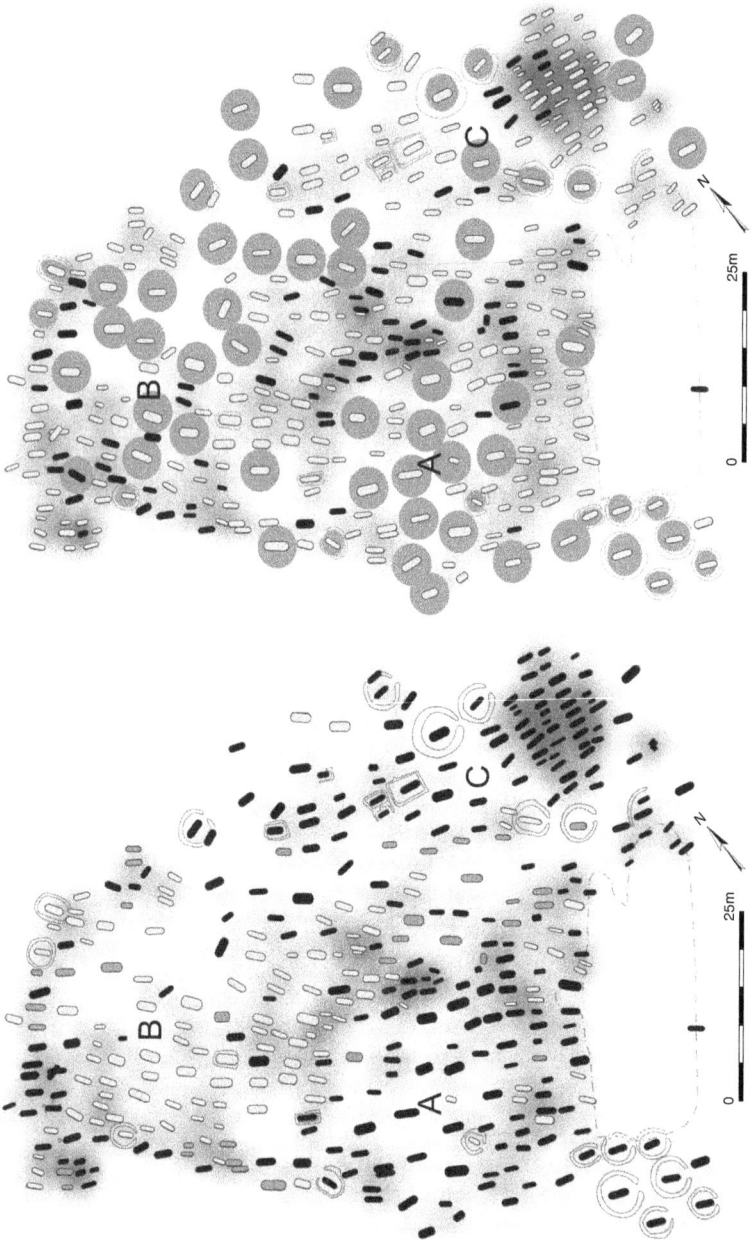

Figure 4.14 St Peters, Broadstairs, eastern Kent. Both plans show the clustering at 4 m. On the left-hand plan the orientation of the graves is marked as black for N-W/S-E, light grey for E/W, and dark grey are graves in-between the two. On the right-hand plan, small barrows have been marked where the graves had a 4 m gap and had satellite graves around them; in black are graves with integral features.

Similarly to St Peters, the large cemetery at Finglesham deployed integral and external features to highlight a number of graves. Finglesham is located about eighteen miles (29 km) from Broadstairs, just south of the village after which it was named. This site was first identified during quarrying and was investigated in 1928 and 1929 when thirty-eight individuals were discovered; unfortunately part of the northern edge of the site had been lost. The remaining cemetery was excavated by Chadwick Hawkes between 1958 and 1967, taking the total up to 254 inhumations, ranging in date across the sixth and seventh centuries. The excavated cemetery is shaped like an irregular quadrilateral, with the eastern and southern edges having been identified (Chadwick, 1958; Chadwick Hawkes, 1977; 1981; 1982; Chadwick Hawkes et al., 1965; Chadwick Hawkes and Grainger, 2006; Sayer, 2009). Burials at Finglesham clustered at 4 m and were divided into four plots A, B, C and D (Figure 4.15). There were significant gaps between the four plots, and even at its narrowest the gap between A and C or D and B this was 4 m.

A number of burials at Finglesham show evidence of having had medium-sized or small barrows over the top of them. During excavation the soils associated with grave 116 indicated the presence of a mound, and many graves sported ring ditches around their periphery (Chadwick Hawkes and Grainger, 2006). At Finglesham, like Orpington or St Peters, some of the sixth-century graves survived with a considerable gap left around them, with other burials that surrounded these spaces fossilising the shape of the now absent barrow. These satellite graves were located deliberately with respect to the barrow burial they encircled. Armed with this knowledge Grainger examined the space around each grave to explore the location of additional barrows. Regrettably, this investigation was never published, but these barrows were presented as part of Chadwick Hawkes' ongoing deliberations about the site (Chadwick Hawkes, 1982). As at St Peters, the Ripley's K-function analysis of Finglesham showed that graves clustered at 4 m, dividing the site into four parts: a northern group, plot A, and three predominantly seventh-century plots, plot B to the west, plot C to the east and plot D to the south. Many of the barrows that Grainger identified had been located within significant gaps in the cemetery plan; that is, 4 m away from other graves. Many of these barrow graves were also positioned with differing orientations to those adjacent. As at Orpington, these graves were placed like this deliberately to distinguish them, sharing their axes as part of a mnemonic strategy which employed a multi-layered visual connotation that created an association between them.

Finglesham also had integral features, and these were used in the same way as at St Peters (Figure 4.15). Plot A included just one grave with a posthole and this was a satellite burial around the northern

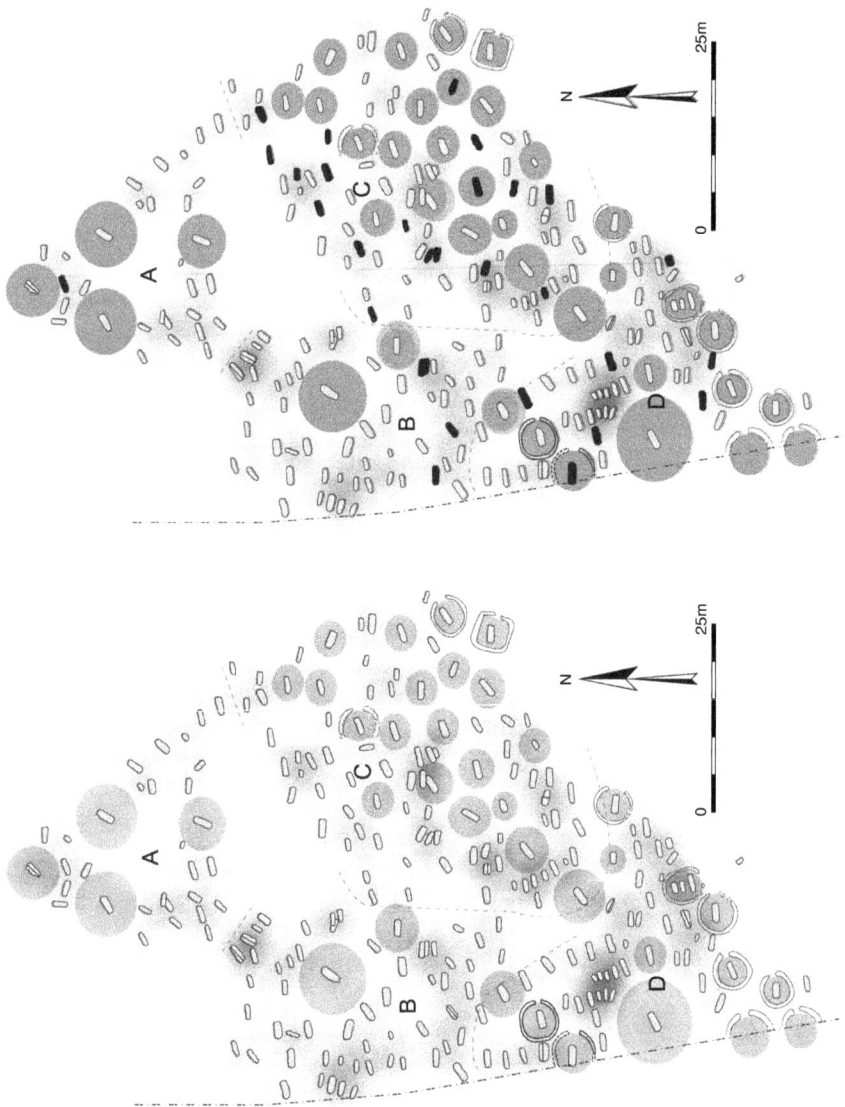

Figure 4.15 Finglesham, eastern Kent. Both plans show the clustering at 4 m, and the left-hand plan shows how the clustering of graves defined four plots, A–D. On the right-hand plan, the location of barrows has been inferred where the graves had a 4 m gap and had satellite graves around them; in black are graves with integral features.

barrow. Plots B and D included a greater quantity and variety of integral features, including five posthole graves, four ledge burials and two with sideboards. All eleven were found between barrow graves; just one grave, 93, included a posthole but it was located under a small barrow within a ring ditch. Most integral-feature graves were found in plot C, and almost all of these were in satellite burials. There were just two exceptions, graves 151 and 161, both the graves of adult women without gendered artefacts. Just as at St Peters, the graves with integral features were not often associated with central places, but surrounded them. In both cemeteries these graves were found in the highest-density parts of the cemetery. Ledges or sideboards supported structures or planks that were used to convey a specific message. In the majority of cases at both Finglesham and St Peters, integral grave structures and external structures, like barrows, were only rarely found on the same grave. As a result the two types of display must have been largely separate and so conveyed similar, but contrasting messages.

The dissimilarity of graves with different types of feature is also seen in how the graves were treated after burial. Alison Klevnäs (2013), identified an intensifying outbreak of deliberate grave robbery in sixth- and seventh-century Kent. This activity targeted wealthy burials, and the robbers' intention was to destroy the artefacts, she argued, and thus obliterate the memory and the power of a grave. This behaviour was not aimed at personal enrichment, but at damaging the reputation and influence of surviving relatives. Grave robbing is seen outside Kent, in cemeteries like Barrington, Cambridgeshire; Spong Hill, Norfolk; Bloodmoor Hill, Suffolk; Apple Down, West Sussex; Winnall II, Hampshire; and Chadlington, Oxfordshire, among others. But in Kent it took place on a larger scale, involving fifteen known sites and over 200 graves; around 20 per cent of the graves may have been robbed. Klevnäs (2013: 83) suggested that this phenomenon was localised, the result of a feud and conflict between competing families. Ozengell, Bradstow School, Finglesham and St Peters were among the most heavily robbed cemeteries (see Table 4.5) and they also contained barrows or integral features (Figures 4.16 and 4.17).

Table 4.5 Targets of grave robbers: barrows and graves with integral features

Cemetery	Graves investigated	Number robbed	Proportion robbed	Barrows robbed (total)	Integral features robbed (total)
Bradstow School	89	18	20%	12 (19)	n/a
Finglesham	237	17	7%	8 (45)	3 (28)
Ozengell	89	39	44%	n/a	2 (12)
St Peters	388	54	14%	26 (66)	5 (83)

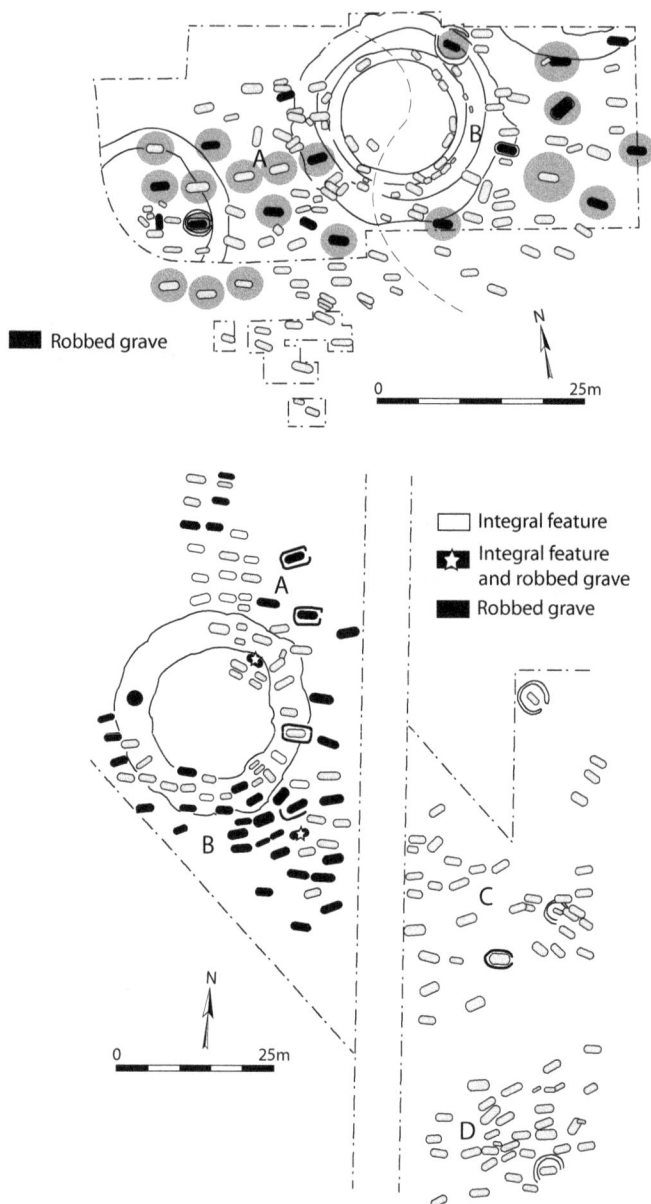

Figure 4.16 Bradstow School (top) and Ozengell (bottom), both in eastern Kent. Both cemeteries had been robbed in antiquity. At Bradstow School, the robbers targeted graves with visible barrows, whereas at Ozengell the robbers appear to have deliberately targeted particular graves: plot B was heavily robbed, but plot A was less heavily robbed and interestingly had more integral features. Just two graves with integral features were robbed. We do not know the extent of robbing in plots C and D.

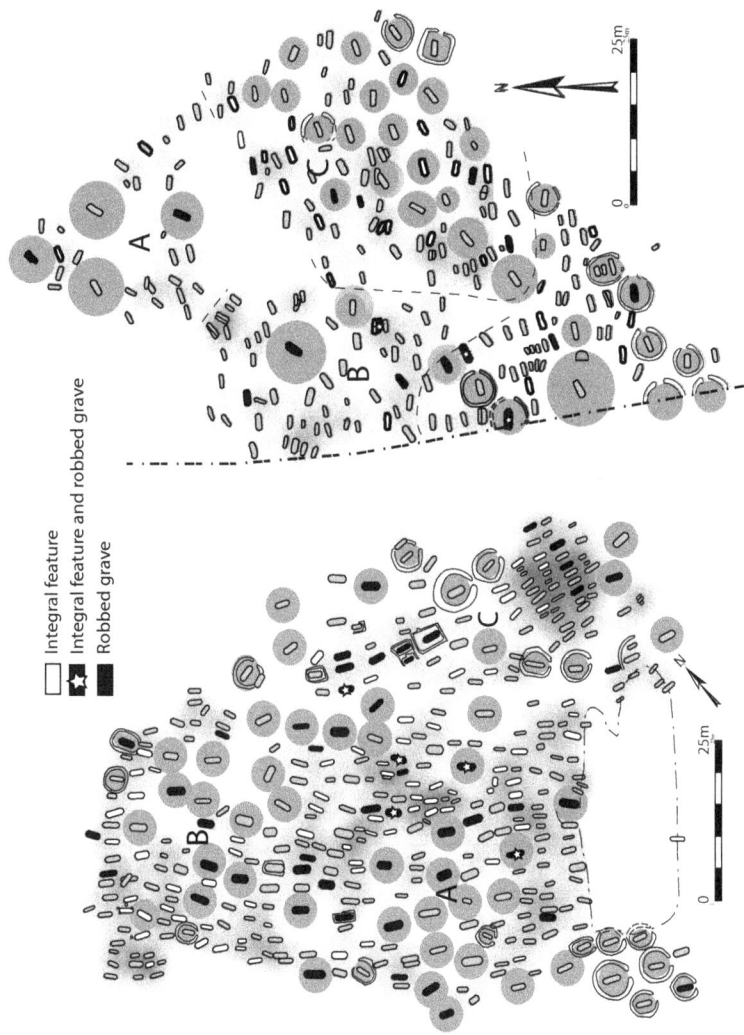

Figure 4.17 St Peters, Broadstairs, and Finglesham, both in eastern Kent. In these cemeteries, robbers were deliberately targeting individuals, particularly those under mounds. The same robbers also avoided graves with integral features. At St Peters, just five graves with integral features were robbed, and at Finglesham just three graves with integral features were robbed.

In the cemeteries at Bradstow School, Finglesham and St Peters, it was possible to use spatial statistics, and the evidence of surrounding graves, to predict the location of additional barrows. The graves with barrows and other external features were more frequently robbed than burials with solely integral features. With forty-six robbed barrows and just ten graves with integral features ransacked, this contrast is striking and statistically significant. The calculation using Fisher's Exact Test ($p = (a+b)!(c+d)!(a+c)!(b+d)!/n!a!b!c!d1$) and the contingency table (Table 4.6) results in a p value of less than 0.0001. So the association between these variables is extremely statistically significant, indicating deliberate selection of barrows over graves with integral features.

Ozengell and Bradstow School are awkward inclusions because publications are still outstanding. It is not known whether they included barrows or integral features, though it is possible to do the same calculation for just Finglesham and St Peters. In that scenario (see Table 4.7) the p value is also less than 0.0001, indicating deliberate selection of barrows over graves with features.

In these east Kent cemeteries, grave robbers were deliberately targeting graves with external features like ditches or barrows. Interestingly, the association between robbing any grave and robbing one with integral features is also significant. The calculation using Fisher's exact test and the contingency table (Table 4.8) results in a p value of 0.0210. So the association between these variables is statistically significant, indicating the deliberate avoidance of graves with integral features by grave robbers.

Table 4.6 Grave robbers' preference: graves with integral features v. barrows at Bradstow School, Finglesham, Ozengell and St Peters

	Robbed	Not robbed	Total
barrow	46	84	130
integral feature	10	113	123
total	56	197	253

Table 4.7 Grave robbers' preference: graves with integral features v. barrows at Finglesham and St Peters

	Robbed	Not robbed	Total
barrow	34	77	111
integral feature	8	103	111
total	42	180	222

Table 4.8 Grave robbers' preference: flat graves v. graves with integral features

	Robbed	Not robbed	Total
flat grave	128	675	803
integral feature	10	113	123
total	138	788	926

Table 4.9 Grave robbers' preference: flat graves v. graves with barrows

	Robbed	Not robbed	Total
barrow	34	77	111
flat grave	128	675	803
total	162	752	914

In a similar vein there was a deliberate selection of barrows over flat graves to rob (Table 4.9) with a p value of less than 0.0001, indicating that the grave robbers were deliberately selecting barrows over other graves to destroy.

Undeniably, raiders targeted rich graves, but they also purposely avoided those which had integral features. The only way someone could know that a burial had integral features is if they participated in the funeral, and so the grave robbers must have been active members of these communities. Graves with barrows and external features were selected because they had been identified as significant places. However, it is unlikely that robbers were aware of internal features in the same way and so the deliberate avoidance of these graves was the result of a related purpose. The robbers were not just selecting noticeable graves; they must have had semiotic knowledge of the cemetery and used this to maliciously target specific individuals – those ancestors important to specific parts of community identity.

The Ozengell cemetery is notable because graves with integral features were more often placed to the north of the site, and robbed graves were found to the south of a pre-existing ring ditch (Figure 4.16). At Finglesham and St Peters, these integral-feature burials were found around central graves, and focused on them, as discussed above (Figure 4.17). Ozengell is reminiscent of cemeteries divided into particular zones, with the northern plots subdivided into two areas, one identity group south of the barrow and one to the north, whereas at Finglesham and St Peters this second identity group was closely associated with certain individuals. In fact, at Finglesham only two of these satellite burials, grave 84, with a pendant, and grave 170, with a single small leaf-shaped spear (type C5; Swanton, 1974) displayed limited gender identity. In these Kentish cemeteries there were three distinct rituals within the cemetery:

1. burials with gendered objects or burial wealth in flat graves or barrows;
2. burials with integral features and objects, but rarely with gendered objects; and
3. burials in flat graves with limited or no gravegoods.

However, not all significant burials included objects, depending on chronological localised trends.

Elaborate funerals with marked graves recreated personhood for the deceased in the eyes of the funerary party and at the same time they reinforced old identities or contributed to the creation of new ones. Marked burials became central places within the cemetery, and their visible destruction was symbolic because it acted as a form of iconoclasm, disempowering the agency of that central place and shared ancestor. External features marked these central grave sites, but integral features were not often incorporated in them; moreover, graves that did have integral features must have been part of a limited funerary ritual carried out by a select group within the community. Perhaps these secondary rites recreated the personhood for the deceased or a select group, but in using integral features this group was not creating a central place. Integral features were perhaps more common among subgroups within the population, but importantly they had enough autonomy to have their own distinctive burial ritual.

Semiotics and social differentiation in cemetery space

One of the most useful analytical tools available to archaeologists is difference, and quite understandably gravegoods provide a useful vehicle to understand the differences that existed between graves. However, gravegoods are not the only difference present within mortuary archaeology. In Chapter 2 we discussed the semiotics of mortuary display, and the subsequent scales at which these tools operated. Body position, for example, is a characteristic of an individual burial, but we rarely find clusters of burials which shared body positions. Body position does not correspond with age, gender, status or time of death, any of which might suggest a wider cultural significance (see Pader, 1982; Faull, 1977 and Chadwick Hawkes, 1977; Mui, 2018). As a result, body position was probably meaningful to the mortuary party and those who laid out a corpse, but not necessarily to the extended narrative which outlived the funeral. Corresponding with that discordance, there are other *leitmotifs* within and between cemeteries – for example, personal characteristics like age and gender – that seem to have been an influence on where an individual was buried, depending on who that person was; the organisation of a cemetery was determined at a community level, and its layout provided a visual mnemonic used as an aid in the narrative description. This created mortuary semiotics which employed lasting devices, like external features, used to turn a cemetery into a scopic regime, a series of culturally constructed ways of seeing. Identities operated dissimilarly at different times. Finglesham and Orpington, for instance, included graves without any burial wealth whatsoever, but these same burials manifested significant agency because later graves, some furnished, were positioned at satellite locations around them. At both Finglesham and Orpington these significant graves were probably covered in small barrow mounds because they commanded some considerable visual authority.

The majority of cemeteries consisted of multiple groups of graves, either densely or loosely arranged into plots. In many graves the distribution of material culture varied between plots, and the density of graves was a way to distinguish between these groups, for example as at West Heslerton (see Chapter 2). Some grave plots included richer graves and this inclusion of visually signalled wealth made a statement about the individual, but also about the social group that constructed that plot. The inclusion of wealth in a grave was a socially coded statement, just like the erection of burial mounds, and seems to have been a significant part of how the plots were organised. Many cemeteries contained one plot which was wealthier than the others – for example, at Wakerley, Apple Down, West Heslerton, Great Chesterford or Holborough. Within many of these plots, wealthy graves were positioned in central zones among similar graves; alternatively they may have been dispersed, marking new focal points for each generation of new interments. However, the presence or absence of gravegoods is only part of the story and the location of graves was an important part of that display. Burial plots were not static entities, but themselves exhibited a number of different characteristics. In any given cemetery these characteristics could include a core of wealthy burials, or significant graves dispersed but identified as central points. Some sites had no core of wealthy graves at all – for example, Holborough.

Previous scholars have suggested that individual graves could be compared and ranked in hierarchal identity bands (Arnold, 1981; Steuer, 1968; Christlein, 1973; and Shephard, 1979). This is problematic, but the idea persists, at least in principle. Archaeologists regularly consider high-wealth burials as being of higher-status individuals (for examples, see Blacknall Field, in Annable and Eagles, 2010). However, gender, age and life course, as well as situational, political, regional and status identities, all played a role within the conglomerate, multi-layered mesh of identities that made up a *persona*. As a result, elements of an individual's identity intersected with artefact selection and spatial, technological and consumption practices during a single commemoration event. Equally, these identities were not internal or individualistic, but rather they resulted from membership of social and community groups and it is these groups who constructed burial events. Plots and satellite burials were mortuary technologies used to highlight group affiliation. Where cemeteries had multiple plots they highlighted nested group affiliations, sub-units within local identities. Core groups and barrow burials highlighted particular individuals within those mortuary populations, many from different generations. Burial plots consisted of many individuals with a mixture of ages, genders and identities, but there was also variation between plots within cemeteries.

As we saw at Leighton Buzzard III, Great Chesterford, Wakerley and Finglesham, there was hierarchy to group affiliation, and some plots had core burials creating mnemonic regimes for regional display, whereas others did not. These local community arrangements highlighted one primary group and one or two subsidiary groups, differentiated because they employed separate plots with less organisation and less focus on funerary narratives for retelling. These systems created a scopic regime for each site, and the messages embedded in these systems extended beyond the local site, creating a regional and pan-regional visual experience that defined each early Anglo-Saxon cemetery, and defined specific groups by their ancestral heritage. Sites like West Heslerton, Broadway Hill in Hereford and Worcester, Winterbourne Gunner near Salisbury, Lyminge II, Westgarth Gardens, Berinsfield, Deal, Bargates, Fonaby or Snell's Corner separated groups of gendered individuals into specific places, highlighting male or female characteristics in central places, and such arrangements may have been a way to define key lines of inheritance within dominant families. These recognisable structures drew on local and cultural tropes, and would have served to distinguish elite individuals and affiliate them with the living community who employed (and returned to) a cemetery for funerals and other social events. In some regions, particular cemeteries became central places for identity groups that existed within a broader community and encouraged the transportation of specific bodies, women and infants, to a specific burial place, probably because lingering associations and identities persisted after marriage, birth and death.

The inherent visual character of each grave cluster, and each cemetery, tells the story of a particular community and a particular social group. Wealthier plots seem to have included a greater depth of hierarchical expression: plots at Finglesham included multiple inhumation rites, barrows, integral features and furnished burials, and at Apple Down these rites included central burials, cremations or peripheral burials, with wealthy graves in a core at the centre of the cemetery. This was part of a cemetery's scopic regime and was used to identify significant community ancestors by their location and visual characteristics, which highlighted multiple aspects of community identities, those that its members felt were important. But with this signalling came a price, and the localised feuds between competing units extended to iconoclasm, leaving graves ransacked and objects broken, targeted because they had been important to how that community defined itself. This was particularly prevalent in Kent, and in Merovingian cemeteries, but it may have had a wider impact on funerary behaviour, affecting local decisions whether to bury the dead with objects, or under mounds, in earthen cemeteries, and eventually led to the decline of the furnished burial.

5

Intonation on the individual

Introduction

As archaeologists working in contemporary theoretical paradigms, we tend to look for the individual through discourses and cultural performances around personhood, material culture, gender or age (Fowler, 2004; Lucy, 1997; Martin, 2014; Felder, 2015). In part this research priority is driven by a twenty-first century perspective, which focuses on social questions through a lens of contemporary individualism. However, the individual may not always have been created within this frame. Who is the individual within a historic lineage, a large household or an extended kinship system, for example? Additionally, despite the specificity of archaeological discourse, social categories do not intersect cleanly with each other and there can be significant overlaps and grey areas.

In the shoe example discussed in the first chapter, a skateboarder had a particular pattern of wear to their skate shoes, and this acted as a semiotic device recognisable to other skaters. However, skating is not just an identity; it is also a pastime and an attitude or a social activity (Hockey *et al.*, 2013; Ingold, 2010). Similarly, like weapon use in the early Anglo-Saxon period, skating may expose a person to injury significant enough to cause skeletal trauma. Skating as an activity may be more common among members of certain ethnic or social/ economic groups, or genders. A professional skater, for example, might have achieved their status helped by their economic background, which allowed them time to practise, or because some value systems of classes or families valued the activity or sporting achievements where others did not. Moreover, an individual skater might be unique, defying the usual social, economic or attitude boundaries of others. Hypothetically, a skateboarder might be buried with the board they had used, but if the people making the decisions at the funeral were not themselves skaters they might not choose to include it, or they might position it without the knowledge of a skater. As an activity, skateboarding may take place outside of, or in parallel with, other identities. It may be linked to life course stages, practised by adolescents or young adults more than children or the elderly. A skateboarder might not be one at all times – for example, when returning home to family or to the household to eat, where their primary identity is that of son or daughter. Skateboarders might have different biological backgrounds, familial or ethnic, and so their bodies might be different heights and/or different shapes to those of their peers. They might socialise with other skaters and so might meet a partner though that activity and might marry that person, but they might also meet their partner though education, employment, social networks or family, or by prior arrangement. Skateboarding is a physical activity, a community and an identity. However, it is also an expression of individuality, and at the same time involves membership of a network of other skaters. But a person does not have to be part of that network to own a skateboard, to skate or to have skating paraphernalia placed in a mortuary context. An aspiration, a gift or a key relationship also might bring skating material culture to the grave.

Similarly, a weapon burial may be one part of an identity which is nested with others alongside social, ethnic or religious values (Hakenbeck, 2007b). A weapon may not mean the same thing in different graves. A sword, for example, may be part of a person's mortuary aesthetic and wrapped up with pluralistic expressions of personhood (Sayer *et al.*, 2019). But would a weapon have been placed in the grave because the person was a warrior, because they occupied a specific social/economic rank, or because they belonged to a specific group, for example, a family with a tradition of weapon burial? How long did that 'tradition' last? Two generations, three, or more? Did having a weapon in the grave mean that that person had used it in life? Or that they could have used it in life? Were they witnessed with it or a similar weapon? And was weapon ownership, practice and use more common in some social or economic groups than others? (Sayer *et al.*, 2019; Brunning, 2017; Martin, 2014; Felder, 2015). Were people who used weapons routinely associated with them? In short, what could a weapon embody – masculinity, war, danger, protection, physical prowess, youth, storytelling, heroics, banditry, wealth, heritage, hunting, *camaraderie*, safety? Is it all of those thing to all people, or some of those things to some people? Material culture can change the body, either with its presentation or by influencing its shape and appearance – muscles and calluses, for example – but for a weapon to change the body it had to be used, and it could not be entirely symbolic or passive. However, the association with weaponry *post mortem* may be about attitude and lifeways, as much as about the physical use of that weapon. An Anglo-Saxon slave might have owned a spear and used it regularly; s/he may have engaged in hunting for food, fighting for protection or participating in aggressive raiding and battles. As a result, the way in which a spear or sword intersected with mortuary identity may have been more dependent on who buried them and their attitude.

With these pluralistic questions in mind this chapter explores biological data because, importantly, it is the body that allows us to penetrate these points of social attitude. At Apple Down, for example, there are two burial configurations. The first group occupied a smaller mortuary space, which was returned to for generation after generation, and it employed a particular orientation for the graves that defined the aesthetics of that space and allowed it to be identified. These people from the first configuration buried their dead with weapons or brooches, and they were buried alongside infants and children. The lives of the people in the second configuration on average were shorter: they did not bury their dead in one space, but instead chose to do so in a chronological sequence, one after the other in a clockwise pattern around the cemetery. They used the mortuary space differently; they may also have had different diets, different biological heritages and different relationships, or had different attitudes towards marriage, the selection of sexual partners or the creation of a union between couples. The differences visible within the cemetery space, and within the bodies of the dead, resulted from different decisions and attitudes. It is by exploring the archaeology of lifeways and attitudes together that we may begin to see where material culture and physical practices intersect.

To explore lifeways and attitudes together, this chapter looks at the presence of skeletal pathology, in particular at trauma and damage caused by work or injury. This chapter looks at diet via isotope data and then at the body through height and teeth metrics. All of these are combined with a detailed chronological, material and spatial examination of the cemeteries under investigation in order to look at social attitudes, which can be explored by understanding a group's exposure to risk or their attitude towards biological relatedness. The actions and material expression of mourners at the graveside might tell us about the individual, but how that person's lived experience compares to others' unlocks a whole range of alternative multi-scaled interpretations. Diet and trauma may provide insight into lifeway, whereas height and teeth metrics may reveal a degree of relative biological connection.

Lifeways

The challenge presented to the social archaeologist is that the evidence available has resulted from a multitude of simultaneous social and environmental factors. It is the prerogative of natural scientists to isolate a particular process for examination, but inevitably this can oversimplify the situation, reducing the complex or pluralistic nature of society. In this section we will be looking at evidence from the body, and situating that within an examination of social situations. For example, rather than investigating the medical or social cause of skeletal trauma and the individual experience, we examine with whom it is found, alongside the mortuary technologies already identified in the preceding chapters. Despite its title, this chapter is not about the individual, but it uses individuals as the building blocks with which to examine the community of which they were a part. By first identifying where different lifeways, and different attitudes, arose it is possible to explore in more depth the place of the individual within early Anglo-Saxon lived experience.

Of the 121 inhumations at Apple Down, twenty showed evidence of skeletal trauma – specifically fractures, periostitis (bone infections) or swollen limb-bone shafts; interestingly, only four of these 121 graves (nos. 14, 19, 28 and 67) belonged to configuration A (as defined in Chapter 1). However, the prevalence of arthritis did not share this pattern, because seven of the thirty-six configuration A burials and twelve of the seventy-five configuration B burials had osteoarthritis. The percentage of individuals with arthritis was very similar to that seen at Finglesham (see below) but, unlike Finglesham, at Apple Down we can conclude that all of the individuals were exposed to a similar amount of risk for acquiring this pathology, for example, exposure to injury, or repetitive or manual labour. Nonetheless, those people belonging to the less well furnished and peripheral burials of configuration B were exposed to a higher risk of physical injury than their peers in configuration A, evidenced by an increased frequency of fractures seen among this group. Perhaps both groups worked, but for the individuals found in a configuration B burial there was a more immediate risk of physical trauma associated with their lifeway; perhaps the labour they engaged in was heavier or more dangerous.

This pattern shows that there were at least two different lifeways present within this site. The configuration A burials included a higher proportion of adults aged over 45 and, if all things were equal, their longer lifespans should have resulted in a higher, not lower, incidence of osteoarthritis and trauma. The configuration A area included a greater proportion of children and furnished graves, and it also had a different chronological character to configuration B. Notably, the individuals

associated with configuration A created genealogies within the immediate, densely packed inhumation space. These people returned time
and again to bury their dead, whether elderly, adult or child, a pattern
also seen at Orpington and West Heslerton. Configuration B burials,
by contrast, did not seem to place emphasis on returning to the same
spaces, nor on the locations of children's graves. This group carried
out more dangerous work, labour which changed their physical bodies;
they dressed their dead differently, placing emphasis on more mun-
dane objects like beads or buckles, and they placed less emphasis on
familial or ancestral history than did their peers. Their cemetery space
developed with a chronological character, and it appears to have been a
more functional space, not loaded with the same symbolism found with
configuration A burials.

At this point it is worth revisiting Finglesham early Anglo-Saxon
cemetery in detail because there were also a number of different lifeways evidenced in this large cemetery. Finglesham contained 254
excavated inhumations, ranging across the sixth and seventh centuries;
these clustered at 4 m and were divided into four plots, A, B, C and
D, with sufficient gaps between them for us to be confident of their
deliberate separation (see Chapter 4, Figure 4.15). A number of burials at Finglesham had medium-sized or small barrows over them, and
some of these graves were furnished burials, while others were less
well furnished. Finglesham also contained graves which used integral
features, as at St Peters (Chapter 4), and it is notable that these graves
with integral features were less likely to have been robbed (7 per cent).
Indeed, there is strong evidence to suggest that the differences between
graves was an expression of social differences. In addition, we saw in
Chapter 4 that there were three distinct rituals within the cemetery: 1)
burials with gendered objects or burial wealth in flat graves or barrows;
2) burials with integral features and objects, but rarely displaying gender
identities; 3) burials in flat graves with limited or no gravegoods.

This was a complex cemetery and the differences in burial ritual highlight cultural differences that were markers of social divisions inherent in
the community. However, these differences were not easily witnessed in
the physical bodies of the deceased, suggesting similar lifeways within,
but not necessarily across, the community who used Finglesham. These
differences in lifeways are apparent in two types of evidence – skeletal
pathology (Figure 5.1) and dental pathology (Figure 5.2). The majority
of cases of identifiable skeletal trauma were seen in plot B, which also
had the longest internal chronology of the groups within the cemetery.
The skeletal trauma was evident in the form of activity-related trauma,
manifesting most evidently in the presence or absence of arthritis among
the burials. However, witnessing this difference is tricky. For example,

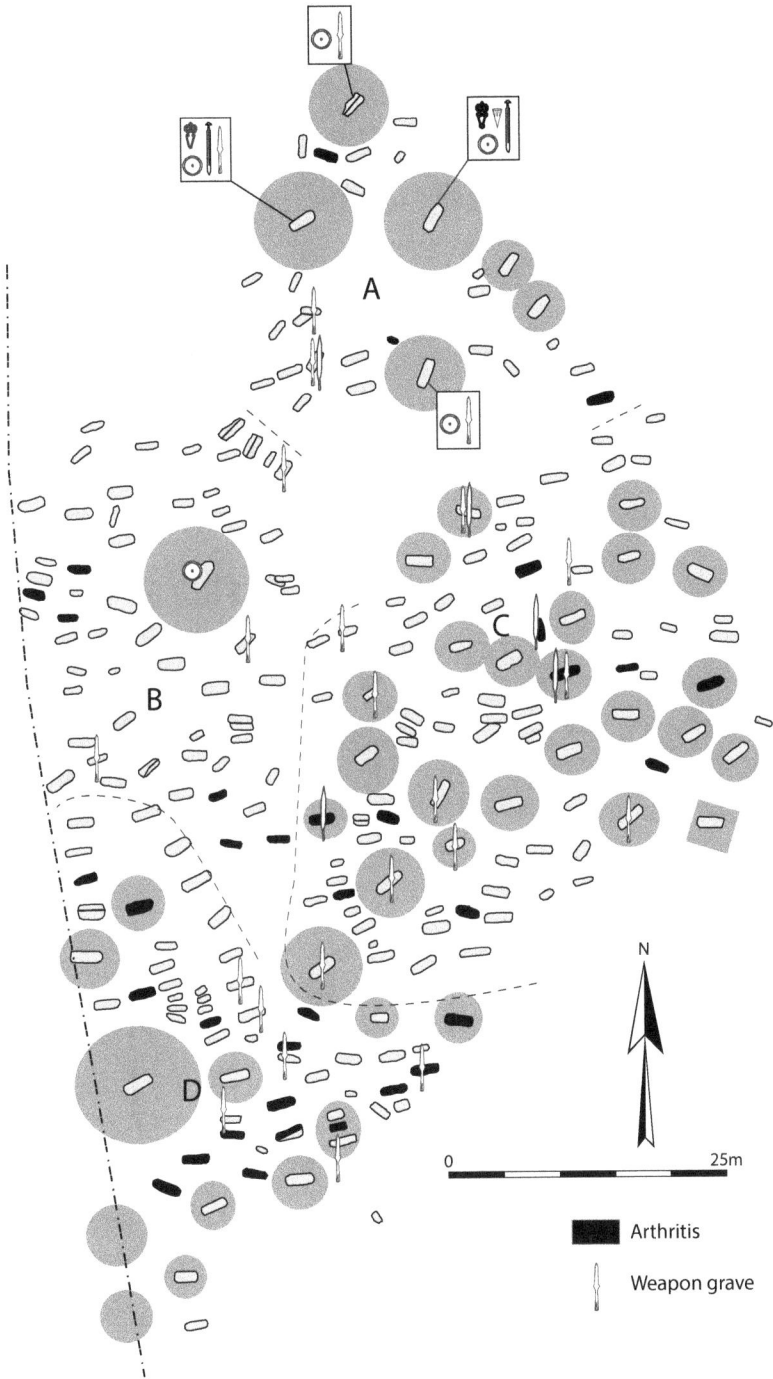

Figure 5.1 Finglesham, Kent: the distribution of arthritis and weapons.

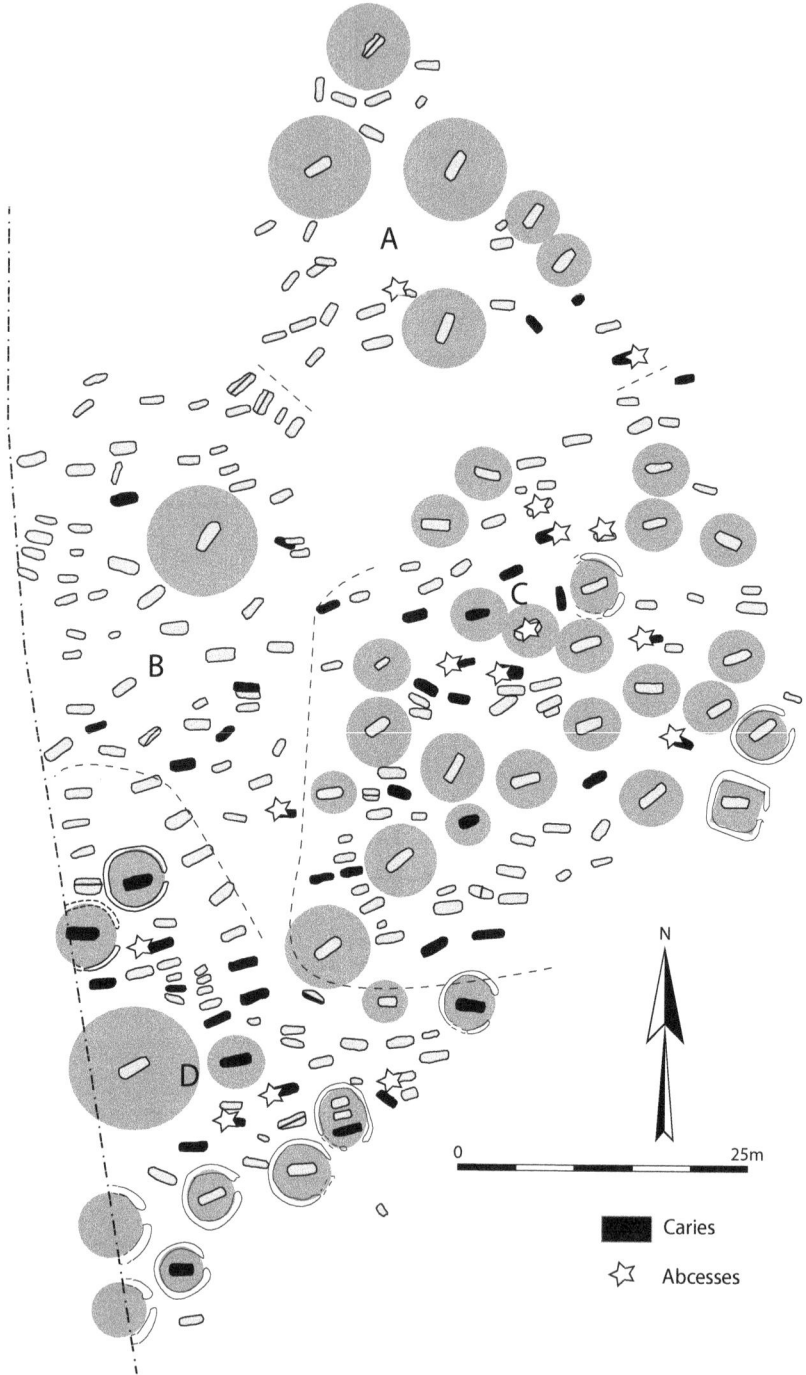

Figure 5.2 Finglesham, dental pathology: caries and abscesses.

there is no significant difference between the numbers of individuals with weapons and the numbers without, or those with arthritis found in flat graves, in graves with integral features, or under barrows. Each category has a proportion of around 16 per cent of the population who manifest arthritis. Similarly, 15 per cent of the male population had arthritis, and around 15 per cent of weapon burials showed evidence of arthritis. However, this flat patterning is not repeated between the spatial groupings, and there were patterns in the frequency of arthritis found between burial areas. In plot A three of thirty-two graves had arthritis, although preservation is poor in this plot (Figure 5.1). In plot B, six of sixty-four grave inhabitants had arthritis, whereas in plot C ten of ninety-five had arthritis. In plot D, however, sixteen of sixty graves showed evidence of arthritis.

This is a ratio of around 10 per cent in plots A, B and C, and 27 per cent in plot D; thus in plot D arthritis was found with almost three times the frequency. These data give a p-value of 0.013537 using Pearson's chi-square test, and this result is significant. Note that this test is appropriate for a 4×2 contingency table, comparing presence and absence of arthritis in each plot; however, given the poor preservation in plot A it has also been calculated for B, C and D, and this comparison gives a p-value of 0.007963 and so is also significant. Pearson's chi-square test is appropriate where there are values over 5 and with a significance of 0.05. Arthritis was therefore more likely in the plot D graves because of patterns in cultural activities and was not due to chance. Just as with Apple Down, these individuals were exposed to a greater risk of developing the disease because of their differential exposure to high-risk activity, work or injury. Therefore in both cemeteries there was evidence of different lifeways, which corresponds to the spatial organisation of the sites and not directly with just the presence and/or absence of material culture. Notably, however, plot D was also the least wealthy part of the cemetery, just as at Apple Down.

Unfortunately, good-quality skeletal data are not available for the earliest phases of the excavation at Finglesham and this can make comparing skeletal particularly dental characteristics in plot A and B more challenging. Nonetheless, there are important differences in dental pathology between plots C and D. Overall, dental pathology showed similar results to arthritis. Dental caries, for instance, had a limited frequency with no particular patterns (Figure 5.2). The thirty-seven examples were proportionally distributed between plot C (20 of 95) and plot D (17 of 60). Abscesses were similar again, with eight examples in plot C and four in plot D. However, enamel hypoplasia was found in fifteen of the sixty graves (25 per cent) in plot D whereas in plot C just nine of ninety-five graves (10 per cent) showed similar evidence (Figure 5.3).

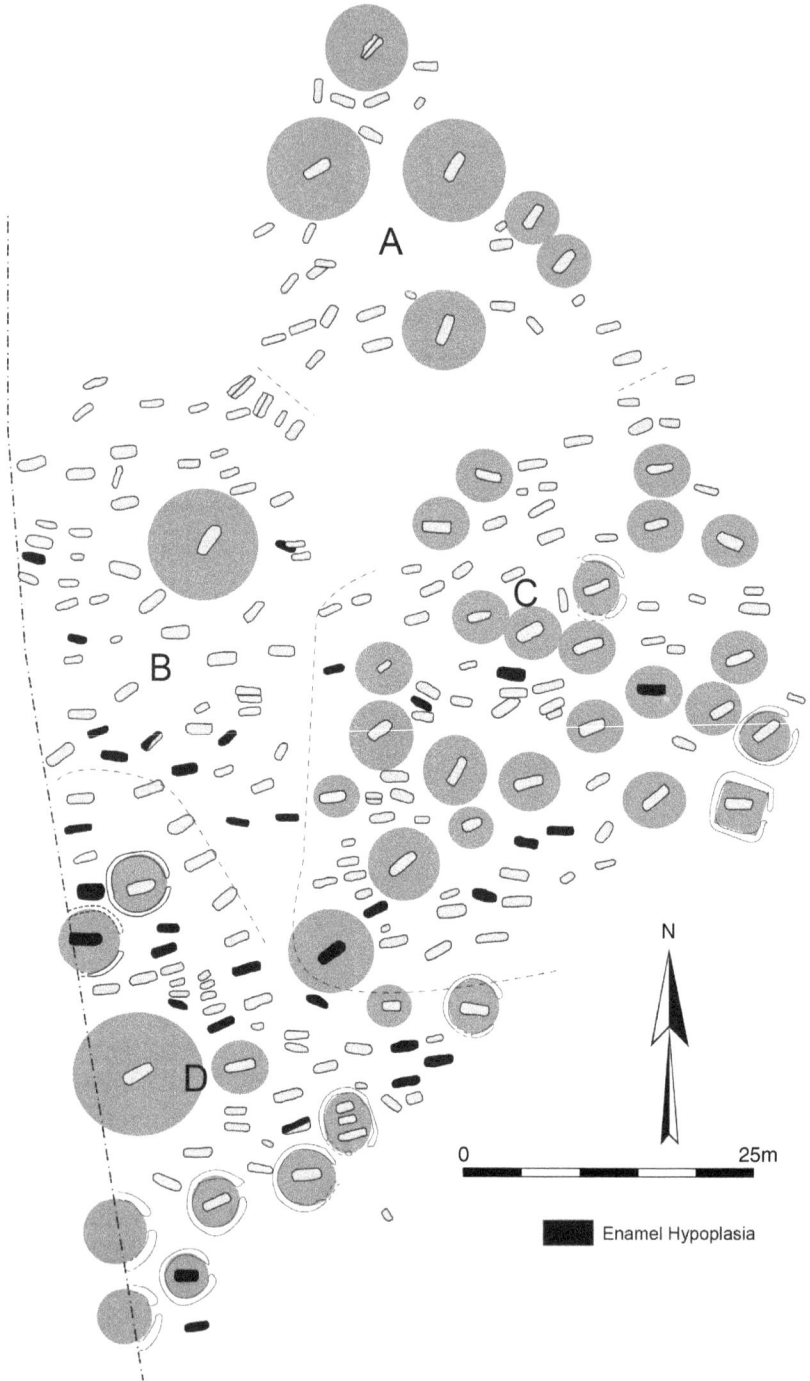

Figure 5.3 Finglesham, dental pathology: enamel hypoplasia.

Enamel hypoplasia occurred with more frequency in plot D. The numbers were small and were thus analysed with Fisher's exact test, which provided a p-value of 0.0122. As a result, this pattern is not random; it is significant and should be understood as the product of cultural activity. Equally, of the thirty-four total cases of enamel hypoplasia, only four occurred among the individuals that were buried under barrows. In other words, 88 per cent of cases of enamel hypoplasia were found on individuals in flat graves; proportionally there were four cases in thirty-nine (10 per cent) in barrows and thirty-three (15 per cent) in the 217 flat graves, but, with a Fisher's exact test p-value of 0.62, this difference does not have statistical significance and should as a result be seen as the product of chance. Enamel hypoplasia is evidence of periods of nutritional stress or disease during infancy and childhood (Roberts and Manchester, 2005). It is not unexpected in an early medieval population, but it is important that this has been identified in significantly higher proportions in plot D than in plot C, suggesting a difference in childhood diet between the populations of the two areas. As a result, it seems reasonable to conclude that these childhoods were somewhat separate, or at least that access to resources and consumption practices were not shared between these groups of people.

The cemetery at Finglesham contained evidence of at least two different life experiences, and these were distinguished by the use of one plot or another within the cemetery. The individuals in plot D were exposed to a higher risk of acquiring arthritis, probably through exposure to physical labour. It is likely that the population of this part of the cemetery was also exposed to nutritional stress or disease in childhood, and in thirty-four examples this manifested as enamel hypoplasia. This developmental deficiency was more frequent in plot D, the inhabitants of which had a poorer childhood diet compared to the rest of the cemetery population. These conditions did not physically manifest in the skeletal remains of all of the people in plot D, but the increased frequency suggests that the risk of acquiring arthritis or enamel hypoplasia was much higher among this specific group because of their lived experience. Thus, if the plots are evidence for different households, or corporate groups, then these groups experienced different lifeways, and there may have been limited intersection between these lifeways. Although high-wealth graves from the whole cemetery were as likely to contain individuals with arthritis or enamel hypoplasia as not, it is conspicuous that the most-wealthy graves were absent from plot D. Deprivation and hard repetitive work were characteristic of the community at Finglesham, and at other early medieval sites such as Apple Down, because these conditions were prevalent across the population as a whole. Nonetheless, the people who were buried in plot D had different physical and cultural experiences to those who were found in plots A, B and C.

Great Chesterford, Essex, is another site with evidence of multiple lifeways within the mortuary population. Great Chesterford was excavated between 1953 and 1955 and a large population was uncovered, with 167 individuals found at the site. This cemetery was notable in a number of ways; in particular, there was a larger proportion of women, infants and children than expected. Unfortunately, only part of the cemetery was excavated. Tony Waldron analysed the human remains, focusing particularly on the pathology and on preservation. His more detailed notes and appendix are available as a Historic Buildings and Monuments Commission of England report, no. 89/88 (Waldron, 1994). These data were reviewed and added to work published by Sarah Inskip (2008), who noted the high degree of tuberculosis among the remains.

As we have seen in previous chapters, Great Chesterford was notable because the aesthetics of the space combined material culture, the orientation of graves and clustering, which were used to define and separate a series of plots and burial areas. In area A there was a central area defined by inhumations of different orientations, which included the wealthiest graves in the cemetery. In area B the core graves were well furnished, and area C consisted of a series of equally spaced, but contrastingly oriented, burials. The graves in area D were widely spaced and poorly furnished. As with the examples at Finglesham and Apple Down, the individuals in this cemetery experienced different lives and chose to bury their dead differently. This was evidenced in the prevalence of arthritis, osteophytes and fractures. Osteophytes are bony projections associated with the degeneration of cartilage at the joints, and are caused by localised inflammation, for example, from degenerative arthritis or tendonitis. As a result they are related to osteoarthritis in their cause, and are primarily the result of stress within the physical environment. Each of the individuals in plots A, B and C had similar proportions of these skeletal traumas, whereas area D had proportionally twice as many instances of arthritis, osteophytes and fractures (see Table 5.1). Indeed, where skeletal preservation was good enough to analyse, 46 per cent of the individuals from area D showed evidence of arthritis. In effect, this means that people in this burial area were twice as likely to develop this condition as those in areas A, B and C. Additionally, 53 per cent of these individuals had developed osteophytes and 23 per cent were found with fractures, having been exposed to more than double the risk of physical injury as those individuals in areas A, B and C, and were treated differently in death. A chi-square test was used to examine if the proportion of individuals with pathology in area D is notably higher than the proportion in areas A, B or C. The p-value for this test, using data

Table 5.1 Skeletal trauma at Great Chesterford

Grave area	% of graves A–D	Arthritis	Osteophytes	Fractures
A	(20) 29%	(7) 25%	(7) 35%	(1) 5%
B	(13) 19%	(2) 15%	(3) 23%	(1) 8%
C	(22) 32%	(4) 18%	(8) 36%	(2) 9%
D	(13) 19%	(6) 46%	(7) 53%	(3) 23%
predicted	100%	25%	36%	10%

from Table 5:1, was $p = 0.006$, which is significant. As a result, we can conclude that the people from area D were exposed to significantly more risk within their lived experience, and these people also chose a different location to bury their dead. In this case, as with the Apple Down and Finglesham plots, we see the cemetery spaces related to groups of people with different lived experiences.

Arthritis is caused when joints are not able to withstand the stresses repeatedly applied to them, for instance through repetitive work, and joint injuries also greatly increase the risk of acquiring arthritis. Individuals such as the occupant of grave 160 from Great Chesterford showed evidence of secondary osteoarthritis of the elbow following fracture (Waldron, 1994: 57). Occupational stress has been seen from sites such as the *Mary Rose* where, from a total of 110 individuals recovered from the submerged wreck, fifteen individuals showed evidence of *os acromiale* (non-fusion of the acromion, a bony process on the scapula). This may have been linked to the use of the rotator cuff (a group of muscles and tendons that stabilises the shoulder joint); the injury/deformity is specific to archery (Stirland, 1986; 2000). Similarly, arthritis may be caused by a mixture of environmental factors resulting from the gradual wear of cartilage in the joints, joint inflammation and imperfect repair mechanisms in response to injury (Roberts and Manchester, 2005). As a result, patterns in the frequency of degenerative joint diseases can be used to differentiate specific occupation patterns within a community, but each of these individuals had different conditions. Therefore it is more appropriate to explore different lifeways resulting in increased exposure to, or frequency of, trauma – that is, that some groups of people were exposed to a greater degree of risk (Samut-Tagliaferro, 1999; White *et al.*, 2012: 441; Johnson, 2008). Arthritis is found at different locations on the skeleton and it has a less specific cause than the *os acromiale* seen on the Mary Rose. As a result of this ambiguity it possible to suggest only that the individuals of Finglesham and Great Chesterford were exposed to a higher risk of acquiring joint injury. This increased risk probably resulted from exposure to injury, as well as repetitive manual labour.

Importantly, there was no correlation between weapon burials and arthritis at these three sites. That is interesting because it means that the semiotics associated with weapons, and probably other gravegoods too, crossed these experiential boundaries. Despite this, the well-furnished, or wealthiest, graves were absent from plot D at Finglesham, where most trauma was found. At Apple Down, and at Great Chesterford too, exposure to a high risk of joint trauma and the absence of wealth in the graves seems to have correlated. It is unfortunate that these numbers are small, but these are the sizes of the cemeteries and the populations we have to work with. Nonetheless, despite these small samples, the patterns are strong, and correlate with spatial as well as wealth differences within the mortuary populations. In combination, these differences are striking and evidence of the different lived experiences. Patterns in skeletal pathology do not seem to correlate with individual variations, for example, the presence or absence of a weapon, but with corporate groups across community-level dynamics. The differences in lifeways that we have seen at Finglesham, Apple Down and Great Chesterford overlapped with differences in mortuary expression. Different corporate groups shared different values which contributed to how they chose to bury their dead, how the deceased were commemorated, and how cemetery space was used. These differences in attitude and in lifeways were embedded in the community for generations and changed only slowly over hundreds of years.

Parallel lifeways

Unfortunately, the majority of early Anglo-Saxon cemeteries have poor preservation, or else (in many cases) the skeletal data have not been recorded to modern standards. This chapter has described a series of sites with evidence for internal differences within the distribution of skeletal or dental pathology, and these corresponded to cultural differences in mortuary treatment at these sites. In each of these cases the numbers were relatively small, reducing confidence in the statistics. However, Fisher's exact test was used to test for significance, a reliable statistical approach where the numbers are low, i.e. below five, and where chi-square would not be accurate. As a result, we can be confident that the differences seen at Finglesham, Apple Down and Great Chesterford were actually the product of lifeway differences between co-operating but separate or unequal corporate groups. Reassuringly, the differences between these groups included skeletal trauma, spatial location and/or variation in the expression of material wealth, and therefore we might infer that these patterns were behavioural and related to differences in lifeways and attitudes to mortuary practice or expression. This is evident because in each site there were distinctly different ways of treating the dead, who were found in different locations, on different orientations, and with different patterns to the chronology of burial. At Apple Down and Great Chesterford this also included or excluded different age groups, more specifically, children. Together these differences and the pathology point to evidence of different lived experiences. Importantly, however, not all cemeteries contained evidence of separate lifeways.

The Anglo-Saxon cemetery at Berinsfield is a good example of a cemetery with the same proportions of pathological evidence between differentiated types of burial. Berinsfield consisted of two contemporary collections of graves and both contained a core group of inhumations, and although these were of similar dates they spanned different generations (Sayer, 2010; see Figure 5.4). The burials at Berinsfield have been dated using the typology method because they were largely too early to reliably use the radiocarbon method – see Chapter 4, and Sayer, 2007. Graves 91, 102, 104 and 107 were part of the northern core and all dated to the early sixth century. Similarly, the southern core burials, 51, 53, 54 and 66, also had a predominantly early/mid-sixth-century date. The exception was grave 52, early seventh-century in date, which was placed on a different orientation, an aesthetic way to distinguish it from its predecessors. The well-furnished burials at Berinsfield were all contemporaneous; however, in the northern cluster inhumation 91 was buried AD 450–566 and was aged 17–25, whereas grave 102 had an identical age range but was interred in the early sixth century. Inhumation 107 was buried AD 500–66 and was of a similar age. Grave 104 was buried between the early and mid-sixth centuries and was also aged between 17 and 25. In the southern group of inhumations grave 51 was a male aged 15–25 years, interred between the later-fifth and sixth centuries, whereas grave 53, buried AD 500–66, was aged between 24 and 35, and burial 54, dated to the later-fifth to early sixth centuries, was aged between 25 and 36. The comparison of biological data and chronological information illustrates that these individuals had contrasting age and chronological characteristics, and so we might conclude that these core areas were returned to repeatedly, generation after generation, for three or four generations. These were places to bury a particular group of people and included one or two individuals from each age cohort, irrespective of gender (Sayer, 2010).

The presence of trauma pathology at Berinsfield is also important, because it was very different to that seen at Finglesham, Apple Down and Great Chesterford. Seventeen sets of human remains showed evidence for osteoarthritis, and these were distributed around the cemetery (Figure 5.5). There was no difference between burials, for example, in the type and style of gravegoods and osteoarthritis. Two of fifteen richly

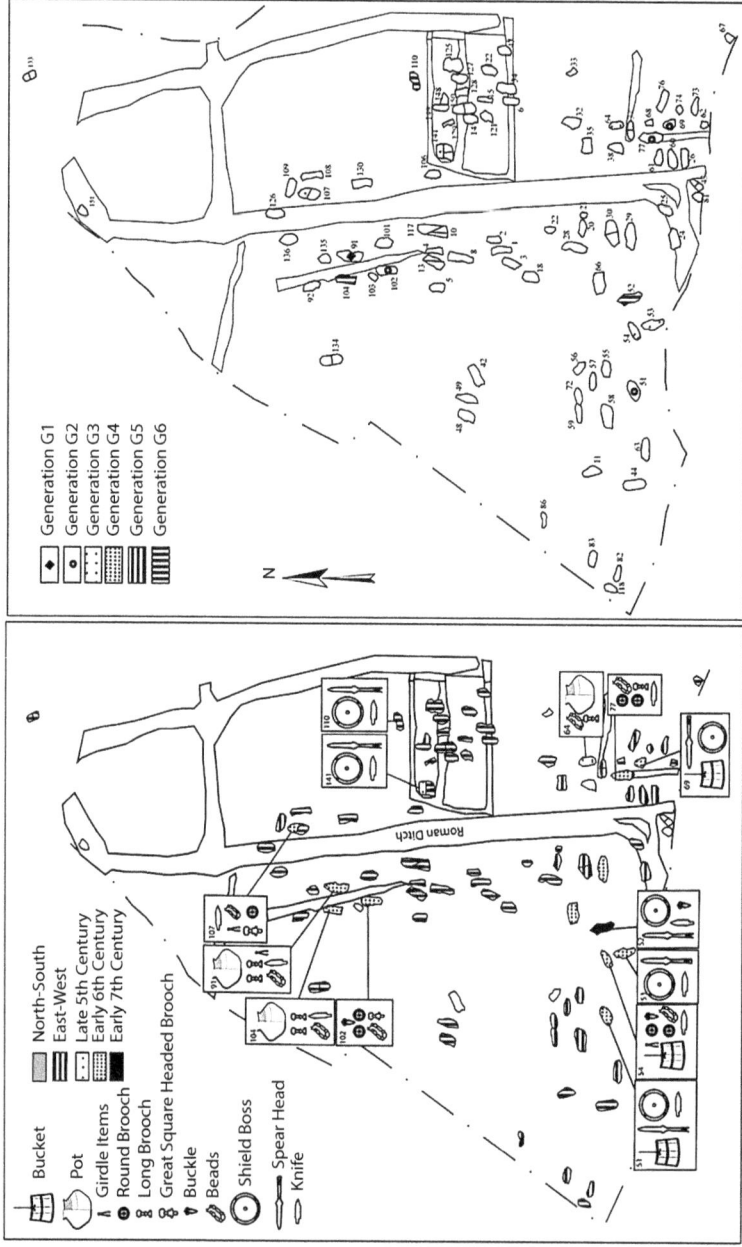

Figure 5.4 Berinsfield, Oxfordshire: the left-hand plan shows distribution and dating of wealthy burials; the right-hand map shows the generations that the burials belong to. The core burials were of similar dates but notably they spanned different generations (Sayer, 2010).

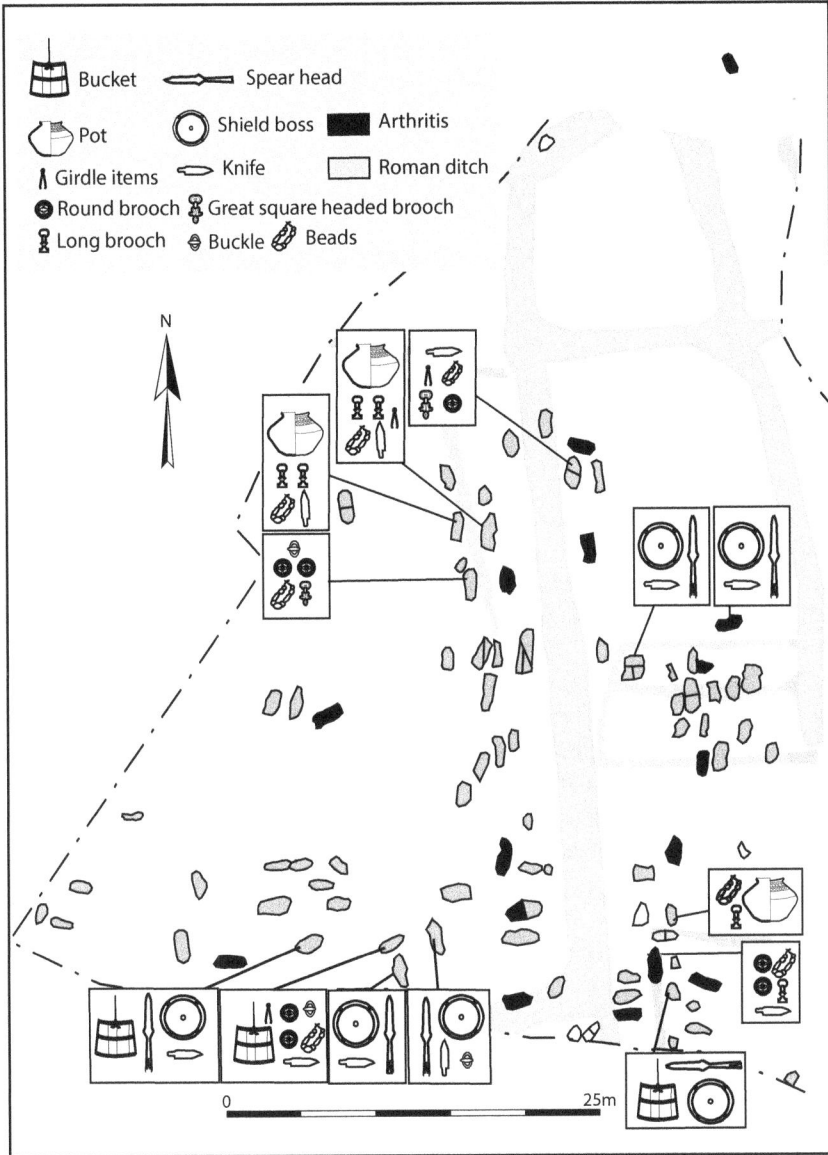

Figure 5.5 Berinsfield: the distribution of arthritis and artefacts.

furnished burials were found with osteoarthritis, and thirteen of eighty remaining burials for which data exists showed evidence of osteoarthritis. Fisher's exact test for this data gave a value of $p = 1$, meaning that both richly furnished and poorly furnished burials had had identical proportions of arthritis. As a result, we can conclude that there were no independent factors which separated the experience of these individuals, based on gravegoods. Equally, the forty-eight burials to the north of the site, which have a primary N/S orientation, included seven individuals with osteoarthritis. In the south there were nine such burials, from a total of forty-nine. The southern burials primarily display an E/W orientation. A Fisher's exact test of these groups gives a p-value of 0.79 which is not significant. As a result, we much conclude that there are no independent factors influencing the presence of osteoarthritis among these individuals. In short, the physical experience, and the lifeways, at Berinsfield were similar for the wealthier burials and the different burial areas.

Deal, like Berinsfield, has no obvious differences within the lived experience. The site was a sixth- and seventh-century cemetery and consisted of three visually separate groups of graves around a Bronze Age barrow. Two plots, A and B, were contemporaneous and sixth-century in date. The third plot, C, was later-sixth- and seventh-century. Plots A and B were organised in similar ways. Plot A, the spatial group south-west of the ring ditch, was a collection of early burials, five of which were similar – inhumation 33, a female adult, was interred in the early sixth century. Burials 17 and 97 were both male and had lived to an age of between 35 and 45 when they were interred in the mid-sixth century. Brugmann (Parfitt and Brugmann, 1997: 106) distinguished between these two, placing them in different phases of local Kentish chronology: burial 17 in phase II and burial 97 in phase III. This provided a mid-sixth-century date for both burials but specifically 17 dated to AD 530–40 and burial 97 to AD 530–70. Graves 17 and 97 were probably consecutive and not contemporary. Inhumations 102 and 25b were both females interred in the mid-sixth century; 25b was aged between 25 and 35, whereas burial 102 was aged between 35 and 45 years. These age and chronological characteristics suggest that these individuals were born around the same time, or belonged to a similar generation (Figure 5.6). Burials from a 'middle' generation included grave 40 which was a particularly well-furnished burial of a male aged between 35 and 45, interred with a full weapon set, including a sword. Of a probably comparable generation was burial 105c, a notably well-furnished female inhumation, aged between 35 and 45 at death. Both were interred in the mid-/later-sixth century and may have been of the same generation. From the latest generation there was just one inhumation, burial 64, an 18- to 25-year-old female interred in the mid-sixth century, before graves 45 and 107c. As a younger individual at death she may have been born some time before them both, perhaps dying when they were children.

Within plot B, burials from the early phase and north-east of and overlying the ring ditch, there were also three generations, which

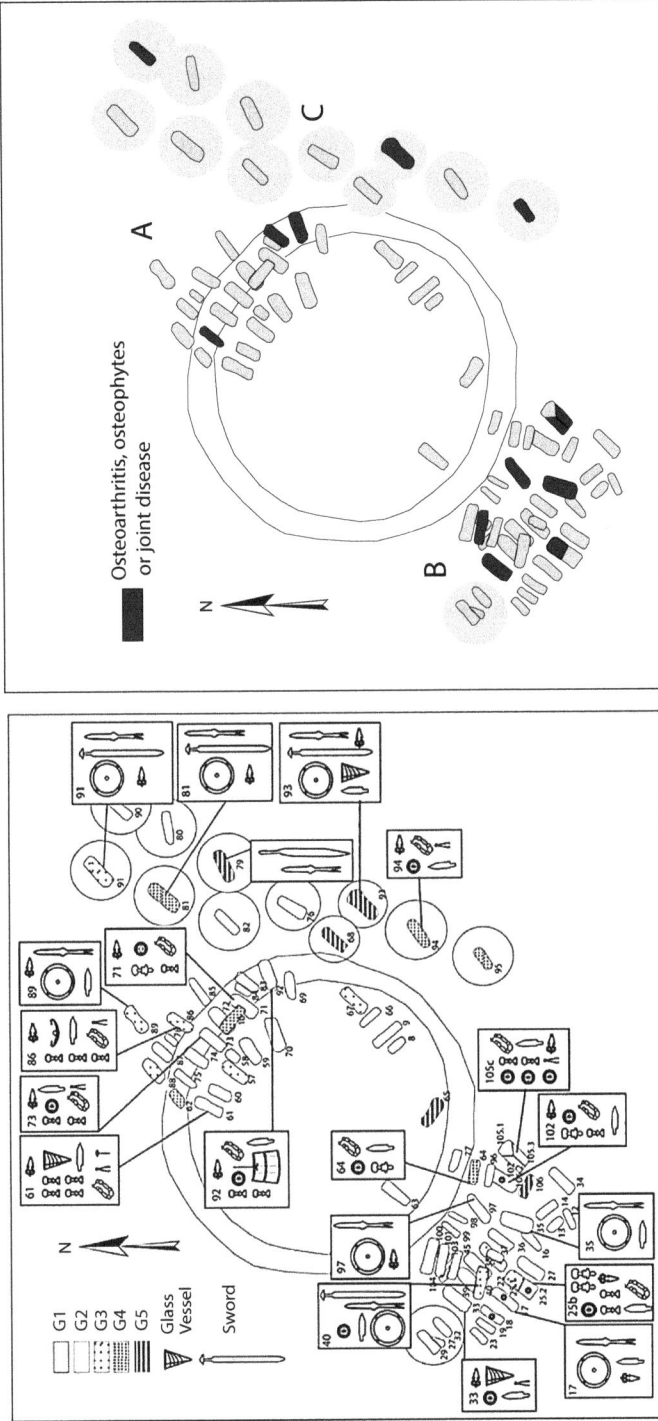

Figure 5.6 Deal, Kent: chronology and generations (after Sayer, 2010).

Osteoarthritis, osteophytes or joint disease

showed a similar pattern to the contemporaneous plot A. The wealthiest burial consisted of a single early sixth-century female, inhumation 92. Following on from this grave were three females interred in the early sixth century – burials 61 and 73 were both aged between 18 and 25 when they died. Burial 71 was a female who died in the middle of the sixth century and was of similar age. Age was the significant factor in all three of these burials, and it is very probable that in this plot was a series of consecutive burials of wealthy young women. The well-furnished burials from the latest generation included burials 86 and 89, which may have been contemporary. These two graves were of a male aged 18 to 25, buried early/mid-sixth century (in grave 89), and a female aged 45 plus and buried mid-sixth century (in grave 86); although they were of different ages at death, the two were probably from the same generation.

The second-phase burials were spatially separated from the earlier two groups described above. These latest graves were interred in a linear fashion underneath small mounds to the east of the ring ditch. This visual distinction indicated a change in the burial rite, and this change saw an increase in the number of male weapon burials. Despite this reorganisation, which emphasised a gender-specific expression, these male burials showed a similar pattern to the previous phases. Specifically, either one or two well furnished inhumations were found from each generation. The earliest well-furnished grave was a single sword burial, inhumation 91, a sub-adult buried in the middle-sixth century. Equally, grave 81 was a sword burial, but from a later generation. Grave 81 was interred in the later-sixth or seventh century, and was over 45 at death. A later group of well-furnished burials included a garnet brooch (burial 94, aged 45 plus and interred in the early/mid-seventh century) and a single sword burial, (grave 93, also over 45 years old and also interred in the early/mid-seventh century). In the next generation there were two high-wealth burials from the same generation, and in addition a notable burial found with a seax, grave 79. This burial was a young man interred in the later-sixth or early seventh century, who was probably from the same generation as burials 93 and 94. The aesthetics of the space changed, the emphasis shifted towards males, but attitudes toward the use of these spaces remained similar, with generations of burials returning to each of these plots to inter their dead as with phase one.

The pathology at Deal is similar to that from Berinsfield; thirteen individuals showed evidence for osteoarthritis, osteophytes or joint disease (Figure 5.6). These included eight from the thirty-one well-furnished graves, and three from fifty-four comparatively poorly furnished burials. However, using Fisher's exact test this difference is not statistically significant (8:23 and 3:51 give a value of p-value = 0.64). Equally, when this is looked at by plot there are three graves with these pathologies versus twenty-two without in plot B; three with versus twelve without in plot C; and six with and forty without in plot A. Using a 3 × 2 contingency table and Pearson's chi-square test, these data have a *p*-value of 0.77, which is not significant. In both cases, skeletal trauma was distributed across the cemetery in roughly comparable proportions (Figure 5.6). Similarly, seven of fifty-seven male burials showed evidence of skeletal trauma, and four of thirty-one females also showed evidence of skeletal trauma, with a Pearson's chi-square *p*-value of 1 and so also has no statistical significance, indeed, the differences are equally proportioned. Similarly, of the seventeen weapon burials at Deal, five showed evidence of skeletal trauma, whereas only two of the forty-nine weaponless burials had evidence of trauma. This result is significant, with a *p*-value of 0.04. It may be that joint disease, and osteoarthritis in particular, are evidence of the higher risk of injury among martially inclined males. At Deal, this situation might be an individual choice, a decision to participate in the masculine lifeways that related to battle, such as one-on-one engagement or weapons practice. Nonetheless, these numbers are very low with just seven individuals with trauma distributed across both weapon and weaponless categories. As a result, we might question if this is a real variation or an artefact of preservation bias across the site. However, it remains important and especially so as it was a characteristic also seen at Apple Down. At these sites, there was a statistical correlation between the active inclusion with a weapon within the mortuary context, and physical change to the body. At Apple Down, non-participant males were larger (Chapter 1 and above), whereas at Deal the males found with weapon graves were exposed to greater risk of physical injury or joint disease.

Isotopic evidence

In the preceding section on pathology we saw two types of cemetery, those that contained groups of individuals with different lifeways and those containing groups of individuals with broadly similar lifeways. Existing skeletal isotope studies allow us to explore this distinction further, because they provide data which can be explored in a different way. The two most comprehensive studies are the comprehensive study of Berinsfield by Karen Privat *et al.* (Privet *et al.*, 2002) and Bradley Hull's PhD thesis, in which he sampled a number of different cemeteries (2007). Both studies looked at dietary information using stable carbon and nitrogen isotope analysis, and both studies investigated social rank, age and biological sex. Hull also explored height and burial position in an attempt to find patterns in the data that could interpreted. Stable isotopes have been used routinely to explore diet in archaeological populations and have been used to explore subsistence practices and social status, as well as health and nutrition (Müldner, 2009). Carbon isotopes are used to explore the ecological foundation for the diet. Nitrogen, by contrast, shows where someone's main diet came from, marine versus terrestrial ecosystems, for example, displaying very different results.

As we have seen, Berinsfield consisted of two contemporary collections of graves organised around a series of Roman features, and these graves were organised into two groups buried on N/S and E/W alignments respectively. Both groups contained a core of relatively wealthy burials, but importantly trauma-related skeletal pathology was distributed around the site, as was evidence of osteoarthritis. Both types of skeletal damage were found in statistically equal proportions in both areas and in both the wealthier and less wealthy graves. The isotope data were similar, and Privat *et al.* concluded that 'the frequent consumption of animal products was not a privilege for any individual or groups at Berinsfield' (Privat *et al.*, 2002: 788). However, there was a trend identified where individuals from burials of lower wealth had scores which showed an elevated level of $\delta15N$, suggesting that their consumption of forest/wild foods was higher. The Thames had a plentiful supply of fish and birds, and Privat *et al.* suggest that this isotope pattern may have resulted from higher consumption of these freely available resources, whereas the wealthier individuals feasted more regularly on omnivores as sources of protein, pigs for example (2002). This pattern was also seen by Hull at Worthy Park and Westgarth Gardens (Hull, 2007: 75, 176). There were no other patterns observed at Berinsfield; when the results from the two burial areas A and B were compared, there was no discernible difference between the two (see Figures 5.7 and 5.8). The slight difference seen in the $\delta15N$ was not significant, as proven in an independent t-test of the data, which produced a value of $p = 0.433$.

As mentioned above, Worthy Park had a slight difference in nitrogen values between wealthy and less wealthy graves (Hull, 2007: 75). This may suggest that the individuals in poorer graves ate more fowl. Perhaps of more importance, however, was the statistically significant difference between carbon isotopes across the three burial areas identified earlier. In terms of height data, the E/W weapon graves in plot A were the most homogeneous, suggesting that there may have been some sort of biological connection between these individuals, which was entwined in the orientation and material display of the dead (see below). No difference was seen in nitrogen isotopes, but carbon isotopes showed a statistically significant distribution between burial areas A, B and C (see Figures 5.9 and 5.10). An Analysis of Variance test (ANOVA) of the $\delta13C$ data yielded a value of $p = 0.044$, which was significant and must be the result of purposeful behaviours. The burials in area A had the highest $\delta13C$ values, and B the second highest; the lowest scores were

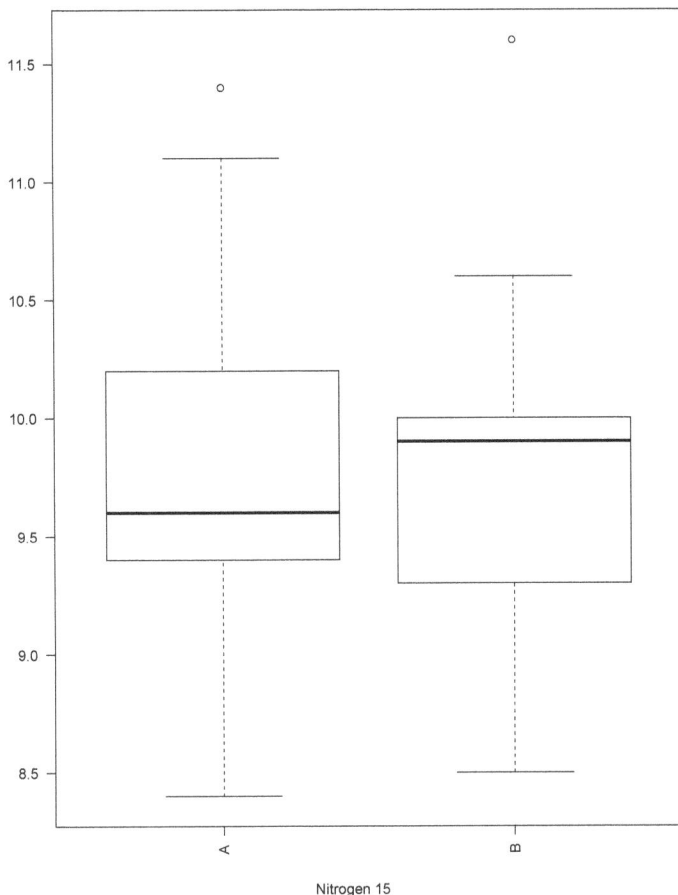

Nitrogen 15

Figure 5.7 Berinsfield: nitrogen isotopes δ15N box plots by burial area. The range within these two burial areas A and B is very similar, showing no obvious dietary difference.

found in the burials of the small area C. Decreased levels of δ13C may be caused by increased consumption of forest resources such as fruit, nuts and fungi, or via the consumption of pigs, whose food consisted of these things. Enriched δ13C levels also may have come from the consumption of grains enriched with carbon, for example through the brewing process (Hull, 2007: 283, 296).

Patterns within these five cemeteries are important but it is only in combination with other types of data that we can start to infer identify or status differences within the living community. By using material, spatial and skeletal evidence we might begin to see differences that can be understood as differences of lifeways that might yield clues about social status. That does not mean social status as defined by the presence

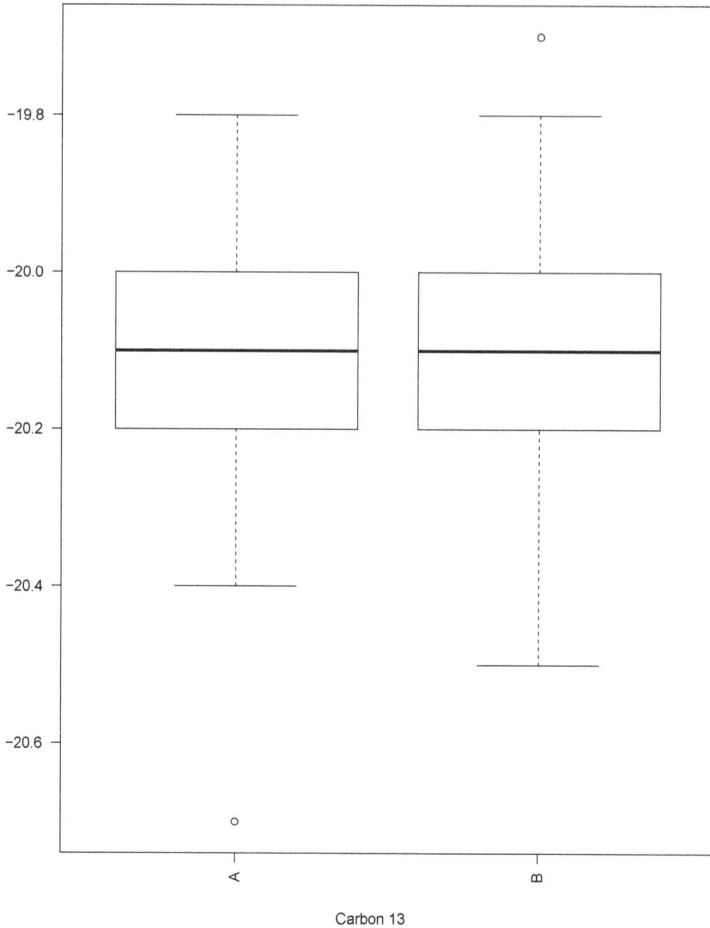

Carbon 13

Figure 5.8 Berinsfield: carbon isotopes δ13C box plots by burial area. Data from these two areas show identical results, except that the lowest result in plot B was was lower than that in plot A.

or absence of precious materials, or by the number of artefacts in graves, but status in dissimilar lifeways and in diverse attitudes towards the dead that indicate that there were a variety of ways of occupying the social landscape. Differentiation is important, and so is similarity. In the examples discussed above, Deal and Berinsfield, there were similar lifeways across the cemeteries suggesting that these sites may have been the mortuary spaces for two similar corporate groups. They defined themselves within the space using different mortuary technologies to create and recreate their own narratives. Ultimately, their bodies suggested similar experiences across both groups. As a result, there are at least two types of behaviour evident from early Anglo-Saxon

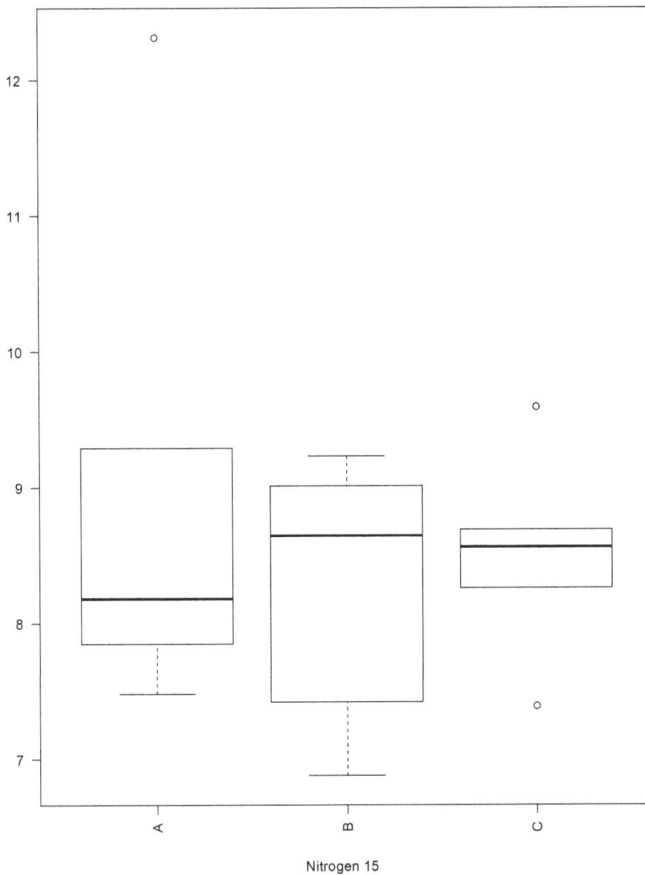

Figure 5.9 Worthy Park, Hampshire: nitrogen isotope δ15N box plots by burial area. The results from these three burial areas are very similar, showing no obvious dietary difference, though the range between highest and lowest results was far smaller in C.

cemeteries: those with broadly comparable lifeways/attitudes, and those in which there was a greater degree of social hierarchy. It is in the different treatments of the dead at Apple Down, Finglesham and Great Chesterford that we can see variations in lifeways. At Great Chesterford, there were three spatially defined groups of graves that shared similar skeletal data. Here the material differences suggested different ways of generating narrative. At the central group, plot A, the wealthiest graves were defined by material culture and by their orientation. Aesthetically, these ancestors became central places within the cemetery and marked out this space, which defined both the adjacent burials and the people who used this plot. There were no children in plot A. The burials

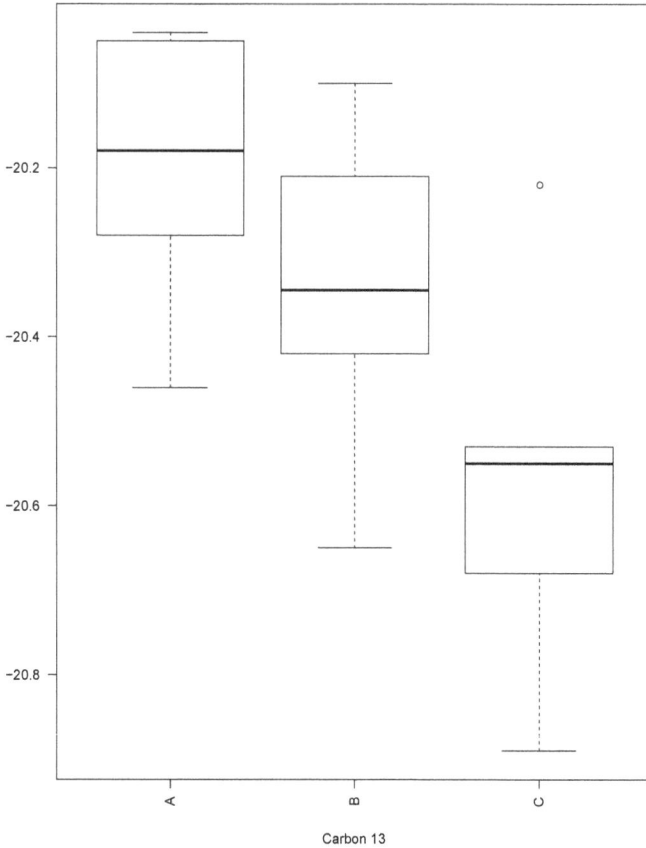

Figure 5.10 Worthy Park: adult carbon isotopes δ13C box plots by burial area. The data from these three plots are statistically different; the distribution perhaps indicates that individuals in area C were more dependent on wild or woodland resources.

in plot D showed little evidence of internal structuring within their mortuary space, and additionally they had experienced a higher risk of trauma in their life. This community contained different lifeways, with different attitudes towards their antecedents and towards the expression of identity. Perhaps these people had different values and so expressed their identities differently within funerary places.

Biological relatedness

Height

Stature data are often recorded from skeletal material, but rarely used to explore social questions. Such data are central to the measurement of size, and they are also important because they are particularly sensitive to environmental conditions (Willey, 2009; Stinson, 2000). Adult stature has been used by health scientists as a measure of the welfare of modern populations (Steckel, 2006; 2009). Biocultural studies which use stature data derived from skeletal material explore hypotheses regarding health and nutrition in ancient societies, in particular how they varied with factors such as social status, subsistence strategy and living conditions (Larsen, 2015: 16–20; Mays, 2016). Heinrich Härke preferred to use stature to discuss ethnicity and described enclaves of British and Anglo-Saxon people which, he argued, showed greater divergence based on stature estimation measurements. He suggested that at Berinsfield there were two non-interbreeding populations with different biological heritages (Härke, 1990). Given that much of the literature on Anglo-Saxon archaeology focuses on ethnicity this is certainly thought-provoking, and must be considered carefully (see, for example, Thomas *et al.*, 2006; Lucy, 2005; Hines, 1997; Härke, 2007). Equally, the small differences in height described, just a few millimetres, could certainly result from nutritional rather than ethnic differences (Tyrell, 2000). However, increasingly we are becoming aware that a large part of stature is determined by genetics, and it is interesting that archaeology often emphasises the environment and health aspects of stature, but does not explore how much variation is attributable to genetic effects, and how much is attributable to biological distance or relatedness (Lai, 2016). Recent genomic studies have tried to connect phenotypical and genetic variation statistically and they suggest that, accounting for nutritional environmental conditions, between 60 and 70 per cent of human height is the result of familial similarity rather than purely environmental factors (Yang *et al.*, 2015: 8). Given this genetic link it might be possible to compare individual height data and discuss degrees of homogeneity or heterogeneity within biological populations. In this section I explore the biological similarities, or differences, that correspond to the mortuary technologies that have been described in previous chapters. As a result it is possible to suggest that the lifeways and attitudes described in the pathology section above can be understood as the results of different patterns of relatedness within the genders and also between groups of people that used the cemetery space in different ways. Due to the genetic component to height we might be able to observe different behaviours in cases where some cemeteries, or some groups within cemeteries, emphasised degrees of relatedness and used this to structure their mortuary space. The chronology and pathology sections of this book have suggested that there were generational burial patterns, that people returned to particular spaces for burial for generation after generation. It would be interesting, then, to explore whether these individuals shared similar statures. The adult human skeleton is not uniformly sexually dimorphic, and as a result males and females are considered separately (Humphrey, 1998).

To explore Härke's (1990) observations it is worth looking at Berinsfield in detail and then comparing it with a series of cemeteries where good-quality stature data have been taken according to Mildred Trotter's methodology (Trotter, 1970; Trotter and Gleser, 1952; 1958; 1977). At Berinsfield there were twenty-one adult male skeletons with height data available, and these ranged between 1.61 m to 1.85 m. The average male at this cemetery was 1.73 m. The individual in grave 117 was 1.85 m tall, which was 0.12 m more than the average. Of that 0.12 m, 60 to 70 per cent was due to genetics; thus between 0.036 m and 0.048 m was likely to be due to environmental factors such as diet and lifestyle. As a result, it is unlikely that the tallest individual (in grave 117 and 1.85 m tall) and the shortest (grave 133/1, 1.61 m) were biologically related. The largest outside influence could have been environmental factors; for example, famine or malnutrition in child-hood could have caused large differences between related individuals. However, the published report does not record any incidences of enamel hypoplasia, Harris lines or any other skeletal changes resultant from childhood malnutrition in a way that can be compared with the height data. As Härke (1990) has already observed, there were no discernible differences in the prevalence of enamel hypoplasia in terms of the health of males interred with or without weapons, which might imply that disease and malnutrition had been felt equally across the population.

Importantly, however, the variations in height data were distributed differently in weapon burials and non-weapon burials at Berinsfield (Figure 5.11). There were fifteen weapon burials with height data, and six non-weapon burials with height data available. Despite the larger number of weapon burials, they had the smaller range of distribution. The average height of a weapon burial was 1.73 m, with the shortest 1.68 m and the tallest 1.78 m. Each of these was just 0.05 m different from the average, and for each of them 0.035 m of this difference could be environmental. As a result, the difference between the tallest and shortest weapon burials suggested that these two might not be directly related, although more distantly related people have a larger degree of difference (Yang *et al.*, 2015). It is noteworthy that these fifteen weapon burials' heights closely cluster together, with just a few centimetres separating them. And it is notable that the five weapon graves from plot B are much less diverse, with a range of just 0.07 m (between 1.71 m and 1.78 m), meaning that these individuals were the most biologically homogeneous group in the cemetery (Figure 5.12). By contrast, the non-weapon burials also had an average of 1.73 m, but a range of 0.24 m, from 1.85 m to 1.61 m, meaning a higher degree of biological diversity within this subgroup of the population.

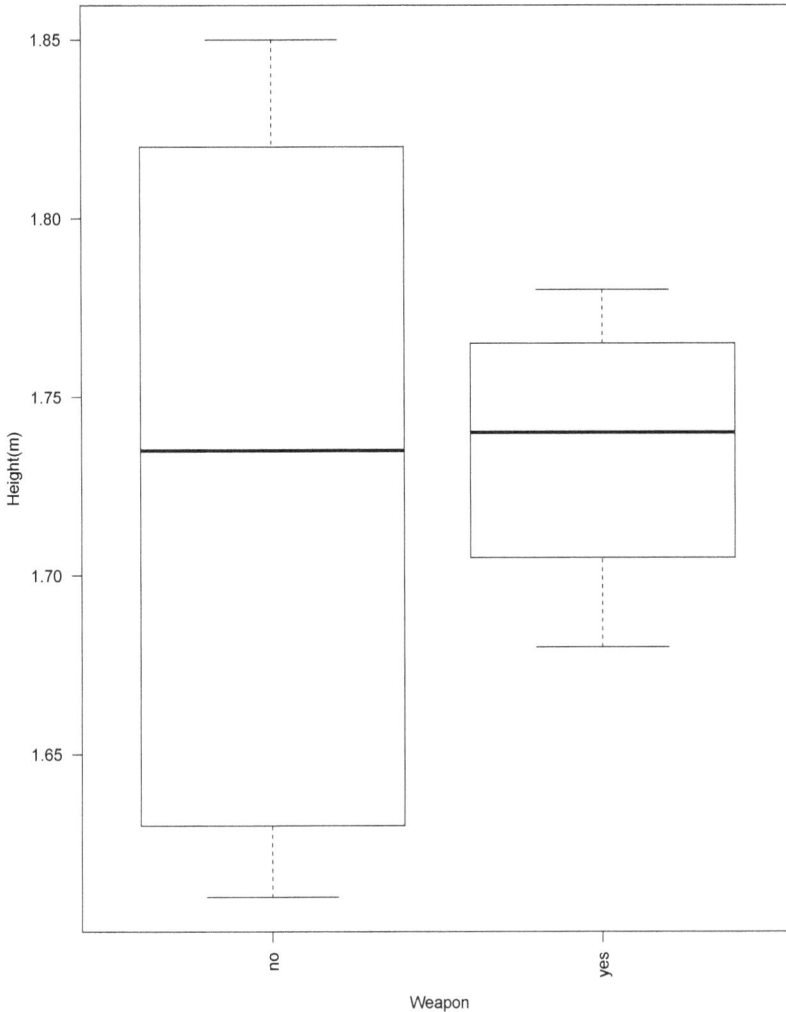

Figure 5.11 Berinsfield: height data differences between weapon and non-weapon burials. This shows that the weapons burials had the smaller range of distribution. The average height of a weapon burial was 1.73 m, with the shortest 1.68 m and the tallest 1.78 m.

The female population of Berinsfield does not seem to have had the same character as that of the male (Figure 5.13). There were sixteen brooch burials among this population, and these showed a greater degree of heterogeneity than there was among the women without brooches (Figure 5.14). The most similar in height were those women without brooches; on average these were shorter than those with brooches and had an average height of 1.60 m, contrasting with 1.63 m

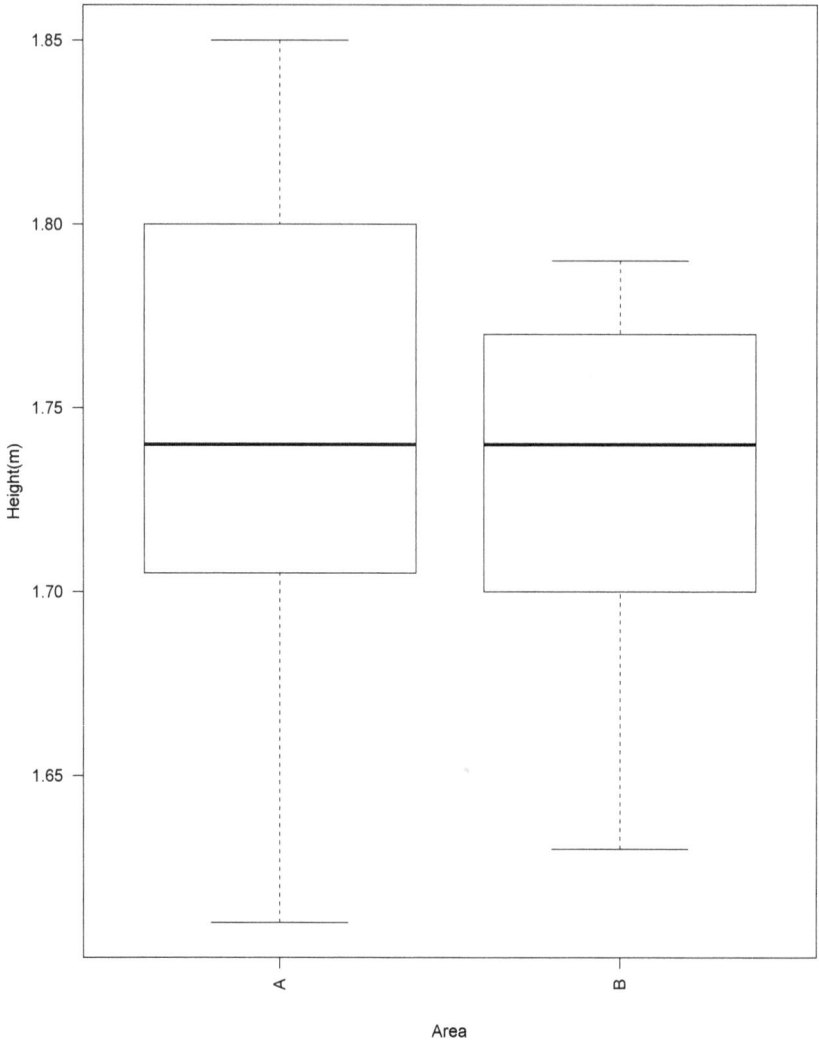

Figure 5.12 Berinsfield: height data differences between weapon burials in plots A and B. The area B weapon burials were less diverse than area A burials.

for those with brooches. The non-brooch burials were eight inhumations between 1.52 m and 1.68 m tall, a range of 0.16 m, but most clustered between 1.58 m and 1.63 m. This variation suggested that these women were diverse, but it is possible that some of these women had a degree of biological relatedness among the non-brooch burials. The brooch burials had a greater degree of heterogeneity, with a range from 1.55 m to 1.72 m, with most being found between 1.59 m and 1.68 m, a wide range suggesting that the use of brooches was not connected to

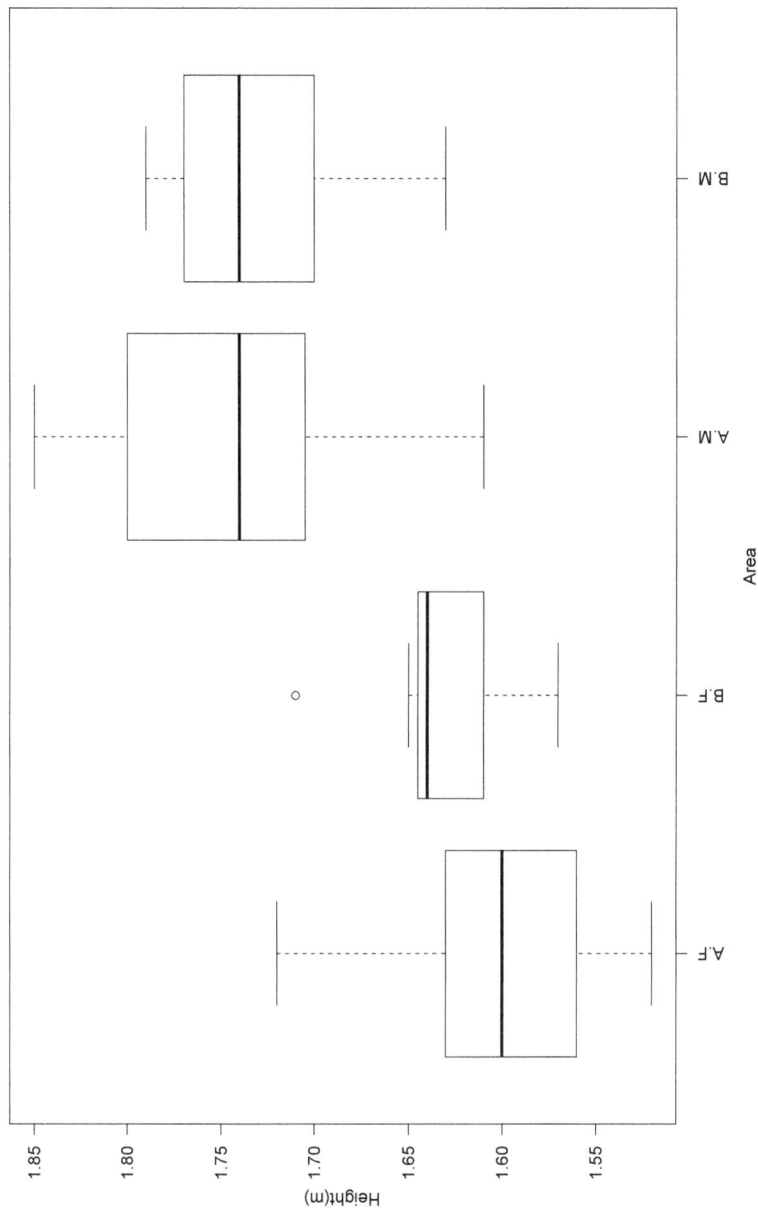

Figure 5.13 Berinsfield: height data by gender. Females in plot B had the narrowest range, and the two female groups had very different height distributions. Males, by contrast, showed a very similar height distribution when comparing these two plots.

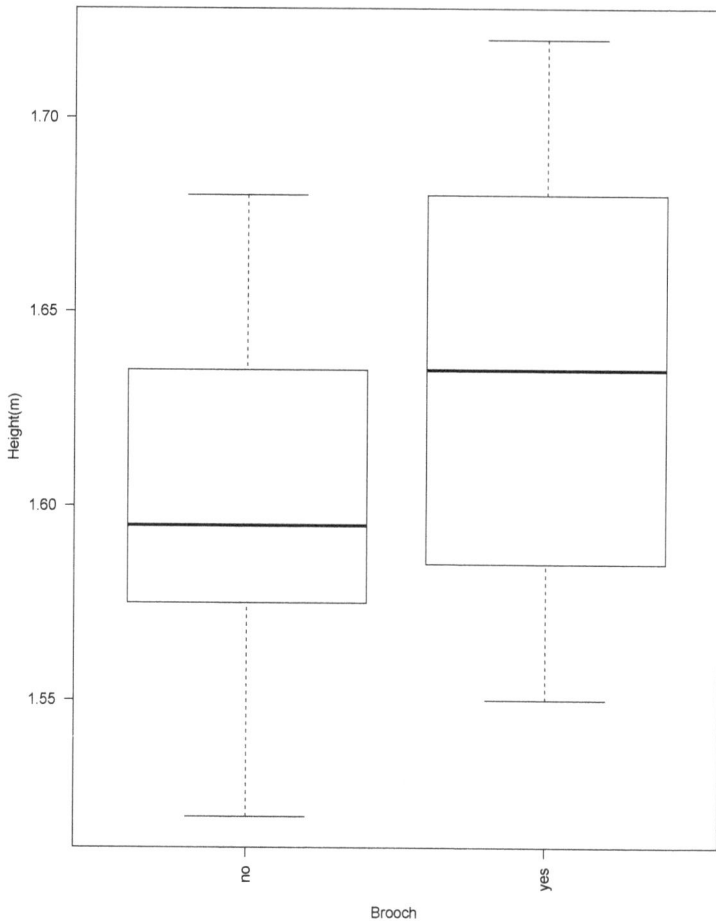

Figure 5.14 Berinsfield: height data with and without brooches. There was more similarity in height among burials of females without brooches than among burials with brooches.

biological relatedness in the same way that it may have been for some weapon graves at this site.

When these same data are expressed by biological sex and spatial grouping, there are some interesting, and contrasting, patterns evident (Figure 5.15). For example, the women in plot B with brooches had the narrowest range, with a concentration between 1.61 m and 1.65 m, and a particular cluster around the top of this range. Graves 77 (1.65 m) and 73 (1.63 m), as well as 25 and 54 (both 1.64 m), were all within 1 cm of the plot's average height and were the most homogeneous female burials. These graves had a variety of different material cultures within them. Notably, the two female plots had very different height

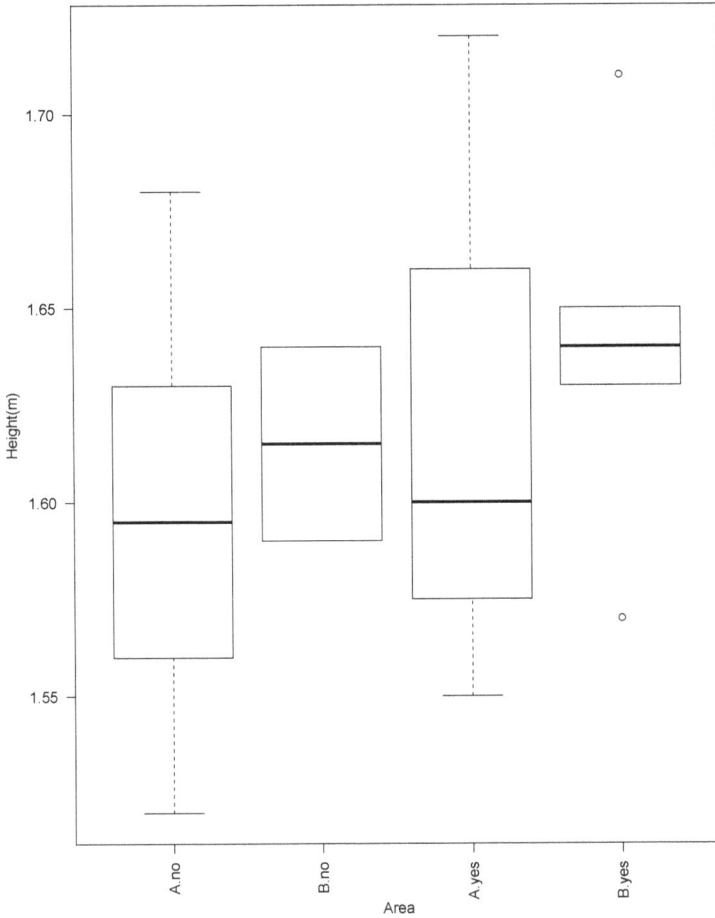

Figure 5.15 Berinsfield: height data by plot, with and without brooches. The burials most similar in height were those of females in Plot B without brooches.

distributions and averages, suggesting a high degree of heterogeneity among these groups. The men, by contrast, showed a range of heights, with the same average figure for both plots, which suggests there was some homogeneity within this population; this degree of cross-plot comparison is probably the result of the similarity between the male weapon burials that we witnessed earlier.

By contrast, the cemetery at Great Chesterford showed greater homogeneity within the female population, with a wide quartile but similar average heights in all four burial areas, suggesting some degree of internal similarity across the female population (Figure 5.16). In comparison the male population was much more diverse, with huge variations within and between burial areas (Figure 5.17). Interestingly,

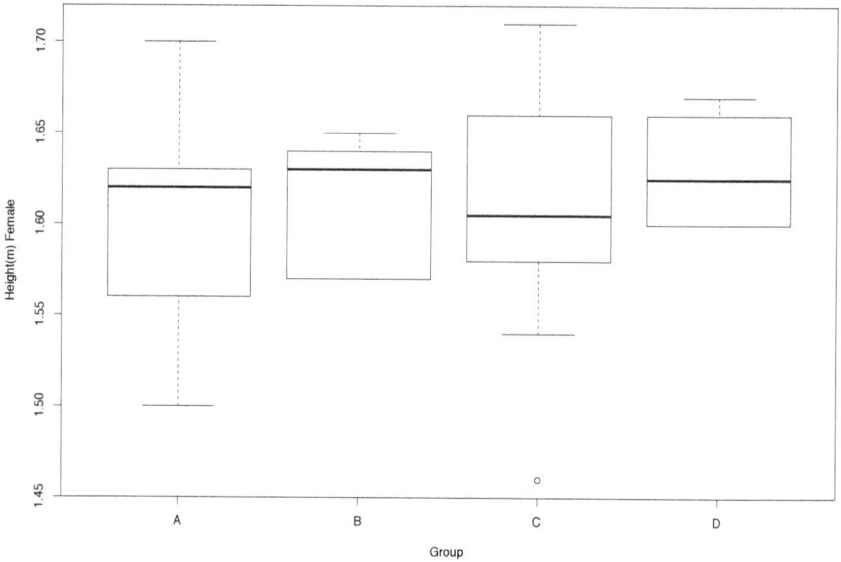

Figure 5.16 Great Chesterford, Essex: female height. With a wide interquartile range, but similar average heights in all four burial areas, there may have been some degree of similarity within the female population. Compare this with Figure 5.18, which shows no such similarity among the males.

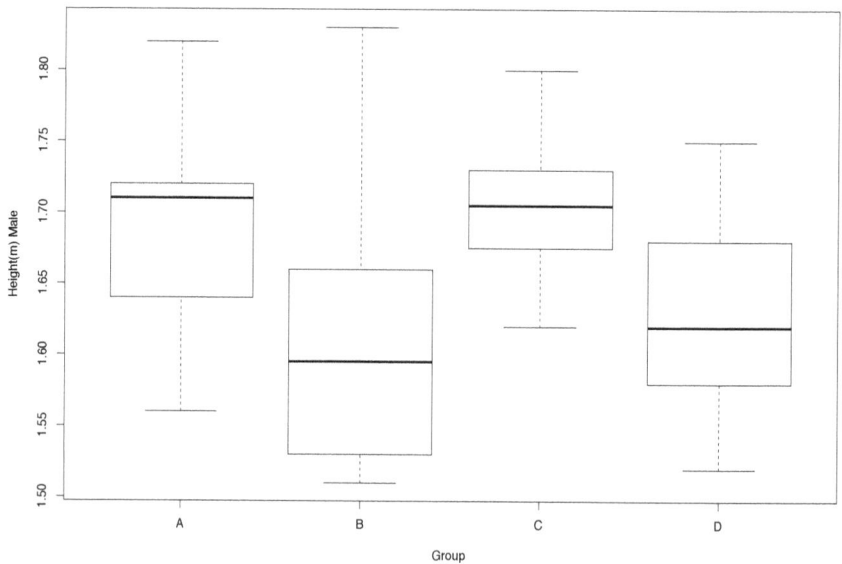

Figure 5.17 Great Chesterford: male height. In contrast to the female heights shown in Figure 5.16, the male heights were very diverse and showed much less similarity between the burial plots.

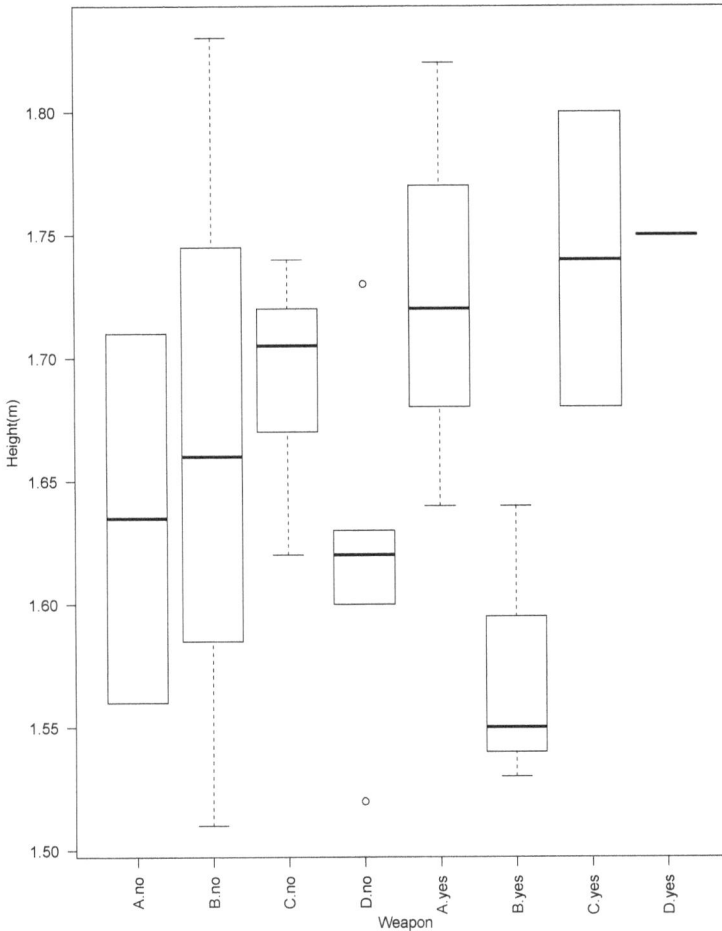

Figure 5.18 Great Chesterford: comparison of the height of men with weapon and non-weapon burials from each plot. The most closely comparable groups of males with weapons were in plots A and C. Weapons burials from area B were the most homogeneous.

the most similar males were those found in areas A and C, with comparable average figures. This degree of similarity was also seen in the distributions of height and weapon burials, where the most similar were men with weapons in A and C, but the greatest degree of homogeneity was present among males with weapons from area B, who were comparatively short (Figure 5.18). The greatest degree of heterogeneity existed within the non-weapon burials. It is not possible to see any patterns within the female data related to the presence or absence of brooches, which suggests that female identity was not expressed using

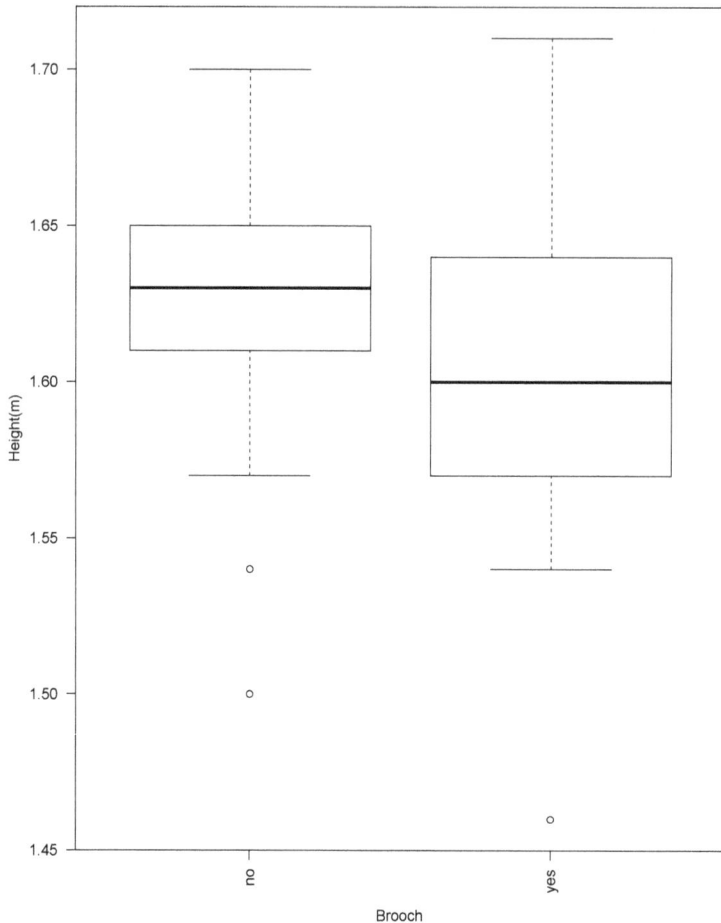

Figure 5.19 Great Chesterford: comparison of the height of women with brooch and non-brooch burials. The heights of brooch burials varied by over 10 cm.

material culture in the same way as it was among the male burials. In a similar way to Berinsfield, at Great Chesterford there was a greater degree of homogeneity within the female population that did not dress with brooches; the majority of these individuals were situated within a 0.04 m height range, a more homogeneous group which probably included many related individuals (Figure 5.19). The brooch burials, however, had a range of over 0.10 m suggesting that they were hetero-geneous, and so had different and diverse biological heritages.

Apple Down is also very interesting. Men with weapons in configura-tion A burials were, on average, taller than men with weapons in configu-ration B burials (Figure 5.20). They were also taller than the men without weapons within both configurations. Men without weapons had a much

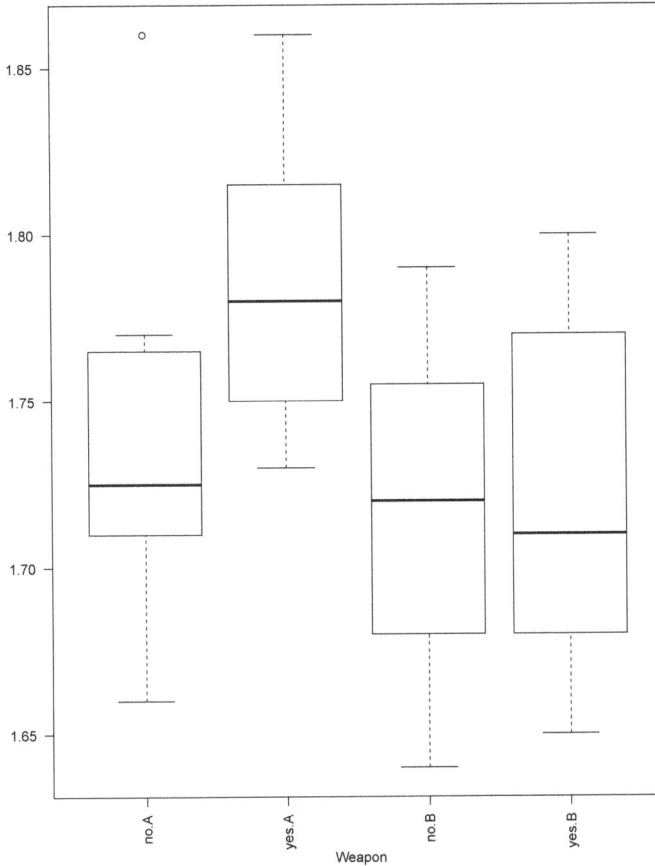

Figure 5.20 Apple Down, Kent: weapon burials by height. Males with weapons in configuration A burials were, on average, taller than males with weapons in configuration B burials and males without weapons.

greater range of heights, which varied over 0.15 m between the tallest and the shortest individuals, and the range was very similar among the different styles of burial. This pattern is most striking in the male weapon burials, but it was also evident in the gender difference according to burial configurations (Figure 5.21). The males from the configuration A graves were a few centimetres taller on average than those from configuration B, regardless of material weapons. Interestingly, the average height of women in groups A and B was very similar, but notably there seems to have been a much greater degree of similarity between the females in the configuration B burials, with most just 0.05 m in difference, as opposed to those in configuration A with around 0.10 m between them. Configuration A females had a total range of 0.18 m between the tallest and the shortest.

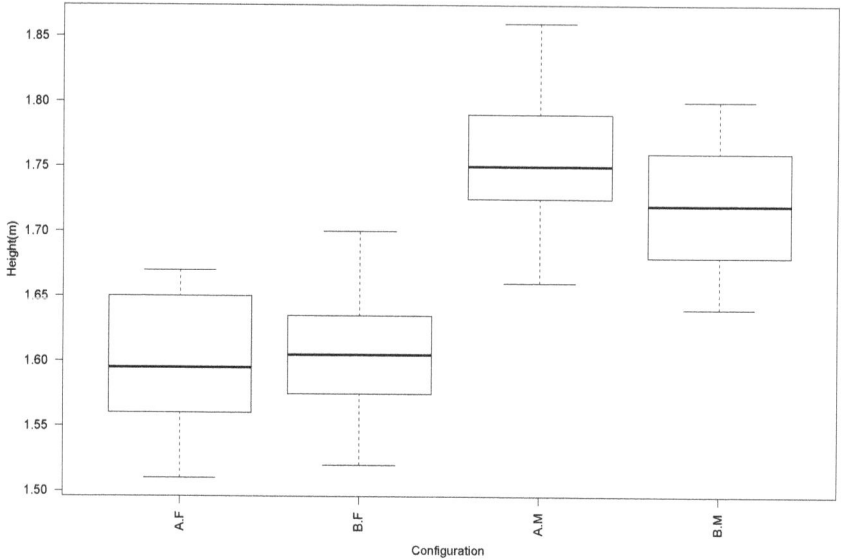

Figure 5.21 Apple Down: height box plot by gender. Males from A graves were a few centimetres taller on average than those from configuration B graves. By contrast, the average height of females in A and B graves was very similar.

This pattern suggests that were differences between the configurations in the homogeneity of males and females. The women were most similar across the whole populations but, significantly, the male weapon burials of configuration A showed the greatest degree of homogeneity, as they did in the burial areas at Berinsfield and Great Chesterford.

Worthy Park had a similar pattern to the male weapon burials. Like Apple Down, Worthy Park had a very masculine feel to the material culture (see Chapter 4); for example, there were just four brooch burials but nineteen male weapon burials. As with Apple Down, there was a pattern within the weapon burials, but it was specific to a particular group. Worthy Park had two burial zones evident in the biological data, A and B. Area A was to the south and had the greatest density; it was characterised by burials of different orientation and had a significant number of intercutting graves. Area B, to the north, was less dense (Figure 5.22). The height data in each area were interesting, and the area A females had the tightest range. These women fitted between 1.50 m and 1.68 m tall, but most were between 1.58 m and 1.64 m, illustrated by the box plot (Figure 5.23). By contrast, the females from area B were wide-ranging between 1.52 m and 1.73 m. The men were similar to those in area A and slightly taller on average. When explored by orientation, both sexes showed diversity, most evident among the E/W oriented female graves

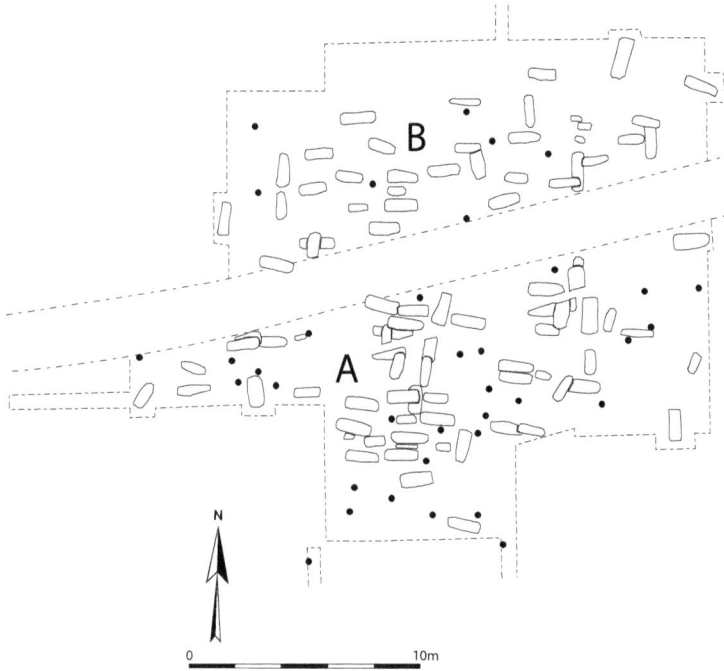

Figure 5.22 Worthy Park, Hampshire: plan to illustrate the layout of the cemetery.

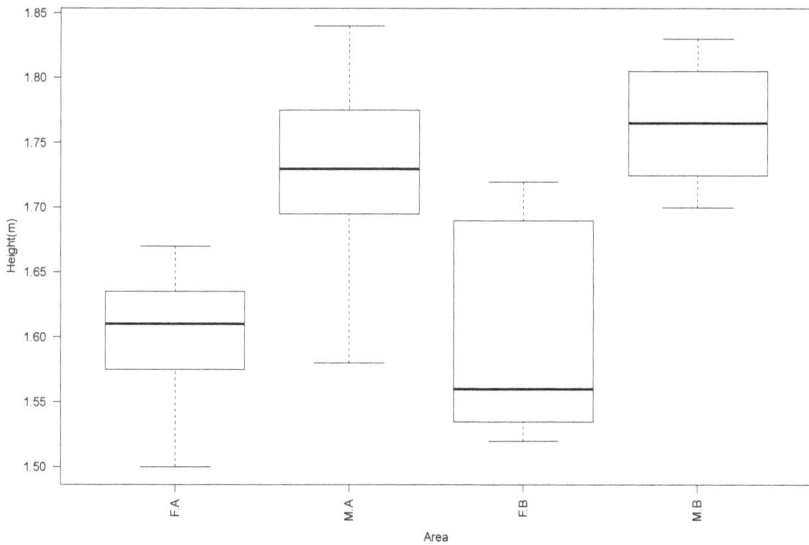

Figure 5.23 Worthy Park: height and biological sex by area. F = female, M = male. Plot A had the most structure to it, but the female graves in plot B showed the greatest diversity in terms of height.

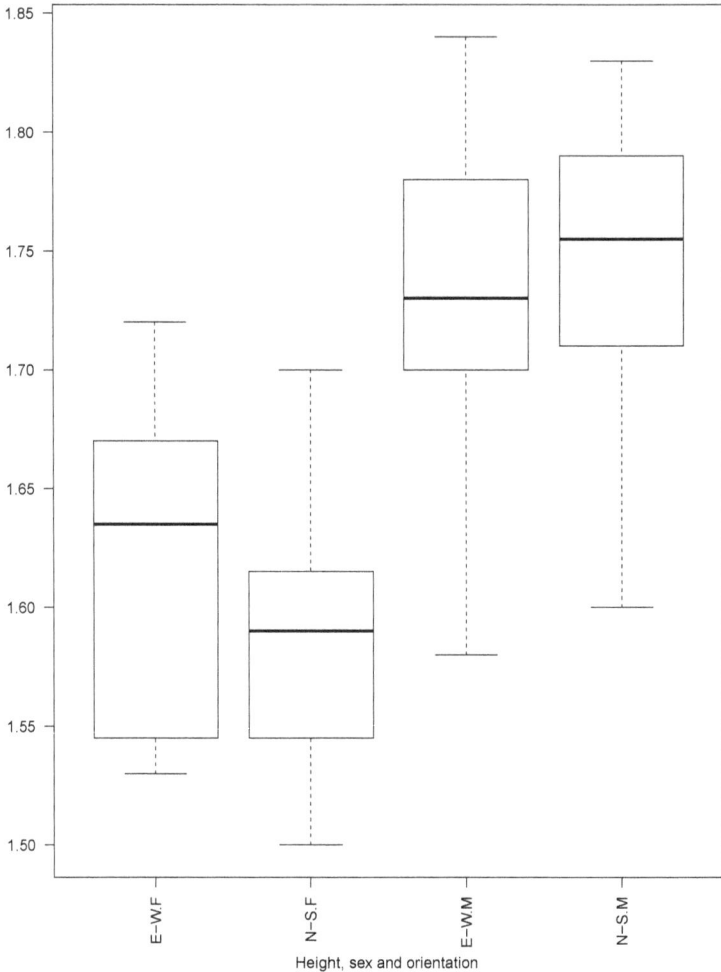

Figure 5.24 Worthy Park: height data by gender and grave orientation. Both sexes showed diversity, with the greatest range evident among the E/W-oriented females.

(Figure 5.24). Male burials were broadly similar based on orientation alone. However, when the male graves were explored by looking at the presence or absence of a weapon, the picture changed dramatically (Figure 5.25). Plot A had the most structure to it, and these males were oriented in different ways, but the graves without weapons showed the greatest diversity in terms of height, which ranged between 1.60 m and 1.80 m. The E/W oriented weapon graves were the tightest group, despite being one of the largest collections of burials, with five graves: nos. 22 (1.72 m), 45 (1.73 m), 46 (1.69 m), 95 (1.75 m) and 44, which was an outlier at 1.84 m (or six foot!). The E/W weapon graves in plot A were

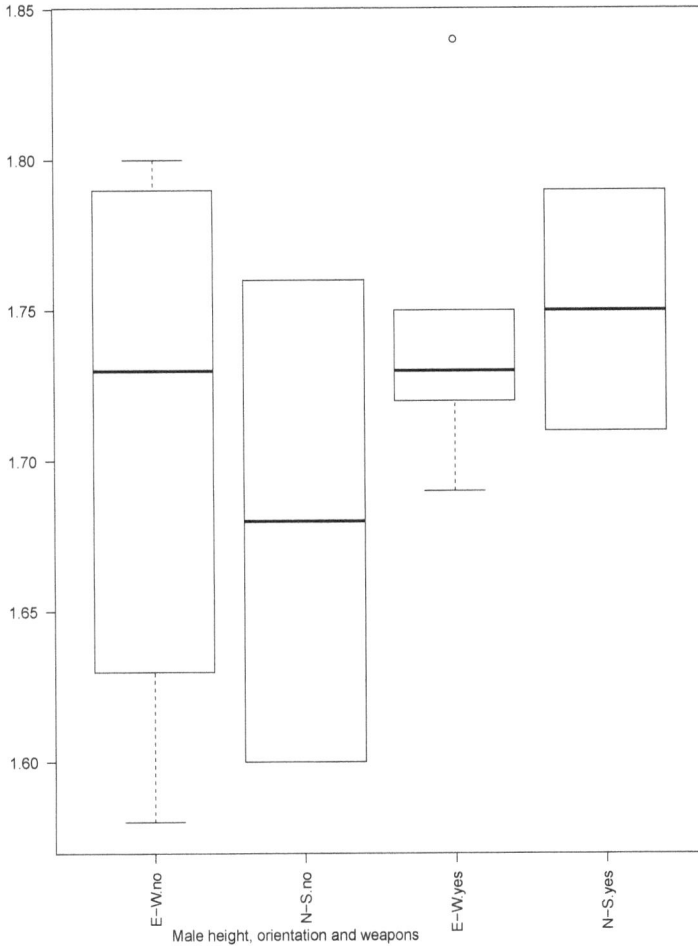

Figure 5.25 Worthy Park: height and weapons by grave orientation in burial area A. The E/W-oriented weapon graves were the most closely related group in the cemetery.

the most homogeneous group in the cemetery, a result which may suggest some degree of biological similarity between them.

At Lechlade, there were five groups of burials, A to E, with A and B separated by a Bronze Age barrow. Group C was a cluster to the east, D was a group of burials partly organised around a row of graves and E was the later phase distributed across the cemetery; many phase E burials were on an E/W orientation at odds with the earlier graves (see Figure 6.9). Notably, each of these burial groups included a range of male and female heights (Figure 5.26). Among the burials in groups A, B, C and E the males had a much greater distribution, with the males

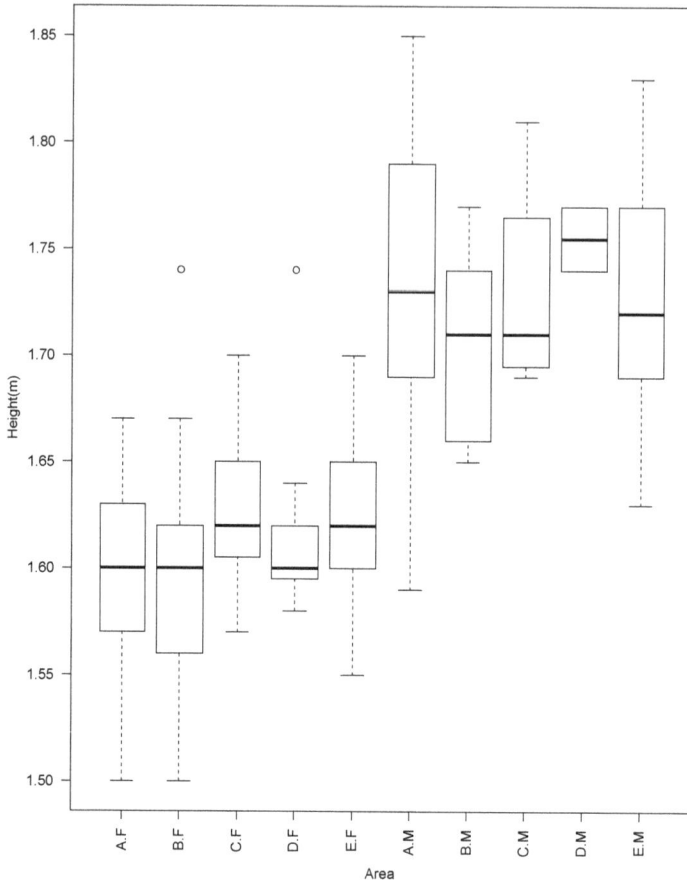

Figure 5.26 Lechlade, Gloucestershire: height by plot and gender. Males in plots A, B, C and E had a large range, females in D the tightest range and in groups A, B, C and E the interquartile range of heights among the females was much smaller than among the males. Plot D contained a small number of males.

from group A varying over 20 cm in height. This height difference suggests these males were a heterogeneous group. The females had a much tighter range, and in groups A, B, C and E the interquartile range varied up to 5 cm (C and E) and 6 cm (A and B) in height. Group D was interesting and consisted of a small group of burials focused around a row. There were only two males with height data, and both were weapon burials: graves 35 (1.77 m) and 92 (1.74 m). However, there were seven females with height data available, and five of these were within 3 cm of each other: burials 18 (1.6 m), 81/1 (1.6 m), 81/4 (1.6 m), 165 (1.59 m) and 167/2 (1.58 m). This was a tight enough cluster of heights that this difference could easily be understood as being the product of

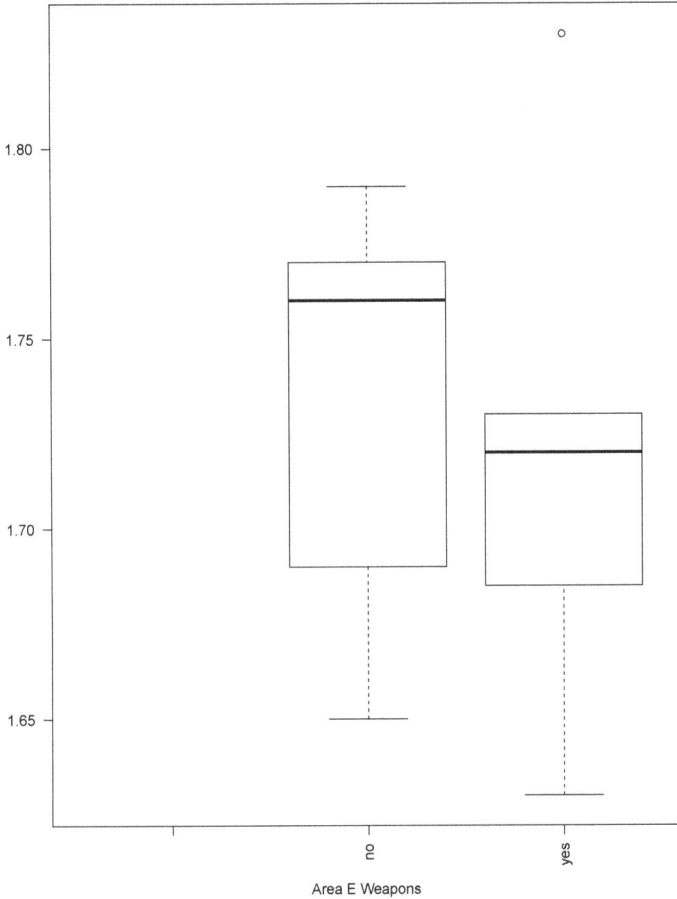

Figure 5.27 Lechlade: weapon burials in seventh-century burial area E. The male weapon burials of this configuration were more homogeneous than the non-weapon graves.

environmental variation. In short, these women were homogeneous and there is a very good chance they were related.

The final-phase burials at Lechlade included group E, which was a very diverse range of inhumations spread across the main burial area, and across a new burial area to the south of the cemetery. Notably, the male weapon burials of this configuration were in the north of the cemetery and were much more homogeneous in nature than the non-weapon graves (Figure 5.27). Certainly, the five weapon graves – 40 (1.72 m), 104 (1.72 m), 155 (1.73 m), 172/3 (1.73 m) and 181 (1.72 m) – all had men within 1 cm of each other in height. There were three outliers – graves 106 and 178 (1.63 m and 1.65 m respectively) and 121, who was very tall at 1.83 m. Although not a completely homogeneous group, it is evident that there was a core community of later-sixth-century and early seventh-century weapon graves at Lechlade with extraordinarily similar heights, indicating that they were almost certainly related. Indeed, across the whole date range, the weapon burials were much more homogeneous than the non-weapon burials; the interquartile range of weapon graves ranged between 1.70 m and 1.74 m, with an average of 1.72 m. The interquartile group of non-weapon graves ranged between 1.69 m and 1.77 m and had an average height of 1.72 m, meaning that although there were similarities between these groups there was a very strong homogeneous component to the male weapon graves at Lechlade.

By way of contrast, this pattern was not seen among the brooch burials (Figure 5.28). The quartile for non-brooch graves varied between

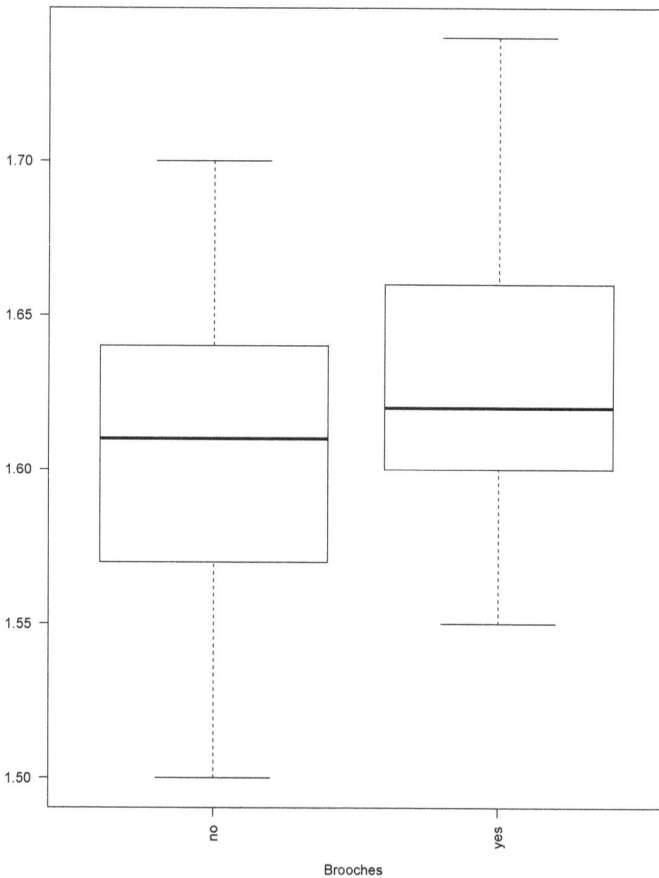

Figure 5.28 Lechlade: height and brooch burials. The brooch and non-brooch burials had a similar degree of heterogeneity.

1.57 m and 1.64 m and the interquartile group of brooch burials ranged
between 1.59 m and 1.66 m. Both brooch and non-brooch burials had
a similar degree of heterogeneity. In particular, among the twenty-five
women in area E there was a much greater degree of difference between
the two brooch burials, graves 127 (1.56 m) and 164 (1.55 m), than
between the non-brooch burials, which had an interquartile cluster
between 1.61 m and 1.65 m (Figure 5.29). This pattern was also seen
across the other cemeteries discussed in this chapter, and as a result it
is very unlikely that brooch burial was used as a way of distinguishing women who belonged biologically to a particular family, whereas
weapon burials appear to have had a high degree of homogeneity.

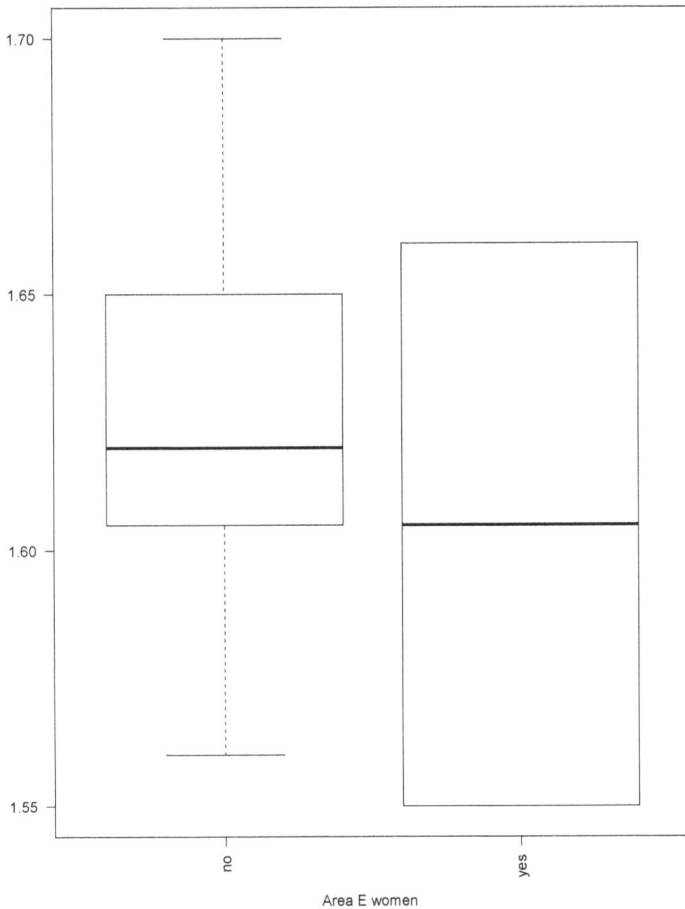

Figure 5.29 Lechlade: height and brooch burials in the seventh-century area E.
There was a much greater degree of difference between the two brooch burials
than among the twenty-five burials without brooches.

Weapon graves may thus have been afforded to male members of particular familial groups, although there is certainly enough variation
within the cemetery data discussed here to suggest this was not the only
reason men were interred with weapons.

The importance of height data in examining the health of past populations is undeniable (Mays, 2016), as is the impact of the environment
on population height. Even more influential, however, are the underlying
genetics. When fully grown, the range into which a person's height will
fall is determined by their parents. Inevitably, their final height will
be determined both by the environment and genetics together, but the
impact of the environment upon this is limited. Obviously, a particular
individual will be most similar to their siblings and their parents when
compared against more distant relatives, and more different still to unrelated individuals. In the examples discussed here there were evident patterns in the distribution of height data. These patterns were not evident
by examining the type of burial, such as a weapon grave, nor were they
evident in the location of burials in a particular plot. They were visible
through a combination of the two types of data. For example, weapon
graves within a particular plot or burial area were often the most homogeneous graves in a cemetery. This is compelling evidence and suggests
that there may have been familial traditions and kinship relations that
underlie patterns within the mortuary spaces. But families are not simple,
and it is important to remember that there would have been a significant
amount of complexity underpinning this. Indeed, in many burial areas,
such as Apple Down's configuration B burials, biological distance may
not have been the most important aspect of identity expressed within the
mortuary rite. To explore this further, we look at information from teeth
metrics. Like individual height, the size and shape of teeth have a strong
genetic component. Moreover, in the absence of extensive ancient DNA
data, height and teeth metrics are powerful ways to begin a discussion of
relatedness within historic population dynamics.

Early Anglo-Saxon teeth metrics

Teeth provide a strong medium through which to investigate familial-
inherited traits because their size and shape are derived from genetics
(Hughes and Townsend, 2013). Teeth form in early life and they do not
remodel like bone, which makes them taphonomically resilient (Galloway
et al., 1997). The potential to explore biological inheritance using dental
features has been reported before via non-metric characteristics, but has
not entered mainstream archaeological analysis because kinship studies
have not been fashionable (Alt and Vach, 1991; 1995; Sayer, 2009).
Nonetheless, we know that people who are closely related will have

proportionally similar sized and shaped teeth (Biggerstaff, 1975; Garn, 1977; Townsend and Brown, 1978a). This means that the teeth of sibling children will appear most similar to one another and their parents compared with more distant relatives, and more different still from unrelated individuals (Townsend and Brown, 1978a; 1978b). As a result, it is possible to compare the measurements of individual teeth within cemeteries, and where we assume that there is a similar biological basis to the population we can expect there to be similarly proportioned teeth.

Allison Stewart studied 145 individuals from four cemeteries; fifty-six from Hatherdene, Cherry Hinton, and forty-eight from Oakington (both in Cambridgeshire) as well as twenty-six from Polhill and fifteen from Eastry (both in Kent) (Stewart and Sayer, forthcoming). This created a combined total of 5,988 measurements for statistical analysis, and from this sample it was possible to identify significant patterns of similarity. For example, the left and right mandibular canines had the most significance in their patterning among the Oakington and Hatherdene males (Stewart and Sayer, forthcoming; Table 5.2). Dental metric data were recorded from all identifiable permanent teeth, focusing on skeletons of later adolescence to adulthood. Biologically male and female remains might be better understood together if studied separately, and this provides a useful way to explore sex-based differences within the teeth data. Moreover, there are more factors influencing tooth size than sex alone.

Table 5.2 Observations from cluster analysis for pooled sex comparisons from the combined cemetery and individual cemetery groups: Hatherdene, Oakington, Polhill and Eastry

Group	No. of clusters at 1	No. of clusters at 3	No. of clusters at 5	% of group split after node 1	Distance of node 2 split	Average size of largest cluster	Proportion of group (%)
Hatherdene							
males	8.50	6.50	4.50	79.6	15	4.50	20.5
females	5.75	5.25	3.50	57.5	9.5	4.25	26.5
Oakington							
males	5	4	3	78.9	8	6.50	43.5
females	6.75	5.25	3.75	68.3	12.25	4.75	27
Polhill							
males	5	4	3	85.7	14	2	29
females	6.50	5	3.50	58.7	11	3	25
Eastry							
males	2	2	2	66.7	4	2	67
females	3.25	3.13	2.63	70.4	8.38	2	49.3

After analysis, clusters were observed (see Table 5.2) and were identified at the squared Euclidean distances of 1, 3 and 5; also identified was
the percentage of the group that split after node 1; the distance of node
2 split; the average size of largest cluster across all teeth; and the proportion of the sample that this cluster comprised overall. Focusing on
significant teeth, a 'hierarchical cluster analysis' (HCA) showed that, at
all four sites, males had fewer clusters than females for the same tooth;
this pattern was observed across all of the significant teeth identified.
Men also appeared to have had more individuals within each cluster
than the females did. At each site, there were small numbers of relatively
large groups of related males, and a larger number of smaller groups of
related females. Such a pattern is very similar to the results described
for height data and, where in some burial areas there was less diversity
within the male population than in the female population, it would
seem that both the height and the teeth data are pointing in the same
direction. In these early Anglo-Saxon cemeteries there were more related
males than related females. Many of the related males included weapons
within their burials; however, caution is needed because membership
of a particular family group was evidently not the only reason to have
been buried with a weapon. Nonetheless, these two studies imply a high
degree of relatedness within the populations of these cemeteries, which
tends to suggest that early Anglo-Saxon cemeteries included a familial
element. The proportion of related men also suggests that among a
particular group there was a strong male residency pattern, which
remained; it seems it was women who moved for marriage. As a result,
though women and their daughters were related, new women came into
the community in each generation – a pattern that would result in small
numbers of biologically similar women. Men remained and so each
generation contained related men, a result seen in the large groups with
high degrees of similarity within the tooth metrics.

Notably, however, in the examples discussed there was not just
a single male group or lineage; indeed, the teeth data appear to be
structured in such a way as to imply that there were several different
communities of people, who shared different degrees of relatedness,
within each site. There may have been several groups of males who
were related to each other, but also to the women within the community. Indeed, the height data suggest that there was greater homogeneity
between the poorly furnished female burials (which were also the smallest); either these individuals had less social worth and so received less
food throughout their lives, or the lower social ranks practised female
residency whereas men from these groups moved to marry, or for
work. Nonetheless, the height and teeth data both suggest that the most
homogeneous group within all of these communities were the males, a

group which contained high degrees of relatedness among the wealthier burial areas within each site. This is especially important because the chronology data described in Chapter 3, suggest that it was to these burial areas that people returned generation after generation to bury their dead.

Conclusion

The world that people occupy exists independently of their knowledge of it. This is particularly true of biosocial problems, where the impact of lifestyle on the physical bodies of groups may not be known to the individual. Comparably, DNA does not respect the institution of marriage but is the combined product of physical parents whose genes were passed on and expressed in their child. This chapter has looked at evidence of both lifeways and relatedness, and has seen patterns in both types of evidence that correlate with both the organisation of the cemetery space and the expression of material culture.

At the time of writing, the methodologies and questions employed in the investigation of ancient DNA are only just catching up with the problems of social archaeology (Sykes, et al. 2019). However, we have an enormous amount of data to investigate by looking at the bodies of past people and, most importantly, by situating the data within each contextual setting. In this chapter we have used trauma pathology, or physical injury, to look at lifeways. The individual experience is important, but by examining the bodies of individuals it is possible to see patterns in lifestyle that were underpinned by social freedoms or attitudes within groups in each cemetery. Importantly, there seem to have been two basic types of cemetery, those with two or more similarly sized, broadly equal groups with similar lifeways, and those with a single core group and a spectrum of other groups with higher risks of trauma and/or less mortuary wealth. Crucially, in a given cemetery, these patterns were visible within and between groups, and not individual graves. For example, it was not possible to see patterns within weapon graves, because the placement of a weapon within a grave was dependent on a host of different decisions. However, it was possible to distinguish some weapon graves that were buried in a similar location within the cemetery. There were different attitudes towards burying the dead, and each cemetery consisted of a host of different approaches that were competing against the use of material culture or space as a form of differential expression contingent on the individual's identity. These attitudes were simultaneous influences on lifeways, chronology and the expression of the mortuary aesthetic.

Importantly, it is differences in attitude which underpin social difference, not wealth or the resources implied with the grave – which were expressions of the individual. This is especially true in archaeological data because the circumstances of death, burial and the disposal of the body vary from one individual to another. To use a well-known example, Richard III was buried without rich gravegoods, in a minor church in the middle of England (King *et al.*, 2014). The circumstance of his death, the shift in political power that resulted from it, and the redistribution of attitudes toward him *post mortem* may have affected the location and circumstances of his grave. Nonetheless, it was his body and its treatment in life and in death that revealed his identity to archaeologists (Appleby *et al.*, 2015). Similarly, in early Anglo-Saxon cemeteries grave location, wealth and style may have been contingent on the specific social context at the point of burial. The chronological point of the burial, who survived the deceased, the cause of death and/or any social or economic effects of that death would potentially change the material expressions involved in commemoration. The most stable *post mortem* communities, those which showed similar patterns across the life of the cemetery, comprised those individuals who had suffered least from exposure to the risk of trauma and had the most homogeneity among their teeth and height metrics. Collectively, these groups may have expressed the greatest wealth, even if individually they did not. At the heart of one or two plots in each cemetery seems to have been a multi-generational group of males with very similar statures and teeth metrics. It was these individuals and their immediate social group that returned to a cemetery generation after generation and created high-density burials areas, core groups or rows of graves. Diet, homogeneous or heterogeneous bodies and the lifeways evident in the archaeological record have provided powerful evidence for attitude in the mortuary context. And it is the attitude behind a burial, not the grave wealth within it, which provides us with a holistic approach to social archaeology. Ultimately, attitude may give us good access to questions about social segregation and/or identity. The exploration of personhood should be based on the social context, as well as at the level of the contents of the grave.

6

Early Anglo-Saxon community

Each early Anglo-Saxon cemetery was unique, the product of multiple agents working at different times, in different spaces and with different visions. Each grave was the end result of a funeral situated within specific chronological and community circumstances, influenced by social agents and their relationships to the deceased and to each other. In many ways each grave was the product of both a social context and of interpersonal relationships. Inhumation graves were cut into the soil and cremation pyres were built by hand. Together some participants had to lower the body into the ground or raise it onto a pyre. These were co-operative actions, they created or recreated bonds and reinforced existing relationships. As a result, a mortuary event included an emotional element in which objects, bodies, relationships and memories intertwined and occupied physical spaces. It was in this context that the dead were situated within the contemporary community narrative, the result of a series of negotiations that adopted locally contingent mortuary technologies, material cultures and spatial locations and which fitted with the expectations of mourners and other participants.

This final chapter brings together the other chapters and situates them within the historical context. It includes two case studies, Morning Thorpe and Lechlade, to demonstrate how the syntax, grammar, metre and intonation of the cemetery can be used to start building a holistic picture combining spaces and people. This study is a multi-dimensional interpretation because it explores space and chronology, and multi-scaled because it looks from gravegoods to individual identities, as well as to local and regional narratives. In particular, this chapter is interested in family, household and kinship, themes that have cropped up throughout this book. It situates the detailed explorations presented in each of the previous chapters alongside an exploration of Anglo-Saxon historical information, with a particular emphasis on contemporary (seventh-century) law codes. After all, the people buried in these sites were alive when the laws were first spoken about and written down, and as a result they were constructed from the same *Zeitgeist*, the same blood, sweat and attitudes of the contemporary cultural context.

Kinship and household

One of the key funerals described in the epic poem *Beowulf* is that of Hildeburh's kin. There was a feud between her father and her husband. Presumably she was married as part of a peace pledge to resolve an earlier phase of the feud, but the situation erupted again and in the ensuing battle both her brother and her son are killed while fighting on opposite sides at the hall of Finn, her husband, who was killed after the joint funeral of his son and his brother-in-law (Sayer *et al.*, 2009; Sebo, 2015; Sebo, pers. comm.). This dual funeral was designed by Hildeburh as an expression of her grief and also of her anger at the conflict. Hildeburh ordered a pyre to be built for her brother, Hnæf, and then placed her son beside him so they were cremated together. The poet's emphasis is on the construction of the pyre and how it allows for a public display of the couple, which focuses Hildeburh's emotional distress:

> *Here-Scyldinga*
> *betst beadorinca wæs on bael gearu·*
> *æt þaam ade wæs eþgesyne*
> *swatfah syrce*
>
> (The war-Scylding,
> The best battle-warrior [Hnæf] was prepared on the pyre,
> At the funeral pile he was easily seen,
> His tunic covered in blood) (Sebo, 2015)

The circumstances dictated the nature of the ritual and its emphasis; it was designed by a wife and mother, with a focus on her brother. Had this mortuary drama been prepared by Hildeburh's daughter-in-law it might have looked quite different. Rather than being cremated in the clothes they died in, they might have been dressed in new clothes and with identifiable gravegoods. The visibility of the injuries they inflicted on each other was important to emphasise loss and grief:

> *hafelan multon·*
> *bengeato burston ðonne blód ætspranc,*
> *láðbite líces· líg ealle forswealg,*
> *gaesta gífrost, þara ðe þaer guð fornam*
> *bega folces· (Beowulf, lines 1120b–1124a)*

(Heads melted.
Wounds burst open, then blood gushed out,
from the body's hate-bites. Fire swallowed everything –
The greediest guest – those who were taken by the battle,
from both sides.) (Sebo, 2015)

According to this description, marriage may have been a somewhat dangerous and unsuccessful device to settle a feud between two kindred (Rosenthal, 1966). In this funeral from *Beowulf*, a grandson had fought on behalf of his maternal grandfather, but died by the hand of his uncle. Uncle and son were cremated together.

Jack Goody (1983: 230) describes Anglo-Saxon society as ego-oriented rather than ancestor-oriented because he suggests that a person's kindred were important for support in feuds. Indeed, the state of feud is heavily cited by scholars of Anglo-Saxon social institutions because it contributed to one of the largest bodies of literature considering kindred. In the collection of *wergild* (the fine for killing a person) the role of direct kin varied according to circumstance, and it is likely that the recovery of this compensation fell to a wider group. The early eleventh-century document *Textus Roffensis* defined the extent of kindred involved in the surety for *wergild* payment; it states that for a twelve-hundred man (a nobleman whose *wergild* was set at 1,200 shillings) twelve men were to act as surety, eight from the paternal kinsmen and four from the maternal kinsmen. It is because of this that Loyn (1974: 204) argued 'we are clearly dealing with a society where great emphasis is placed on the individual and his household and the inner kin', because both paternal and maternal kindred were involved.

In the Textus Roffensis however, it was not a given that these kinsmen would support the slayer. In Edmund's earlier code (AD 939–49), concerning the blood feud, it affirms this:

[1.1.] If, however, the kindred abandons him, and is not willing to pay compensation for him, it is then my will that all that kindred is to be exempt from the feud, except the actual slayer, if they give him neither food nor protection afterwards. (Whitelock, 1955: 391)

These documents allow the kin to abandon the agitator and, provided they give him no support in the form of food and protection, then he alone bears the responsibility for the feud and its compensation. Notably:

[1.] If henceforth anyone slays a man, he himself to bear the feud, unless he can with the aid of his friends within twelve months pay compensation at the full *wergild*, whatever class he [the man slain] may belong to. (Whitelock, 1955: 391)

It is interesting that the term 'friends' (*freond* or *frynd*) is used here, and that this group was able to aid in the payment of compensation, demonstrating that by at least the tenth century the payment of *wergild* was not restricted to kin groups. Nevertheless, the details of these *frynds* are not specified and so may refer to less-defined kinship arrangements (Lancaster, 1958b: 375). These later texts were a form of social engineering intended to dismantle powerful kin alliances and shift responsibility for conflict resolution from the family to the institutions of kingship. Another early eleventh-century document, 'The ordinance of the bishops and reeves of the London district' (VI Athelstan), states:

> [8.2.] And if it happens that any kindred is so strong and so large, ... we are to ride thither with all our men with the reeve in whose district it is.

> [8.3.] And also we are to send in both directions to the reeves and request help from them of as many men as may seem to us suitable in so great a suit, so that the guilty men may stand in greater awe on account of our association; and we are all to ride thither and avenge our injury and kill the thief and those who fight with him and support him, unless they will desert him. (Whitelock, 1955: 389)

This is contradictory, in that it demonstrates the state's intention to control kindred, but it also proves how strong those kindred could be if reeves from several directions were potentially needed for support (Lancaster, 1958a; 1958b; Bloch, 1962; Loyn, 1974; Goody, 1983; Murray, 1983; Drew, 1988).

If later-Saxon England saw the deliberate decline in the power of the elite kindred, undermined by the emerging power of the Church and the King, it has been assumed that early Anglo-Saxon England was a 'Golden Age' of the kin and, indeed, that the laws did not need to mention their importance because they were taken for granted. But this assumption probably reveals more about evolutionary approaches to historical anthropology than it does about early Anglo-Saxons. It is therefore worth considering some of these laws.

Some of the earliest laws we have date from the seventh century. In the Laws of Æthelbert, King of Kent (recorded AD 602–3) it stated that 'If anyone kills a man he is to pay as an ordinary *wergild* 100 shillings' (Whitelock, 1955: 358; Oliver, 2002: 53/67), of which twenty shillings were to be paid at the open grave, and if the killer left the land his kin were responsible for paying half the *wergild*. There is no indication that the kin should pay any of the *wergild* unless the guilty man ran away and there is, significantly, no indication of who was present at the open grave of the deceased. In the Laws of Ine, King of Wessex (recorded AD 688–94), if a foreigner was slain then a third of his *wergild* would go either to his son or to his kinsmen (Whitelock, 1955: 366), the rest to the king, and if he (the foreigner) had no kinsmen then it was to go his *gesith* (lord). Importantly, this blood-price was paid first to his son or his household, then to the kinsmen and finally to his lord. It was not until the later Laws of Alfred (recorded AD 871–99) that we start to see evidence of the sharing of *wergild* payments between kin: '[8.3.] if her [of a nun stolen from a convent] child is killed, the share of the maternal kindred is to be paid to the King; the paternal kindred are to be given their share' (Whitelock, 1955: 375). This is interesting in that, as the child is illegitimate, it cannot inherit from its father, but it still requires the protection of the paternal kindred. There are further definitions within the Laws of Alfred:

> [30 (27).] If a man without paternal kinsmen fights and kills a man, and if then he has maternal kinsmen, those are to pay a third share of the *wergild* [and the associates a third]; [for the third part] he is to flee.
>
> [31 (28).] If anyone kills a man so placed, if he has no kinsmen, he is to pay half to the King, half to the associates. (Whitelock, 1955: 377–8)

Here again there is reference to people other than the kin – the 'associates' – though there is also reference to the maternal kin. But perhaps, rather than seeing this as evidence of legal bilateralism (Lancaster, 1958b), we should be cautious. The written statement of this responsibility tends to imply that it was not assumed, suggesting that the maternal kin did not routinely take responsibility for their daughter's children or her husband.

As we saw earlier in Æthelbert's law, the payment of *wergild* was due at the graveside, which suggests that an individual present at that grave would receive payment, or at least part of it. If we assume that this means literally at the graveside, and is not a reference to the time by which the compensation must be paid, the funeral becomes paramount. The funeral was when a community might redefine itself following the loss of one or more of its members (Metcalf and Huntington, 1991). At the graveside that relationship was defined and redefined, and division of the *wergild* might be as much a ritualised action, separated into parts by those present, as it was a legal responsibility. However, this also seems a peculiar clause, for surely the most dangerous (or insulting) or simply problematic time for a slayer or their kin to redress this death was when the family had gathered to remember their loss and their pain. As Lisi Oliver argues, this part payment forced the pronouncement of murder, and its settlement, at the most emotive time possible and at precisely the point where blood feud was likely to break out (Oliver, 2002: 97). As the example of Hildeburh's kin illustrates, it is likely that these

feuds took place between entwined groups among whom the boundaries
of relatedness and obligation were not always clear. In other words, it is
likely that the murderer was known to the kindred, and was even part of
it or its extended network.

Another source of information that the law codes dealt with might be
described as family law (Drew, 1988). In these documents, marriage was
a surprisingly secular business, conducted between families to the sat-
isfaction of the woman and her kindred and, interestingly, marriage
did not seem to interfere with a woman's *wergild* because she retained
the status of her father (Loyn, 1974: 206). Nonetheless, it was clearly
important to create and maintain a relationship with affinal kin, who
had their own distinct terminology, for example, father-in-law (*sweor*)
and mother-in-law (*sweger*) (Lancaster, 1958a: 247–8). This terminology identified the maternal kin group, suggesting that they had a role
post-marriage but perhaps also a different social function. Lorraine
Lancaster argued that they remained less important than the paternal
kindred (Lancaster, 1958a: 248).

Equally, marriage was not the only institution of union, and concubines may have been commonplace until the Conversion, when they
were discouraged by the Church (Ross, 1985). A concubine was legally
a member of the man's household, and this state may suggest a degree of
intra-kin or incest coupling where marriage would otherwise have been
forbidden (Clayton, 2008: 136; Goody, 1983; Ross, 1985). The early
Church's desire to quell these unions is undeniable, but the extent of
incest or concubinage remains unclear (Clayton, 2008). By contrast,
Æthelbert's seventh-century Kentish laws listed penalties for adultery
but omitted incest (Oliver, 2002), whereas the seventh-century canons
of Theodore, Archbishop of Canterbury, had provision for dealing with
homosexuality, incest, sex between siblings and mother–child incest
(Gravdal, 1995; Frantzen, 2008). Strikingly, these two sources illustrate a difference in how household practice collided with an emerging
Christian morality.

One aspect of marriage that was discussed in detail was the break-
down of marriage. Æthelbert's Law devoted a few clauses to dealing
with the inheritance of a wife (Oliver, 2002: 79). These suggested
that, if a woman had a healthy baby she would be entitled to half
of the household goods should her husband die first. If she left her
husband and took the children, she was also to have half of his goods,
but if she wished to take another husband the inheritance was split
between mother and child. They also indicate that if she was childless
her paternal kinsmen would obtain her goods and the 'morning-gift'
(the gift from her husband on the morning following the marriage).
These laws, numbered 76, defined a woman's inheritance, but only if

she bore children; they were more concerned with her husband's kin and protecting his inheritance. The Laws of Hlothhere and Eadric, Kings of Kent (they ruled jointly between AD 679 and 685), provided a clause stating that a widow should return to her kindred with the child, leaving someone from his father's kin to maintain the child's property until he was ten years old (the law refers to the child as he) (Oliver, 2002: 129). These laws imply that a woman's role in a man's household was not necessarily permanent, and that her family remained paramount in her welfare and her life.

Ine's Law also described the situation of a widow and child:

[38.] If a husband and a wife have a child together, and the husband dies, the mother is to have her child and rear it; she is to be given six shillings for its maintenance, a cow in summer, and ox in winter; the kinsmen are to take charge of the paternal home, until the child is grown up. (Whitelock, 1955: 367)

This clause, like those of Hlothhere and Eadric, was concerned with maintaining the husband's inheritance, and providing for the child's protection while the child remained in the care of his/her maternal kinsmen. It is noteworthy that there were no clauses for the maintenance of a child if its mother died, because the father's inheritance remained with the paternal kindred. This shows that the matrilineal kin only had a secondary kinship association with the child. It also suggests that the paternal kindred took priority in legal guardianship of inheritance, and it implies a degree of patrilocality among the social elite. In all of these cases it seems that the woman has travelled for marriage, and then returned to her family to rear her child following divorce or the death of her husband.

Extant Anglo-Saxon wills provide further evidence of male and female family responsibilities; a woman's obligation may have been to see her father's wishes completed (Crick, 2000). Women may not always have been independent of their father's or husband's wishes, but they were not totally dependent agents either and did not always follow the directions of men. Indeed, the will of Ælfflæd (will XV: 39–43, AD 1000–02) completes the bequests of her father, Ælfgar (will II: 103–8, AD 941–51), and although she honoured many of his land grants, some of which also passed from her sister, Æthelflæde (will XIV: 35–7, AD 971–91), her actions were not always in line with her father's wishes as outlined in his will (Whitelock 1930). Ælfflæd had many estates 'from her ancestors' which were not mentioned in the wills of her sister or father, and she also held many estates which should have passed directly from her sister to a monastic foundation but did not: Cockfield and Ditton, Suffolk, are two examples. Her estate at Totham, Essex, was supposed to go to a religious foundation at Mersea, Essex, but instead she split it up and the forest went to Stoke in her bequest. Waldingfield was supposed to pass to a monastery in a place called Crawe but Ælfflæd bequeathed it to one called St Georges instead. These actions were not those of a passive female, whose function was to carry out her father's wishes, and they show that women ran estates consisting of many households and were able to make executive decisions. Ælfflæd had the influence to alter the passage of land (Crick, 2000).

Households

Family was not the only domestic scenario, and references to house-holds are a part of Anglo-Saxon language. For example, David Pelteret has argued that the word *inhired* was used to refer to the sociological household in a societal and not a legal sense. In this case *in-* is a prefix which denoted the household association, *inpeow* therefore being a slave associated directly with the household (Pelteret, 1995: 43). Terms like this defined a household slave, meaning there were also non-household slaves not situated within the immediate household but still under the charge of the household head. Even so, it was the household and the state of being responsible for it which conferred status.

A household was a separate entity from family and may have con-sisted of servants; for those with some means, this might have included a reeve, a priest or military people who were not related or only distantly related to the core family. The early Law of Æthelbert supports this and refers to a serving woman (cup-bearer) of a nobleman, as well as other female slaves of second and third class (Oliver 2002: 67). The compen-sation to the owner if a man slept with an enslaved woman depended on the slave's status and the status of their owner. Further, Æthelbert's Law states: '26. If anyone kills a freeman's loaf eater [dependant], they are to pay six shillings compensation' (Oliver, 2002: 69). Hlothhere and Eadric's Laws 1 and 2 referred to the responsibility a person had for their servants; they indicate that if an unfree person (a slave, or household dependant) killed a freeperson of rank then their owner was responsible for paying the compensation and handing over the killer (Oliver, 2002: 127). If a servant killed another servant then the owner had to pay for that action (Æthelbert's Law, clause 76, Oliver 2002: 79). Ine's Law, clauses 19 and 22, referred to a *geneat*, who was a tenant or dependant, and was described by Whitelock as a member of the household; this *geneat* may have had a high *wergild* value, suggesting that not all members of a household were slaves or servants (Whitelock, 1955: 366). Also in Ine's Law a *gesith*, who was a member of the household and was of noble birth, had their own reeve, a smith and a nanny, as well as unfree workers (Whitelock, 1955: 371). The household of a person of high status could include individuals of many different functions, but a royal household might have had bondspersons who were themselves of substantial rank by virtue of having their own households. Effectively, important or wealthy households would have had satellite households associated with them. A reeve, a priest or a smith, for example, might have had his or her own marriage, servants and slaves.

As we have seen, responsibility for a household lay with the head of that household, but legally its members may not always have been responsible for the actions of the head of the household, witness Ine's Law:

[7.] If anyone steals without his wife and children knowing, he is to pay 60 shillings fine.

[7.1.] If, however, he steals with the knowledge of all his household, they are all to go into slavery. (Whitelock, 1955: 365)

These ordinances of Ine suggest that the immediate family were not responsible for the crimes of another unless they had become party to them.

Anglo-Saxon England had a legal system of compensations and some of these may tell us about the function of household. Æthelbert's Laws defined the compensation for offences against a person's house. Number 79 dealt with a man taking a 'maiden' or woman by force (Oliver, 2002: 79, 106). The head of the house was responsible for applying the fine, and clauses and responsibilities like this make it hard to see the servants or slaves described in these laws as simply objects (Pelteret, 1995: 42). Therefore, while a household may have consisted of the immediate family, partner or concubines, children and possibly otherwise unconnected/unmarried kindred, it will also have included individuals who contributed to the production of food and clothing, childcare and the maintenance of land, as well as metalworkers and skilled labourers. Some of these individuals may have had their own families, and even their own households consisting of family, free associates and servants.

Many of these legal descriptions are contemporary with the early Anglo-Saxon cemeteries, and so if they described family situations, and household responsibilities, it is not unreasonable to assume that we might see some evidence of these complexities within the archaeological record.

Space, place and material culture

Each early Anglo-Saxon cemetery appears different: they had varied overall forms, they were different sizes and they contained different assemblages of material culture. Nonetheless, the communities that used and returned to these sites drew from a comparable repertoire of mortuary syntaxes to subdivide the cemetery. In doing this they created and reproduced a number of underlying but comparable narratives that defined the organisation of space. How this narrative changed is visible in the evolution of mortuary space. The users of the cemetery created, structured and shared in a constantly changing semiotic knowledge. This book has shown that early Anglo-Saxon cemeteries were chaotic and lived spaces, that each grave was the product of different agents acting under dissimilar influences, and that each agent made a unique contribution to the funeral; because of this inherent fluidity, cemetery spaces encapsulated and reflected the contemporary context. In short, they can be understood today because they were meant to be understood by mortuary participants while they were in use. Cemetery aesthetic was used locally to communicate at a cultural level; it provided the physical space to support the narrative discourse of a particular community, and even though each space and each narrative was different it is likely that people from different communities, near or far, would have understood the messages and narratives embedded there. To these unfamiliar participants some aspects of the site would seem outlandish, even alien, while others would have been familiar or even comforting.

Within early Anglo-Saxon cemeteries, materials and spaces had multiple meanings, and people concurrently expressed diverse and disparate identities, which created a muddle of messages. As a result, archaeological investigation cannot isolate just one factor, like social status, for example. What was social status but the product of a series of relationships between people? A head of a household was not that without servants to work the land, or a family to offer legal support. Likewise, a slave without a master was not a slave. Individuals were not singular entities but were entangled within a social complex. These relationships empowered the mortuary *actants* with differential agency in creating a material expression that was the product of a range of contextually contingent conceptual tools unique to that place and those people. Importantly, mortuary expression was communication, which produced *leitmotifs* that were meant to be understood because they communicated shared cultural experiences. Early Anglo-Saxon cemeteries were dynamic and complex places. Yet they are often depicted in reconstruction drawings as insipid, not colourless per se, but empty of emotion or involvement – individuals are spaced apart, inert and not interacting, bodies separated (Williams, 2009).

Instead, each funeral event was different; the dead were dissimilar people, situated within social relationships which were played out by participants. The graves were earthen and cut through the soil by hand. Together some participants had to lower the body into the ground and in doing so their bodies mingled with that of the deceased; they blended with each other and with the soil. These people laid out arms and legs, arranged clothing, faces, heads, hands and feet. To place objects in the grave the mortuary participants must have also climbed into it, and sat or lain next to the body. This experience involved physical and emotional interactions, creating an intimacy between people living and dead (Figures 6.1 and 6.2).

Despite these unique experiences, each mortuary event contained similarities: the participants had relationships, and in these interactions their social world was reproduced though communication and collaboration. Their individual attitudes towards status, gender, age and kinship were shaped by relationships created or defined by existing social structures in the form of agreed canons. These principles had been renegotiated as these were confirmed or challenged by social situations, creating new semiotic knowledge shared between participants. Objects were symbiotic to this situation because they were an aesthetic essential and part of these layered and textured experiences. Cultural perspectives towards gender, for example, added to a mixture of other forces, which included kinship, age, status or family and which might have acted on people's behaviour or perceptions. The social world was not a fixed entity, but changed and evolved in a state of constant negotiation, and this renegotiation and dynamism are evidenced by the variation within and between each cemetery.

As described above, the sixth-century cemetery resulted from an aggregate of multiple perspectives and within this space the syntax of the cemetery could change over time. In a second phase in the later-sixth and seventh century, the southern and eastern coasts of England witnessed a new phase which was probably partly inspired by Merovingian burial practice. Rows of graves gave the impression of order, but in both phases cemetery arrangement was augmented by existing topographies in the form of old features – barrows, Roman buildings or earlier ditches – or new ones such as key burials or central locations within the cemetery.

Thinking of these spaces as either monocentric or polycentric, based on the clustering of graves, is useful but simplistic. As this study has shown, it was only the smallest sites that included just one technology to organise the space. Visible features divided cemeteries into areas,

Figure 6.1 A reconstruction based on archaeologists working at Oakington in 2014. Kayla, Alison, Shanice and Anna are excavating a sixth-century grave. Gravegoods and Anglo-Saxon clothing have been added to this image to resemble the creation of a burial, providing a dynamic experiential reconstruction. Just like the archaeologists working here, the team of people who laid out the burial and the gravegoods would have had to climb into the grave, and would have got on their hands and knees to lay out the body and gravegoods. Like the team here, led by Kayla at the foot of the grave, there may have been hierarchies of people instructing and negotiating the arrangement.

Figure 6.2 A busy excavation scene. This reconstruction is based on an open day at Oakington in 2012. It includes site directors, excavation supervisors, excavators, members of the public and my father, with a spear. Each of these people's experiences and knowledge of the archaeology here was different. Like Figure 6.1, this image conveys the interaction of people engaged in multiple different tasks. In the foreground the body is laid out, some people are interacting with the corpse and negotiating the objects to place within the burial. To the left of the grave, visitors look on, while in the middle a group of people go over the soil preparing to use it to build a mound over the body. Behind them a man kills a pig to prepare a feast, and others watch the whole scene away from the grave, or from the nearby settlement. This image conveys the physicality of the mortuary drama, and illustrates a multitude of ways that people could participate in the funeral events, at different levels and with different degrees of engagement or knowledge.

groups or plots. This included clusters of graves that could be observed and defined by spatial statistics, or by changes in the density of burial, which defined specific groups of graves either between or within clusters. Alternatively, the cemetery architects might use contrasting orientations, as at Berinsfield, Petersfinger, Apple Down and Great Chesterford, to define separate groups or to visually identify outliers dividing spaces; or orientation might have been used to distinguish a few burials within a larger plot, as also seen at Great Chesterford. The choice whether to cremate or inhume also contributed to the shape of burial space, as with Spong Hill, Springfield Lyons, Apple Down and Andover; but, just like orientation or density, cremation could also distinguish or identify an individual's grave or a small group of graves within a larger burial area.

How a corpse was dressed, which objects went into the grave or were withheld, how a corpse was prepared, whether it was cremated or inhumed, and how a corpse was laid out were all locally mediated decisions based on the expectations of mortuary participants. The result was a continually negotiated expression which depended on who was alive to participate. Cemetery chronology might allow us to see this cadence or metre, allowing us to explore the biography of cemetery space and with that the specific groups or identities within it (Hines and Bayliss, 2013: 560). At Orpington a single grave provided a central point around which generations of subsequent weapon graves, child graves and cremations were located. Equally, at Oakington and at Dover Buckland, the emphasis of several burial areas was around key individuals marked by small barrows. This pattern was also seen in several later-sixth- and seventh-century sites, which may have had more uniformity, for example, St Peters, Lechlade and Finglesham. Other cemeteries contained plots with higher densities of graves, creating a concentric pattern. In comparison, at Morning Thorpe, West Heslerton, Apple Down and Deal, or the core areas of plot F at Dover Buckland and plot C at Wakerley, burials were densely packed. The same place may have been used to inter key individuals for generation after generation. But not all burial areas contained this chronological focus: configuration B burials at Apple Down, plots H–I, B or Di at Dover Buckland and the excavated plot at Sewerby all used a horizontal stratigraphy, where contemporary graves were positioned together and adjacent to their predecessors, so that the burial space moved over time. These plots had no obvious central core (Figure 6.3). A number of smaller sixth-century burial plots – at Dover Buckland (plots L, E or G), the westerly graves at Orpington or the dispersed graves at West Heslerton and Polhill – did not seem to have a chronological character. This difference was part of an attitude to burial space and mortuary commemoration, and these attitudes towards cemetery space seem to have differed between different burial areas, and

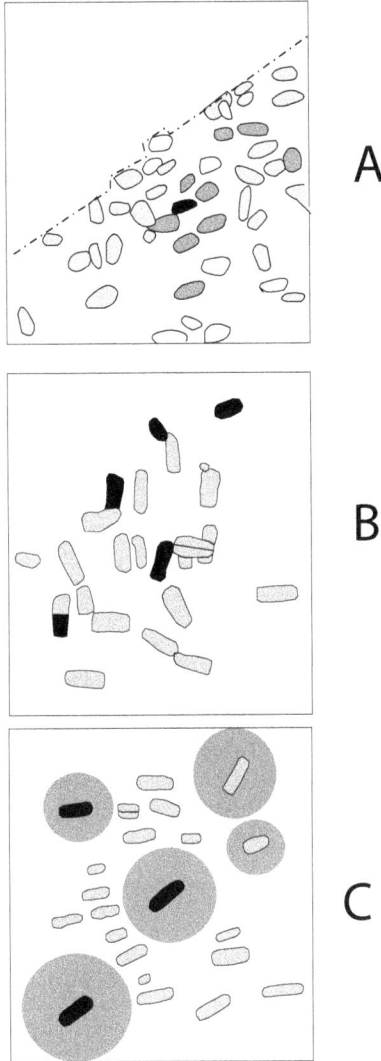

Figure 6.3 Different types of core graves within plots: the darker the grave, the more gravegoods were identified. Plot A was a focused plot with a central core of furnished burials surrounded by well-furnished darker burials and lighter less well-furnished burials – this example is West Heslerton. Plot B was a dispersed core from Lechlade, and C consisted of a series of barrow burials with satellite graves from Finglesham. These burial forms seem to indicate that there were alternative attitudes towards the dead, with different communities/groups valuing different forms of mortuary expression, even within the same cemetery space.

between groups of people with different lifeways. Indeed, as we saw in Chapter 3, each of these burial plots at Dover Buckland had a different style. Some were densely packed, some were marked by barrows, while others used external features or had internal divisions along age or gender lines.

This differential attitude was defined by significant variations within the cemetery spaces. These included a whole host of attitudes towards the dead. But, notably, attitudes seem to have been contained within two basic types of cemetery: those with two or more similarly sized, broadly equal groups with similar lifeways; and those cemeteries with a burial area that had some internal structuring, for example a core area, as well as a spectrum of other areas without similar structure. In the examples discussed here, these less-structured areas also contained those individuals with a higher risk of trauma and with less overall mortuary wealth. Importantly, these patterns were visible within and between groups within the cemetery, and not just between types of graves. For example, it was not possible to see patterns within weapon graves because the placement of a weapon within a grave was dependent on a host of different decisions, many of which may have been about the personal situation of the deceased. Their age, gender, identity, cause and time of death, and who was alive at the time of that death, directly affected how they were seen and interacted with. This is important, because within specific burial areas it was the type of grave that shared key biological characteristics like diet, morphologically similar dentition or correspondence in height which showed similarities.

Indeed, the most stable *post mortem* communities, namely those that showed less internal variation, also had similar patterns across the life of the cemetery, where those individuals who suffered least from exposure to the risk of trauma had the most homogeneity among their tooth and height metrics. Collectively, these groups may have expressed the greatest wealth, even if individually graves may not have been furnished. Many cemeteries contained one plot that was wealthier than the others, for example; Wakerley, Apple Down, West Heslerton, Great Chesterford and Holborough. Within these examples the wealthy graves were positioned in central zones or core areas which included similar, often more densely packed, graves that created an aesthetic focus. These core areas within plots or burial areas seem to have been multigenerational. The women of these same areas also may have included the wealthier graves, for examples those buried with brooches, but they had much more biological variety between them than the male graves. The women seem to have been more heterogeneous in their origin, but it was a group of people with specific social attitudes who returned to a cemetery generation after generation and created an area with a high density of burials, with groups, clusters or rows of graves. Importantly, it was the attitude towards burial – location, orientation, chronology – and not just the wealth within it that provides us with the best evidence for social difference.

As we saw at Leighton Buzzard III, Great Chesterford, Wakerley and Finglesham, there was hierarchy to group affiliation, and some plots contained core burials which created mnemonic regimes for regional display. The males within these areas may have been of similar height and may have shared comparable lifeways. Other plots, or groups of graves, did not exhibit the same biological similarity, and did not employ a core area for burial. These local community arrangements seem to imply that there was one primary group with one or two subsidiary groups, differentiated because they had different attitudes towards the dead. These groups may also have had subtly different life experiences. These secondary or tertiary plots employed separate burial areas, and may have placed less emphasis on gender, or life stages or childhood, and as a result they employed less internal structuring within the mortuary spaces. Along with less organisation there seems to have been less focus on funerary narratives for retelling. These systems created and reinforced differences in attitude highlighted and underpinned by the lived experience. These attitudes were not just towards the treatment of ancestors or the dead, but included attitudes towards the expression and communication of gender and age. Importantly, at sites like West Heslerton, Broadway Hill, Winterbourne Gunner, Lyminge II, Westgarth Gardens, Berinsfield, Deal, Bargates, Fonaby and Snell's Corner, there was evidence of gender separation, highlighting male or female characteristics in central places in specific groups of burials. These recognisable structures drew on local and cultural tropes, and it was these attitudes, not the presence of objects, which served to distinguish the elite individuals from each generation.

In this volume, the syntax of the cemetery, the grammar of the grave, the metre of burial practice and the biological evidence for interconnectedness have been reviewed separately. In this final chapter it is worth visiting two important and complex sites to illustrate how these elements come together. Morning Thorpe was an extremely important cemetery where, like Deal and Wakerley, there were very strong patterns in the distribution of material culture that correlated with the spatial arrangement of the site, and as a result corresponded with differences in attitude and lifeways. Lechlade has been discussed before, but it is one of the most complex cemeteries in the corpus of early Anglo-Saxon sites. Here, spatial data correspond with mortuary ritual and height data across the long duration of the fifth to later-seventh century. At both cemeteries the evidence points to the origination of the sites along family and household lines, where attitudes towards burial corresponded with social groups with different lifeways. Male kinship, wealth and ancestry mattered more to some than to others. It was these social groups that correspond with the early Anglo-Saxon family at the core of the households described in the historical literature.

Morning Thorpe: the material repertoire

Morning Thorpe was excavated in 1974 as a rescue excavation and recorded 320 inhumations and nine cremations (Green *et al.*, 1987). Kenneth Penn and Birte Brugmann (2007) suggested some evidence for the clustering of the graves into groups that included males, females and the smaller graves of children, but not to the extent that would justify describing them as clusters of a nuclear family variety. Indeed, the graves at Morning Thorpe were extremely tightly crowded but not homogeneous, with statistically significant clustering around 1.5 m. As a result, there were four groups of graves, with a narrow but nonetheless visible gap separating them; notably, the central two groups had a particularly high density of graves (Figure 6.4). As at Wakerley, these four groups (from left to right: A, B, C and D) were also associated with subtly different material culture. Notably, group A and D graves were more likely to contain long knives, with a blade length of over 10 cm, with ten associated with group D and twelve with B, and just two examples each associated with groups A and C. The same is true of belt buckles that have copper-alloy loops, which were found in group B and D burials, with only one example in group C (Chadwick Hawkes and Dunning, 1961, type 1 buckles; Penn and Brugmann, 2007: 32; Figure 6.5). Girdle hangers were more common in area B with ten examples, and only three in group C and two in group D; burials in area C were more likely to have a bucket or 'tub' suggesting a ritual unique to this group. These are fascinating distributions, and perhaps they show that there were slightly different ways to dress the dead among each group, with a memory of different methods passed separately within each group between generations.

Perhaps though the most remarkable thing about the Morning Thorpe cemetery was the spatial groupings among the stamped pottery vessels that were found in more than one grave (Penn and Brugmann, 2007: 40). These groupings paralleled the spatial groups identified with the Ripley's K-test and subsistent kernel density plot. These groupings principally correspond with plots B and C. Stamps 'Ih', 'Ik', 'Iic' and 'Ivd' were found in plot B and 'Ia' was primarily found in plot C with some examples in plot B (Figure 6.6). Interestingly, plot D contained a mixture of stamps found more frequently in plots B and C, whereas

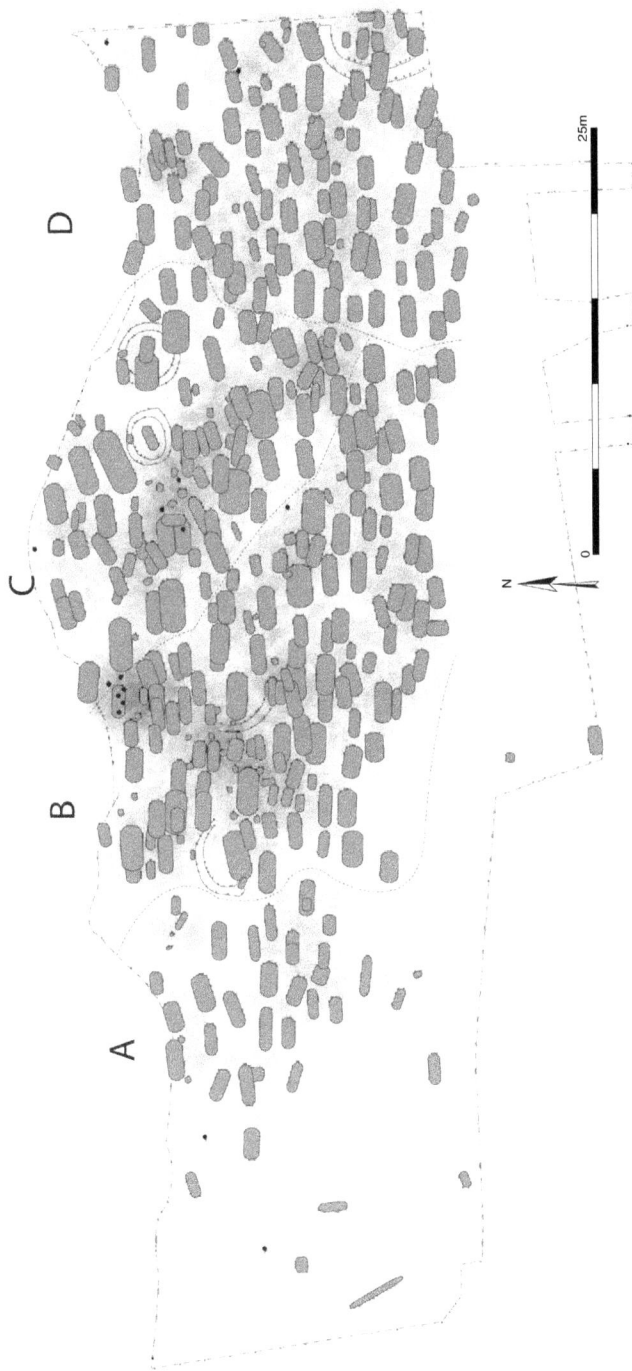

Figure 6.4 Morning Thorpe, Norfolk: kernel densities illustrated at 2 m. There was a narrow, but nonetheless visible, gap separating each of these plots, illustrated by the dashed lines. Notably, the central two groups, B and C, had particularly high-density concentrations of graves.

Figure 6.5 Morning Thorpe: material culture. Note that each of the burial areas had subtly different assemblages of material culture. Areas A and D were less dense and contained burials with one or two weapons or penannular brooches. Area B had the most numerous weapon burials and was bounded on each side with a line of weapon burials. The light grey graves had few gravegoods. The dark grey were double weapon or brooch pair burials and the black graves were the wealthiest.

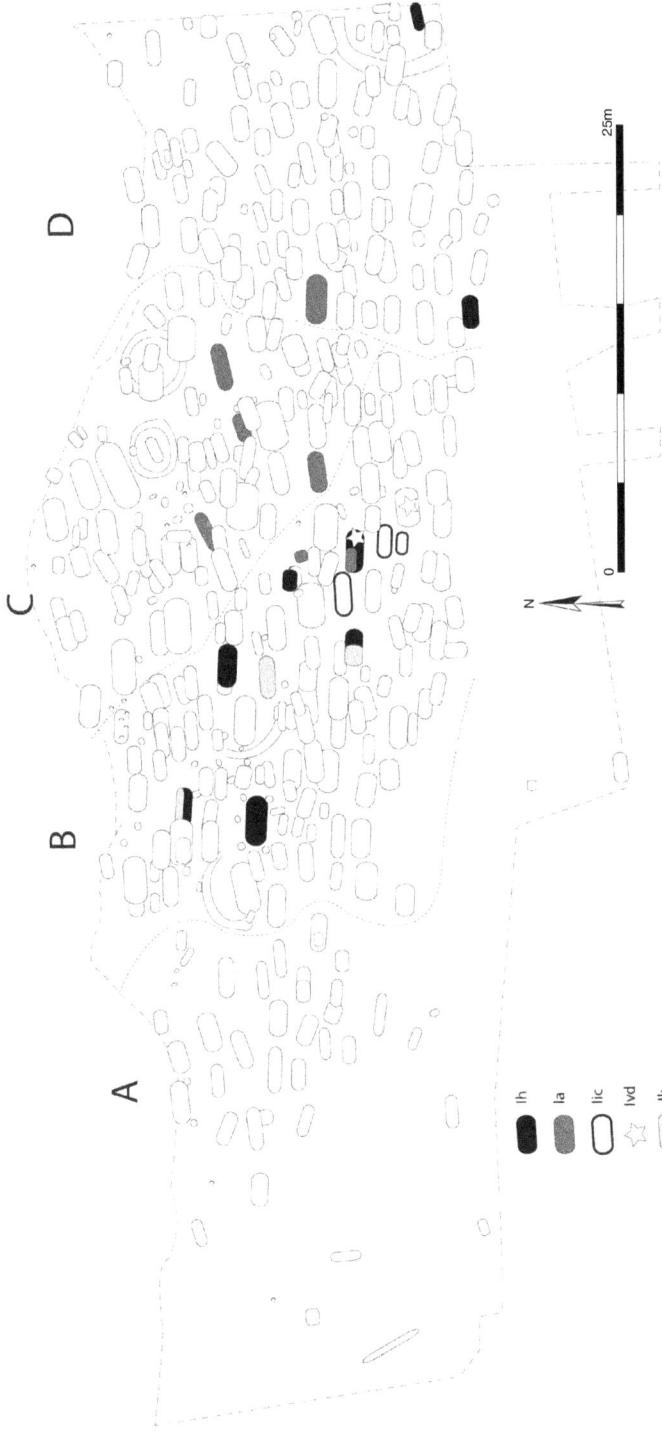

Figure 6.6 Morning Thorpe: distribution of pottery stamps (where they were used for more than one pot). Note the contrast between plots B and C, where B had the most variety and C just a single type (after Penn and Brugmann, 2007: 37, Fig. 4.7).

plot A contained no parallel stamps despite having eight pottery vessels; the sole stamp found in plot A was not paralleled in the other three. Nowell Myres (1937: 391) rather unfairly suggested an 'unimaginative potter' or 'housewife' may have used the same stamps to mark family pots, evidenced at Brighthampton (Oxfordshire) by two identical pots from adjacent graves. Similar stamps were also shared between cemeteries; Myers (1937), for example, also points out similar vessels from Lackford and West Stow (both in Suffolk). Indeed, the uniform use of prints on pottery has been suggested as the result of a clan use of stamps (Hills, 1978: 148), and at Spong Hill stamp groups A, B and C had noticeable spatial distributions linked with the cemetery chronology (Hills and Lucy, 2013: 217–18).

The distribution of material culture at Morning Thorpe was complex, and there were clear differences between the types of object found within each plot. Morning Thorpe is one cemetery, and so the individuals placed within it were interconnected, and probably shared a similar regional perspective. For the most part the funerary rite was constant, annular or penannular brooches for women and spears for men, but even here there were different funerary traditions evident throughout the site. Plots B and C were by far the wealthiest and contained the majority of burials with either weapon sets or brooch sets. B and C also had the more elaborate graves, for example, grave 35 with spearhead, shield boss, shield studs, knife, buckles, pottery vessel and tub. Grave 35 was also a double burial with a small-long brooch and wrist clasps (Figure 6.5). Importantly then, just as with Apple Down (see Chapter 1), the funerary ritual varied between these different areas. Plots B and C were the most marked in their difference and were also the wealthiest plots, and each used different strategies for their internal arrangement. In plot B, the majority of wealthy weapon sets or brooch sets were located around the edges of the group, defining its boundaries; and the highest density of burials was found between barrow graves 157 and 170, within the boundary defined by the majority of the weapon and brooch burials. Indeed, the smaller graves, presumably infants and children, were found in the interior of this row of graves. Only the later graves in plot B, in the south-eastern corner (phase FB, AD 530/550–650, Penn and Brugmann, 2007: fig 5.12), were notably wealthy, with three great square-headed brooches.

Plot C was organised very differently and had a number of wealthy graves throughout its interior, with many less wealthy inhumations found buried around them. Many of these burials may have had small barrows erected over them, marking them as central points (Figure 6.7). Two of these graves, 38 and 277, were evident because of ring ditches, whereas burials 2, 200, 208, 233, and 333 had satellite inhumations

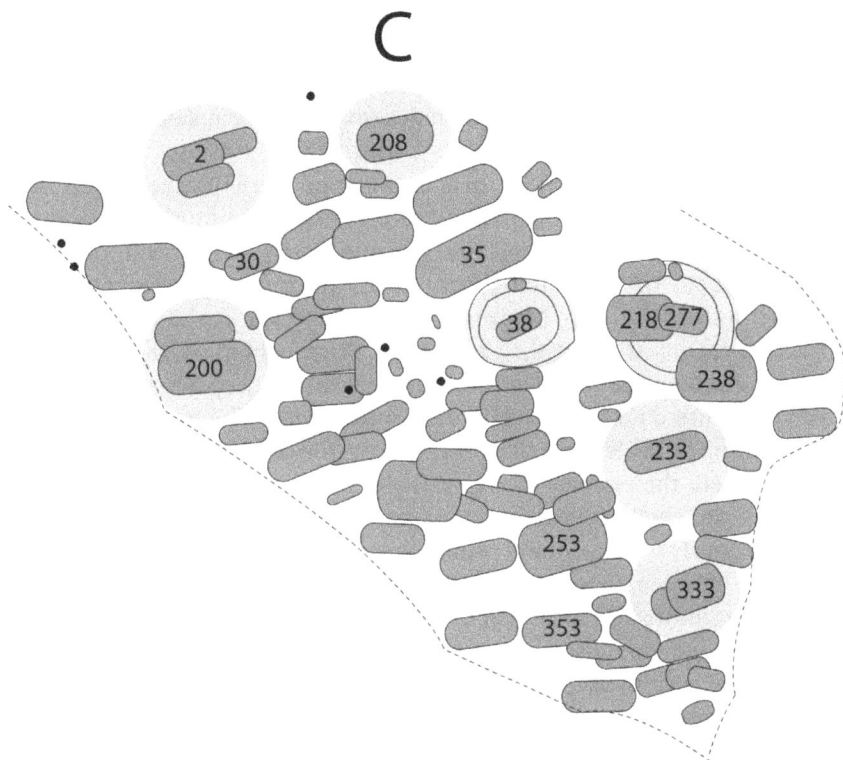

Figure 6.7 Morning Thorpe: barrows in plot C. The light-grey circles illustrate the location of barrows, based on the presence of satellite graves that appear to circle around them. Graves whose date is discussed are also marked.

that seem to have traced around a now-lost barrow; unfortunately neither grave 38 nor 277 was easily datable. The smaller graves were of infants and children, and were positioned centrally to the burial area. Of the datable graves, 35 and 238 were MA2 (AD 510–60/70), whereas 218 was MB (AD 560–650); female graves 30 and 353 were both FA1 (c. AD 480–500) and 253 was FA2 (AD 500–50) (Penn and Brugmann, 2007: 69). These dates imply that the wealthy barrow burials belong to different generations, and so plot C was organised around a series of individual graves creating successive central points around which later graves were placed. Indeed, the highest density of graves in this plot was found between the wealthy barrow burials.

Plots A and D did not contain the wealth of plots B and C, and no structuring was evident within plot A. However, plot D seems to have had a row of graves oriented N/S on its western edge. These graves define the plot's edge or boundary and visually separate it from plots B and C. Internally, plot D had a row of gendered graves positioned diagonally across it SW/NE, with spear burials on the western side and annular/penannular brooch burials on the eastern. On the southern edge of this row were four spear and four annular/penannular brooch burials. These were divided, with males on the western side and females on the eastern. Each of these plots had different attitudes towards, or local traditions behind, their origination and perhaps these were the product of family traditions, a way of preparing and interring the dead which was transmitted though practice and storytelling within different family groups. Unfortunately, because of poor bone preservation we have no stature data for Morning Thorpe, and the pathology data are limited to teeth (Green *et al.*, 1987: 189). Bradley Hull's (2007: 149–56) isotopic analysis identified limited dietary difference, but he was only able to acquire data from twenty-two individuals. The most convincing difference in δ15N levels existed between the wealthiest and the poorest graves, where the poorest graves showed the greatest variation. This is similar to the patterns visible in Chapter 5, in that the individuals without gravegoods or with smaller numbers of gravegoods showed the most variation between them, and the individuals with most artefacts had the least variation in their diets. Unfortunately, the numbers involved were small, but this also did correspond with the outlines of the plots, because the wealthiest burials were mostly found within two burial areas. It is therefore probable that the attitude difference was also supported by different lifeways between burial areas within this cemetery.

The repertoire of mortuary syntax at Lechlade: a material and biological approach

Lechlade is situated in the Upper Thames Valley, Gloucestershire, and archaeological rescue excavation took place in the summer of 1985. The cemetery consisted of 223 skeletons in 200 grave cuts, as well as twenty-nine cremations, and can be split into two phases, the late-fifth and sixth century and the seventh century AD (Boyle *et al.*, 1998; 2011). Lechlade has been referred to throughout the book, but not discussed in detail. Unlike many of the previous case studies, Lechlade was big and complex with multiple phases. It was the result of a plurality of simultaneous, continuous and broken narratives, and therefore the syntax at this site appears to be muddied and complex. It is therefore advantageous to consider the cemetery alongside the whole repertoire of mortuary devices employed in it.

The graves at Lechlade came from two distinct phases and can be understood on the basis of orientation, stratigraphy and datable grave-goods (Boyle *et al.*, 1998: 49; 2011: 129; Figure 6.8). As a result there were enough burials to treat the furnished and the final-phase burials

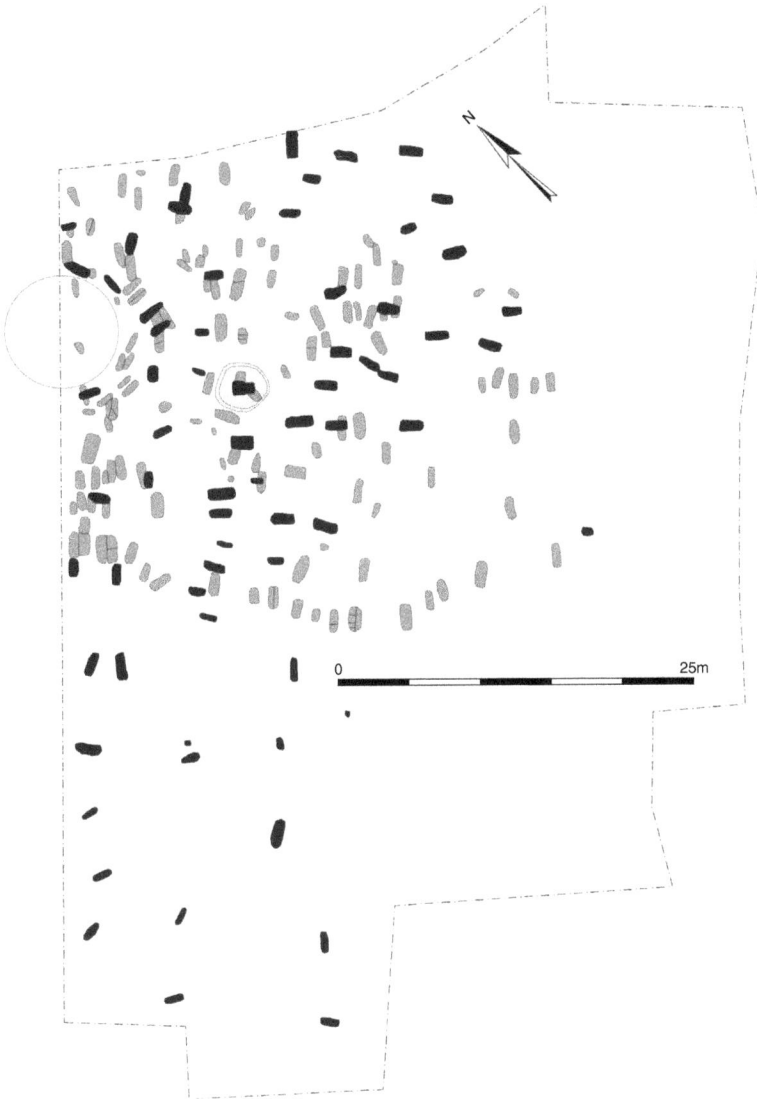

Figure 6.8 Lechlade, Gloucestershire, was split into two phases: grey are fifth/sixth-century graves and black are the seventh-century graves.

separately. The Ripley's K statistical assessment indicates that there was significant clustering at 0.75 m for the fifth- and sixth-century burials and at 8 m for seventh-century burials (Sayer and Wienhold, 2012). The fifth- and sixth-century graves seem to have been organised into three burial plots, a northern, a southern and an eastern plot (Figure 6.9). The northern (A) and southern (B) plots were positioned on

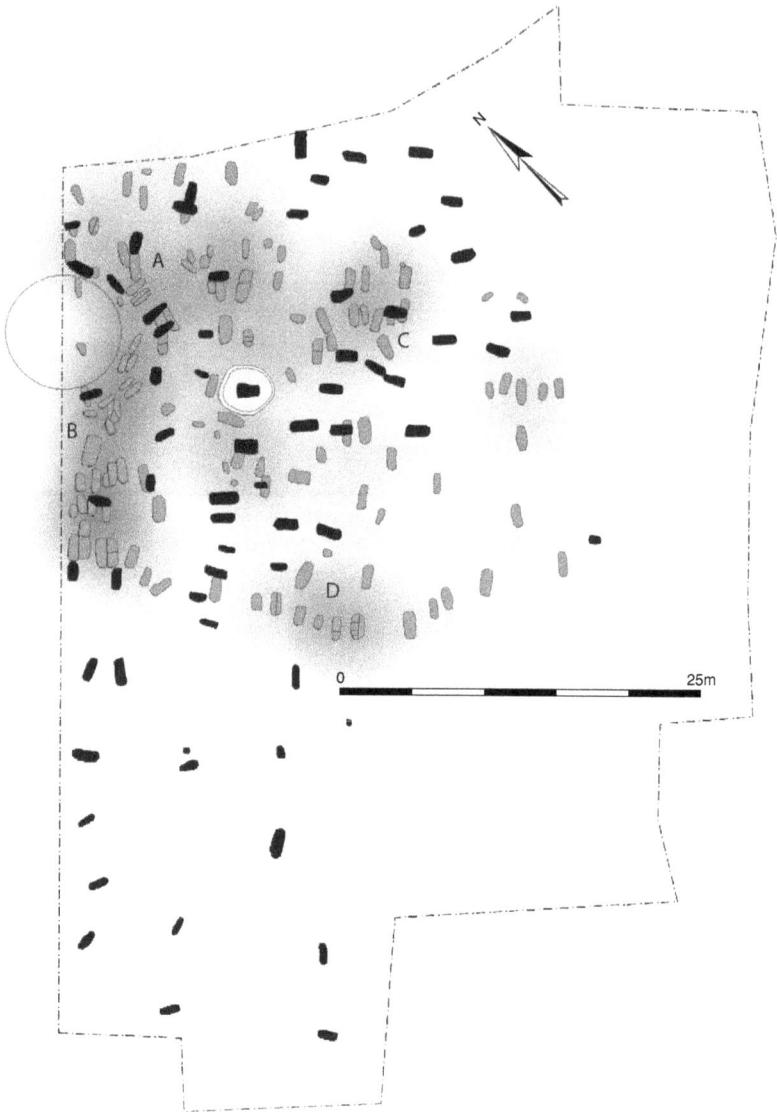

Figure 6.9 Lechlade, fifth- and sixth-century graves with kernel density set at 5 m to highlight the clustering of the graves. The Ripley's K analysis identified significant clustering between 0.75 m and 8 m.

either side of a Bronze Age barrow to the west of the site, and the density of these graves seen with Ripley's K analysis makes this area seem to be a continuous group of burials. However, the wealthy graves were clustered to the south of the southern group and to the middle of the northern group, and the Bronze Age barrows separated these two zones, one to the north-east and one to the south-east. The eastern plot (C) was isolated, with a visible gap in the density of inhumation graves between those graves to the west and to the east of the site. It was also the only plot that contained both types of burial ritual in significant numbers, suggesting that this group was purposely internally divided using inhumation or cremation burial. Consequently, in this first phase the spatial organisation and topography of the site was its primary organising element, and the selection of inhumation or cremation was the result of a localised attitude to the treatment of the dead, which subsequently distinguished the internal groups.

The final-phase burials had a notably sparser distribution and were some ten times less dense than for the earlier phase. The densest concentration of graves was to the north of the site, and these graves were primarily oriented on an E/W axis; interestingly, they create a Y-shape based on their density (Figure 6.10). This orientation and their location within the bounds of the fifth- and sixth-century cemetery contrasted with a series of multiple-orientation graves interred to the south of the site. It is also notable that this southern group contained very few artefacts. Moreover, the later-phase weapon graves were all located to the north.

Lechlade was a complex cemetery and at least initially does not appear to have had the 'kind of spatial or linear succession that has been used to phase cemetery development elsewhere' (Boyle *et al.*, 2011: 129). However, the site did employ a combination of modes of burial from the repertoire of mortuary syntax available throughout the early Anglo-Saxon period. This repertoire included different burial plots, different rituals, and organisation around earlier barrow monuments. Each of these technologies had been employed differently, suggesting that they were using specific semantic knowledge – this division of three groups within the early phase suggests an inherited rite specific to a societal subgroup, each one deliberately differentiated within the cemetery space while still part of the larger cemetery. In the seventh century, the number of groups decreased and the densely clustered plots were abandoned in favour of structured but dispersed placement of E/W oriented burials. The core part of this cemetery remained in the north, within the boundaries of the sixth-century cemetery, but some new unfurnished graves were placed deliberately outside the sixth-century boundaries and to the south of the site.

The excavators identified some biological evidence that, they argued, suggests related people were buried in close proximity (Harman, 2011: 48) – for example, three of the four people with asterionic ossicles (burials 95/1, 170, and 105) were all near to each other. Burial 95/1 was a later-phase female burial, aged between 35 and 40, with a gold

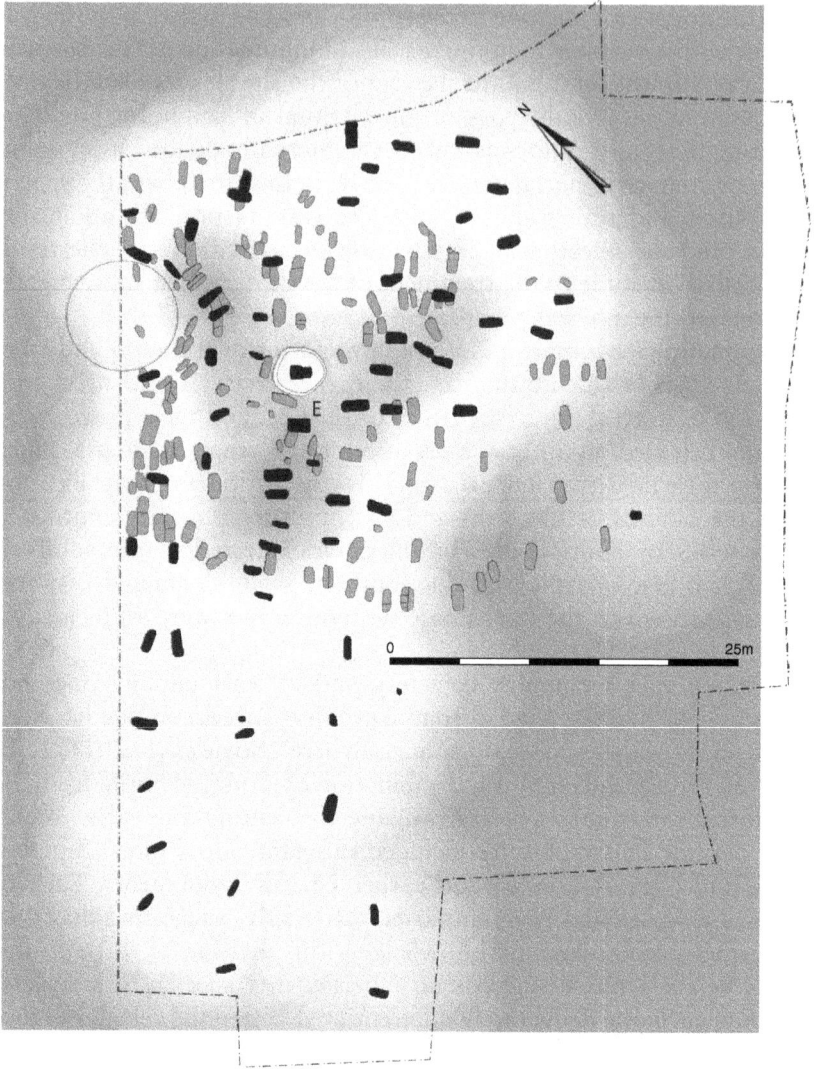

Figure 6.10 Lechlade, seventh-century graves with the kernel density set at 8 m. Note the 'Y' shape created by this density plot; the male weapon burials were predominantly found at the top left arm of the Y.

disc pendant and with a long spearhead that had been converted into a weaving baton found at her waist, which was not the usual place for a spearhead in the grave. Burial 170 was of an adolescent with an undatable knife, and 105 was a young man aged between 16 and 18 and found with a large leaf-shaped spearhead. Inhumations 78, 104 and 115 all had *sacral spina bifida occulta*, and 78 and 115 also had an extra sacro-lumbar vertebra. Notably, grave 78 had a pair of decorated saucer brooches dating it to the middle-sixth century (Hines and Bayliss, 2013: 367, 221). Burials 114 and 115 both had separate acromion process on the left-hand side (Harman, 2011: 48). From this study the height data detailed in Chapter 5 also indicated that there were strong degrees of biological relatedness within the cemetery.

In Chapter 5 we identified group D, which consisted of a row of graves and a few burials which were satellite to that. There were only two males with available height data, both weapon burials, 35 (1.77 m) and 92 (1.74 m). Unfortunately, grave 35 was not datable, whereas 92 contained an early spear and shield-type putting it into the first half of the sixth century. Remarkably, five of the biologically female burials were within 3 cm of each other's height – graves 18 (1.6 m), 81/1 (1.6 m), 81/4 (1.6 m), 165 (1.59 m) and 167/2 (1.58 m). Grave 18 was aged between 25 and 35 and contained saucer brooches and a great square-headed brooch, dating it to the early/middle-sixth century. Inhumation 81/4 was in the same range, and may have been earlier than grave 18; based on a pair of relatively plain disc brooches, it may have dated to the later-fifth or early sixth century. Female burial 165 was aged between 20 and 25 and contained a small buckle, and 167/2 was also a young woman, aged between 19 and 22, found with two annular brooches and a copper ring.

Notably, the male weapon burials of the later-sixth- or seventh-century phase were all located in the north of the cemetery and were much more homogeneous than the non-weapon graves from the same phase (Figure 5.29). Certainly, the five weapon graves – 40 (1.72 m); 104 (1.72 m); 155 (1.73 m); 172/3 (1.73 m); and 181 (1.72 m) – were all within 1 cm of each other in height. Grave 40 contained an adult male aged between 30 and 35 and two small spears; the older adult in grave 104, aged between 40 and 45, connected this group with the young woman in grave 78 and with the earlier male weapon burial 115, who was incidentally 1.73 m tall. Like 78 and 115, the 30- to 35-year-old male in 172 also had an extra vertebra. Burial 155 was also aged between 30 and 35, and was buried with a seax and spearhead. The occupant of grave 181 was aged over 45, and had an additional vertebra and asterionic ossicles on the right-hand side of his skull. He was found with a spearhead, bone pin and knife.

Among these later-phase weapon burials there were three outliers whose heights were significantly different from the others – the adult male in grave 106 was aged between 40 and 45 years and was buried with a spear and shield boss; he was 1.63 m in height. The male in grave 178 was 1.65 m tall and over 45 years in age, and he was found with a seax and knife. Grave 121 contained a very tall individual, at 1.83 m, with a knife and small spearhead. Although not a completely homogeneous group, these later weapon burials were remarkably standardised. Indeed, across both the first and second phases the weapon burials were much more homogeneous than the non-weapon burials and the furnished female burials. As we saw in Chapter 5, the interquartile group of weapon graves ranged between 1.70 m and 1.74 m in height, with an average of 1.72 m. The interquartile group of non-weapon graves ranged between 1.69 m and 1.77 m, and also had a 1.72 m average, but with much more internal variety. Notably, though the weapon burials contained a core group with very similar heights, there were also a number of outliers. Evidently biological kinship was not the only qualification necessary for weapon burial, and importantly the weapon graves themselves varied tremendously in their material composition with seaxes, small spearheads and long spearheads. Some also included shields and/or other material culture.

Material and textual perspectives on Anglo-Saxon kinship

The early Anglo-Saxon cemeteries at Morning Thorpe and Lechlade illustrate very nicely how sites could use a variety of different methods and techniques to convey complex, but similar, messages. The biological data from these sites, and those discussed in Chapter 5, imply a very strong kinship element within these cemeteries. While there were almost certainly a number of biological relationships within these communities, the strongest evidence points to similarity between weapon burials found within particular burial areas. Chapter 5 also pointed to a number of female burials with similar heights, and these were in different burial areas. Indeed, the most similar females were found in the less wealthy burial areas at Great Chesterford, Worthy Park area A and Lechlade area E.

The English Anglo-Saxon scholarly tradition has, since the nineteenth century, assumed a role for the family and kinship in early Anglo-Saxon England. Authors like John Kemble (1849), Charles Elton (1890) and Frederic Seebohm (1905) described Anglo-Saxon society as small-scale, locally based and tribal. They used descriptions that had all of the geographic conformity you might expect from larger national societies, including a central unifying administration. The early Anglo-Saxon cemeteries we have discussed in this book were not standardised, and contained considerable amounts of internal variation. The most obvious of these was the opposition created by the cemeteries that contained a small number of roughly equal groups – for example, Wakerley or Berinsfield – versus the cemeteries with differences in hierarchy or attitude evident in their use of space or their approach to chronology, such as Apple Down or West Heslerton. The contemporary written sources described at the beginning of this chapter suggest that the paternal kindred took priority in legal guardianship of inheritance, which implied a degree of patrilocality among the social elite. The implication is that Anglo-Saxon women travelled for marriage and that if the marriage broke down or the husband died she would return to her family to rear her child. Certainly, the cemetery data seem to support this: the tooth metrics and the height data point towards more homogeneity within the male populations than in the female populations, which would be expected in a patrilocal society where women from different kinship groups moved into a community each generation for marriage.

However, this is not the only story. Some cemeteries – like West Heslerton, Broughton Lodge, Castledyke, Norton and Sewerby – had a distinctly female-gendered character because more female graves contained gendered objects than male graves. This might imply that these communities contained women who maintained a strong sense of gender identity across several generations. Alternatively, given that West Heslerton had a series of male weapon graves at the core of plot A, it could imply that the male weapons grave and gender identity were reserved for a specific group of people. Indeed, the female height data from Great Chesterford, Worthy Park and Lechlade, and the tooth metric data from Eastry, Polhill, Oakington and Hatherdene, indicate that there were female biological relationships, that there were more of these and they included fewer people than the male kindred. Perhaps the seventh-century legal documents only describe the male elite family. Moreover, this pattern may in archaeology data suggest that there were different residency patterns depending on your social attitude.

According to the laws discussed above, the Anglo-Saxon family seems to have been at the core of the community, and important heads of families were also heads of the extended households that made up the local and regional elite. Elite marriage patterns and the law surrounding inheritance and kinship relationships seem to have assisted the protection of a specific lineage at the core of community. These kin married across similar families, and women moved for marriage, evidenced by their return in the case of divorce or bereavement. Nevertheless, the chronological information from Berinsfield, Deal or Apple Down seems to imply that men or women were buried in core areas within these cemeteries with one or two of each gender per generation. Perhaps women could be the heads of the household in their own right, or in the case of the death of the male head. It would be interesting to know who these women were. Were they the sisters of male kindred, or their daughters as the Anglo-Saxon wills suggest? Probably both, depending on localised circumstance. But a household did not just consist of its leaders; it was supported by family who remained locally within the extended family. Who were these people? Unmarried women, women whose husbands had moved into their community for marriage, brothers, cousins, elderly relatives? Perhaps ancient DNA evidence can tell us more about the elite Anglo-Saxon female – but we must also be aware that DNA is determined by biology, and it is social relationships that drive household prosperity. Indeed, a large part of the anthropology of relationships studies fictive kinship that might include fostering, adoption and other ways of creating relations (Carsten 2004).

At West Heslerton, Westgarth Gardens, Broadway Hill, Winterbourne Gunner and Lyminge II, burial areas with wealthier gravegoods also included the densest concentration of inhumations. These areas displayed the most gender disparity among them, even going so far as to separate male- and female-gendered graves into different spaces within the core burial area. That the emphasis of mortuary expression was on family is perhaps evidenced by the location of more children at Orpington, Apple Down and Westgarth Gardens in these core areas, or as satellite graves around barrow burials. Among these families, gender was important because it helped to determine social rules of inheritance, courtship and power.

In their mortuary treatment the members of less well-furnished areas placed less emphasis on chronology, on children's graves and on gender display. It is important that, at least where the evidence is available, there was stronger biological similarity between women in these areas. Perhaps some of these people, whose lifeways may have exposed them to more risk of skeletal trauma, did not routinely practise patrilocality, and residency may have varied or even favoured women who stayed within the wider extended community. Perhaps these people's households were secondary, the daughters or brothers of the primary house, the families and households of reeves, smiths or other significant members of the community. Notably, the core burial at West Heslerton plot B contained a man buried with metalworking tools, not weapons. Additionally, a third group is evident via the unstructured burial areas at Lechlade, Buckland, West Heslerton, Apple Down and Polhill. These groups may be better described as tertiary burial areas, and these contained the least gravegoods of all, along with the most biological diversity. These areas do not seem to have had a continual narrative associated with their burials.

Mortuary attitude and the different visual aesthetics described above underpinned differences in lifeways and in the attitude towards the expression of ancestry within the mortuary space. Perhaps the people in the lower-wealth areas of a cemetery did not need (or use) a lineage or key ancestors as part of the construction of their identity. Frederic Seebohm described early Anglo-Saxon 'households [which] might quite possibly be, from the first, embryo manors with serfs upon them. They might be settlements precisely like those ... [manorial estates] described by Tacitus' (Seebohm, 1905: 366). This interpretation was of its time and was situated within a cultural-historical or social evolutionary paradigm. Nonetheless, the two different types of cemetery – 1. those with two or more similarly sized, broadly equal groups with similar lifeways, and which contained primary or secondary burial areas; and 2. those cemeteries with a burial area that had some internal structuring, for example a core area, as well as a spectrum of other areas without similar structure that might include primary, secondary and tertiary burial areas – might imply different ways to organise an early Anglo-Saxon estate: either relying primarily on family and their households, as in type 1, or including a greater diversity of households and people, with type 2. Notably, these type 2 cemeteries became more common in the seventh century (Sayer, 2009), with a change in emphasis towards the ego-centred burial style without gravegoods and under small barrows, alongside unstructured zones which did not emphasise the individual. These second-phase cemeteries seem to have included more social stratification, and perhaps the greater stratification in the seventh century created heightened social tensions which can be witnessed by the presence and extent of grave robbery evident in large, stratified cemeteries in Kent, for example Bradstow School, Ozengell, St Peters or Finglesham (Klevnäs, 2013).

Conclusion

The early Anglo-Saxon era was one of the most dynamic periods in Britain's past. For some locally or regionally important families, the emphasis of mortuary ritual was on reinforcing kinship identities and reproducing family narratives in the ordering of antecedents into lineages. These ancestral landscapes were used to display and legitimise narratives around social stratification and elite identities locally, and for a regional network who used feud and marriage to reinforce male lineage and property ownership. This was the Anglo-Saxon family, patrilocal, hierarchical but ultimately flexible, with male and female heads of household as needed. The cemetery evidence suggests that the household was a diverse place, containing a multiplicity of different lifeways, burial styles and ways to express identity. Notably, however, there were scales of expression from the person created with a connection or emotional bond via the objects selected for inclusion, the dressing of the corpse, and the positioning of the body or the construction of the wooden pyre or earthen grave. The household might be explored by way of the location of burial, the use of space, its orientation, cremation or inhumation, or by differential density and the use of rows of graves. Interestingly, the objects usually associated with ethnicity seem more comfortably situated within familial or household, rather than regional, identities. Indeed, it may not be possible to see regional ethnicity at all, because by far the most important organisational principle seems to be local situation. Ultimately, it is the archaeologist and historian who have framed the Early Middle Ages in that mode; whereas Anglo-Saxon cemeteries, stories, laws and poetry were about family, personal relationships and belonging.

Family was expressed in the mortuary space using chronologically contingent narratives, which may have included returning to a space repeatedly or building small barrows for key members of each generation. For some people, mortuary behaviour conveyed family attitude in the expression of gender identity and attitude towards ancestors and children. This was more keenly conveyed among the core burials of the early Anglo-Saxon family than the plain inhumations of their dependants. Children and infants were treated differently by the family, more often located next to core areas, or around individual antecedents within family spaces than in the wider household areas. Ultimately, Anglo-Saxon burial practice was about the expression of identity, hierarchy and group belonging; not via wealth or gravegoods, which may have been contingent on time, place and person, but by utilising the mortuary performance, and the variety of mortuary technologies available to create, recreate and perform community narratives. These narratives were supposed to be understood via the aesthetics of mortuary space, and the construction of semiotic language. They were meant to be understood by multiple participants at the graveside, at the burial, days later at the funeral or years later as community members returned to the site to tell stories about themselves and their past. They were meant to be understood because they were designed to carry community narratives. Stories about the dead and the living, who they were and what they did. These narratives can be understood by archaeologists because we are simply latecomers to the mortuary drama. With the use of contextual, holistic, multi-scalar and multi-dimensional approaches, it is possible to see some small part of the narratives that these sites conveyed.

Epilogue

Social identity is a term which has been employed by archaeologists in a variety of different ways over the last forty or more years. It refers not only to individual perceptions but also to the external categorisation of individuals and groups. As a result, social identities are a nexus of pluralistic interpersonal and intergroup relationships, which change over time (Williams and Sayer, 2009: 2). In the mortuary context these identities were mediated via funerary events, and so no two events could be the same. Different actors contributed to a funeral that was meaningful to them, and which reflected their experience and their outlook. The specific contribution from individuals depended on their social influence, which was in turn mediated by their identity and was reliant on the chronological context because social attitudes and relationships are determined by an individual's situation and circumstances. The resultant expression of mortuary identities was inherently complex and multi-faceted; but most of all the expression of identity was inherently relational.

It is vital to remember that 'the dead did not bury themselves' (Parker Pearson, 1993: 203; 1999: 3), because the decisions and attitudes which contributed to the aesthetics of display and the expression of the deceased's identity were selected by a unique mortuary party within a historically contingent event. The mortuary events were knitted together by a group of people who had been fragmented following the death of one of their members (Metcalf and Huntington, 1991). The decisions that this community made dictated the mode of burial – cremation or inhumation – and the location of the grave within a cemetery (assuming it was in one), as well as the orientation of the grave and its relationship with earlier graves and the use of markers, feature or structures, the inclusion of objects, the dress a person wore, how they were positioned and whether they were alone. The mortuary party also dictated the length of the mortuary event, the stories told, and how the person was remembered. These decisions were directed by the participants and influenced by their approaches and attitudes, and so each event was the result of the contemporary societal context created by such factors as local and regional politics, religion, family and wealth. Material and social things like dress, weapons, wealth, children and the past were reflections of that contemporary attitude. This complexity is hard to see in the archaeological record, because individual approaches to life course, gender or status cannot capture that relational *Zeitgeist*. It is vital therefore that this study proposes a holistic approach, creating a relational mortuary archaeology in which the spatial location of a grave was as important as the chronological date, the objects and the gender display within. Indeed, subtle questions like attitudes to gender in the past cannot be understood unless the social context is first explored.

In the introductory sections of this volume we discussed the materiality of shoes. This discussion revealed different attitudes towards shoes or dress mediated by class, status, gender, life course and individual or group expression. Indeed, social science understands that our contemporary attitude towards gender, for example, is mediated by generation, personal experience, education, class and regional or national situation (Kopytoff, 1986). It is puzzling therefore that archaeology continues to explore social questions in binary or chronological fashion. In the case studies presented in the book, the early Anglo-Saxons did not have one attitude towards status or gender, age or identity. Moreover, social attitudes and therefore the resultant funerary expression were dictated by different attitudes towards children, women, men, wealth, ancestors or the past. Importantly, different attitudes towards these things could be seen in different funerals, among different groups from the same cultural and chronological contexts. In short, to understand the social dimensions of mortuary expression we need to explore difference in terms of 'social class', attitude and aesthetics, and not via two-dimensional entities like social status based on wealth. Today, attitudes dictated by background or family might influence someone's attitudes, determining things like the age when you have children and how to approach books, marriage, student loans, family history or social obligations. For example, the middle classes might move for work, whereas those with a more regional background might remain near home to be close to an extended family network (Carsten 2004). If your parents moved for university, for a job or a career, you might be more willing to do so yourself. I am not suggesting that the past contained differences comparable to contemporary social classes, but that the past contained equally complex social institutions. I am proposing that background, attitude and approaches to key social institutions varied according to a person's situation, and approaches to these institutions would have been expressed differently by different funerary parties.

Early Anglo-Saxon archaeology has the advantage of a small number of texts dating to the seventh century. In many ways, these muddy the waters more than they aid interpretation. Nonetheless the holistic method proposed in this volume combines an exploration of space, the immediate or more ancient past, gravegoods, chronology, grave features, mortuary aesthetics, skeletal archaeology, gender and life course to look at *leitmotifs* in cemetery construction and narrative creation. It explores mortuary technologies specific to the period and looks at the local adaptation and use within over one hundred sites. This approach is equally relevant to the mortuary context of the prehistoric Levant, post-medieval USA or the Roman East. In short, the aesthetics of burial, the use of mortuary technologies and their local adaptation, and the exploration of mortuary party attitudes can reveal a complex pluralistic and multi-dimensional past no matter the context to which it is applied.

This book has built on a series of published papers to propose an original approach to horizontal stratigraphy that builds on the wider contemporary archaeological context to explore local history and family narratives; its focus is on the holistic social context at the heart of the ancient community (Sayer and Dickinson, 2013; Schiffels *et al.*, 2016; Sayer and Wienhold, 2012; Sayer, 2009; 2010; 2014). This approach matters because understanding that community tells us about status and dynamism, since community is both the agent of change and at the same time the conservative and traditional. Creating a place in archaeological dialogue for community, family and kinship is vital if we are going to fully utilise the data available from emerging technologies such as the exploration of ancient DNA. As technology becomes more sophisticated so must archaeological approaches to the social situations and social dynamics of past peoples.

Appendix: Dover Buckland chronology

Grave no	Beads	Buckles	Brooches	Spears	Shield	Other	Date	Phase	Correlation	Corrected
C		I.10e		SP2b2d			450–570			
D		I.3			SB3b4		525–570			
F			BR2-c				565–645	5–7	no	
1	B2		BR2-b3				580–650	3b	yes	
4		I.3		SP2a2b2			525–570	3a	no	
5		I.11a-i								
6	C						650–720	5–7	yes	
8		II.9		SP2a1b2			525–615	3	yes	550–615
9		I.10a-I, I.11a0ii								
10							525–595	5–7	no	
12				SP2a2c						
13	A2	I.9	small long, small square				450–530	1b	yes	
14		I.10d-i	BR2b2				525–645	2	overlap	525–560
15	A2	I.2					480–555	2	overlap	480–530
18	B2	II.24a					580–650	3b–5	overlap	510–555
20	A2	I.2	small square			scutiform-style 1	480–555	2a	overlap	510–555
21								1a	No	450–530
23		I.4	rosette brooch				550–580	2a	No	
27		II.z, I.11a-i		SP2b1a2	SB4a		565–570			
28		I.2				bucket FA-B	510–650	2a–3a	overlap	510–600

29	B2	BR2b4, PE7a, PE4	BR2-b4			580–610	3b	yes	
30	B2	I.6a	BR2b3			580–650	3a	No	
32	B2		BR2b3			580–650	3b	Yes	
33		II.24a		SP3a		525–645	3–7	overlap	550–600
34		II.24b-i					3a		
35	B2	PE2c, BR2b3, II.24a				580–650	3b	Yes	
36	A2		BR2b3			525–555	2b–3a	No	
38		II.15b		SP2a2c	SB4a1	565–595			
39		II.24a		SP1a2		525–615			
41						525–615	1b–2a	No	525–550
42	B2	I.2				580–650	3	overlap	
46	B2					580–650	3b	Yes	
48	A2	I.5a, I.1a Button (B), Saucer				480–530	1b	Yes	500–530
50		I.2		SP1b		nd	2–3a		
52		II.24b-i					5–7		
53	C				Bucket FC	650–720	5–7	yes	
55	B2			SP3b		580–650	3b–5	overlap	
56		II.23b-ii				525–590	3a	Yes	
57		II.24b-ii		SP2a1b1		585–680			
59	B1		BR2b3	SP1b		555–580	3a	Yes	
60	B2					580–650	3	overlap	
61		II.24a				nd			
62	B1			SP1b		555–580	3a	Yes	
63		I.11a-i				nd			

(Continued)

Grave no	Beads	Buckles	Brooches	Spears	Shield	Other	Date	Phase	Correlation	Corrected
65		I.2		SP2b1a4		SX-1c	525–570	3a	No	560–580
67	C						650–720	3b–5	overlap	
71		II.24a		SP2a2c	SB4a2		565–595			
75	C						650–720	5–7	Yes	
76	C	I.11a-i					650–720	5–7	yes	
85										
87				SP2b1a1			450–570	1–2	yes	
90				SP4	SB4a2		565–645			
91		I.2		SP2b1a1	SB3b4		525–570	2–3a	overlap	
92	A2b	I.5b	BR2b2				530–565	2	yes	
93	A2b			SP5	SB3b3		530–570	2b–3a	Yes	
96a		I.2		SP2a1a2	SB3b3		525–570	2–3a	overlap	
96b				Doesn't fit		SW6-e	525–570	2–3a	overlap	
98		II.15a			SB3b2		525–570	3	overlap	
107	C						650–720	5–7	Yes	
108		II.24b-ii								
110	C						650–720	5–7	Yes	
113		II.24a						5–7		
114				SP2a1a1			525–570			
124	C						650–720	3b–5	No	
126			BR2c				565–645	3b	overlap	
127	C						650–720	5–7	Yes	
128		II.24b-ii		SP2b1b			525–570	3–7	No	
129	C	II.24b-ii					650–720	5–7	Yes	
131		I.11c, I.12a-i		SP2b1a2			525–570			
132	C						650–720	5–7	Yes	

133	C			650–720	3b–5	overlap	
134	C			650–720	5–7	No	
135		II.22b-ii	SP1a2	525–615	3–7	No	
137		II.24a	SP1b1		5–7		
141	C			650–720	5–7	yes	
144		II.22b-ii, II.24a			5–7		
145		II.24a					
146		II.24a			5–7		
148		II.24b-i					
149		II.23a, II.24b-ii			3–7		
155	C	I.9		650–720	5–7	yes	
156					5–7		
157	C	II.23b-ii, II.24b-ii		650–720	5–7		
158		II.24b-i			5–7		
159		I.12a-i		650–720	5–7	yes	
160	C			535–565			
164		Great Square Headed					
204	A2			480–580	2b	overlap	530–560
205					2–3		
207	A			450–580			
209	A1				1b–2		
217				450–530	1	yes	

(Continued)

Grave no	Beads	Buckles	Brooches	Spears	Shield	Other	Date	Phase	Correlation	Corrected
218	A1						450–530			
219	A1						450–530	1a	yes	450–510
220				SP2b1a2			450–570			
221								1b		
222	B2						580–650	3a	no	
223	A1						450–530	2b–3	no	
228A								3a–7		
230				SP2b1a3	SB1B		525–570	2b–3a	Yes	
231								3b		
232	B2						580–650	3b	Yes	
233				SP2a3			525–645	1–3a	no	
235										
238A								1–2		
238b								1–2		
239	A1						450–530	1a	Yes	
240				SP4			525–645			
245	A2						480–555	3a	no	
247	A2						480–555	2a		
249				SP2b1b			450–570	2–3	yes	510–570
250	B1						555–580	3a	Yes	
251				SP3a			525–645	3	overlap	550–580
254	A2						480–555	1	Yes	
255								1b		
256				SP1a5			610–680			
257	A1						450–530	1	Yes	
259				SP2a2a			550–615	1		
261								1		

262		SP2a1b2		525–615	2–3	overlap	
263A					1b–2a		
263b					1b		
264		SP1b	SB3B3	525–570	3	no	
265A					3–7		
265B		SP2b1a2	SB3a	525–570	3a	no	
266					1b–2a		
271					2–3a		
276					2–7		
281					1b		
290					1		
293	A2			480–555	1b–2	Yes	
294	A			450–580	1	overlap	
296	A2			480–555	2a	overlap	510–555
297		SP2b1b	SB3B3	525–570	2	Yes	
299		SP2a2b2		525–570			
300		SP2b1a3		525–570			
301		SP3a		525–645			
302							
303A	B2/C			580–720	2–3a	overlap	
303B					3b		
306	A1			450–530	1–3	yes	
308	A1			450–530	1	yes	
319	c			650–720	1b–3a	No	
323	A1	SP3b	SB3B3	525–570	3	overlap	
324					1–3		
325					2b–3		
326					2–7		
327					1b–2a		

(Continued)

Grave no	Beads	Buckles	Brooches	Spears	Shield	Other	Date	Phase	Correlation	Corrected
331	B1						555–580	3a	Yes	
333								1b–2		
334								1a		
335								1b–2		
336								2b		
337				SP3a			525–645			
338								3a		
339	A2b						530–580			
339	B1						555–580			
334								1b		
335								2b–7		
337								3		
346				SP2a2d			585–680			
347	A2						480–555	2a	overlap	510–555
348								1b–2a		
349	A2b						530–580	1	No	
350A								1b–3a		
350B	A2						480–555	1–2	Yes	
351A								1–2		
351B								1		
352								1–3a		
353	B2						580–650	3a	No	
354	A2b						530–555	2b	Yes	
355								1		
356										
359								1–3		
360	B2						580–650	3b	Yes	

	great square-headed brooch							
361						1–3b		
363		SP2b1a3			525–570	1b–2		
366						2a		
372						2b–3a		
373	B1	SP1b			555–580	2b–3a	Yes	580–645
374								
375		SP3a	SD4b2		525–645	3b	overlap	
376	B2				580–650	5–7	No	
377						1–2		
381						1b–2a		
384						1b–7		
391B	A2			bucket FA	480–555	2	overlap	510–555
392	A2				480–555	2	overlap	510–555
393		SP2b1b			525–570			
398						2b–3a		
400		SP2bib			525–570			
405						1b–7		
406						1b–7		
407	A2				480–555	2	overlap	530–555
408						1b		
409	A2				480–555	1b	overlap	480–530
411		SP2a2b1			450–525			
412	A2b				530–580	2b–3a	yes	
413	C				650–720	5–7	yes	
414		SP1b			525–595	2b–3a	yes	
417	A		SB3c		450–580	2a	overlap	530–550

(*Continued*)

Grave no	Beads	Buckles	Brooches	Spears	Shield	Other	Date	Phase	Correlation	Corrected
418								1–2		
419	A2						450(530)–580(550)	2a	overlap	
420								2–3a		
422								1–2		
423				SP2b1a3			525–570	2–3a	yes	
425	A2						480–555	1b–2	yes	
426								2		
427A	A2						480–555	1b–2	yes	
428	A2						480(510)–555	2	overlap	
432	A2						480–555	1b–2	yes	
433								1		
435								2–3a		
436								1b–2		
437								2		
440								1b–2a		
441	A2						480–555	1b–2	yes	
442								1b–2		
443								1b0–2		

References

Åberg, N. (1926) *The Anglo-Saxons in England*, Uppsala: Almqvist & Wiksell.

Adams, B. and Jackson, D. (1988–9) 'The Anglo-Saxon cemetery at Wakerley, Northamptonshire: Excavations by Mr D. Jackson 1968–69', *Northamptonshire Archaeology* 22: 69–178.

Ager, B. M. (1985) 'The smaller variants of the Anglo-Saxon quoit brooch', *Anglo-Saxon Studies in Archaeology and History* 4: 1–58.

Akerman, J. Y. (1855) 'An account of excavations in an Anglo Saxon burial ground at Harham Hill, near Salisbury', *Archaeologia* 35: 259–78.

Alcock, L. (1981) 'Quantity or quality: the Anglian graves of Bernicia', in V. I. Evison (ed.), *Angles, Saxons, and Jutes*, Oxford: Oxford University Press, pp. 168–86.

Alt, K. W. and Vach, W. (1991) 'The reconstruction of "genetic kinship" in pre-historic burial complexes – Problems and statistics', in H.-H. Bock and P. Ihm (eds), *Classification, Data Analysis, and Knowledge Organization: Models and Methods with Applications*, Berlin: Springer, pp. 299–310.

Alt, K. W. and Vach, W. (1995) 'Odontologic kinship analysis in skeletal remains: Concepts, methods, and result', *Forensic Science International* 74: (1–2), 99–113.

Alvesson, A. and Sköldberg, K. (2010) *Reflexive Methodology: New Vistas for Qualitative Research*, 2nd edn, London: Sage.

Annable, F. K. and Eagles, B. N. (2010) *The Anglo-Saxon Cemetery at Blacknall Field: Pewsey, Wiltshire*, Wiltshire Archaeology and Natural History Society Monograph 4, Devizes: Wiltshire Archaeology and Natural History Society.

Appleby, J., Rutty, G. N., Hainsworth, S. V. *et al.* (2015) 'Perimortem trauma in King Richard III: a skeletal analysis', *The Lancet* 385 (9964): 17–23.

Ariès, P. (1974) *Western Attitudes towards Death: From the Middle Ages to the Present*, London: Johns Hopkins University Press.

Ariès, P. (1981) *The Hour of Our Death*, New York: Alfred A. Knopf.

Arnold, C. J. (1981) 'Wealth and social structure: A matter of life and death', in P. Rahtz, T. Dickinson and L. Watts (eds), *Anglo-Saxon Cemeteries 1979: The Fourth Anglo-Saxon Symposium at Oxford*, Oxford: British Archaeology Reports 8: 81–142.

Arnold, C. J. (1997) *An Archaeology of the Early Anglo-Saxon Kingdoms*, London: Routledge.

Avent, R. (1975) *Anglo-Saxon Garnet Inlaid Disc and Composite Brooches*, Oxford: British Archaeology Reports 11.

Bantelmann, N. (1988) *Süderbrarup I. Archäeologische Untersuchungen*, Bücher 63, Neumünster: K. Wachholtz.

Barber, M. (2011) *Introduction to Heritage Assets: Pre-Christian Cemeteries*, London: English Heritage.

Barrett, J. (1988) 'Fields of discourse: reconstructing a social archaeology', *Critique of Anthropology* 7 (3): 5–16.

Behmer, E. G. (1939) *Das zweischneidige Schwert der germanischen Völkerwanderungszeit*, Stockholm: Tryckeriaktiebolaget.

Bennet, M. (2009) 'The Wolds before AD 100', in D. N. Robinson (ed.), *The Lincolnshire Wolds*, Oxford: Oxbow.

Bhaskar, R. (1998) *The Possibility of Naturalism: A Philosophical Critique of the Contemporary Human Sciences*, 3rd edn, London: Routledge.

Biggerstaff, R. H. (1975) 'Cusp size, sexual dimorphism, and heritability of cusp size in twins', *American Journal of Physical Anthropology* 42 (1): 127–39.

Binford, L. (1971) 'Mortuary practices: their study and their potential', in J. Brown (ed.), *Approaches to the Social Dimensions of Mortuary Practices*, Memoir of the Society for American Archaeology 25. Washington DC: Society for American Archaeology, pp. 6–29.

Bloch, M. (1962) *Feudal Society*, translated L. A. Manyon, London: Routledge & Kegan Paul.

Boddington, A. (1990) 'Models of burial, settlement and worship: the final phase reviewed', in E. Southworth (ed.), *Anglo-Saxon Cemeteries: a Reappraisal*, Stroud: Sutton, pp. 177–99.

Böhme, H. W. (1974) *Germanishche Gradfunde des 4. Bis 5. Jarhrhunderts zwischen unter Elbe und Loire*, Munich: Beck.

Böhner, K. (1958) *Die fränkischen Altertümer des Trierer Landes*, Germanische Denkmäler der Völkerwanderungszeit Serie B 1, Berlin: Mann.

Bone, P. (1989) 'The development of Anglo-Saxon swords from the fifth to the eleventh century', in S. Chadwick Hawkes (ed.), *Weapons and Warfare in Anglo-Saxon England*, Oxford: Oxford University Committee for Archaeology, pp. 63–70.

Boyle, A., Dodd, A., Miles, D. *et al.* (1995) *Two Oxfordshire Anglo-Saxon Cemeteries: Berinsfield and Didcot*, Thames Valley Landscapes Monograph 8, Oxford: Oxford Archaeological Unit.

Boyle, A., Jennings, D., Miles, D. *et al.* (1998) *The Anglo-Saxon Cemetery at Butler's Field, Lechlade, Gloucestershire, Volume 1*, Thames Valley Landscapes Monograph 10, Oxford: Oxford Archaeological Unit.

Boyle, A., Jennings, D., Miles, D. *et al.* (2011) *The Anglo-Saxon Cemetery at Butler's Field, Lechlade, Gloucestershire, Volume 2: The Anglo-Saxon Grave Goods Specialist Reports, Phasing and Discussion*, Thames Valley Landscapes Monograph 33, Oxford: Oxford Archaeological Unit.

Brown, D. (1977) *Firesteels and Pursemounts Again*, Bonn: Bonner Jahrbücher 177.

Brown, M. A. (1983) 'Grave orientation: a further view', *Archaeological Journal* 140: 322–8.

Bruce-Mitford, R. L. S. (1978) *The Sutton Hoo Ship-Burial, Volume 2: Arms, Armour and Regalia*, London: British Museum Publications.

Brugmann, B. (1999) 'The role of continental artefact-types in 6th-century Kentish chronology', in J. Hines, K. Høilund Nielsen and F. Siegmund (eds), *The Pace of*

Change: Studies in Early-Medieval Chronology, Cardiff Studies in Archaeology, Oxford: Oxbow, pp. 37–64.

Brugmann, B. (2004) *Glass Beads from Early Anglo-Saxon Graves*. Oxford: Oxbow Books.

Brugmann, B. (2012) 'Buckland cemetery chronology', in K. Parfitt and T. Anderson (eds), *Buckland Anglo-Saxon Cemetery, Dover, Excavations 1994*, The Archaeology of Canterbury New Series 6, Canterbury: Canterbury Archaeological Trust, pp. 323–60.

Brunning, S. (2017) 'Crossing edges?: "Person-like" swords in Anglo-Saxon England', in S. Semple, C. Orsini and S. Mui (eds), *Life on the Edge: Social, Religious and Political Frontiers in Early Medieval Europe*, Neue Studien zur Sachsenforschung 6. Braunschweig: Braunschweigisches Landesmuseum with Internationales Sachsensymposion, pp. 409–18.

Brunning, S. (2019) *The Sword in Early Medieval Northern Europe: Experience, Identity and Representation*, Woodbridge: Boydell.

Bruns, D. (2003) *Germanic Equal Arm Brooches of the Migration Period*, British Archaeological Reports, International Series 1113, Oxford: Archaeopress.

Brush, K. (1988) 'Gender and mortuary analysis in pagan Anglo-Saxon archaeology', *Archaeological Review from Cambridge* 7 (1): 76–89.

Buckberry, J. (2000) 'Missing, presumed buried? Bone diagenesis and the under-representation of Anglo-Saxon children', *Assemblage 5*.

Bullough, D. (1983) 'Burial, community and belief in the early Medieval West', in P. Wormald (ed.), *Idea and Reality in Frankish and Anglo-Saxon Society*, Oxford: Oxford University Press, pp. 177–201.

Cameron, E. A. (2000) *Sheaths and Scabbards in England, AD 400–1100*, BAR British Series 301, Oxford: Archaeopress.

Carsten, J. (2004) *After Kinship*. Cambridge: University of Cambridge Press.

Carver, M. (2005) *Sutton Hoo: A Seventh-Century Princely Burial Ground and its Context*, London: British Museum.

Carver, M., Hills, C. and Scheschkewitz, J. (2009) *Wasperton: A Roman, British and Anglo-Saxon Community in Central England*, Woodbridge: Boydell & Brewer.

Chadwick, S. (1958) 'The Anglo-Saxon cemetery at Finglesham, Kent', *Medieval Archaeology* 2: 1–71.

Chadwick Hawkes, S. (1969) 'Early Anglo-Saxon Kent', *Archaeological Journal* 126: 186–92.

Chadwick Hawkes, S. (1977) 'Orientation at Finglesham: Sunrise dating of death and burial in an Anglo-Saxon cemetery in East Kent', *Archaeologia Cantiana* 92, 33–51.

Chadwick Hawkes, S. (1981) 'Recent finds of inlaid iron buckles and belt-plates from seventh-century Kent', *Anglo-Saxon Studies in Archaeology and History* 2, British Archaeological Reports 92, pp. 49–70.

Chadwick Hawkes, S. (1982) 'Finglesham. A cemetery in East Kent', in J. Campbell, E., John and M. Wood, (eds), *The Anglo-Saxons*, London: Penguin Books, pp. 24–5.

Chadwick Hawkes, S. and Dunning, G. C. (1961) 'Soldiers and settlers in Britain, fourth to fifth century; with a catalogue of animal-ornamentation buckles and related belt-fittings', *Medieval Archaeology* 21: 167–76.

Chadwick Hawkes, S. and Grainger, G. (2003) *The Anglo-Saxon Cemetery at Worthy Park, Kingsworthy, near Winchester, Hampshire*, Oxford University School of Archaeology Monograph 59, Oxford: Oxford University School of Archaeology.

Chadwick Hawkes, S. and Grainger, G. (2006) *The Anglo-Saxon Cemetery at Finglesham, Kent*, Oxford University School of Archaeology Monograph 64, Oxford: Oxford University School of Archaeology.

Chadwick Hawkes, S., Ellis Davidson, H. R. and Hawkes, C. (1965) 'The Finglesham Man', *Antiquity* 39 (153): 17–32.

Chapman, R. W., Kinnes, I. and Randsborg, K. (eds) (1981) *The Archaeology of Death*, Cambridge: Cambridge University Press.

Cherryson, A. (2000) 'Bones, beads and buckles: An analysis of funerary provision in the South Saxon cemeteries at Apple Down, West Sussex', unpublished MA thesis, University of Southampton.

Christlein, R. (1973) 'Besitzabstufungen zur Merowingerzeit im Spiegel reicher Grabfunde aus West- und Süddeutschand', *Jahruch des Römisch-Germanisches Zentralmuseum*, Mainz 10: 147–80.

Clayton, M. (2008) 'The Old English Promissio regis', *Anglo-Saxon England* 37: 91–151.

Cook, A. M. and Dacre, M. W. (1985) *Excavations at Portway, Andover, 1974–5*, Oxford: Oxford University Committee for Archaeology.

Cook, J. (2004) *Early Anglo-Saxon Buckets: A Corpus of Copper Alloy- and Iron-Bound, Stave-Built Vessels*, Oxford University School of Archaeology Monograph 60, Oxford: Institute of Archaeology, University of Oxford.

Cook, J. M. (1958) 'An Anglo-Saxon cemetery at Broadway Hill, Broadway, Worcestershire', *Antiquaries Journal* 38 (1–2): 58–84.

Corbett, R. (2009) *The Grammar and Syntax of the Dead: A Regional Analysis of Chumash Mortuary Practice*, Saarbrucken: Lambert Academic.

Corney, A., Ashbee, P., Everson, V.I. *et al.* (1967) 'A prehistoric and Anglo-Saxon burial ground, Ports Down, Portsmouth', *Proceedings of Hampshire Field Club Archaeological Society* 24: 20–41.

Crawford, S. (1991) 'When do Anglo-Saxon children count?' *Journal of Theoretical Archaeology* 2: 17–24.

Crawford, S. (1993) 'Children, death and the afterlife in Anglo-Saxon England', in W. Filmer-Sankey and S. Chadwick Hawkes, S. (eds), *Anglo-Saxon Studies in Archaeology and History* 6, Oxford: British Archaeological Reports, pp. 83–91.

Crawford, S. (1999) *Childhood in Anglo-Saxon England*, Stroud: Sutton Publishing.

Crawford, S. (2000) 'Children, grave goods and social status in early Anglo-Saxon England', in S. Derevenski (ed.), *Children and Material Culture*, London: Routledge, pp. 169–79.

Crawford, S. (2011) 'The disposal of infants in Anglo-Saxon England: an overview of the archaeology', in M. Lally (ed.), *(Re)thinking the Little Ancestor: the Archaeology of Infant Burial*, British Archaeological Reports, International Series 2271, Oxford: Archaeopress, pp. 75–84.

Crick, J. (2000) 'Women, wills and movable wealth in pre-Conquest England', in M. Donald and L. Hurcombe (eds), *Gender and Material Culture in Historical Perspective*, Basingstoke: Macmillan, pp. 17–37.

Davies, D. (2005). *A Brief History of Death*, Oxford: Blackwell.

Davison, A., Green, B. and Milligan, B. (1993) *Illington: The Study of a Breckland Parish and its Anglo-Saxon Cemetery*, East Anglian Archaeology 63, Dereham: Norfolk Museums Service.

Dean, M. J. and Kingsley, A. G. (1993) *Broughton Lodge: Excavations on the Romano-British Settlement and Anglo-Saxon Cemetery at Broughton Lodge, Willoughby-on-the-Wolds, Nottinghamshire 1964–8*, Nottingham Archaeology Monographs 4, Nottingham: Department of Classical and Archaeological Studies, University of Nottingham.

Devlin, Z. (2007a) 'Social memory, material culture and community identity', in S. Semple and H. Williams (eds), *Early Medieval Mortuary Practices*, Anglo-Saxon Studies in Archaeology and History 14, Oxford: Oxford University Committee for Archaeology, pp. 38–46.

Devlin, Z. (2007b) *Remembering the Dead in Anglo-Saxon England: Memory Theory in Archaeology and History*, British Archaeological Reports 446, Oxford: Archaeopress.

Dickinson, T. (1976) 'The Anglo-Saxon burial sites of the Upper Thames Region, and their bearing on the history of Wessex, circa AD 400–700', unpublished DPhil thesis, University of Oxford.

Dickinson, T. (1979) 'On the origin and chronology of the Early Anglo-Saxon disc brooch', *Anglo-Saxon Studies in Archaeology and History* 1, Oxford: British Archaeological Reports 72, pp. 39–80.

Dickinson, T. (1982) 'Fowler's type G penannular brooches reconsidered', *Medieval Archaeology* 26: 41–68.

Dickinson, T. (1993) 'Early Saxon saucer brooches: a preliminary overview', *Anglo-Saxon Studies in Archaeology and History* 6: 11–44.

Dickinson, T. (2011) 'Overview: Mortuary ritual', in H. Hamerow, D., Hinton and S. Crawford (eds), *The Oxford Handbook of Anglo-Saxon Archaeology*, Oxford: Oxford University Press, pp. 221–37.

Dickinson, T. and Speake, G. (1992) 'The seventh century cremation burial in Asthall Barrow, Oxfordshire: a reassessment', in M. Carver (ed.), *The Age of Sutton Hoo*, Woodbridge: Boydell & Brewer, pp. 95–130.

Dickinson, T. M. and Härke, H. (1992) *Early Anglo-Saxon Shields*, Archaeologia Monographs 110, London: Society of Antiquaries.

Dilley, R., Hockey, J., Robinson, V. *et al.* (2014) 'Occasions and non-occasions: identity, femininity and high-heeled shoes', *European Journal of Women's Studies* 22 (2): 143–58.

Down, A. and Welch, M. (1990) *Chichester Excavations VII: Apple Down and the Mardens*, Chichester: Chichester District Council.

Drew, K. F. (1988) *Law and Society in Early Medieval Europe: Studies in Legal History*, Aldershot: Variorum.

Drinkall, G. and Foreman, M. (1998) *The Anglo-Saxon Cemetery at Castledyke South, Barton-On-Humber*, Sheffield Excavation Reports 6, Sheffield: Sheffield Academic Press.

Dunning, G. C. and Evison, V. I. (1961) 'The Palace of Westminster sword', *Archaeologia* 98: 123–58.

Eckardt, H. and Williams, H. (2003) 'Objects without a past? The use of Roman objects in early Anglo-Saxon graves', in H. Williams (ed.), *Archaeologies of Remembrance: Death and Memory in Past Societies*, London: Plenum, pp. 141–70.

Elton, C. (1890) *Origins of English History*, London: Quaritch.

Evison, V. I. (1955) 'Early Anglo-Saxon inlaid metalwork', *Antiquaries Journal* 35: 20–45.

Evison, V. I. (1956) 'An Anglo-Saxon cemetery at Holborough, Kent', *Archaeologia Cantiana* 70: 84–141.

Evison, V. I. (1967) 'The Dover ring-sword and other sword-rings and beads', *Archaeologia* 101: 63–118.

Evison, V. I. (1972) 'Glass cone beakers of the "Kempston" type', *Journal of Glass Studies* 14: 48–66.

Evison, V. I. (1977) 'Supporting-arm and equal-armed brooches in England', *Studien zur Sachsenforschung* 1: 127–48.

Evison, V. I. (1979) *Wheel Thrown Pottery in Anglo-Saxon Graves*, London: Royal Archaeological Institute.

Evison, V. I. (1982) 'The Anglo-Saxon glass claw beakers', *Archaeologia* 107: 43–76.

Evison, V. I. (1987) *Dover: The Buckland Anglo-Saxon Cemetery*, London: Historic Buildings and Monuments Commission for England.

Evison, V. I. (1994) *An Anglo-Saxon Cemetery at Great Chesterford, Essex*, Council for British Archaeology Research Report 91, York: Council for British Archaeology.

Evison, V. I. and Hill, P. (1996) *Two Anglo-Saxon cemeteries at Beckford, Hereford and Worcester*, Research Report 103, York: Council for British Archaeology.

Faull, M. L. (1977) 'British survival in Anglo-Saxon Northumbria', in L. Laing (ed.), *Studies in Celtic Survival*, British Archaeological Report 37, Oxford: British Archaeological Reports, pp. 1–55.

Felder, K. (2015) 'Networks of meaning and the social dynamics of identity. An example from early Anglo-Saxon England', *Papers from the Institute of Archaeology* 25: 1–20.

Filmer-Sankey, W. and Pestell, T. (2001) *Snape Anglo-Saxon Cemetery: Excavations and Surveys 1824–1992*, East Anglian Archaeology 95, Ipswich: Archaeological Service, Suffolk County Council.

Fisher, R. A. (1922) 'On the interpretation of χ2 from contingency tables, and the calculation of P', *Journal of the Royal Statistical Society* 85 (1): 87–94.

Fowler, C. (2001) 'Personhood and social relations in the British Neolithic, with a study from the Isle of Man', *Journal of Material Culture* 6 (2): 137–63.

Fowler, C. (2004) *The Archaeology of Personhood: An Anthropological Approach*, London: Routledge.

Fowler, C. (2010) 'Pattern and diversity in the early Neolithic mortuary practices of Britain and Ireland: contextualising the treatment of the dead', *Documenta Praehistorica* 37: 1–22.

Fowler, E. (1960) 'The origins and development of the penannular brooch in Europe', *Proceedings of the Prehistoric Society* 26: 149–77.

Fowler, E. (1963) 'Celtic metalwork of the 5th and 6th centuries AD: a reappraisal', *Archaeological Journal* 120: 98–160.

Frantzen, A. J. (2008) *Anglo-Saxon Penitentials: A Cultural Database*, at www.anglo-saxon.net/penance [accessed March 2020].

Gaimster, M. (1992) 'Scandinavian gold bracteates in England: Money and media in the Dark Ages', *Medieval Archaeology* 36: 1–28.

Gale, D. (1989) 'The seax', in S. Chadwick Hawkes (ed.), *Weapons and Warfare in Anglo-Saxon England*, Oxford University Committee for Archaeology Monograph 2, Oxford: Oxford University, pp. 71–83.

Galloway, A., Willey, P. and Snyder, L. (1997) 'Human bone mineral densities and survival of bone elements: A contemporary sample', in W. D. Haglund and M. H. Sorg (eds), *Forensic Taphonomy: The Postmortem Fate of Human Remains*, Boca Raton, Florida: CRC Press, pp. 295–317.

Garn, S.M. (1977) 'Genetics of tooth development', in: J. A. McNamara (ed.), *The biology of occlusal development (Craniofacial growth series)*. Ann Arbor, MI: Center for Human Growth and Development, University of Michigan, pp. 61–88.

Geake, H. (1992) 'Burial practice in seventh- and eighth-century England', in M. Carver (ed.), *The Age of Sutton Hoo*, Woodbridge: Boydell & Brewer, pp. 83–94.

Geake, H. (1994) 'Anglo-Saxon double-tongued buckles', *Medieval Archaeology* 38: 164–6.

Geake, H. (1997) *The Use of Grave-Goods in Conversion-Period England*, British Archaeological Reports 261, Oxford: Archaeopress.

Gell, A. (1992) 'The technology of enchantment and the enchantment of technology', in J. Coote and A. Shelton (eds), *Anthropology, Art, and Aesthetics*, Oxford: Oxford University Press, pp. 40–63.

Gell, A. (1998) *Art and Agency*, Oxford: Clarendon Press.

Gero, J. M. and Conkey, M. W. (1991) *Engendering Archaeology: Woman and Prehistory*, Oxford: Blackwell.

Gibson, C. (2007) 'Minerva: an early Anglo-Saxon mixed-rite cemetery in Alwalton, Cambridgeshire', in S. Semple and H. Williams (eds), *Early Medieval Mortuary Practices*, Anglo-Saxon Studies in Archaeology and History 14, Oxford: Oxford University, pp. 238–350.

Gilchrist, R. (1991) 'Women's archaeology? Political feminism, gender theory and historical revision', *Antiquity* 65 (248): 495–501.

Gilchrist, R. (2009) 'Rethinking later medieval masculinity', in D. Sayer and H. Williams (eds), *Mortuary Practice and Social Identities in the Middle Ages*, Exeter: Exeter University Press, pp. 236–52.

Gilchrist, R. (2012) *Medieval Life: Archaeology and the Life Course*, Woodbridge: Boydell & Brewer.

Glass, H., Garwood, P., Champion, T. *et al.* (2012) *Tracks through Time: The Archaeology of the Channel Tunnel Rail Link*, Oxford: Oxford Archaeology.

Goody, J. (1983) *The Development of the Family and Marriage in Europe*, Cambridge: Cambridge University Press.

Gosden, C. (2005) 'What do objects want?', *Journal of Archaeological Method and Theory* 12 (3): 193–211.

Gosden, C. and Marshall, Y. (1999) 'The cultural biography of objects', *World Archaeology* 31 (2): 169–78.

Gowland, R. and Knüsel, C. (2006) *Social Archaeology of Funerary Remains*, Oxford: Oxbow.

Gravdal, K. (1995) 'Confessing incests: Legal erasures and literary celebrations in medieval France', *Comparative Literature Studies* 32 (2): 280–91.

Green, B., Rodgerson, A. and White, S. G. (1987) *The Anglo-Saxon Cemetery at Morning Thorpe, Norfolk, volume 1: Catalogue*, East Anglian Archaeology 36, Dereham: Norfolk Archaeological Unit.

Green, E. (2017) *London Craft Week – The Art of Handsewing*, at www.edward green.com/journal-article/london-craft-week-art-handsewing [accessed March 2020].

Guido, M. (1999) *The Glass Beads of Anglo-Saxon England c. AD 400–700. A Preliminary Visual Classification of the More Definitive and Diagnostic Types*, Woodbridge: Boydell & Brewer.

Hadley, D. M. (2011) 'Late Saxon burial practice', in H. Hamerow, D., Hinton and C. Crawford (eds), *The Oxford Handbook of Anglo-Saxon Archaeology*, Oxford: Oxford University Press, pp. 288–314.

Hakenbeck, S. E. (2007a) 'Identitätsbildungsporzzesse im Gräberfeld von Altenerding', in C. Grünewald and T. Capelle (eds), *Innere Strukturen von Siedlungen und Gräberfeldern als Spiegel gesellschaftlicher Wirklichkeit?*, Akten des 57. Internationalen Sachsensymposiums, Veröffentlichungen der Altertumskommission für Westfalen 17, Münster: Aschendorff, pp. 89–97.

Hakenbeck, S. E. (2007b) 'Situational ethnicity and nested identities: New approaches to an old problem', in Semple, S. and Williams, H. (eds), *Early Medieval Mortuary Practices*, Anglo-Saxon Studies in Archaeology and History 14, Oxford: Oxford University School of Archaeology, pp. 19–28.

Hakenbeck, S. E. (2009), 'Hunnic modified skulls: Physical appearance, identity and the transformative nature of migrations', in D. Sayer and H. Williams (eds), *Mortuary Practice and Social Identity in the Middle Ages*, Exeter: University of Exeter Press, pp. 64–80.

Hakenbeck, S. E. (2011) *Local, Regional and Ethnic Identities in Early Medieval Cemeteries in Bavaria*, Contributi di Archaeologia Medievale/Premio Ottone d'Assia e Riccardo Frankovich 5, Firenze: All'Insegna del Giglio.

Halsall, G. (1995a) *Early Medieval Cemeteries. An Introduction to Burial Archaeology in the Post-Roman West*, Glasgow: Cruithne Press.

Halsall, G. (1995b) *Settlement and Social Organisation: The Merovingian Region of Metz*, Cambridge: Cambridge University Press.

Harden, D. B. (1956) 'Glass vessels in Britain and Ireland AD 400–1000', in D. B. Harden (ed.), *Dark Age Britain: Studies Presented to E.T. Leeds*, London: Methuen, pp. 132–67.

Harden, D. B. (1978) 'Anglo-Saxon and later medieval glass in Britain: Some recent developments', *Medieval Archaeology* 22: 1–24.

Härke, H. (1989a) 'Knives in early Saxon burials: blade length and age at death', *Medieval Archaeology* 33: 144–8.

Härke, H. (1989b) 'Early Saxon weapon burials: frequencies, distributions and weapon combinations', in S. Chadwick Hawkes (ed.), *Weapons and Warfare in Anglo-Saxon England*, Oxford University Committee for Archaeology Monograph 21, Oxford: Oxford University School of Archaeology, pp. 49–61.

Härke, H. (1990) 'Warrior graves? The background of the Anglo-Saxon weapon burial rite', *Past and Present* 126: 22–43.

Härke, H. (1992) *Angelsächsische Waffengräber des 5. bis 7, Jahrhunderts ZAM Beiheff 6*, Köln/Bonn: Rheinland-Verlag/Habelt.

Härke, H. (1995) 'Weapon burials and knives', in A. Boyle, A., Dodd, S. Miles *et al.* (eds), *Two Oxfordshire Anglo-Saxon Cemeteries: Berinsfield and Didcot*, Thames Valley Landscapes Monograph 8, Oxford: Oxford Archaeology Unit, pp. 67–74.

Härke, H. (1997) 'Early Anglo-Saxon social structure', in J. Hines (ed.), *The Anglo-Saxons from the Migration Period to the Eighth Century: An Ethnographic Perspective*, Studies in Archaeoethnology 2, San Marino: Boydell Press.

Härke, H. (2000a) 'Social analysis of mortuary evidence in German protohistoric archaeology', *Journal of Anthropological Archaeology* 19: 369–84.

Härke, H. (2000b) 'The circulation of weapons in Anglo-Saxon society', in F. Theuws and J. L. Nelson (eds), *Rituals of Power from Late Antiquity to the Early Middle Ages*, The Transformation of the Roman World 8, Leiden/Boston/Köln: Brill, pp. 377–99.

Härke, H. (2007) 'Ethnicity, race and migration in mortuary archaeology: an attempt at a short answer' in S. Semple and H. Williams (eds), *Early Medieval Mortuary Practices*, Anglo-Saxon Studies in Archaeology and History 14, Havertown PA: Oxbow Books, p. 12.

Härke, H. (2011) 'Gender representation in early medieval burials: ritual re-affirmation of a blurred boundary?', in S. Brookes, S. Harrington and A. Reynolds (eds), *Studies in Early Anglo-Saxon Art and Archaeology: Papers in Honour of Martin Welch*, British Archaeological Reports 527, Oxford: British Archaeology Reports, pp. 98–105.

Härke, H. (2014) 'Grave goods in early medieval burials: messages and meanings', *Mortality* 19 (1): 1–21.

Harman, M. (2011) 'The human remains' in A. Boyle, D. Jennings, D. Miles *et al.* (eds) (1998), *The Anglo-Saxon Cemetery at Butler's Field, Lechlade, Gloucestershire*, Vol. 1, Thames Valley Landscapes Monograph 10, Oxford: Oxford Archaeological Unit, pp. 43–8.

Harper, S. (2012) '"I'm glad she has her glasses on. That really makes the difference": grave goods in English and American death rituals', *Journal of Material Culture* 17 (1): 43–59.

Haughton, C. and Powlesland, D. (1999a) *West Heslerton: The Anglian Cemetery Volume I: The Excavation and Discussion of the Evidence*, Yedingham, Yorkshire: Landscape Research Centre/English Heritage.

Haughton, C. and Powlesland, D. (1999b) *West Heslerton: The Anglian Cemetery Volume II: Catalogue of the Anglian Graves and Associated Assemblages*, Yedingham, Yorkshire: Landscape Research Centre/English Heritage.

Hills, C. M. (1978) 'Sachsische und Angelsachsische Keramik', in J. Ypey and C. Ahrens (eds), *Sachsen und Angelsachsen*, Veroffentlichungen des Helms-Museums 32, Hamburg: Helms-Museums, pp. 135–52.

Hills, C. M. (1994) 'The chronology of the Anglo-Saxon cemetery at Spong Hill, Norfolk', in B. Stjernquist (ed.), *Prehistoric Graves as a Source of Information: Symposium at Kastlosa, Oland, May 21–23, 1992*, Stockholm: Historie Och Antikvitets Akademien Kungl. Vitterhets.

Hills, C. M. (2017) 'The Anglo-Saxon migration to Britain: an archaeological perspective', in H. H. Meller, F. Daim, J. Krause *et al.* (eds), *Migration and Integration from Prehistory to the Middle Ages*. Halle: Tagungen Des Landesmuseums Für Vorgeschichte Halle Volume 17, pp. 239–54.

Hills, C. M. and Lucy, L. (2013) *Spong Hill Part IX: Chronology and Synthesis*, Cambridge: McDonald Institute for Archaeological Research, University of Cambridge.

Hills, C. M., Penn, K. and Rickett, R. (1984) *The Anglo-Saxon Cemetery at Spong Hill, North Elmham Part III: Catalogue of Inhumations*, East Anglian Archaeology Report 21, Dereham: Norfolk Archaeological Unit in conjunction with the Scole Archaeological Committee.

Hines, J. (1984) *The Scandinavian Character of Anglian England in Pre-Viking Period*, British Archaeological Reports 124, Oxford: British Archaeological Reports.

Hines, J. (1994) 'The becoming of the English: identity, material culture and language in early Anglo-Saxon England', in W. Filmer-Sankey and D. Griffiths (eds), *Anglo-Saxon Studies in Archaeology and History* 7, Oxford: Oxford University, pp. 49–59.

Hines, J. (1997) *The Anglo-Saxons From the Migration Period to the Eighth Century: An Ethnographic Perspective*, Studies in Archaeoethnology 2, San Marino: Boydell Press.

Hines, J. and Bayliss, A. (eds) (2013) *Anglo-Saxon Graves and Grave Goods of the 6th and 7th Centuries* AD: *A Chronological Framework*, Society of Medieval Archaeology Monograph 33, York: Society of Medieval Archaeology.

Hines, J., Høilund Nielsen, K. and Siegmund, F. (eds) (1999) *The Pace of Change: Studies in Early-Medieval Chronology*, Oxford: Oxbow Books.

Hirst, S. (1985) *An Anglo-Saxon Inhumation Cemetery at Sewerby, East Yorkshire*, York University Archaeological Publications 4, York: Department of Archaeology.

Hirst, S. and Clark, D. (2009) *Excavations at Mucking. Volume 3, the Anglo-Saxon Cemeteries: Parts i and ii*, London: Museum of London Archaeology.

Hockey, J. and James, A. (2003) *Social Identities across the Life Course*, Basingstoke: Palgrave.

Hockey, J., Dilley, R., Robinson, V. *et al.* (2013) 'Worn shoes: Identity, memory and footwear', *Sociology Research Online* 18 (1): 20, at https://journals.sagepub.com/doi/full/10.5153/sro.2897 [accessed March 2020].

Hockey, J., Dilley, R., Robinson, V. *et al.* (2014) 'The temporal landscape of shoes: A life course perspective', *Sociological Review* 62 (2): 255–75.

Hockey, J., Dilley, R., Robinson, V. *et al.* (2015) 'There's not just trainers or non-trainers, there's like degrees of trainers': Commoditisation, singularisation and identity', *Journal of Material Culture* 20: 21–42, at https://doi.org/10.1177/1359183514560665 [accessed March 2020].

Hogarth, A. (1974) 'Structural features in Anglo-Saxon graves', *Archaeological Journal* 130: 104–19.

Hope-Taylor, B. (1977) *Yeavering: An Anglo-British Centre of Early Northumbria*, London: Her Majesty's Stationery Office.

Huggett, J. (1996) 'Social analysis of early Anglo-Saxon inhumation burials', *Journal of European Archaeology* 4: 337–65.

Hughes, T. and Townsend, G. C. (2013) 'Twin and family studies of human dental crown morphology: Genetic, epigenetic, and environmental determinants of the modern human dentition', in G. R. Scott and J. D. Irish (eds), *Anthropological Perspectives on Tooth Morphology: Genetics, Evolution, Variation*, Cambridge: Cambridge University Press, pp. 31–68.

Hull, B. D. (2007) 'Social differentiation and diet in early Anglo-Saxon England: stable isotope analysis and archaeological human remains', unpublished PhD thesis, University of Oxford.

Humphrey, L. T. (1998) 'Growth patterns in the modern human skeleton', *American Journal of Physical Anthropology* 105 (1): 57–77.

Hurd, H. (1913) *Some Notes on Recent Archaeological Discoveries at Broadstairs*, Broadstairs: Broadstairs and St Peter's Archaeological Society.

Hurd, H. and Smith, R. (1910) 'An Anglo-Saxon burial ground at Broadstairs', *Proceedings of the Society of Antiquarians of London* 23: 272–82.

Hyslop, M. (1964) 'Two Anglo-Saxon cemeteries at Chamberlains Barn, Leighton Buzzard, Bedfordshire', *Archaeological Journal* 120: 161–200.

Ingold, T. (2010) *Bringing Things to Life: Creative Entanglements in a World of Materials* (ESRC National Centre for Research Methods, Realities Working Paper 15), Manchester: University of Manchester, at http://eprints.ncrm. ac.uk/1306/ [accessed March 2020].

Inskip, S. (2008) 'Great Chesterford: a catalogue of burials', in M. Brickley and M. Smith (eds), *Proceedings of the Eighth Annual Conference of the British Association for the British Association for Biological Anthropology and Osteoarchaeology*, British Archaeological Reports 1743, Oxford: Archaeopress, pp. 57–66.

James, E. (1979) 'Cemeteries and the problem of Frankish settlement in Gaul', in P. H. Sawyer (ed.), *Names, Words and Graves: Early Medieval Settlement*, Leeds: University of Leeds, pp. 55–89.

Jarvis, K. S. (1983) *Excavations in Christchurch 1969–1980*, Christchurch: Dorset Natural History and Archaeological Society, pp. 102–44.

Johnson, G. (2008) 'Biomechanics of joints', in P. Revell (ed.), *Joint Replacement Technology*, Cambridge: CRC Press, pp. 3–30.

Jørgensen, L. (1987) 'Family burial practices and inheritance systems: The development of an Iron Age society from 500 BC to AD 1000 on Bornholm, Denmark', *Acta Archaeologica* 58: 17–54.

Joy, J. (2009) 'Reinvigorating object biography: reproducing the drama of object lives', *World Archaeology* 41 (4): 540–56.

Kemble, J. M. (1849) *The Saxons in England. A History of the English Commonwealth till the Period of the Norman Conquest*, London: Longman.

Kendall, J. M. (1982) 'A study of grave orientation in several Roman and post-Roman cemeteries from Southern Britain', *Archaeological Journal* 139: 270–83.

Kennett, D. H. (1970) 'Pottery and other finds from the Anglo-Saxon cemetery at Sandy, Bedfordshire', *Medieval Archaeology* 14: 17–33.

King, T. E., Gonzalez Fortes, G., Balaresque, P. *et al.* (2014) 'Identification of the remains of King Richard III', *Nature Communications* 5: 5631.

King, C. and Sayer, D. (eds) (2011), *The Archaeology of Post-Medieval Religion*, Woodbridge: Boydell and Brewer.

Klevnäs, A. (2013) *Whodunnit? Grave Robbery in Anglo-Saxon England and the Merovingian Kingdoms*, British Archaeological Reports, International Series 2582, Oxford: Archaeopress.

Koch, A. (1998) 'Fremde Fibeln im Frankenreich. Ein Beitrag zur Frage nichtfränkischer germanischer Ethnien in Nordgallien', *Acta Praehistorica et Archaeologica* 30: 69–89.

Kopytoff, I. (1986) 'The cultural biography of things: commoditization as process', in A. Appadurai (ed.), *The Social Life of Things*, Cambridge: Cambridge University Press, pp. 64–91.

Lai, C.-Q. (2016) 'How much of human height is genetic and how much is due to nutrition?', *Scientific America* (11 December 2006), at www.scientificamerican.com/article/how-much-of-human-height/ [accessed March 2020].

Lancaster, L. (1958a) 'Kinship in Anglo-Saxon society: I', *British Journal of Sociology* 9 (3): 230–50.

Lancaster, L. (1958b) 'Kinship in Anglo-Saxon Society: II', *British Journal of Sociology* 9 (4): 359–77.

Larsen, C. S. (2015) *Bioarchaeology: Interpreting Behaviour from the Human Skeleton*, Cambridge: Cambridge University Press.

Latour, B. (1996) *Aramis, or The Love of Technology*, trans. C. Porter, Cambridge MA: Harvard University Press.

Latour, B. (2005) *Reassembling the Social: An Introduction to Actor Network Theory*, Oxford: Oxford University Press.

Leahy, K. (1998) 'Cleatham, North Lincolnshire, the Kirton-in-Lindsey cemetery', *Medieval Archaeology* 42: 94–5.

Leahy, K. and Bland, R. (2009) *The Staffordshire Hoard*, London: British Museum Press.

Leeds, E. T. (1913) *The Archaeology of the Anglo-Saxon Settlement*, Oxford: Clarendon.

Leeds, E. T. (1936) *Early Anglo-Saxon Art and Archaeology*, Oxford: Clarendon.

Leeds, E. T. (1945) 'The distribution of the Angles and Saxons archaeologically considered', *Archaeologia* 91: 1–106.

Leeds, E. T. (1949) *A Corpus of Early Anglo-Saxon Great Square-Headed Brooches*, Oxford: Clarendon.

Leeds, E. T. and Harden, D. B. (1936) *The Anglo-Saxon Cemetery at Abingdon, Berkshire*, Oxford: Ashmolean Museum.

Leeds, E. T. and Pocock, M. (1971) 'A survey of Anglo-Saxon cruciform brooches of the florid type', *Medieval Archaeology* 15: 13–36.

Leeds, E. T. and Short, H. de S. (1953) *An Anglo-Saxon Cemetery at Petersfinger, near Salisbury, Wiltshire*, Salisbury: South Wiltshire and Blackmore Museum.

Leigh, D. (1980) 'The square-headed brooches of sixth-century Kent', unpublished PhD thesis, University College Cardiff.

Lethbridge, T. C. (1947) *A Cemetery at Lackford, Suffolk: Report of the Excavation of a Cemetery of the Pagan Anglo-Saxon Period*, Cambridge: Cambridge Antiquarian Society.

Loyn, H. R. (1974) 'Kinship in Anglo-Saxon England', *Anglo-Saxon England* 3: 197–209.

Lucy, S. (1994) 'Children in early medieval cemeteries', *Archaeological Review from Cambridge* 13 (2): 21–34.

Lucy, S. (1997) 'Housewives, warriors and slaves? Sex and gender in Anglo-Saxon burials', in J. S. E. Moore and E. Scott (eds), *Invisible People and Processes: Writing Gender and Childhood into European Archaeology*, Leicester: Leicester University Press, pp. 150–68.

Lucy, S. (1998) *The Early Anglo-Saxon Cemeteries of East Yorkshire. An Analysis and Reinterpretation*, British Archaeological Reports 272, Oxford: British Archaeological Reports.

Lucy, S. (2000a) 'Early medieval burial in East Yorkshire: Reconsidering the evidence', in H. Geake and K. Kenny (eds), *Early Deira: Archaeological Studies of the East Ridings in the Fourth to Ninth Centuries AD*, Oxford: Oxbow Books, pp. 11–18.

Lucy, S. (2000b) *The Anglo-Saxon Way of Death*, Stroud: Sutton.

Lucy, S. (2005) 'Ethnic and cultural identities', in M. Díaz-Andreu, S. Lucy, S. Babic *et al.* (eds), *The Archaeology of Identity: Approaches to Gender, Age, Ethnicity, Status and Religion*, London: Routledge, pp. 86–109.

Lupton, D. N. (1998) *The Emotional Self: A Sociocultural Exploration*, London: Sage.

Lyotard, J. F. and Benjamin, A. E. (1989) *The Lyotard Reader*, Oxford: Blackwell.

Mackeprang, M. B. (1952) *De Nordiske Guldbrakteater*, Jysk Arkaeologisk Selskabs Skrifter 2, Åarhus: Universiteitsforlaget.

Malim, T. (2006) 'A Roman-British temple complex and Anglo-Saxon burials at Gallows Hill, Swaffham Prior', *Proceedings of the Cambridge Antiquarian Society 95*: 91–114.

Martin, T. F. (2014) '(Ad)dressing the Anglo-Saxon body: corporeal meanings and artefacts in early England', in P. Blinkhorn and C. Cumberbatch (eds), *The Chiming of Crack'd Bells: Recent Approaches to the Study of Artefacts in Archaeology*, British Archaeological Reports International Series 2677, Oxford: Archaeopress, pp. 27–38.

Martin, T. F. (2015) *The Cruciform Brooch and Anglo-Saxon England*, Woodbridge: Boydell & Brewer.

Marzinzik, S. (2003) *Early Anglo-Saxon Belt Buckles (Late 5th to Early 8th centuries AD): Their Classification and Context*, British Archaeological Reports 357, Oxford: Archaeopress.

Matthews, C. L. (1962) 'The Anglo-Saxon cemetery at Marina Drive, Dunstable', *Bedfordshire Archaeological Journal* I: 25–47.

Mayes, P. and Dean, M. (1976) *An Anglo-Saxon Cemetery at Baston, Lincolnshire*, Occasional Papers in Lincolnshire History and Archaeology 3, Sleaford: Society for Lincolnshire History and Archaeology.

Mays, S. (2016) 'Estimation of stature in archaeological human skeletal remains from Britain', *American Journal of Physical Anthropology* 161: 646–55.

McHugh, F. (1999) *Theoretical and Qualitative Approaches to the Study of Mortuary Practice*, British Archaeological Reports, International Series 785, Oxford: Archaeopress.

McLean, L. and Richardson, A. (2010) 'Early Anglo-Saxon brooches in Southern England: the contribution of the Portable Antiquities Scheme', in S. Worrell, G. Egan and J. Naylor (eds), *A Decade of Discovery Proceedings of the Portable Antiquities Scheme Conference 2007*, British Archaeological Reports 520, Oxford: Archaeopress, pp. 161–72.

Meaney, A. (1964) *A Gazetteer of Early Anglo-Saxon Burial Sites*, London: George Allen & Unwin.

Meaney, A. and Chadwick Hawkes, S. (1970) *Two Anglo-Saxon Cemeteries at Winnall*, London: Society for Medieval Archaeology.

Menghin, W. (1974) 'Schwertortbänder der frühen Merowingerzeit', in G. Kossack and G. Ulbert (eds), *Studien zur vor- und frühgeschichtlichen Archäologie*, Werner-Festschrift, München: Beck, pp. 435–69.

Metcalf, P. and Huntington, R. (1991) *Celebration of Death: The Anthropology of Mortuary Ritual*, 2nd edn, Cambridge: Cambridge University Press.

Moore, J. and Scott, E. (1997) *Invisible People and Processes: Writing Gender and Childhood into European Archaeology*, Leicester: Leicester University Press.

Moreland, J. (2001) *Archaeology and Text*, London: Duckworth.

Morris, I. (1991) 'The archaeology of ancestors: The Saxe/Goldstein hypothesis revisited', *Cambridge Journal of Archaeology* 1: 7–40.

Morris, J. (1974) 'Review of Myres and Green 1973', *Medieval Archaeology* 18: 225–32.

Mortimer, C. (1990) 'Some aspects of early medieval copper-alloy technology, as illustrated by a study of the Anglian cruciform brooch', unpublished DPhil thesis, University of Oxford.

Mortimer, J. R. (1905) *Forty Years' Researches in British and Saxon Burial Mounds of East Yorkshire: Including Romano-British Discoveries, and a Description of the Ancient Entrenchments on a Section of the Yorkshire Wolds*, London: A. Brown & Sons.

Mortimer, R., Sayer, D. and Wiseman, R. (2017) 'Anglo-Saxon Oakington: A central place on the edge of the Cambridgeshire Fen', in S. Semple, C. Orsini and S. Mui (eds), *Life on the Edge: Social, Religious and Political Frontiers in Early Medieval Europe*, Neue Studien zur Sachsenforschung 6, Braunschweigisches Landesmuseum with the Internationalen Sachsensymposion, Wendeburg: Verlag Uwe Krebs, pp. 305–16.

Mui, S. (2018) 'Dead Body Language: Deciphering Corpse Positions in Early Anglo-Saxon England', unpublished PhD dissertation, University of Durham.

Müldner, G. H. (2009) 'Investigating medieval diet and society by stable isotope analysis of human bone', in R. Gilchrist and A. Reynolds (eds), *Reflections: 50 Years of Medieval Archaeology*, Leeds: Maney, pp. 327–46.

Murray, A. C. (1983) *Germanic Kinship Structure: Studies in Law and Society in Antiquity and the Early Middle Ages*, Toronto: Pontifical Institute of Medieval Studies.

Musty, J. and Stratton, J. E. D. (1964) 'A Saxon cemetery at Winterbourne Gunner, near Salisbury', *Wiltshire Archaeology and Natural History Magazine* 59: 86–109.

Myres, J. N. L. (1937) 'Some Anglo-Saxon potters', *Antiquity* 11 (44): 389–99.

Myres, J. N. L. (1969) *Anglo-Saxon Pottery and the Settlement of England*, Oxford: Clarendon Press.

Myres, J. N. L. (1977) *A Corpus of Anglo-Saxon Pottery of the Pagan Period*, Gulbenkian Archaeological Series, Cambridge: Cambridge University Press.

Myres, J. N. L. and Green, B. (1975) *The Anglo-Saxon Cemeteries of Caistor-by-Norwich and Markshall, Norfolk*, London: Society of Antiquaries.

Myres, J. N. L. and Southern, W. H. (1973) *The Anglo-Saxon Cremation Cemetery at Sancton, East Yorkshire*, Hull: Hull Museum Publications.

O'Brien, E. (1999) *Post-Roman Britain to Anglo-Saxon England: Burial Practices Reviewed*, British Archaeological Reports 289, Oxford: Archaeopress.

Office of National Statistics (2012) *Census 2011 – Population and Household Estimates for the United Kingdom*, at www.ons.gov.uk/ons/rel/census/2011-cen

sus/population-and-household-estimates-for-the-united-kingdom/index.html [accessed March 2020].

Oliver, L. (2002) *The Beginnings of English Law*, Toronto: University of Toronto Press.

Owen-Crocker, G. R. (1986) *Dress in Anglo-Saxon England*, Woodbridge: Boydell & Brewer.

Owen-Crocker, G. R. (2004) *Dress in Anglo-Saxon England*, revd edn, Woodbridge: Boydell & Brewer.

Pader, E.-J. (1980) 'Material symbolism and social relations in mortuary studies', in P. Rahtz, T. Dickinson and L. Watts (eds), *Anglo-Saxon Cemeteries 1979: The Fourth Anglo-Saxon Symposium at Oxford*, British Archaeological Reports 82, Oxford: British Archaeological Press, pp. 143–69.

Pader, E.-J. (1982) *Symbolism, Social Relations and the Interpretation of Mortuary Remains*, British Archaeological Reports, International Series 130, Oxford: British Archaeological Reports.

Palmer, S. (1984) *Excavation of the Roman and Saxon Site at Orpington, Kent, 1871–1987*, London: London Borough of Bromley.

Parfitt, K. and Anderson, T. (2012) *Buckland Anglo-Saxon Cemetery, Dover: Excavations 1994*, Canterbury: Canterbury Archaeological Trust.

Parfitt, K. and Brugmann, B. (1997) *The Anglo-Saxon Cemetery on Mill Hill, Deal, Kent*, The Society for Medieval Archaeology Monograph Series 14, London: Society for Medieval Archaeology.

Parker Pearson, M. (1982) 'Mortuary practices, society and ideology: an ethnoarchaeological study', in Hodder, I. (ed.), *Symbolic and Structural Archaeology*, Cambridge: Cambridge University Press, pp. 99–113.

Parker Pearson, M. (1984) 'Economic and ideological change: cyclical growth in the pre-state societies of Jutland', in D. Miller and C. Tilly (eds), *Ideology, Power and Prehistory*, Cambridge: Cambridge University Press, pp. 69–92.

Parker Pearson, M. (1993) 'The powerful dead: archaeological relationships between the living and the dead', *Cambridge Archaeological Journal* 3 (2): 203–29.

Parker Pearson, M. (1999) *The Archaeology of Death and Burial*, Stroud: Sutton.

Pelteret, D. (1995) *Slavery in Early Medieval England: From the Reign of Alfred until the Twelfth Century*, Woodbridge: The Boydell Press.

Penn, D. (2000) *Excavations on the Norwich Southern Bypass 1989–91, Part II: the Anglo-Saxon Cemetery at Harford Farm, Markshall, Norfolk*, East Anglian Archaeology Report 92, Gressenhall, Norfolk: East Anglian Archaeology.

Penn, K. and Brugmann, B. (2007) *Aspects of Anglo-Saxon Inhumation Burial: Morning Thorpe, Spong Hill, Bergh Apton and Westgarth Gardens*, Gressenhall, Norfolk: East Anglian Archaeology Report 119.

Petts, D. (2011) *Pagan and Christian: Religious Change in Early Medieval Europe*, Bristol: Bristol Classical Press.

Philp, B. (1973) *Excavations in West Kent 1960–1970: The discovery and excavation of 30 prehisotric, Roman, Anglo-Saxon and medieval sites, mainly in the Bromley area and in the Darent Valley*, Dover: Kent Archaeological Rescue Unit for the West Kent Border Archaeology Group.

Philp, B. (1979) 'Four more Anglo-Saxon graves discovered at Polhill, Kent', *Kent Archaeological Review* 58: 178–88.

Philp, B. (2002) *The Anglo-Saxon Cemetery at Polhill near Sevenoaks, Kent, 1964–1986*, West Wickham, Kent: Kent Archaeological Rescue Unit.

Price, N. (2010) 'Passing into poetry: Viking-age mortuary drama and the origins of Norse mythology', *Medieval Archaeology* 54: 123–56.

Privat, K. L., O'Cobbell, T. C and Richards, M. P. (2002) 'Stable isotope analysis of human and faunal remains from the Anglo-Saxon cemetery at Berinsfield, Oxfordshire: dietary and social implications', *Journal of Archaeological Science* 29 (7): 779–90.

Rahtz, P. (1978) 'Grave orientation', *Archaeological Journal* 135: 1–14.

Ravn, M. (2003) *Death Ritual and Germanic Social Structure (c. AD 200–600)*, British Archaeological Reports, International Series 1164, Oxford: Archaeopress.

Reay, D. (1998) 'Rethinking social class: qualitative perspectives on class and gender', *Sociology* 32 (2): 259–75.

Reynolds, A. (2009) *Anglo-Saxon Deviant Burial Customs*, Oxford: Oxford University Press.

Richardson, A. (2005) *The Anglo-Saxon Cemeteries of Kent: Volume 2, Catalogue*, British Archaeological Reports 391, Oxford: Archaeopress.

Robb, J. (1998) 'The interpretation of skeletal muscle sites: A statistical approach', *International Journal of Osteoarchaeology* 8: 363–77.

Robb, J. (2010) 'Beyond agency', *World Archaeology* 42: 493–520.

Roberts, C. and Manchester, K. (2005) *The Archaeology of Disease*, 3rd edn, Ithaca NY: Cornell University Press.

Rosenthal, J. T. (1966) 'Marriage and blood feud in "heroic" Europe', *British Journal of Sociology* 17 (2): 133–44.

Ross, M. C. (1985) 'Concubinage in Anglo-Saxon England', *Past and Present* 108 (1): 3–34.

Saggau, H. E. (1981) *Bordesholm. Der Urnefriedhof am Brautberg bei Bordesholm in Holstein, vol. 2: Katalog, Tafeln und Plan des Gräberfeldes*, Offa-Bücher 48, Neumünster: K. Wachholtz.

Saggau, H. E. (1986) *Bordesholm. Der Urnenfriedhof am Brautberg bei Bordesholm in Holstein, vol. 1: Text und Karten*, Offa-Bücher 60, Neumünster: K. Wachholtz.

Salin, E. (1952) *La Civilisation Merovingienne 2: les sépultures*, Paris: Picard.

Samut-Tagliaferro, J. (1999) 'The archaeology of joint disease', *Rheumaderm* 455: 463–7.

Saxe, A. A. (1970) 'Social dimensions of mortuary practice', unpublished PhD thesis, University of Michigan.

Sayer, A. (1992) *Method in Social Science: A Realist Approach*, 2nd edn, London: Routledge.

Sayer, D. (2007) 'Drei südenglische Gräberfelder aus angelsächsischer Zeit und ihre Organisation' in Grünewald, C. and Capelle, T. (eds), *Innere Strukturen von Siedlungen und Gräberfeldern als Spiegel gesellschaftlicher Wirklichkeit?*, Akten des 57. Internationalen Sachsensymposiums. Veröffentlichungen der Altertumskommission für Westfalen 17, Münster: Aschendorff, pp. 79–84.

Sayer, D. (2009) 'Laws, funerals and cemetery organisation: the seventh-century Kentish family', in D. Sayer and H. Williams (eds), *Mortuary Practice and Social Identities in the Middle Ages*, Exeter: Exeter University Press, pp. 141–66.

Sayer, D. (2010) 'Death and the family: developing a generational chronology', *Journal of Social Archaeology* 10 (1): 59–91.

Sayer, D. (2011) 'The organization of post-medieval churchyards, cemeteries and grave plots: Variation and religious identity as seen in Protestant burial provision', in C. King and D. Sayer (eds), *The Archaeology of Post-Medieval Religion*, Woodbridge: Boydell and Brewer, pp 199–214.

Sayer, D. (2012) 'Christian burial practice in the early Middle Ages: Rethinking the Anglo-Saxon funerary sphere', *History Compasses* 11 (2): 133–46.

Sayer, D. (2014) 'Sons of athelings given to the earth: infant mortality within Anglo-Saxon mortuary geography', *Medieval Archaeology* 58: 83–109.

Sayer, D. and Dickinson, S. D. (2013) 'Reconsidering obstetric death and female fertility in Anglo-Saxon England', *World Archaeology* 45 (2): 285–97.

Sayer, D. and Wienhold, M. (2012) 'A GIS-investigation of four early Anglo-Saxon cemeteries: Ripley's K-function analysis of spatial groupings amongst graves', *Social Science Computer Review* 31 (1): 70–88.

Sayer, D., Sebo, E. and Hughes, K. (2019) 'A double-edged sword: Swords, bodies and personhood in early medieval archaeology and literature', *European Journal of Archaeology* 22 (4): 542–66.

Schiffels, S., Haak, W., Paajanen, P. *et al.* (2016) 'Iron Age and Anglo-Saxon genomes from East England reveal British migration history', *Nature Communications* 7: 10408, at www.nature.com/articles/ncomms10408 [accessed March 2020].

Sebo, E. M. (2015) '*Ne Sorga*: Grief and Revenge in "Beowulf"', in J. Wilcox, A. Jorgensen and F. McCormick (eds), *Anglo-Saxon Emotions: Reading the Heart in Old English Language, Literature and Culture*, London: Ashgate, pp. 177–92.

Seebohm, F. (1905) [1876], *English Village Community*, London: Longmans, Green & Co.

Sexton, J. (2006) 'Saint's Law: Anglo-Saxon sanctuary protection in the *Translatio et Miracula S. Swithuni*', *Florilegium* 23 (2): 61–80.

Shephard, J. F. (1979) 'The social identity of individuals in isolated barrows and barrow cemeteries in Anglo-Saxon England', in B. C. Burnham and J. Kingsbury (eds), *Space, Hierarchy and Society: Interdisciplinary Studies in Social Area Analysis*, British Archaeology Reports, International Series 59, Oxford: British Archaeological Reports, pp. 47–79.

Sherlock, S. J. (2012) *A Royal Anglo-Saxon Cemetery at Street House, Loftus, North-East Yorkshire*, Hartlepool: Tees Archaeology.

Sherlock, S. J. and Welch, M. (1992) *An Anglo-Saxon Cemetery at Norton Cleveland*, CBA Research Report 82, London: Council for British Archaeology.

Šmejda, L. and Turek, J. (2004) *Spatial Analysis of Funerary Areas*, Plzeň: University of West Bohemia.

Sofaer, J. R. (2006) 'Gender, bioarchaeology and human ontogeny', in R. Gowland and C. Knüsel (eds), *Social Archaeology of Funerary Remains*, Oxford: Oxbow, pp. 155–67.

Sørensen, M. L. S. (1992) 'Gender archaeology and Scandinavian Bronze-Age studies', *Norwegian Archaeology Review* 25 (1): 31–49.

Stapel, A. (2007) 'Betattungsbrauchtum auf dem Gräberfeld Dortmund-Wickede', in C. Grünewald and T. Capelle (eds), *Innere Strukturen von Siedlungen und Gräberfeldern als Spiegel gesellschaftlicher Wirklichkeit?*, Akten des 57. Internationalen Sachsensymposiums. Veröffentlichungen der Altertumskommission für Westfalen 17, Münster: Aschendorff, pp. 63–9.

Steckel, R. H. (2006) 'Biology and culture: assessing quality of life', in H. Schutkowski (ed.), *Between Biology and Culture*, Cambridge: Cambridge University Press, pp. 67–104.

Steckel, R. H. (2009) 'Heights and human welfare: recent developments and new directions', *Explorations in Economic History* 46: 1–23.

Steele, V. (1998) *Shoes: A Lexicon of Style*, London: Scriptum Editions.

Steuer, H. (1968) 'Zur Bewaffnung und Sozialstruktur der Merowingerzeit', *Nachrichten aus Niedersachsens Urgeschichte* 37: pp. 18–87.

Stewart, A. and Sayer, D., forthcoming, *Necrogeneology and Mortuary Topography: Dental Metrics and Kinship in the Early Anglo-Saxon Mortuary Landscape.*

Stinson, S. (2000) 'Growth variation: biological and cultural factors', in S. Stinson, B. Bogin, R. Huss-Ashmore *et al.* (eds), *Human Biology: An Evolutionary and Biocultural Perspective*, Chichester: Wiley-Liss, pp. 423–63.

Stirland A. (1986) 'A possible correlation between os acromiale in the burials from the "Mary Rose"', in *Proceedings of the 5th European Meeting of the Palaeopathology Association*, pp. 327–34.

Stirland, J. (2000) *Raising the Dead: The Skeleton Crew of Henry VIII's Great Ship, the Mary Rose*, Chichester: John Wiley & Sons.

Stoodley, N. (1999) *The Spindle and the Spear: A Critical Enquiry into the Construction and Meaning of Gender in the Early Anglo-Saxon Burial Rite*, British Archaeological Report 288, Oxford: Archaeopress.

Stoodley, N. (2000) 'From the cradle to the grave: Age organization and the early Anglo-Saxon burial rite', *World Archaeology* 31: 456–72.

Stoodley, N. (2011) 'Childhood to old age', in H. Hamerow, D. Hinton and S. Crawford (eds), *The Oxford Handbook of Anglo-Saxon Archaeology*, Oxford: Oxford University Press, pp. 640–66.

Suzuki, S. (2000) *The Quoit Brooch Style and Anglo-Saxon Settlement*, Woodbridge: Boydell & Brewer.

Swanton, M. J. (1973) *The Spearheads of the Anglo-Saxon Settlements*, London: Royal Archaeological Institute.

Swanton, M. J. (1974) *A Corpus of Pagan Anglo-Saxon Spear-Types*, British Archaeological Reports 7, Oxford: British Archaeological Reports.

Sykes, N., Spriggs, M. and Allowen Evin (2019) 'Beyond curse or blessing: the opportunities and challenges of a DNA analysis', *World Archaeology*, 51 (4): 503–16, doi: https://doi.org/10.1080/00438243.2019.1741970

Taylor, A., Duhig, C. and Hines, J. (1997) 'An Anglo-Saxon cemetery at Oakington, Cambridgeshire', *Proceedings of the Cambridge Antiquarian Society* 86: 57–90.

Tester, P. J. (1968) 'An Anglo-Saxon cemetery at Orpington. First interim report', *Archaeologia Cantiana* 83: 125–50.

Tester, P. J. (1969) 'Excavations at Fordcroft, Orpington. Concluding report', *Archaeologia Cantiana* 84: 39–77.

Tester, P. J. (1977) 'Further notes on the Anglo-Saxon cemetery at Orpington', *Archaeologia Cantiana* 93: 201–2.

Theuws, F. (2013) 'Do all the burials we excavate allow an archaeology of individuality and individualism?', in L. Babette (ed.), *Individual and Individuality? Approaches towards an Archaeology of Personhood in the First Millennium*, Neue Studien zur Sachsenforschung 4, Stuttgart: Theiss, pp. 9–15.

Thomas, M. G., Stumpf, M. P. H. and Härke, H. (2006) 'Evidence of apartheid-like social structure in early Anglo-Saxon England', *Proceedings of the Royal Society of Biological Sciences* 273: 2651–7.

Timby, J. R. (1996) *The Anglo-Saxon Cemetery at Empingham II, Rutland*, Oxbow Monograph 70, Oxford: Oxbow.

Townsend, G. C. and Brown, T. (1978a) 'Heritability of permanent tooth size', *American Journal of Physical Anthropology* 49 (4): 497–504.

Townsend, G. C. and Brown, T. (1978b) 'Inheritance of tooth size in Australian Aboriginals', *American Journal of Physical Anthropology* 48 (3): 305–14.

Trotter, M. (1970) 'Estimation of stature from intact limb bones', in T. D. Stuart (ed.), *Personal Identification in Mass Disasters*, Washington DC: National Museum of Natural History, pp. 71–84.

Trotter, M. and Gleser, G. C. (1952) 'Estimation of stature from long bones of American whites and negroes', *American Journal of Physical Anthropology* 10: 463–514.

Trotter, M. and Gleser, G. C. (1958) 'A re-evaluation of estimation of stature based on measurements of stature taken during life and of long bone after death', *American Journal of Physical Anthropology* 16: 79–123.

Trotter, M. and Gleser, G. C. (1977) Corrigenda: 'Estimation of stature from long limb bones of American whites and negroes', *American Journal of Physical Anthropology* 47: 355–6.

Tyler, S. (1996) 'Early Saxon Essex AD 400–700', in O. Bedwin (ed.), *The Archaeology of Essex. Proceedings of the Writtle Conference*, Chelmsford: Essex County Council, pp. 108–16.

Tyler, S. and Major, H. (2005) *The Early Anglo-Saxon Cemetery and Later Saxon Settlement at Springfield Lyons, Essex*, East Anglian Archaeology Report 111, Norwich: East Anglian Archaeology.

Tyrell, A. (2000) 'Corpus Saxonum: Early medieval bodies and corporeal identity', in W. O. Frazer and A. Tyrell (eds), *Social Identity in Early Medieval Britain*, Leicester: Leicester University Press, pp. 137–56.

Ucko, P. J. (1969) 'Ethnography and archaeological interpretation of funerary remains', *World Archaeology* 1 (2): 262–80.

Vanmechelen, R. and Vrielynck, O. (2009) 'Bossut-Gottechain et Haillot (Belgique): Deux cimetières mérovingiens, deux expressions de le sépulture privilégiée', in Alduc-Le Bagousse, A. (ed), *Inhumations de Prestige ou Prestige de L'inhumation?* Caen: Publications du CRAHM, pp. 23–67.

Vrielynck, O. (2012) 'The Merovingian cemetery of Bossut-Gottechain (Grez-Doiceau, Belgium)', in A. S. M. Panhuysen and B. Ludowici (eds), *Transformations in North-Western Europe (AD 300–1000)*, Neue Studien zur Sachsenforschung 3, Hannover: Niedersaächsisches Landesmuseum, pp. 259–65.

Wahl, J. (1988) *Süderbrarup. En Gräberfeld der römischen Kaiserzeit und Völkerwanderungszeit in Angeln. II: Anthropologische Undersuchungen*, Offa-Bücher 64, Neumünster: K. Wachholtz.

Waldron, T. (1994) 'The human remains', in V. I. Evison (ed.), *An Anglo-Saxon Cemetery at Great Chesterford, Essex*, Council for British Archaeology Research Report 91, York: Council for British Archaeology, pp. 52–66.

Walter, T. (1994). *The Revival of Death*. London: Routledge.

Walton Rogers, P. (2007) *Cloth and Clothing in Early Anglo-Saxon England,* AD *450–700,* York: Council for British Archaeology.

Warhurst, A. (1955) 'The Jutish cemetery at Lyminge', *Archaeologia Cantiana* 69: 1–40.

Welch, M. G. (1983) *Early Anglo-Saxon Sussex,* British Archaeological Reports 112(i), Oxford: British Archaeological Reports.

Wells, C. (1960) 'A study of cremation', *Antiquity* 34: 29–37.

Wells, C. and Green, C. (1973) 'Sunrise dating of death and burial', *Norfolk and Norwich Archaeological Society* 35 (4): 435–42.

West, S. E. (1988) *The Anglo-Saxon Cemetery at Westgarth Gardens, Bury St Edmunds, Suffolk: Catalogue,* East Anglian Archaeology Report 38, Norwich: East Anglian Archaeology.

White, R. (1988) *Roman and Celtic Objects from Anglo-Saxon Graves: A Catalogue and an Interpretation of Their Use,* British Archaeological Reports 191, Oxford: British Archaeological Reports.

White, R. (1990) 'Scrap or substitute: Roman material in Anglo-Saxon graves', in E. Southworth (ed.), *Anglo-Saxon Cemeteries: A Reappraisal,* Stroud: Alan Sutton, pp. 125–52.

White, T., Black, M. and Folkens, P. (2012) *Human Osteology,* Oxford: Elsevier.

Whitelock, D. (1930) *Anglo-Saxon Wills,* Cambridge: Cambridge University Press.

Whitelock, D. (1955) *English Historical Documents c. 500–1042,* London: Eyre & Spottiswoode.

Willey, P. (2009) 'Stature estimation', in S. Blau and D. H. Ubelaker (eds), *Handbook of Forensic Anthropology and Archaeology,* World Archaeological Congress Research Handbooks in Archaeology, Walnut Creek CA: Left Coast Press, pp. 236–45.

Williams, H. (1997) 'Ancient landscapes and the dead: The reuse of prehistoric and Roman monuments as early Anglo-Saxon burial sites', *Medieval Archaeology* 41: 1–32.

Williams, H. (1998) 'Monuments and the past in early Anglo-Saxon England', *World Archaeology* 30 (1): 90–108.

Williams, H. (2002a) 'Cemeteries as central places: Landscape and identity in early Anglo-Saxon England', in B. Hardh and L. Larsson (eds), *Central Places in the Migration and Merovingian Periods,* Papers from the 52nd Sachsensymposium, Lund: Almqvist, pp. 341–62.

Williams, H. (2002b) '"The Remains of Pagan Saxondom"? Studying Anglo-Saxon cremation practices', in S. Lucy and A. Reynolds (eds), *Burial in Early Medieval England and Wales,* London: Society for Medieval Archaeology, pp. 47–71.

Williams, H. (2005) 'Keeping the dead at arm's length: memory, weaponry and early medieval mortuary technologies', *Journal of Social Archaeology* 5 (2): 253–75.

Williams, H. (2006) *Death and Memory in Early Medieval Britain,* Cambridge: Cambridge University Press.

Williams, H. (2007) 'The emotive force of early medieval mortuary practices', *Archaeological Review from Cambridge* 22 (1): 107–23.

Williams, H. (2009) 'On display: envisioning the early Anglo-Saxon dead', in D. Sayer and H. Williams (eds), *Mortuary Practices and Social Identities in the Middle Ages,* Exeter: University of Exeter Press, pp. 170–206.

Williams, H. (2011) 'Mortuary practices in early Anglo-Saxon England', in H. Hamerow, D. A. Hinton and S. Crawford (eds), *The Oxford Handbook of Anglo-Saxon Archaeology*, Oxford: Oxford University Press, pp. 238–59.

Williams, H. and Sayer, D. (2009) 'Hall of mirrors: Death and identity in medieval archaeology', in D. Sayer and H. Williams (eds), *Mortuary Practice and Social Identities in the Middle Ages*, Exeter: Exeter University Press, pp. 1–22.

Wilson, D. (1992) *Anglo-Saxon Paganism*, London: Routledge.

Wilson, D. M. (1965) 'Some neglected late Anglo-Saxon swords', *Medieval Archaeology* 9: 32–54.

Wiseman, R. (2015) 'Social distance in settled communities the conceptual metaphor, SOCIAL DISTANCE IS PHYSICAL DISTANCE, in action', *Journal of Archaeological Method and Theory* 23: 1023–52.

Yang, J., Bakshi, A., Zhu, Z. *et al.* (2015) 'Genetic variance estimation with imputed variants finds negligible missing heritability for human height and body mass index', *Nature Genetics* 47 (10): 1114–20. doi: 10.1038/ng.3390 [accessed March 2020].

Index

Abingdon I 8, 11, 40–1
aesthetics xvi, 2, 108, 192, 200, 208, 270, 272–275
age xv, xvii, 1, 2, 21, 31, 33, 35–6, 43, 74, 89, 143, 145, 149, 160–1, 172–6, 186–7, 190, 203, 206, 249, 254–5, 274
Alfriston 8, 11
Alwalton 8, 70–1, 85, 172
Ancaster 8, 68
ancestor xvii, 20, 84, 89, 95, 129, 139, 140, 149, 185–6, 189, 213, 241, 245, 255, 270, 272, 274
Andover 8, 11, 18, 70–3, 82, 85, 149, 252
Anglo-Saxon Wills 245, 269
animal art 91, 99, 109, 116, 131
antecedent 88–9, 92, 95, 103, 115, 131, 138, 140, 142, 214, 271, 272
Apple Down xvi, 8, 22–8, 30, 33, 35, 36, 62, 66, 70, 78, 79–82, 85
art-historical 91, 96
arthritis 193–202, 205
Asthall 8, 67, 147
attitude, social 1, 28–9, 85, 90, 190–2, 202, 238, 254–5, 262, 269–70, 272
  toward the dead 90, 139, 142, 238, 252, 255, 265
audience xv, 6, 75, 77, 148, 171

Bargates 8, 40, 85, 156, 167, 171, 188, 255
Barrington 8, 169, 181
barrow, Anglo-Saxon 19–20, 37, 39, 44, 47, 50, 52, 67, 88, 95, 121–2, 126–9, 134, 138–40, 142, 156–8, 160, 163, 176, 177–89, 194, 197, 199, 206, 229, 249, 252–4, 260–1, 270–2
Bronze Age 14, 39–44, 62, 64, 77, 84, 134–9, 264–5
  mounds 3, 20, 27, 59, 62, 179, 251
Baston 8, 68
beads, burial 4–6, 23, 78, 138, 146–7, 150, 152–3, 161, 194, 204–5
  chronology 91–2, 97–9, 107–9, 112–21, 127–36
Beckford B 8, 62, 169
bed burial 59
Belgium 9, 87, 107
Beowulf 240–1
Bergh Apton 8, 10–11, 22, 43, 62, 156, 163
Berinsfield 8, 12–15, 40, 42, 45, 62–6, 69–74, 78, 85, 88, 140, 149, 151, 156, 161, 167–9, 171, 177, 188, 203–12, 215–21, 224, 226, 252, 255, 268, 269
Bidford-on-Avon 8, 60–61
Bifrons 8, 147
biological sex xvii, 32, 145, 160–3, 169–71, 209, 216, 220, 226–8, 235
  asexual identity 31, 161
  sexy, material culture 31–2, 161
  sexuality 32, 244
Blacknall Field 8, 10, 47–8, 69, 169, 187
Bloodmoor Hill 8, 181
body position 4, 10, 43, 62, 66, 78, 144, 161, 172, 186
Bordesholm 9, 171
Bossut-Gottechain 9, 87, 103, 107, 108, 140
boundary, cemetery 60–1, 174, 260–1

Boxford 9, 10
bracteate 116, 129
Bradstow School 8, 176, 181–4, 271
Brettenham 8, 68
Brighthampton 9, 260
Broadstairs I 8, 11, 171
Broadway Hill 9, 164, 165, 188, 255,
    270
Bronze Age 14, 40, 41, 43, 52, 58, 62,
    82, 88, 134, 152, 153, 158, 206,
    229, 264
brooch, burial
  annular 75, 92, 96, 98, 109, 114,
    116, 152, 258, 260, 262, 267
  applied 73, 95, 116, 120
  bird 23, 78, 96, 97, 109
  bow 23, 92, 97, 114
  button 23, 73, 96, 112, 132–3
  cognate 73, 96, 114, 118
  composite 92, 96, 100
  cruciform 62, 73, 75–6, 92, 94, 97,
    103, 109–10, 114, 116–17, 119,
    152, 153, 159
  disc 23, 73, 75, 91–2, 95–6, 121,
    129, 131, 134, 136, 267
  elaborate 74, 75–7, 96–7, 100–21,
    149, 186, 260
  equal armed 97
  keystone (garnet) 78, 92, 96, 123,
    129, 131–2, 136, 208
  penannular 96, 109, 116, 118, 152,
    258, 260, 262
  plated 96
  quoit 96
  radiate 23, 128, 130
  saucer 23, 95, 96, 114, 116, 120,
    127, 128, 150, 267
  square headed, 23, 75, 76, 78, 97,
    109, 114, 118, 128, 130, 132–4,
    150, 152, 159, 204–5, 260,
    267
Broomfield 9, 147
Broughton Lodge 9, 169, 171, 269
Brugmann, Birte xx, 22, 44, 69, 97,
    123, 128–9, 131, 132, 134, 167,
    172, 206, 256
Buckland, Dover 10–11, 55, 62, 87–95,
    111, 123–6, 129–42, 163, 252,
    254, 276–85
buckles 20, 23, 75–78, 90–4, 99,
    108–9, 112–18, 121, 127–8,
    131–2, 146–7, 150, 153, 159, 176,
    194, 204–5, 256, 260, 267

Bülach, Cologne 9, 57
cadence of burial 87, 89, 95, 139, 142,
    252
Caenby 9, 147
Caistor St Edmund 9, 43, 85
Caistor-by-Norwich 9, 70–3, 82, 85
Castle Acre 9, 68
Castledyke 9, 169, 171, 269
Chadlington 9, 181
Chadwick Hawkes, Sonja 7, 99, 179
Chamberlains Barn II 9, 62
Cherryson, Annia xxi, 25, 27
children 5, 14, 19, 20, 25, 27, 33, 43–5,
    89, 97–8, 128, 132, 140, 145, 158,
    167, 172–5, 191–4, 200, 203, 206,
    213, 235, 243–7, 256, 260–1, 270,
    272, 274
chronology, artefact typologies
    87–94, 96, 108
  cemetery 10–16, 36–8, 85–9,
    92–114, 123–42, 160, 176, 203,
    206–7, 237, 252, 255, 260,
    269–70, 275
  Hines and Bayliss 91–4, 96–101,
    123, 144
  Kentish 93, 206
Church 30, 238, 242, 244
Churchyard 172
class, social 1, 29, 31, 36, 274
Cleatham 9, 68
clustering, grave 7, 10, 43–7, 52, 54–5,
    68, 71, 80–1, 84–6, 106, 108, 136,
    149, 150, 155–6, 166–7, 178, 180,
    200, 249, 256, 263, 264
Collingbourne Ducis 9, 11
combs 100, 103
compound cemeteries 79–84
concentric burials/plot 103, 110–11,
    116–17, 140
concubine 244
Coombe 9, 147
core graves xvii, 14, 15, 65, 80,
    107–13, 116, 134, 139–41, 145,
    149–60, 167–8, 71–2, 174,
    187–9, 200, 203–4, 210, 238,
    252–6, 265, 269–72
cow, burial 121
cremation 16, 19, 22–3, 26, 36, 42, 45,
    47, 53, 64, 66–73, 79, 80–3, 85,
    90, 100, 102–6, 111, 140, 156,
    158, 171, 174, 176, 189, 239, 252,
    256, 262, 265, 271, 273
urns 43, 103–6

cremation, cemetery 10, 12, 67–8, 71, 171
Cuddesdon 9, 147

Deal, Mill Hill 9, 14–15, 40, 50–2, 55, 57, 62, 66, 74, 77–9, 86–9, 97, 125–6, 137–8, 146–7, 156, 163–4, 166, 169, 171–2, 188, 206–9, 212, 252, 255, 269
deviant burial 66, 161
Devlin, Zoe 74
Dickinson, Tania 91, 95–98, 101
diet xvii, 192, 199, 209–11, 213, 216, 238, 254, 262
dispersed graves 17, 20, 23, 50–2, 55, 60, 65, 78, 83, 85, 103, 124–5, 134–7, 155–6, 159, 163, 187, 252–3, 265
ditch, enclosure 40, 80, 82–3
   ring 14, 40, 43, 50, 52, 54, 55, 58, 62, 83, 134, 136, 152–3, 163, 176, 179, 181, 185, 206, 208, 260
   Roman 40, 42, 205
Dortmund-Wickede 9, 59
double burial xvi, 161, 121, 140, 260
Drayton 9, 68
dressing (dressed) the dead 6, 78–9, 148, 271
Driffield 9, 62
Droxford 9, 43

Eastry 9, 235, 269
Eccles 9, 40
egocentric burial (ego-focused) 122, 129, 158, 241, 271
elite, family 70, 85, 171, 188, 242, 270
   political 90
   social 70, 145–7, 167–8, 245–55, 269, 271
   material culture 32
emotion xiv, 249
Empingham II 9, 40, 161, 163, 169
enamel hypoplasia 197–9, 216
ethnicity 37, 62, 66, 73–4, 215, 272
Evison, Vera 10, 14, 20, 44, 64, 91, 99–100, 102, 123–5, 136
external grave structures 176–7, 181, 273

family 1, 2, 10, 17–18, 29, 33, 38, 60, 64, 74, 138, 143, 145, 167, 171, 191, 233, 236, 239, 242–9, 255–6, 260, 262, 268–72, 274–5

field cemeteries 172
final-phase 85, 142, 231, 262, 265
Finglesham 11–13, 88, 121, 140–1, 147, 156, 163, 169–70, 176, 179–85, 187–8, 193–203, 213, 252–5, 271
firesteels 77–8, 99
flat chronology 137, 140–1
flat graves 185–6, 194, 197, 199
focal point 12, 19–20, 88, 122, 158, 177, 187
Fonaby 9, 167, 171, 188, 255
food 7, 192, 210–11, 236, 241, 247
founder's graves 17, 156
fractures, bone 25, 193, 200, 201
France 9, 56–7
funeral costume 5, 22, 75, 77–9, 89, 144, 147–8, 152, 161, 170, 256

Gallows Hill, 9, 40
Garton Slack II 9, 40, 57–8, 85, 141
Gateway, artefacts 94, 98
gender xv, xvii, 7, 10, 21, 28–36, 74, 79, 88—95, 123, 127–8, 130, 131, 134–8, 143, 145, 148–9, 160–72, 181, 186–8, 190, 194, 203, 208, 215, 219, 225–6, 228, 230, 249, 254–5, 261, 269–70, 272, 274–5
genealogies, mortuary 38, 194
generations xvii, 6, 12, 16–17, 19, 21, 29, 38, 43, 52, 55, 75, 86–90, 95, 98–9, 103, 110–11, 113, 115, 118–22, 125–6, 129, 131–2, 134, 137–41, 146, 159, 187–8, 191–2, 200, 202–8, 215, 236–8, 252, 254–6, 261, 269, 272, 274
genetics 215–16, 234
Germany 9, 56–57, 59, 97, 171
girdle hangers 73, 77, 99–100, 109–10, 116, 118, 121, 256
Goody, Jack 241–2, 244
grave density 37, 50, 55, 81, 84, 144
grave features 177, 275
grave goods xvi, 7, 12, 18–19, 23, 25, 28, 30, 32–3, 39, 62, 74, 78, 86, 91, 100, 102, 114–18, 120–1, 137–8, 144–7, 160, 169, 171, 186–7, 194, 202–3, 206, 238–40, 250, 253, 258, 262, 270–2, 275
grave plots (burial plots) xvi, 36, 43, 45, 50, 52, 75, 84, 85, 87, 138, 145, 159, 171, 187
grave robbery 181, 271

grave structure 141, 176, 181
grave, rows xvi, 37, 39, 40, 45, 56–60,
    62, 64, 84, 108, 177, 238, 249,
    252, 254–5, 271
graveside 4, 6, 19, 78, 79, 192, 243,
    272
Great Chesterford 9, 34, 44, 62, 64–5,
    68, 85, 153–6, 169–71, 174–5,
    177, 187–8, 200–3, 213, 221–4,
    226, 252–5, 268–9

Hall Hill 9, 68
Harford Farm 9, 74
Härke, Heinrich xiii, xx, 11, 12, 34, 44,
    47, 85, 101, 148, 160, 215, 216
Hatherdene 9, 140, 235, 269
height xvii, xxi, 93, 101, 192, 209–210,
    214–34, 236, 238, 254–5, 267–9
heirloom, objects 3, 91, 94, 115, 148
Hills, Catherine xvi, xx, xxi, 87, 103
Hines and Bayliss 91, 92, 93, 94,
    96–101, 123, 144
Hines, John xvi, xx, 87, 94, 97, 99, 148
Hirst, Susan xxi, 17, 18, 44 92, 96, 109
Høilund Nielsen, Karen xx, 101, 112
Holboroug 9, 49–50, 155–6, 187, 254
holistic approach xiii, xvi, 1, 28, 31,
    36, 238
Holywell Row 9–11, 43
homogeneity, grave 44–5, 47, 50, 86,
    108, 215, 221, 223–4, 226, 233,
    236, 238, 254, 269
Hope-Taylor, Brian xiv, 10, 12, 17–18,
    85, 89
horizontal stratigraphy 1, 10–12, 14,
    17–18, 87–8, 103, 140, 252, 275
horse, burial 107, 120–1, 153
household 1–2, 26, 78, 164, 190–1,
    239–48, 256, 269–72
Howletts 9, 162
Hull, Bradley 209–11

iconoclasm 186, 189
Illington 9, 68
infants 172–6, 188, 192, 200, 260–72
injuries 25, 190, 192–3, 197, 200–1,
    209, 237, 242
    see also trauma
integral features, ledges, sideboards
    176–86, 194, 197
intercutting, graves 15, 108, 129, 131,
    138, 140, 226
isotope studies 192, 209–12

Junkersdorf 9, 57, 60

Kentish cemetery 77, 123, 163, 186
kernel density map 44, 80, 86, 256,
    264, 266
kingdoms 90, 147–8
kingship 29, 242
Kingston-on-Soar 9, 68
Kingsworthy 9, 169
kinship xiii, xvii, 2, 28, 33, 36, 74, 190,
    234, 239–40, 242, 245, 249, 256,
    268–71, 275
Klevnäs, Alison 181
knife 19, 114, 120–1, 145–7, 150, 153,
    204–5, 260, 266–268
knowledge, semiotic xvi, 31–2, 34–9,
    84–5, 185, 248–9
    selective 6, 7, 31–6, 79, 84–5, 143–4,
    190, 237, 251

Lackford 9, 68, 260
Lavoye 9, 57
laws, Anglo-Saxon 27, 240, 242–7, 272
    Edmund's law 241
    laws of Æthelbert 242–4, 246–7
    laws of Alfred 243
    Canons of Theodore, Archbishop of
        Canterbury 244
    laws of Hlothhere and Eadric 27,
        245,
    laws of Ine 21, 27, 242, 247
Lechlade 9, 12, 45, 57, 60–1, 66, 79,
    95, 121, 126, 137, 140–1, 156–8,
    160, 162–3, 169–71, 176, 229–33,
    239, 252–3, 255, 262–6, 268–70
Leeds, Edwin Thurlow 91, 96–7
Leighton Buzzard II and III 9, 155–6,
    188, 255
leitmotifs xvii, 2, 36, 145, 160, 186,
    248, 275
less well furnished graves 151, 154,
    157, 193–4, 253, 270
life course xvii, 1, 6–7, 21, 31–2, 34,
    160, 172, 187, 191, 274–5
lifeways xv, xvii, 4, 25–8, 32, 191–4,
    197, 199–203, 206, 209, 211–15,
    237–8, 254–6, 262, 270–1
lived experience xvii, 192–3, 199,
    201–3, 206, 255
localisation xv, xvii, xix, 1–2, 6, 37,
    75–9, 87, 163–4, 169–71, 176,
    181, 186, 189, 200, 265
Lucy, Sam xvi, xxi, 37, 73, 87, 89, 160

Lyminge x, 9, 147, 164–5, 171, 188, 255, 270

Marina Drive 9, 40, 57
Market Lavington 9, 169, 245, 247, 269–71, 274
Marzinzik, Sonja 91, 99, 121, 176
Meaney, Audrey 67–8
memory 3, 6, 21, 36, 38–39, 74–5, 143, 164, 181, 256
Merovingian xix, 17, 59–60, 84–5, 91, 95, 100–1, 103, 107, 146, 189, 249
mixed rite cemetery 22, 42, 47, 67–8, 70, 80, 85, 102
mnemonics 20, 39, 85, 108, 159, 179, 187–8, 255
monocentric cemeteries 10, 85, 103, 139
monument 10, 39, 40, 83, 138, 158, 200, 265
Morning Thorpe 9, 22, 39–40, 50, 52–3, 60–2, 66, 78–9, 86, 140, 174, 239, 252, 255–62, 268
mortuary syntax 84, 248, 262, 265
mortuary technology 67, 70, 73, 88, 249
mourners 32, 87, 88, 126, 137, 192, 239
Mucking xxi, 9, 11, 39–42, 52–5
multiple generational, 3, 20, 87, 95, 139, 159, 215, 238, 254
Müngersdorf 9, 57
Myres, Nowell 102, 116, 260

narratives, community xvii, 4, 39, 86–7, 89, 145, 239, 248, 271–2, 275
   mortuary 3, 6–7, 17, 20, 39, 79, 83–4, 88, 103, 108, 122–3, 132, 140, 167, 176–7, 186–8, 212–13, 248, 255, 262, 270, 272, 275
Newark 9, 68
Norton 9, 44–7, 57, 62, 68, 70, 85, 153, 154–6, 167, 169, 171–2, 269

Oakington xiv, xvi, xx, 4–5, 9, 30, 36, 66, 87, 88, 118–19, 120–2, 126–7, 129, 140, 156–8, 160, 174–6, 235, 250–2, 269
obliteration, earlier burial 88, 95, 131, 135, 138, 140, 181
Oliver, Lisi 243

orientation, grave xvi, 7, 19, 23, 25–6, 36–7, 40, 60–6, 73, 81, 84–6, 107–8, 111, 114, 127, 136, 138–9, 144, 153, 174, 177–8, 192, 200, 203, 206, 210, 213, 226–9, 252, 255, 262, 265, 271, 273
Orpington xvi, 9, 14, 16, 19–20, 27–8, 30–1, 33, 35–6, 38–41, 47–8, 57, 87–9, 128, 139–41, 156–8, 164, 171, 176, 179, 187, 194, 252, 270
Orsett 9, 176
Osteophytes 200–1, 207–8
over 45 (age) 20, 25, 173, 175, 193, 208, 267
Ozengell 9, 176, 181–5, 271

pace of change 89–90, 141
Pader, E.J. 10, 43, 44, 74, 161
participants, funeral 4, 6, 28, 33, 36, 38, 74, 139, 144, 146, 167, 177, 239, 248–9, 252, 272–3
participation 4, 6, 37–8, 75, 77, 79, 185, 209, 251–2
pathology 192–203, 208–10, 215, 237, 262
patrilocality (male residence) 245, 269–70
Pelteret, David 246
performance, funerary 3, 6, 36, 143, 272
   social/cultural 32, 60, 190
personhood xiv, xvii, 29, 32, 35, 149, 186, 190–1, 238
Petersfinger 9, 18, 40, 63–66, 70, 85, 149, 177, 252
Pewsey 9, 11, 47, 163, 172
pins xvi, 17, 28, 36, 74–9, 87, 98, 112, 170
plurality 37, 74, 77, 139, 262
Polhill 9, 11, 50–2, 55, 137, 141, 156, 162–4, 171, 235, 252, 269, 279
polycentric cemeteries 10–11, 85, 103, 139, 249
Ports Down I 9, 40
pregnant woman 66, 119
preparing the corpse xiv, 4, 6, 22, 28, 75, 78–9, 90, 116, 139, 144, 148, 170, 177, 186, 251–2, 271
princely graves 147
Prittlewell 9, 147
prone burial 4, 5, 62, 66, 121, 158
pyre 67, 239, 240, 271

radial cemeteries 62
radiocarbon dates 92–6, 98, 100, 102,
    118–21, 123, 144, 302
Ravn, Mads 43, 70
reconstruction drawings 248, 250–1
regional, traditions 34, 38, 79, 262
relatedness, biological 6, 192, 214–15,
    218–20, 234, 236–7, 244, 267
relationship xiii–xvi, 2, 4, 7, 21, 28–31,
    35–6, 74, 86, 122, 128, 131,
    143–145, 148, 163, 191–2, 239,
    243–4, 248–9, 268–70, 272–3
religion 1, 29, 60, 62, 66, 90, 274
reuse, monument 39–40, 80–1, 83
Richard III 238
Roman, coin 127, 116, 118, 153
    building 40–1, 249
    burial rites 80
    cremations 64
    features 40, 42, 64, 80, 205, 210
    objects 96, 98, 102, 121

Salin style animal art 91, 95, 99, 109,
    116, 131
Saltwood 9, 43
Sancton 9, 68
Sarre 9, 147
satellite graves 47, 50, 80, 82, 121,
    126–9, 138, 157–8, 176, 181,
    185, 187–8, 247, 253, 260–1, 267,
    270
Saxe, Arthur xv, 145
Scandinavian xvii, 97–8
scopic regime xvii, 187–9
scutiform pendent 98, 109, 116,
    277
Seax 23, 57, 102, 114, 134, 150, 208,
    267–8
Seebohm, Frederic 268, 270
semiotic knowledge xvi–xvi, 31–9,
    84–5, 185, 248–9
semiotics 7, 31, 39, 66, 70, 73, 190,
    272
seventh-century, artefacts 92–4, 96,
    98–102, 147, 231–3
    cemetery 40, 57, 85, 155–6, 167,
    206, 271
    graves 11–16, 39, 43, 45, 52, 60,
    63–4, 77–8, 84, 88, 90, 109–11,
    114–15, 117, 119, 125–6,
    130–142, 158, 163–4, 170, 176,
    179, 203, 206, 208, 249, 252,
    262–7, 271

Sewerby xvi, 4, 9, 11, 18, 49–50, 66,
    87, 92, 96, 108–11, 134, 140, 169,
    171, 252, 269
shield boss 19, 23, 77, 101, 115,
    117–18, 121, 123, 128, 131–2,
    136, 153, 160, 204–5, 260, 267
shoes xvi, xxi, 31–5, 190, 191, 274
Shudy Camps 9, 40
slaves 1, 21–2, 28, 191, 246–8
Snape 9, 18, 34, 40, 68
Snell's Corner 9, 11, 47, 49–50, 167,
    171, 188, 255
social archaeology xx, 36, 237, 238
social status 1, 18, 28, 145, 148–9,
    160, 211, 215, 248, 274
social stratification 18, 271
South Elkington 9, 68
spear 3, 19–23, 26–8, 33–6, 77, 91–4,
    100–1, 112, 114–18, 127–8,
    131–2, 134–6, 142, 144, 150,
    152–3, 161, 164, 170, 185, 191–2,
    204–5, 251, 260, 262, 266–8, 277,
    279, 281, 283, 285
Spong Hill xvi, xxi, 9, 11, 22, 39, 43,
    66, 68–71, 73, 79, 82, 85, 87, 100,
    102–6, 108, 142, 176, 181, 252,
    260
Springfield Lyons 9, 43, 79, 83, 85,
    176, 252
Springhead 9, 57
stamps, pottery 102–6, 256, 259–60
St Peters x, xii, 9, 57, 121, 140, 176–9,
    181, 183–5, 194, 252
statistics
    Bayesian 92, 144
    box plots 211–14
    chi-square 93, 170, 197, 200, 202,
    209
    Fisher's exact test 93, 169–70, 184,
    199, 202, 205–6, 208
    Ripley's K function 44, 86, 179
    spatial xvi, xx, 184, 252
stature 214–216, 238, 262
Stewart, Allison xx, xxi, 235
Stifford Clays 9, 176
Stoodley, Nick 18, 44–5, 91, 149, 160,
    164, 172
storytelling 79, 191, 262
Street House 9, 57, 59, 84, 141, 156
Stretton-on-Fosse 9, 11
stufe groups 94
subdivided, plots of graves 50, 55, 60,
    80, 84, 98, 149, 164, 185

Süderbrarup 9, 171
Sutton Hoo 9, 67–8, 147
sword 21–2, 34, 77–8, 100, 102, 123,
    127, 131, 136, 148, 152–3, 164,
    170, 191–2, 206–8

Tanner's Row 9, 172
Taplow 9, 147
teeth xvii, xx, 192, 234–6, 238, 262
tempo of burial 137
Textus Roffensis 241
third gender 161
Thurmaston 9, 68
tradition, mortuary xvi, 20, 38–39, 55,
    59–60, 64, 75–9, 129, 137, 139,
    191, 234, 260, 262
transformation xvi, 28, 50, 87
transitional plots 141
trauma xvii, 25–27, 190, 192–4, 200–3,
    209–10, 214, 237–8, 254, 270
tropes, cultural 36, 188, 255

unfurnished graves 27, 60, 112, 129,
    149, 163, 265

Wakerley xvi, 9, 11, 45–47, 70, 75–79,
    85, 87, 112, 114–15, 117–19,
    124–5, 140, 149–50, 156, 159,
    167, 169, 187–8, 252, 254–6,
    268
warrior graves 7, 18, 191
Wasperton 9, 39, 79–82
wealth, burial 18–20, 57, 77, 134, 138,
    145–54, 158, 164, 181, 186–9,
    194, 197, 199, 202, 204, 206,
    208–10, 237–8, 254–6, 260–2,
    264, 268, 270, 272, 274
wealthiest, grave 7, 17, 27, 55, 138,
    150–1, 154, 156–7, 166, 174,
    199–200, 202, 213, 258, 260, 262,
    270
weapon, burial 14–16, 18–21, 25–8,
    34–6, 74, 77–8, 88–9, 91, 93–4,
    127, 131–4, 136–8, 140, 144,
    146–8, 152–3, 161–6, 170, 191,
    195, 197, 202, 206, 208–10,
    216–18, 220–1, 223, 225–34,
    236–7, 252, 254, 258, 260, 265–9
weapon, set 16, 19, 144, 147–8, 166,
    206, 260
Welch, Martin 62, 80–91, 96–8
wergild 241–4, 246
West Heslerton 9, 34, 39, 52, 54–5, 66,
    86, 150, 152, 155–6, 161, 164,
    166, 169, 171, 187–8, 194, 252–5,
    269–70
Westgarth Gardens 9–11, 22, 43,
    163–4, 167–9, 171–4, 188, 210,
    255, 270
Williams, Howard xviii, 67, 73–4,
    78–9, 164
Winnall II 9, 47, 50, 181
Winterbourne Gunner 9, 164–5, 171,
    188, 255, 270
Wold Newton 9, 68
Worthy Park 9, 11, 70, 73, 85, 162,
    210, 213–14, 226–9, 268–9
wrapped, objects 34, 74, 79
wrist clasps 4, 73, 99, 109–10, 114,
    116–18, 120–1, 260

EU authorised representative for GPSR:
Easy Access System Europe, Mustamäe tee 50,
10621 Tallinn, Estonia
gpsr.requests@easproject.com